When Simon Kuznets was awarded the Nobel Prize in Economics in 1971, his citation read, in part, ". . . his empirically based scholarly work has led to a new and more profound insight into the economic and social structure and the process of change and development." These qualities are evident in the essays in this volume, drawn from Professor Kuznets's work of the past eight years.

The essays center on a few broad themes: population and its relation to economic growth, capital formation in long historical perspective, the broader features of modern economic growth, and recent changes in the gap between the rich and poor countries. The themes are clearly interrelated. Even a selection on the supply of and demand for economic data bears on the others, since it deals with the conditions that limit the quantitative study of economic growth. Included in the volume and published for the first time in book form is Professor Kuznets's Nobel Laureate address, "Modern Economic Growth: Findings and Reflections."

Population, Capital, and Growth

Population, Capital, and Growth

Selected Essays

Simon Kuznets

W · W · Norton & Company · Inc ·

New York

COPYRIGHT © 1973 BY

W. W. NORTON & COMPANY, INC.

All Rights Reserved

Published simultaneously in Canada
by George J. McLeod Limited, Toronto

Library of Congress Cataloging in Publication Data

Kuznets, Simon Smith, 1901–
  Population, capital, and growth.

  Includes bibliographical references.
  1. Economic development—Collected works.
2. Population—Collected works.   3. Capital—Collected
works.   I. Title.
HD82.K875   330   73-12145
ISBN 0–393–05497–7

Printed in the United States of America

1 2 3 4 5 6 7 8 9 0

Contents

Preface

The essays in this volume were written over the last eight years. Most of them were prepared for presentation at various conferences, others were lectures delivered on special occasions.

Despite their ad hoc character, the essays are limited to a few broad themes: population and its relation to economic growth, capital formation in long historical perspective, the broader features of modern economic growth, and recent changes in the gap between the rich and poor countries. The themes are obviously interrelated. Even the essay on problems in the supply of and demand for economic data has some bearing on the others, since it deals with the conditions that limit the quantitative study of economic growth.

As with most such collections, publication of this one is primarily for the convenience of having the interrelated essays assembled between two covers. On re-reading them, I found need for stylistic changes alone, and for minor revisions to reduce duplication.

I am grateful to Mrs. Lillian Weksler, who helped me in the original preparation of the papers, as well as in the review for re-publication. I am also indebted to my colleague, Professor James S. Duesenberry, for advice on papers to be included (and excluded). Finally, thanks are due to the publishers, as indicated in footnotes to the essays, for permission to reprint.

January, 1973   SIMON KUZNETS

Population, Capital, and Growth

Population and Economic Growth

1. Introduction

Modern economic growth, as revealed by the experience of the developed countries since the late eighteenth or early nineteenth century, reflects a continuing capacity to supply a growing population with an increased volume of commodities and services per capita. The increase in both population and per capita product is not the unique feature of recent growth: even in pre-modern times the population of several countries grew and enjoyed a rising per capita product. The distinctive features of modern economic growth are the extremely high rates of increase—at least five times as high for population and at least ten times as high for per capita product as in the observable past.[1] Both high rates of increase imply rapid shifts in the structure of production and patterns of life, suggested by the terms industrialization and urbanization. Underlying these high aggre-

[1] For the underlying data and relevant discussion see my *Modern Economic Growth* (New Haven, Conn.: Yale University Press, 1966), Chapter 2, "Growth of Population and Product," pp. 34–72. See also footnote 3 in a later paper in this volume, "Modern Economic Growth: Findings and Reflections."

Reprinted from *Proceedings of the American Philosophical Society,* Vol. III, no. 3, June, 1967, pp. 170–93. A shorter version was presented at the meeting of the Society on November 11, 1966.

gate rates and rapid structural shifts is the extended application
to problems of health and economic production of a vast and
rapidly growing stock of tested knowledge and inventions. The
knowledge, which relates not only to natural conditions of the
universe in which we live but also to the characteristics of social
groups, affects the values and beliefs of the societies that possess
and apply it; and the inventions contribute to the advance not
only of material technology but also of social institutions.

That modern economic growth meant a strikingly accelerated
rise not only in product per capita but also in population does
not imply that the latter was a necessary condition for the
former. To be sure, until the 1930's there was a broad positive
association: population grew more rapidly in the developed
countries than in the underdeveloped rest of the world [2]; and in
some countries, particularly the European offshoots overseas, a
substantial population increase seemed to be indispensable for
the rapid growth in per capita product. But the association was
quite loose: in some countries high rates of growth in per capita
product were accompanied by high rates of population increase,
and in others by low rates. Besides, historical association is a

---

[2] In the volume from which this paper is reprinted, Professor Durand's
discussion (in his paper, "The Modern Expansion of World Population,"
pp. 136–59) indicates that it would be an over-simplification to attribute
higher rates of population growth largely to economic growth. Yet the estimates he gives (with the 1930 figures interpolated and the 1960 figures extrapolated on the basis of the source cited in footnote 1) show that until
1930 population grew more rapidly in the area of European settlement,
dominated by the more developed countries, than in the rest of the world
(the rates below are percentages per decade based upon the "medium" estimates).

	1750–1850	1850–1930	1930–1960
Latin America included in area of European settlement			
1. A. E. S.	6.3	10.1	10.3
2. Rest of world	4.1	4.2	13.7
Latin America included in rest of world			
3. A. E. S.	6.0	9.6	7.7
4. Rest of world	4.3	4.8	14.3

For comparison of developed with underdeveloped parts of the world,
lines 3 and 4 are more relevant than lines 1 and 2. The higher rate of population growth in the developed parts of the world for the period before
1930 and the striking reversal thereafter are clearly indicated.

treacherous guide to invariant relations. Clearly, in this case the rise in the knowledge and technological power of human societies meant greater control over health and economic production problems and resulted in an accelerated growth of both population and per capita product. But today and in areas with conditions quite different from those that characterized the presently developed countries in their past, rapid population growth may be an obstacle to, rather than a condition of, an adequate rise in per capita product.

Indeed, the question that we wish to examine is that emphasized in the widespread discussion of the current population "explosion." To what extent does a high rate of population growth impede the growth of per capita product? This question is explored here in general terms; yet such general treatment is required if we are to avoid *ad hoc* empiricism and plausible but casual inferences from currently pressing problems that may, in fact, incorrectly identify the causes of observed low and stagnant levels of economic performance in many parts of the world.

2. The Limits to Rising Productivity— Natural Resources

The central question may be put sharply by asking why, if it is man who was the architect of economic and social growth in the past and responsible for the vast contributions to knowledge and technological and social power, a larger number of human beings need result in a lower rate of increase in per capita product? More population means more creators and producers, both of goods along established production patterns and of new knowledge and inventions. Why shouldn't the larger numbers achieve what the smaller numbers accomplished in the modern past—raise total output to provide not only for the current population increase but also for a rapidly rising supply per capita?

The usual answers indicate limits to the productive power of a larger population, limits that either did not operate or were less restrictive with smaller numbers, and that prevent the attainment of the high rate of increase in per capita product that would otherwise be possible. We examine these limits briefly, distinguishing between those related to scarcity of natural, non-reproducible resources—to be discussed here—and those represented by greater requirements of capital investment for the sustained or increased productivity of the larger population and labor force—to be discussed in the next section.

The fixed supply of natural resources, especially land, which limits the productivity of a larger labor force and per capita supplies of a larger population, was the major theme of Malthus, particularly in the first edition of his *Essay on Population* in 1798. In subsequent editions, second and third thoughts shaded the stark confrontation of the geometric rate of growth of population endowed with "fixed passions" with the arithmetic rate at which the limited natural resources kept the increase in necessary subsistence. And the theme has persisted, with varying intensity, ever since—with the focus of scarcity shifting from land to other natural, non-reproducible resources such as depletable minerals, to water, and finally to space on our planet. Implied in the theme was the assumption that discovery and innovation, and their extended application, could not significantly remove or raise the limits—except at heavy material costs that would necessarily reduce or stop the rate of growth of per capita product or indeed bring it down to a point where the Malthusian positive checks would operate.

The one and three-quarters centuries since the publication of the first edition of Malthus's *Essay* have seen the assumption of the inability of human knowledge and technology to cope with the constraints imposed by the scarcity of natural resources proven wrong—despite a rate of population growth that by the mid-twentieth century was more than double that of Malthus's time. And the same fate befell several other long-term prognoses made by the Classical and Marxian schools of economics from a model in which the keystones were scarcity of land and diminishing returns as an historical tendency: the iron law of wages, the falling rate of profit and increasing exploitation, the "immiseration" and proletarianization of the masses, the increasing violence of economic crises. Furthermore, for the developed part of the world, which accounted for a rising share of world population, the disparity between the reality of rapid growth of population and per capita product and the vision of the Malthusian threat has become progressively wider.

But the important question relates to the present situation, to the limits that scarce natural resources impose upon current and prospective rises in productivity, given current and prospective population numbers. Rather than attempt to answer this question myself, let me quote two summary statements by Professor Joseph J. Spengler, who recently reviewed the field.

The first statement was made in a Presidential Address to the American Economic Association in December, 1965, and describes the present thinking of economists as follows:

> Perhaps the greatest reversal of opinion in the period 1930–65 is that relating to the role played by land and other natural resources in economic development and the disenthralling of populations from Malthusian traps. The importance of this role has been played down for a variety of reasons. First, investment in scientific discovery, applied technology, and education has been found to account for a major fraction of the increase in output in advanced countries, although recently the need to complement this type of investment with physical capital has again begun to be emphasized. Second, input of the services of land and natural resources per unit of GNP has greatly decreased in advanced countries. . . . Third, discovery and technological change, together with substitution at producer and consumer levels, have greatly augmented both the visible and the immediately potential stock of fuel, mineral, and related sources of natural-resource services. Man, it is supposed, is confronted by chains of natural-resource substitutes which modern molecular engineering and alchemy can subvert to his purposes, replacing links that weaken and elevating inferior sources (e.g., taconite rock) as well as substituting less expensive for more expensive sources of particular natural-resource service needs. For example, energy should prove producible in large amounts through fission assisted by breeder reactors, and in almost unlimited amounts should fusion prove technologically and economically feasible.[3]

Professor Spengler qualifies this consensus of economists as overly influenced by the favorable experience of advanced countries and insufficiently cognizant of the difficulties of underdeveloped countries and of the depressing effects of population growth on the amenities of life. However, in a summary paper on population and natural resources for the United Nations World Population Conference in the fall of 1965, he suggests that, given skills, capital, and effective use of technology, scarcity of natural resources does not impose serious constraints on

[3] See "The Economist and the Population Question," *American Economic Review*, Vol. 56, no. 1, 1966, 9.

population growth, present and presumably in the discernible future. The following quotations support this conclusion.[4]

On agricultural production: "Because it is becoming increasingly difficult to increase arable land, especially in the more densely populated regions, emphasis will be placed almost exclusively upon increasing yields per acre, though some acreage may be shifted to the production of output with a high protein yield per acre (e.g., cereal instead of meat) . . ." (p. 29); and "Food production in most underdeveloped countries could eventually be trebled or quadrupled, given good fertilization, together with improved seed, cultivation, and control of pests and diseases" (p. 30).

On mineral and other depletable resources: "Supplies of many non-fuel minerals will be depleted within a century or two, and it will become increasingly necessary to resort to substitutes or to synthetic production. Fossil fuel reserves may be used up in two centuries or less though the use of fuel cells could extend this period. Improvement in fission procedures and enlargement of sources of fission materials could meet energy needs for several millennia, while the development of feasible, economic ways for using fusion materials would virtually remove limits imposed by shortage of energy. Given adequate supplies of energy, exploitation of sources of heavy-volume minerals, or of substitute materials, which abound in the surface of the earth (iron, aluminum, crushed rock, etc.) would be economically feasible and the costs of desalinization and transportation of sea water would be reduced" (p. 31).

As Professor Spengler indicates, judgments like these are necessarily approximate and partly conjectural. Nor is it clear how such judgments, even if made by technical authorities, are best combined into a reliable consensus with firm quantitative results. But it seems warranted to assume that such a consensus, even if put in moderate terms and shorn of exuberant claims for technology, affirms the feasibility in the proximate future of substantial population growth without such pressure on scarce natural resources as would prevent a substantial rise in per capita product. And "warranted" means that the consensus carries far

[4] See "Population and Natural Resources," mimeographed and listed as prepared on behalf of the United Nations, Background paper /B.10/6/E/447.

more weight in its appraisal of possibilities than dogmatic *obiter dicta* of the Malthusian type.

The content of the consensus should not be misinterpreted. The judgments tell us that it would be technologically feasible to triple or quadruple food production in most underdeveloped countries, presumably within a limited time horizon; in other words, that the capital and skill requirements are not beyond reach of these countries. And if we accept these judgments, doubling of the population of less-developed areas in the world between 1965 and 2000, indicated in the medium projection of the United Nations,[5] would still leave a substantial margin for a rise in food production per capita. But the statement does not mean that the technologically feasible will necessarily be realized, even though capital and skill requirements are not excessive. And, although population growth is feasible at the rate projected, we have no assurance that the rate of growth in food supply or total product per capita will be as high as it might be with a lower rate of population growth.

Even in this sense, and disregarding for the moment other conditions necessary for the realization of technological potentials (to be discussed below), the feasibility of continued population growth should not be accepted without examining several

---

[5] See *World Population Prospects, as Assessed in 1963* (New York: United Nations, 1966), Table A3.2, p. 134.

In connection with its Freedom from Hunger Campaign, the Food and Agriculture Organization explored the problem in its Basic Study No. 10, *Possibilities of Increasing World Food Production* (Rome, 1963). The food requirements that constituted the target allowed not only for the population increase as projected to year 2000, but also for rises in per capita food consumption in the underdeveloped countries above their 1958 level—by 67 per cent in Asia and the Far East, 28 per cent in Africa, 17 per cent in the Near East, and 5 per cent in Latin America (see Table 2, pp. 24–25). The conclusion of the exploration was that not only for the developed countries, but also for Latin America, Africa, and the Near East, meeting the food requirements was technologically feasible. Only for the Far East "the balance between future food needs and known potentialities for production may well prove to be delicate" (pp. 222–23). But even in the Far East a substantial increase, if not 67 per cent, in per capita food supplies was also presumably technologically feasible.

Like most evaluations of this kind, this one assumes that growth in food production will not be at the expense of adequate growth in per capita supplies of other economic goods (see pp. 7–8).

For further discussion, see the next paper in this volume, "Economic Capacity and Population Growth."

possible qualifications. First there is the question of the time horizon. The reference above to the next three to four decades was
by design; and even that period may be too long. It is only for a
limited span ahead that we can evaluate current but not yet
fully applied discovery and invention and gauge their contribution to increased productivity (offsetting scarcity of resources);
and also suggest plausible population growth rates. As the time
span is extended, it becomes increasingly difficult to assess the
cumulative interaction of additions to knowledge and technology, some of which are still to be made; far more difficult, in
fact, than to extrapolate further into the future the geometric
rates of increase in population. If, in facing the complexity of
the long-term projection of technological capacity, we retain
some obvious limits—e.g., the limits of our planet, refusing to
consider the science-fiction possibilities of extra-planetary existence of mankind—then we must admit that at some future time
population growth will have to slow down and eventually come
to a standstill. This eventuality is sufficiently plausible (if we disregard atomic holocausts and other calamities), for all countries
and the world at large, to warrant imaginative exploration of social devices for channeling individual passions and choices into
demographically desirable patterns of population constancy in a
world society for which a range of significant variants would
have to be projected. But it qualifies our conclusions only by
limiting the consensus on technological potentials to a restricted
time span ahead. Extension of the span suggests tasks, in exploration either of long-range technological progress or of social
adjustment to unchanging population numbers, that are beyond
the scope of the discussion here.

The second possible qualification is that in some countries,
particularly among the underdeveloped, the relative scarcity of
natural resources may be so acute that the pressures of further
population growth may be too costly to be borne even by advanced technology. For example, a high rate of increase in the
number of Eskimos in the Arctic wilderness, or of nomads in the
Sahara Desert, may prohibit a rise in per capita product that
might be possible otherwise. And because many underdeveloped
countries, particularly in Asia, are densely populated, relative
scarcity of natural resources may seem to be the typical
condition—suggesting that the Malthusian limit should be

raised for developed countries only. But the scarcity of natural resources in the underdeveloped countries is primarily a function of underdevelopment; underdevelopment is not a function of scarce natural resources. Although the natural resources of Japan and Switzerland are limited compared with those of Indonesia, Nigeria, and the Congo, the former managed to attain high levels of economic performance and growth. Many underdeveloped countries are unaware of their wealth of natural resources since such knowledge is itself a function of economic development. These countries may possess more resources than they realize; practically all of them have sometime in their history enjoyed comparative advantage with respect to some commodity in world demand; and the population density of many of them is in itself evidence that the natural conditions are not drastically unfavorable—as they are in the Arctic or in the desert, where population is thinly spread out. Moreover, the expansion of the international trade network to the whole world has made each country less dependent upon its own specific range of natural resources. It seems legitimate to assume that the supply of natural resources relative to population in most underdeveloped countries is sufficient for technologically feasible advanced methods to provide a larger population with higher per capita product—an assumption that warrants the use of the term "underdeveloped," i.e., below the feasible potential, rather than "undevelopable."

The last possible qualification, a variant of the one just discussed, is formulated explicitly since it bears directly upon the limits represented by greater capital investment requirements associated with increased population. As already indicated, effective use of technology calls for material capital and a new range of skills, as well as the more important institutional adjustments that will be stressed below. As far as capital investment is concerned, whether in material capital or in skills, the conclusion of the discussion of the second qualification in the paragraph above may be taken to read that the removal of limitations of natural resources by the use of advanced technology will require relative inputs of investment into material capital or human skills no greater than those that have occurred in the presently developed countries in the course of their growth. In the course of the growth of the presently developed countries the increasing pressure of population on natural resources was also lifted to permit substantial rises in both population and per capita product, and their incremental capital-output ratios can be considered relevant to further growth—either in the developed or in the underdeveloped countries. Indeed, as will be suggested below, there may be grounds for arguing that in the underdeveloped countries, the latecomers on the scene of industrialization, the wider choice of available technological alternatives may permit, despite the apparent scarcity of resources under *traditional* technology, a lower capital input, i.e., a lower investment in capital (whether material or in skills) per unit of additional output deliverable by *modern* technology, lower than was needed in the earlier phases of growth of the presently developed countries.

3. Limits to Rising Productivity— Capital Requirements

Larger population and labor force mean, in the first instance, additional workers who must be equipped with material capital if their productivity is not to fall below that of those already equipped and engaged. Hence, whatever our assumptions concerning desirable net rises in productivity per worker (and per capita), the higher the rate of increase in population and labor force, the greater the requirement for material capital to equip the additional workers. Thus, if in one case, population and labor force grow 1 per cent per year, while in another they grow 3 per cent per year, and the incremental capital-output ratio, i.e., the ratio of additions to material reproducible capital stock needed to produce an additional unit of output (say net domestic product), is 3.0, the proportion of product that has to be devoted to net capital formation or investment is 3×0.01, or 3 per cent in the first case, and 3×0.03, or 9 per cent in the second case—if the per worker and per capita product in the case of higher population growth is not to fall below the per capita product in the case of lower population growth. And unless the share of government consumption in total product is reduced, this means that current consumption by households would, with the higher share of capital formation, drop by 6 per cent of total product (and a larger percentage of household consumption proper).

This is the rationale for lines 1–5 of the Illustrative Calculation 1, a demonstration of the effects of the rate of population growth on capital and other requirements, and hence on household consumption per unit. Case A assumes a population growth rate of 1 per cent and Case B, a rate of 3 per cent. Within A and B, A–1 and B–1 assume an annual growth in per capita product of 2 per cent whereas A–2 and B–2 assume only 0.1 per cent.

Greater material capital requirements, in terms of a higher share of total product to be devoted to net capital formation, is only one effect of a higher rate of population increase. The second is the consequence for the age structure *if* population growth is due exclusively to natural increase, i.e., balance of births over deaths, and not at all to immigration; and it is with the rate of natural increase of a closed population that we are concerned here. The effect on the age structure of the population, under these conditions, of differences in the growth rates assumed (i.e., between 1 and 3 per cent per year) is shown in lines 7–9 of the exhibit, which we derived by relating the age distribution to population growth rates over the preceding 15 years, in countries for which international migration was negligible. A country with a high population growth rate has a higher proportion of population under 15 than a low growth country—40 per cent compared with 26; a somewhat lower proportion of population of working ages, i.e., 15 through 64—56 per cent compared with 64; and a much lower proportion of older population, 65 years old and older—4 per cent compared with 10.

This shift in age structure, associated with the rate of natural increase of the population, is a long-term result; and Cases A and B represent two patterns of population growth, each persisting long enough to reveal its eventual consequences. Three aspects of such a shift in age structure must be noted. First, the proportion of the population in the working ages is distinctly lower in the case with the higher rate of population growth. Hence, if total populations in the two cases are equal (which we assume to simplify the illustration), total output should be lower in Case B, with a higher rate of population growth and a lower

	A–1 (1)	B–1 (2)	A–2 (3)	B–2 (4)
1. Assumed rate of growth of population, % per year	1.0	3.0	1.0	3.0
2. Assumed rate of growth of per capita product, % per year	2.0	2.0	0.1	0.1
3. Rate of growth of total net product, % per year (from lines 1 and 2)	3.02	5.06	1.101	3.103
4. Net capital investment required as % of net product (Incremental net capital–output ratio, ICOR, assumed to be 3.0)	9.06	15.18	3.303	9.309
5. Government consumption as % of net product (assumed)	10.0	10.0	10.0	10.0
6. Private consumer expenditures as % of net product (100 minus lines 4 and 5)	80.94	74.82	86.70	80.69
Age Structure of Population (based on UN selected data) *Total population = 100*				
7. 0–14 years old	26	40	26	40
8. 15–64 years old	64	56	64	56
9. 65 and over	10	4	10	4
10. Equivalent consumer units (lines 7 and 9 weighted by 0.6; line 8 by 1.0)	85.6	82.4	85.6	82.4
11. Private consumer expenditures, % of total net product per equivalent consumer unit (line 6 ÷ line 10)	0.946	0.908	1.013	0.979
12. Total net product (assuming output of 100 per worker, i.e., per member of line 8)	6,400	5,600	6,400	5,600
13. Consumption per equivalent unit (line 11 × 12 ÷ 100)	60.54	50.85	64.83	54.82

The ICOR in line 4 (3.0) is the figure customarily used in economic analysis of capital-output ratios. The entries in lines 7–9 are the only other empirical coefficients and their derivation is indicated here.

In general, given a rate of natural increase of population and a set of age-sex-specific death rates, the birth rate and the age structure can be derived. For recent years, we have the age structure for a number of countries, with differing rates of population growth over an immediately preceding long period (of say 15 years); and that structure appears to be dominated, at least for the wide age brackets used here, by the population growth rate. This is shown in a recent study of the total dependency ratio (defined as the ratio of population under 20 and 65 and over to one between 19 and 65, a ratio dominated by the younger age brackets) by David R. Kamerschen, "The Total Dependency Ratio Approach to Overpopulation," *Social and Economic Studies,* Vol. 13, no. 4, 1964, 488–501.

From the recent *Demographic Yearbooks* we derived both the shares of population under 15 in a recent year (usually 1960 or later) and the rate of population increase for the preceding 15 years for several countries not much affected by international migration. Several examples, covering the range of population growth from low to high, with the first figure indicating the rate of growth and the second the share of the group under 15 are: Costa Rica—3.88 and 47.6; Chile—2.25 and 39.8; the Netherlands—1.44

proportion in the working ages, than in Case A, which has more workers. On the assumption that per worker product is the same in both cases, total product (and product per capita) is lower in Case B than in Case A in the proportion of the working age shares in population in the two cases.

Second, the higher growth rate, which makes for a higher share of population under 15 in Case B, also means a higher share of younger age groups *within* the total span of working ages. In other words, the labor force is more youthful in Case B than in Case A. The effect of this greater youthfulness on productivity cannot be measured without further specification of the productive processes involved and of the precise age structure of the labor force. Thus, greater emphasis on mobility, on recent education, etc., would favor the more youthful labor force; greater emphasis on experience, acquirable only with practice and age, would favor the older labor force. But I do not feel competent to deal with this question; nor is the answer likely to have major quantitative effects under the simple conditions of the illustration. This aspect of the shift in age structure associated with a higher rate of population growth is therefore neglected.

Third, the greater proportion of population in ages under 15 in Case B means a greater burden of dependency, but this is partly offset by the lower consumer requirements per head of the young. The reduction to equivalent consumer units would therefore be proportionately greater in Case B than in Case A. Neglecting the complex question of consumer equivalence by age and sex, we assigned a weight of 0.6 to the dependent population, i.e., ages under 15 and over 65, and a weight of 1.0 to the population in the working ages.[6] We then calculated the total of

---

and 30.7; Sweden—0.80 and 22.0. The figures in our calculations are derived from this association, and are similar to those given in Jan L. Sadie, "Demographic Aspects of Labour Supply and Employment," prepared for the 1965 World Population Conference (No. A.5/19/E/484), where for industrialized countries, with a birth rate (BR) of 20 and life expectation at birth (E_0) of 70, the shares of the three successive age groups are 27, 63, and 10; whereas for the agricultural countries (BR—38; E_0—46) they are 39, 57, and 4 (see Table 1, p. 4).

[6] These weights were derived from data in Ansley J. Coale and Edgar M. Hoover, *Population Growth and Economic Development in Low-Income Countries* (Princeton, N.J.: Princeton University Press, 1958). For

equivalent consumer units in all cases, and arrived at the ultimate result—per consuming unit supply of total product which remains after the requirements for material capital and the changing proportions of working-age population have been satisfied.

We may now list, seriatim, the conclusions that the calculation suggests concerning the effects of higher population growth rates on capital and other requirements, and on consumption per equivalent consumer unit.

First, a 3 per cent rate of population growth, compared with a 1 per cent rate, raises capital requirements; and, all other conditions being equal, reduces per unit consumption. With government consumption set at 10 per cent of total product in all cases, and with an incremental net capital-output ratio of 3.0, the residual for consumption is reduced 7.56 per cent in Cases A–1 and B–1, with annual growth in per capita product of 2.0 per cent, and 6.93 per cent in Cases A–2 and B–2, with annual growth in per capita product of 0.1 per cent (line 6).

Second, the lower proportion of working-age population to total in Case B, resulting from the higher rate of natural increase in total population, means under the simple assumptions used here a corresponding reduction in total product and in total consumption. This amounts to a drop from 64 to 56, or 12.5 per cent—in both pairs of cases (line 8).

Third, the shift in age structure reduces the number of con-

India "the number of males over ten is multiplied by 1, the number of females over ten is multiplied by 0.9, and the number of children under ten by 0.5" (see footnote 1, p. 238). This calculation was based essentially upon scales of dietary requirements discussed in *ibid.*, pp. 88 ff.; and implies a weight for children under 10 of 0.5 divided by roughly 0.95 for people over 10, or 0.53 to 1.0.

We used these estimates since we had in mind an underdeveloped country; raised the fraction to 0.6, to allow for extension of age to 15 and for non-food consumption; and applied it also to ages of 65 and over, since per head consumption in these ages is also probably lower than for the working population. Assigning the full consuming weight to ages 65 and over would only strengthen the conclusion suggested by the illustrative calculation, viz., the limited reduction in consumption per consumer unit, under the conditions stated, necessitated by a higher rate of population growth.

Our calculation is similar to that in Chapter XVII of the Coale-Hoover volume but uses illustrative figures rather than realistic projections for a specific country.

sumer equivalent units more when population growth is high than when it is low. In our illustration equivalent consumer units drop from 85.6 in Case A to 82.4 in Case B, or 3.74 per cent (line 10).

Fourth, the effect on consumption per equivalent consuming unit is the cumulative result of the two reductions in total product flowing to consumers referred to above, and the one rise represented by the smaller number of equivalent consumer units. Thus for the A–1, B–1 pair the difference in consumption per consuming unit is $100 - [(100-7.56) \times (100-12.5) \div (100-3.74)]$, which works out to a decline of 16.0 per cent, and is equal to the percentage drop from 60.54 to 50.85 (higher figure as base) in line 13, columns 1 and 2. For the second pair of cases (A–2 and B–2) the difference is $100 - [(100-6.93) \times (100-12.5) \div (100-3.74)]$, which works out to a decline of 15.4 per cent, and is equal to the fall from 64.83 to 54.84 (higher figure as base) in columns 3 and 4.

Fifth, the percentage reduction in per consuming unit supply of consumer goods, caused by a higher rate of population growth, is roughly the same whether the annual rate of increase in per capita product is 2.0 or 0.1 per cent—which means that results would be similar for a wide range of rates of growth of per capita product.

Finally, attempts to accommodate both a higher rate of population growth and a higher rate of increase in per capita product would not reduce per unit consumption much more. Thus if we compare Case A–2 (population growing at 1.0 per cent; per capita product at 0.1 per cent) with Case B–1 (population growing at 3.0 per cent; per capita product at 2.0 per cent), the difference in per consumer unit supply is between 64.83 and 50.85, or 21.6 per cent of the higher figure.

These calculations suggest that raising the rate of population growth from 1 to 3 per cent per year can presumably be accommodated by a reduction of about a seventh in consumption per unit; and that a few more percentage points taken from ultimate consumption would permit a much higher rate of growth of per capita product. Before we ask what such reduction in consumption would mean, and how revealing this kind of analysis is, let me note that the analysis follows the traditional lines of the economic discipline—even if in a crude form (using capital-output ratios and simple assumptions concerning labor inputs, rather than linear production functions, whose use, however, would not change the results significantly). The results could easily be modified within a limited range either by raising or lowering the fractions of consumption that would have to be foregone as a result of accelerated population growth. Consumption would be reduced more if *gross* capital-output ratios were used, provided that the rates of increase of *gross* product per capita are the same; or if some part of the government consumption fraction were assumed to be related either to capital investment required or to population, so that a higher rate of population growth would call for a larger fraction for government consumption (a point to which we shall return below). On the other hand, the net incremental capital-output ratio of 3.0 used here may be too high: in the early phases of growth distinctly lower ratios prevailed in several countries.[7] If we set it at 2.0, and apply the full weight of 1.0 to the numbers in age groups of 65

[7] The ratio (NDCF/NDP) for Japan from the late 1890's to World War I was 1.6; for Denmark, from 1870 to 1914—2.4; for Sweden from 1861 to 1911–20—2.6. See "Quantitative Aspects of the Economic Growth of Nations: VI. Long-Term Trends in Capital Formation Proportions," *Economic Development and Cultural Change*, Vol. 9, no. 4, Part II, 1961, Table 5, pp. 17–18.

The choice between the gross and net capital-output ratios depends upon our judgment of the extent to which capital consumption charges represent an absolute reduction in the productive capacity of the fixed capital goods. Consumption charges that represent physical deterioration or greater maintenance costs, and thus a reduction in absolute productivity, ought to be subtracted and capital-output ratios net of these charges should be used in our analysis. Charges representing obsolescence due to changes in taste (e.g., in residential housing), almost inevitably associated with rising per capita income and a growing economy, should be similarly treated. But most of the consumption charges for durable capital goods in the hands of producers, at least in a modern economy, do not represent deterioration in absolute productivity but rather technical obsolescence, i.e., loss in relative earning power due to technical progress that brings constantly new and more productive producer goods into being; so that even zero net capital formation represents a *rise* in productive capacity (about equal to the average rate of technical progress). In this case, gross rather than net capital-output ratios should be used in our analysis. (For further discussion of this problem, particularly in application to pre-modern times, see a later paper in this volume, "Capital Formation in Modern Economic Growth".)

With gross capital-output ratios between 4 and 5.5, compared with net ratios between 2.4 and 3.3 (see the source in the first paragraph of this footnote), the relevant ratios might perhaps be closer to 4 than to 3 (used in the illustrative calculation), but the use of the 4.0 ratio would modify the results only slightly.

and over, the entries in line 13 for consumption per equivalent unit would be, in the order of columns 1–4, 59.97, 53.25, 62.71, and 55.86. In this case a rise in population growth rates from 1 to 3 per cent per year can be accommodated by a decline in per unit consumption of about 11 per cent; and even with the additional shift from low to high growth rates in per capita product (i.e., cols. 2 and 3), consumption per unit would have to be reduced only 15 per cent.

If the orders of magnitude derived in the illustrative calculation are acceptable, and there is no reason to reject them outright, the puzzling results cast doubt upon the adequacy of the underlying analytical structure. That the results are puzzling need hardly be stressed. They suggest that with a growth in per capita product of 2.0 per cent per year a rise in the rate of population growth as large as that from 1 to 3 per cent per year can be met by a reduction in consumption of about 16 per cent—which means that the sacrifice of half of the long-term increase of 2 per cent in per unit consumption for about a decade and a half would bring the country to the high level of per capita product that it would have achieved with only one-third of the population growth rate—and thereafter the growth in per capita product would continue at 2.0 per cent. Likewise, with a given population growth rate, raising the rate of increase in per capita product from 0.1 to 2.0 per cent apparently reduces per unit consumption only about 7 per cent—which would be made up in about three years. One may ask why, if this is a realistic model of economic growth, so few countries have become developed, for surely the sacrifice of a small fraction of rapidly growing consumption would hardly tax the energies or social capacity of the least-developed economies and societies.

The analysis is clearly deficient because it assumes that material capital is the sole agent of increases in per capita product, and that the input of labor is proportional to numbers in the labor force. Since material capital formation is a small fraction of total output, major changes in the former mean minor changes in a large component of output like consumption, and these minor changes can consequently work seeming miracles in the way of producing economic growth. Since limitations of natural resources have also been translated into reproducible capital requirements, without materially raising their share in product (at least for purposes of present analysis, and reasonably so in view of the experience of the developed countries), the dominant role of material capital in the simple model served to remove all limitations to rising productivity and growing population. Consequently a wholly unrealistic picture of the possibilities, and of the problems associated with population and economic growth, is presented.

While the effort cannot lead to firm conclusions at the present stage of our knowledge, we must attempt to repair the omissions in the above analysis by re-examining the nature of capital and other requirements.

4. Capital and Other Requirements Re-examined

The realization that material reproducible capital and labor input unadjusted for quality differentials explain little of the rise in total product and much less of the rise in productivity has led, within recent years, to an attempt to identify and quantify the other factors involved. One direction followed in economic research has been to specify more explicitly various qualities of labor and different aspects of the organization of input into production. This approach is exemplified by Edward F. Denison's study, in which the effects of education of the labor force, length of workday, sex of workers, economies of scale, spread of knowledge, etc. were estimated in an attempt to allocate *fully* the growth of product in the United States among the relevant factors.[8] The other direction emphasizes the extension of the concept of capital beyond material stocks, reproducible or not, to investment in human beings in the form of education—formal or training on the job—as a major growth-promoting factor omitted in the conventional analysis of economic growth. The effort to measure investment in education has been pioneered by Theodore W. Schultz, and followed by Gary Becker and Jacob Mincer among others.[9]

[8] See "The Sources of Economic Growth in the United States and the Alternatives Before Us," Committee on Economic Development, *Supplementary Paper No. 13* (New York, 1962).

[9] See Theodore W. Schultz, "Capital Formation by Education," *Journal of Political Economy*, Vol. 68, no. 6, 1960; *The Economic Value of Education* (New York: Columbia University Press, 1963); and the collection of papers by Schultz, Becker, Mincer, and others under the title "Investment in Human Beings," which appeared as a supplement to *Journal of Political Economy*, Vol. 70, no. 5, Part 2, 1962.

The element common to and prominent in both approaches is the emphasis on investment in knowledge and in the quality of human beings as an integral component of capital formation, i.e., the part of current product diverted from ultimate consumption for the purpose of contributing immediately, or with some time lag, to the increase in output and productivity. We consider this element first in connection with the analysis in the illustrative calculation above—if only to see whether extension of the capital concept effectively repairs the obvious omissions and inadequacies of that analysis.

Undoubtedly both government and household consumption, as defined and measured in current national accounting, contain numerous elements that should be viewed as capital formation rather than government overhead services or ultimate consumption. Such capital-like uses of product range from obvious cases like research and development services (now *not* included under capital formation unless embodied in material capital goods), education and training activities, and services contributing to health, whether curative or recreational, to the more doubtful items of supplies of various commodities over and above a minimum viewed as indispensable for existence, which may contribute to better quality and hence higher productivity of persons engaged in economic production.[10] Needless to say, problems arise in drawing the line between these capital-like components and the pure consumption items; and these will be briefly exam-

[10] The activities in question are to be treated as capital whether performed by government and now included under government consumption, or by households and quasi-households and now included under private consumer expenditures.

Consumers' durable commodities—furniture, other house-furnishings and equipment, passenger cars, and the like—warrant specific mention, to avoid confusion. These could be considered capital goods, as residential housing is at present, and their purchases classified as capital investment rather than as consumer expenditures. But if this procedure were followed the household would be treated as a business unit producing consumer-good services, just as it is now treated as a business unit producing services of owner-occupied residences; and the definition of total product would be changed to include only the net income from consumers' durables, not the gross value of purchases.

In order to avoid complications, we retain the current concept of product and prefer the gross product and capital formation totals to the net (as indicated in the text discussion below). And since we retain the current concept of product, we do *not* classify all consumers' durable commodities, other than residential housing, as capital. Some of them will be so classified, in accordance with our text discussion, if they are seen as contributing to greater product, as product is now defined.

ined below. But any component of government or household consumption that we do identify as a capital item must be transferred to capital formation.

Such transfers, which clearly add to capital formation and capital stock, also affect the definition and scope of net and gross product; and these effects should be indicated. If some items of what is now classified as government consumption or private consumer expenditures are classified as capital, the current expenditures on these items represent capital formation—presumably gross. Hence, for net product, one would have to *subtract* the proportion of such expenditures that represents replacement of currently consumed capital (whether it is stock of education, of consumer durables, etc.) and *add* the net returns on the stock of items newly classified as capital. For gross product the procedure is less complicated: one would only have to add the net returns on the items newly classified as capital stock. Thus, if, for illustration, we assume that the result of the reclassification is a doubling of the gross capital formation proportion and of the net capital returns before reclassification, and if gross capital formation and net capital returns were each 20 per cent of GNP before reclassification, an original gross capital-output ratio of 5 to 1 becomes 10 to 1.2, or 8.5.

To demonstrate how the rise in the incremental capital-output ratio modifies the effects of a rise in the rate of growth of either population or per capita product on the supply of consumer goods per consumer unit, we prepared Illustrative Calculation 2. The ICOR ranges from 2.5 to 20.0; and, by design, we do not specify whether it is a net or gross capital-output ratio, a decision that depends largely upon whether it facilitates further analysis.

Of course, as the capital-output ratio rises, the reduction in the supply of consumer goods per consumer unit due to any rise in the growth rate of population (or of per capita product) becomes more marked. And this reduction is rapidly magnified as the capital-output ratio reaches the higher values. With the population growth tripling, and the ICOR doubling from 2.5 to 5.0, the reduction in per unit consumption increases from 14.0 or 14.4 per cent to about 20 per cent, i.e., by less than half (lines 5 and 6, cols. 1 and 2); with the next doubling, from 5.0 to 10.0, the reduction widens to 38 or 31 per cent, respectively, i.e., by

Illustrative Calculation 2. EFFECTS OF RISE IN RATE OF POPULATION GROWTH, OR OF GROWTH IN PER CAPITA PRODUCT ON PER UNIT CONSUMPTION, DIFFERENT VALUES OF CAPITAL-OUTPUT RATIO
Assumptions: (1) income per capita = 100; (2) government consumption (excl. all implicit capital) = 5% of total product

	Values of incremental C/O ratio				
	2.5 (1)	5.0 (2)	10.0 (3)	15.0 (4)	20.0 (5)
Consumption per equivalent consumer unit					
Growth of per capita product = 2.0%					
1. Population growth = 1% (Case A–1)	65.38	59.74	48.45—	37.16	25.87
2. Population growth = 3% (Case B–1)	55.97	47.37	30.17	12.98	−4.21
Growth of per capita product = 0.1%					
3. Population growth = 1% (Case A–2)	68.97	66.91	62.80	58.68	54.56
4. Population growth = 3% (Case B–2)	59.29	54.02	43.47	32.93	22.39
% reduction in consumption per consumer unit associated with rise in population rate of growth					
5. Growth in per capita product = 2% (lines 1 and 2)	14.4	20.7	37.7	65.1	116.3
6. Growth in per capita product = 0.1% (lines 3 and 4)	14.0	19.3	30.8	43.9	59.0
% reduction in consumption per consumer unit associated with rise in per capita product rate of growth					
7. Population growth = 1% (lines 1 and 3)	5.2	10.7	22.9	36.7	52.6
8. Population growth = 3% (lines 2 and 4)	5.6	12.3	30.6	60.6	118.8
% reduction in consumption per consumer unit associated with rise in population and in per capita product rates of growth					
9. Lines 2 and 3	18.8	29.2	52.0	77.9	107.7

more than a half (lines 5 and 6, col. 3); with the next doubling, from 10.0 to 20.0, the reduction widens to 116 or 59 per cent, i.e., tripling or doubling (lines 5 and 6, col. 5)—and indeed shows negative consumption in line 5. The point relevant to our analysis is that when the ICOR is high, say over 10, any acceleration of the growth rate of either population or of per capita product is severely limited; and, in fact, at those ICOR levels where consumption is reduced to negative values or to values close to 0, the rates of growth of product involved are impossible (e.g., a population growth rate of 3.0 per cent and a per capita product growth rate of 2.0 per cent for an ICOR of 20.0; see line 2, col. 5).

Three major problems are involved in identifying capital items, i.e., those contributing to the increase in output and productivity. First, an activity or product may serve both to increase output and to satisfy basic consumption or related needs. In commonly recognized capital goods, such as machinery, the element of consumption (e.g., vanity of the producer) is usually viewed as minor and is neglected. But in the case of education or health, the question as to how much is a consumption good and how much a production tool is complex. Second, there is the decision between gross and net, i.e., whether to try to establish the uses of product that contribute both to replacement of existing capital stock (however capital is defined) and to net additions, or only to the latter. As footnote 7 indicated, this decision is difficult even for the narrowly defined capital goods; and it becomes even more so when we deal with investment in knowledge and human beings. Third, there is the problem of the period elapsing between the time of the capital investment and the time at which it can be reasonably expected to contribute to product and productivity. In our calculations we disregarded this lag, and it is relatively short for material capital; but it may be far longer for investments in knowledge like basic research, or education and training.

We propose to simplify the analysis by neglecting the time lag between capital investment and its effect on output and by dealing with gross capital formation. Empirical evidence on the lag is scanty; and it would complicate analysis unduly to try to take account of it. Furthermore, the major results sought here are not likely to be affected, however important this question may be in policy decisions concerning investment priorities. The choice of a gross capital and product basis is largely governed by the desire to keep the present product concept, and utilize the available empirical knowledge concerning its rate of growth. As already indicated, if we were to use net capital and net product, outlays for education, if education is classified as capital, would be gross; and we would have to estimate the current consumption of the stock of education to derive net capital formation, and subtract it from the present product total to obtain net product. The difference between gross and net product is slight when we limit capital to reproducible material stock, and capital consumption to current charges against this capital—so that at present the two product totals differ by 6 to 8 per cent, and their growth rates are similar. An allowance for current consumption of the capital stock of education, health, basic research, etc., might amount to a substantial fraction of gross product as now defined; and net product, after subtraction of such consumption, might be appreciably smaller than the present net product, and might move at rates appreciably different from those of gross product. In short, we propose to view the capital-output ratios in Illustrative Calculation 2 as gross ratios, with capital investment acting instantaneously, and then ask what the plausible orders of magnitude would be, given a reasonable interpretation of the scope of capital formation.

The answer to this question, uncertain as it will be, can be sought in an examination of the structure of government and household consumption, in both developed and underdeveloped countries. This might suggest the extent to which the capital-output ratio would be raised by the inclusion in capital of some items now classified as consumption. We could then ask whether the capital-output ratios, based on the experience of the developed countries, are fully relevant to the underdeveloped countries.

Summary data on the structure of government and household consumption in recent years in the developed countries show that of the 14 per cent share of government consumption in GNP, 6 percentage points may be allocated to direct services to consumers, in the way of educational, curative, recreational, and similar services—and should be added to private consumer expenditures to form total consumption.[11] Of the latter total, the components (expressed as percentages of GNP) are: food, beverages, and tobacco—24 per cent; clothing—8 per cent; household, including rent, water, light, fuel, domestic services, furniture and furnishings—16 per cent; and the remaining services—health and personal care, education, recreation, transportation and communication, etc.—23 per cent. The total is 71 per cent of GNP, with the residual accounted for by gross capital formation (21 per cent) and the remainder of government consumption, essentially intermediate services (8 per cent). In the case of the underdeveloped countries, consumption, includ-

---

[11] These and other data in the paragraph are from my "Quantitative Aspects of the Economic Growth of Nations: VII. The Share and Structure of Consumption," *Economic Development and Cultural Change*, Vol. 10, no. 2, Part II, 1962, Table 6, p. 12 and Table 10, p. 24.

The discussion here deals only with use of current product, and disregards the "income foregone" component in the usual calculation of investment in education. In order to include the latter we would have to consider the changing relation of labor force to total population, a relation that we treat as constant in order to simplify the analysis.

ing direct services of government, is roughly 78 per cent of GNP, with 14 per cent allocated to gross capital formation, and 8 per cent to government intermediate product. The structure of consumption is, however, distinctly different: food, beverages, and tobacco account for 42 per cent of GNP; clothing for 8; the household and its furnishings for 14; and the residual services —of education, health, transportation, etc.—for 14 per cent. Perhaps more important than the differences in structure is the much larger per capita consumption in the developed than in the underdeveloped countries, ranging, in a rather conventional translation to U.S. dollars, from 5 to 1 for food to 22 to 1 for recreation and amusement, or 16 to 1 for all the services. Granted that the inadequate conversion exaggerates the difference, the effective disparity in consumption per capita, absolute and relative, must be large for all categories.

How much of the much greater consumption in developed countries of all items, not merely those that contain large capital elements, facilitates and induces further growth of output and production? In attempting an answer, we could adopt one of two approaches. In one we would argue that a larger per capita consumption of *any* commodity or service, except those classed as pernicious and illegal (such as narcotics), may have an element of capital, i.e., output-increasing capacity, within a wide range of per capita volume; but that this capital-content of consumption changes markedly with changes in per capita use of the goods in question, as well as with the requirements of the productive structure of the economy. Thus an increase in daily calorie consumption per capita from 1,800 to 2,200 may have a marked positive effect on the productivity of the labor force, and in that sense additional food consumption is a capital item; but the effect would be less marked with a rise from 2,500 to 3,100 calories per day, and might prove negative with a rise to more than 3,500 calories. (The figures are illustrative, and no knowledge of nutrition is claimed.) At some early stage in an economy's development a greater input into education may fail to contribute to increased output because the productive structure, even though developing, is not advanced enough to accommodate the higher skills involved; whereas at a later stage of development the demand for the products of more education may be great, and the incremental capital-output ratio of this type of use may be quite high. This approach would emphasize not only the capital element in all uses now classified as ultimate consumption, but also the variability, in the course of growth and of changes in absolute levels of consumption and product, in the proportion of such capital elements in the various categories of what are now viewed as consumer goods. The second approach, a crude variant of the first, would, in application to developed countries, begin by assuming that the capital element in most consumer commodities and services is close to zero, given the high levels of per capita consumption and no significant decline in them; and would then identify and estimate the capital elements in a few important consumption categories, e.g., research, education, and possibly health care.

Unfortunately, we cannot assign any values, even orders of magnitude, to incremental capital-output ratios that include indispensable growth-promoting uses, other than material capital formation. Indeed, such estimates would require extensive study of aspects of economic growth still barely known—and for a wide range of phases of economic performance. As the preceding discussion indicates, we would also need to know the net yield to be imputed to the items newly classified as capital stock, since it would have obvious effects on the capital-output ratio. However, two conclusions pertinent to our problem of relating population to economic growth immediately follow.

First, at any level of economic growth and at any time, material capital stock is not the only use of product indispensable for an increase in output and productivity; some elements in consumption are capital items in that sense; and hence the effective incremental capital-output ratio is significantly greater than that in which material capital formation is the numerator. In other words, material capital stock effectively increases output and productivity *only* if it is supplemented by some uses of product now classified as consumption; and, even then, other conditions may be essential—a point to which we shall return below. But if we consider for the moment uses of economic product alone, when we calculate the effects of a higher rate of population growth, this higher effective incremental capital-output ratio means much larger reductions in consumer goods per unit (as a proportion of per capita product)—whether from an attained or from a potential high level.

Second, the identity of the capital elements within the conventional classification of consumption shifts with changes in per capita consumption and in the productive structure of the economy. At one phase and level of economic growth the growth-promoting capital element may lie in consumption of food or in health services above a minimum; at another phase, it may lie in research and higher education. Consequently, in considering the effects of higher population growth, these capital-like items in consumption must be identified; otherwise the attempt to reduce consumption might have the undesirable effect of stifling growth. Thus, as with material capital formation, choices must be made regarding the particular types of investment to favor for growth to be maximized, so that those consumption items that contribute to increase of output and productivity should hopefully rise and those that will be reduced, absolutely or relatively, should have the least restricting effect on further growth.

In view of these conclusions the conventional capital-output experience of the developed countries is only a limited guide in the study of the effects of population increase on economic growth—in the developed countries and particularly in the underdeveloped. Not only material capital formation but also other uses of product must be examined to observe their relation to population increase and to growth in per capita product; and the higher relevant capital-output ratios have a numerator whose changing identity is important. Consequently the raising of the growth rate of total product intended to accommodate the combination of a higher rate of population increase and the same growth rate of per capita product involves more substantial and more selective reductions in the proportion of product flowing into "pure" consumption.

One other aspect of the relevance of even the expanded capital-output ratios to the analysis must be explicitly noted before we are ready to ask what all this means for the population growth problems of either underdeveloped or developed countries in the world today. The material capital-output ratios, for which we have a fair amount of long-term data for the developed countries and some for recent years for the underdeveloped countries, differ even among developed countries, and have changed over time (disregarding short-term fluctuations).

For the developed countries the gross ratios ranged from less than 3 to more than 7, for the long period before World War I; and from more than 4 to more than 7 for the half-century since the beginning of the twentieth century (see the paper cited in footnote 7, Table 5, pp. 17–18). Nor is there any reason to expect these ICOR's to be the same for the different countries, or constant in the course of a country's economic growth. There is no *technological* basis for a fixed relation between additions to material capital and increase in output, except in the sense, hardly relevant to economic experience, that without some low minimum capital addition a sustained rise in output and productivity is impossible—in a given specific field. A railroad cannot operate without track and rolling stock; mechanical spindles and looms are essential to the efficient production of cotton textiles. But a track can be two streaks of rust in the desert, or heavily ballasted high-speed rails cutting through mountains; and rolling stock or textile machinery can be new and expensive or secondhand and cheap. And if one has a choice among means of transport (railroads or trucks) or textile materials (cotton or synthetic fabrics), even greater variability is introduced into the material capital-output ratio. Most important, a capital stock can be run 24 hours a day, with high intensity of utilization, or on an 8-hour day—with obvious effects on the average and incremental material capital-output ratios. Furthermore, conditions existing in economic and social institutions vary and may affect differently the long-term capital-output ratios of individual countries: in general, the material capital-output ratios tend to rise over time, perhaps because a greater supply of capital permits a less intensive rate of utilization and an increase in the proportion of long-lived capital, or because the opportunities for strategic use of the stock of innovations available in the early phases of growth to follower countries (and all but one developed country are followers) are reduced.

These statements concerning the narrower capital-output ratios probably apply also to the extended ratios, since decisions regarding the items of use now classified under consumption but with significant capital elements are unlikely to eliminate differences among countries in the increases in total or per capita output that they attain with the same inputs of a given additional capital total, including both conventional and non-conventional components; or to cancel the significant trends over time observed in the material capital-output ratios. Differences in efficiency caused by differences in economic and social institutions would persist, as would those related to effects of low absolute levels of economic performance and degrees of backwardness; and the trends associated with economic growth and changes in the structure of both material capital and other uses of product would hardly be affected.

Given the variability even of the extended capital-output ratios, the values to be used in measuring the effects of a high rate of population growth, or of a desired higher rate of growth of per capita product—for a given country at a given time—cannot be determined mechanically. No matter how approximate the result will be, it necessitates the examination of all the conditions affecting the economic efficiency of a given country and of any other, apparently relevant countries over their relevant past. And obviously these conditions encompass economic and social factors, complementary to, but not identical with, the determinants embodied even in the wider definition of capital, in its relation to output—factors that should not be neglected, and yet are outside the conventional limits of the economics discipline.

5. *Bearing upon Underdeveloped Countries*

The above discussion can be summarized briefly. First, economic analysis which uses the conventional definitions of material capital and of labor uncomplicated by quality differentials, is inadequate for the exploration of the relations between population increase and economic growth, and, in effect, leads to unwarrantedly easy and optimistic conclusions. Second, while these limitations have been recognized for some time, and attempts have been made to expand the concept of capital either by including non-conventional capital inputs or taking account directly of qualities of labor and of some aspects of economic organization, the empirical evidence is still scanty.[12] Moreover, the difficult problems in distinguishing between capital formation, defined broadly, and pure consumption, and between gross

---

[12] Our discussion has been in terms of the concept of capital, but it could as well have been in terms of the quality of labor input.

and net value of non-conventional capital inputs, are still to be resolved. Third, while this conclusion is tentative, pending further study of additional capital-like uses of product and of qualities of labor, even with the extension of the concepts in any economic analysis of the relations between input and output, effective treatment of the bearing of such relations upon the interaction between population increase and economic growth would probably still involve broader economic, social, and technical conditions, in the given country and elsewhere—conditions that cannot be classified and measured under economic inputs.

With such a prognosis, intellectual caution and modesty should compel one to stop right here—with this confession that economic analysis alone is inadequate in dealing with such a fundamental aspect of economic growth as its relation to population increase. One could, of course, list the economic arguments for and against population increase as an instrument in raising per capita product; or describe past conditions of the presently developed countries where a high rate of population growth seemed indispensable for the achievement of high rates of growth in per capita product (as evident in much of the nineteenth- and early twentieth-century economic growth of this country and other European offshoots overseas, and possibly also of France); or where, on the contrary, a lower rate of population growth might have meant a higher rate of growth in per capita product than was attained (as might have been the case in the Netherlands). However, the history of economic growth, past and current, suggests strongly the importance of noneconomic factors not amenable to economic analysis—the broader social, political, and international decisions that set the conditions for the purely economic decisions and factors. Consequently, in dealing with the relation of population to economic growth, whether in underdeveloped or developed countries, we must note, in addition to the familiar economic factors, some of the broader aspects of social organization, national and international.

In turning now to the underdeveloped countries, we find that the definition affects the size of the group, its economic characteristics, and its diversity. Thus, if per capita product is taken as the most relevant criterion (even if we omit such exceptional cases as the Arab sheikdoms, where high product may be due to

an unusual endowment having little to do with the native economy) and the line is drawn at the low level of $100 GDP per
capita, in 1958 the countries with per capita product below $100
accounted for 1,530 million of the world population of 2,887 million, somewhat over a half.[13] The non-Communist developed
countries (North America, Europe, Australia and New Zealand,
and Japan) had a population of about 550 million and a per
capita product of about $1,400 in that year. And nine-tenths of
the population of the underdeveloped countries live in Asia and
account for most of the population of Asia, excluding Japan and
Asiatic U.S.S.R.; most of the remainder live in Africa and account for some 60 per cent of the population of that continent
(excluding South Africa and the regions assigned to the Middle
East). If we raise the limit to $200, the population total for un-
derdeveloped areas rises to 1,800 million, or about six-tenths of
world population; and it covers almost all of Asia and Africa,
about 60 per cent of the population of the Middle East, and
about half of the population of Latin America.

It seems advisable to accept a dividing line of $200 per head
or thereabout, in order to include the areas in which relatively
low per capita income is associated, in recent years, with high
rates of population growth. The underdeveloped group, in that
case, includes the population of almost all of Asia, Africa, the
Middle East, and most of Latin America (with the usual exclusions of Japan, South Africa, and Israel), but practically none of
Europe, North America, or Oceania (where population outside
Australia and New Zealand is quite small). The per capita product of this group, which accounts for almost two-thirds of world
population, still shows a range from 1 to 3 (i.e., from less than
$100 to more than $200); and the distribution is skewed in the
sense that the bulk of the population, dominated by the populous countries of Asia, has a per capita product below $100.

Several economic characteristics of the underdeveloped countries bear closely on the question of population growth as a pos-

[13] The data are largely from the United Nations, *Yearbook of National
Accounts Statistics* for gross domestic product (at factor cost) and the *Demographic Yearbook* for population, both for recent years. A convenient
summary is provided in my *Modern Economic Growth*, Tables 7.1 and 7.2,
pp. 360–64 and 368–69. In Chapter 7, I discuss the problems of converting per capita product to comparable units, for countries that differ greatly
in level and structure of economic performance.

sible obstacle to a rise in per capita product. First, per capita product is low, relative to that of the developed countries; and at the lower end of the range it is apparently significantly lower than the per capita product of the presently developed countries (with the exception of Japan) on the eve of their industrialization (i.e., the late eighteenth to the mid-nineteenth century) which, as suggested in footnote 1, may have been about $200. Second, the present low per capita product of underdeveloped countries is *not* the result of a recent decline from some higher level in the past. On the contrary, the little available long-term evidence suggests that, at worst, their per capita income was constant (as appears to have been true of Egypt from the early nineteenth century until recently), but that it probably rose, appreciably in some countries in Latin America and Africa (e.g., Ghana) and significantly even in India, although the rates of growth were much lower than in the developed countries. Third, the low per capita product in the underdeveloped countries is not due to a lower ratio of labor force to total population, i.e., a higher dependency ratio of the type shown in our illustrative calculations. The orders of difference between the underdeveloped and the developed countries with respect to per capita product are far too great to be explained by the limited fractional disparities that emerge in the ratio of labor force to total population due to differences in rate of natural increase, and even to differences in social practices with respect to use of labor. Fourth, in both underdeveloped and developed countries, product per worker in the A sector (agriculture, forestry, and fisheries) is distinctly lower than product per worker in the I sector (broadly defined to include mining, manufacturing, construction, light and power, etc., and transport and communication); but the relative differences in product per worker between the A and I sectors are greater in the underdeveloped than in the developed countries. Hence, the backwardness of the underdeveloped countries, if measured by per worker product, is appreciably greater when we compare product per worker in the A sector than when we compare product per worker in the I sector—partly because more modern technology has been introduced into the industry sector of the underdeveloped countries than into their agriculture. Finally, since per worker and per capita product are low, the structure of domestic demand favors foods and other prime necessities, primarily products of the A sector; and these would have to be produced at home rather than imported, except in the few underdeveloped countries that may have some valuable natural resource exportable in quantities that are large relative to the population. But with a high proportion of domestic demand for products of the A sector and low per worker productivity in the A sector, the share of the A sector in the total product and especially in the total labor force will be much larger in the underdeveloped countries than in the developed. Indeed, the share of the A sector in labor force in the low-income, underdeveloped countries may be as high as 60 to 70 per cent, whereas it is less than 10 per cent in the developed countries; and yet some of the latter (e.g., the United States) have a surplus of agricultural production over and above wasteful standards of domestic consumption. Obviously, the economic backwardness of the underdeveloped countries is due partly to lower productivity per worker within both the A and the I sectors, and partly to the greater weight of the A sector, with product per worker in both sets of countries lower than the countrywide average. It follows that in the course of growth per capita and per worker product rises partly because of growth in intra-sectoral productivity, and partly because of shifts in labor force (and other resources) from lower to higher productivity sectors. Such inter-sectoral shifts usually accompany and are indispensable for a sustained and significant rise in per capita product.

The low per capita and per worker output in the underdeveloped countries is due to the failure to apply modern technology, to exploit the productivity potential available in the stock of knowledge used by the developed countries. It is not due to scarcity of natural resources, climatic constraints, or deficiencies in genetic endowments, which would either bar the use of modern technology or result in a low product *despite* it. This proposition, which was advanced in part in our earlier discussion of natural resource limits, cannot be elaborated further here and must be accepted. It is fundamental to all our discussion: if it is rejected, the economic growth problems of underdeveloped countries cannot be solved with presently existing technology and must await some major innovational developments in the uncertain future.

The proposition is fundamental also in that it points to the advantages of economic backwardness that the underdeveloped countries possess. If their low productivity is due to failure to exploit modern technology effectively, the accessibility of most modern knowledge and technical know-how means a large stock of tested technology, material and social, available for future exploitation. In other words, all other conditions being equal, the incremental capital-output ratios, however capital is defined, in the underdeveloped countries should be much lower than either the current or past ratios in the developed countries, as long as production goals in the underdeveloped areas are similar to those of the developed at similar phases or levels of growth. In an economically advanced country, a large proportion of the expansion in output is in new directions and reflects recent innovations rather than the old, tried and true; and the costs of innovations in the early phases of their development are reflected in greater input of material capital, new types of education and training, and wider experimentation with new organizational and social devices. This proportion of the relatively new and untried tends to raise the proportion of capital investment, defined broadly, to new output; and the effect on the capital-output ratio is the greater, the more advanced the country. An underdeveloped country, on the other hand, has at its disposal a variety of what for the developed countries is the old technology. It should be able to attain the increased output that it desires with a relative input of material and other capital that is far smaller than was required in the developed countries in the past when the product or the technology in question was new, and smaller, too, than the capital requirements of the developed countries today, since, as already stated, the latter devote a large proportion of their resources to recent innovations.

The magnitude of this advantage of economic backwardness in relatively low capital-output ratios for the underdeveloped countries cannot be gauged. Given the marked rise in efficiency, i.e., the marked reduction of real inputs per unit of output, accomplished by modern technology in the developed countries since the early phases of the technological innovations, the required incremental capital-output ratios for the underdeveloped countries must be substantially lower, *if* they do not try to emulate developed countries in the pursuit of new and untried technological goals. To put it differently, the purely economic requirements for increasing output significantly—the relative requirements, even when capital is defined broadly to include investment in man—are comparatively moderate. Since the per capita product in underdeveloped countries has been growing in the past, even though slowly in most countries, they should be able to generate enough savings, diverting product to uses other than "pure" consumption, to permit high and sustained rates of growth of total and per capita product.

Yet neither in the long-term past, when population in the underdeveloped countries grew at distinctly lower rates than in the developed areas, nor in recent decades, has the growth rate of the underdeveloped countries exceeded that of the developed. If any underdeveloped country had attained a greater rate of growth of product, particularly on a per capita basis, and had sustained it over a fairly long period, it would have joined the ranks of the developed countries, as Japan did. The historical fact that since the mid-nineteenth century only a few countries were added to the small group of already developed (e.g., the United Kingdom, the United States, France, and Germany, to name the larger units), and only one of these was outside Europe and its offshoots overseas, suggests that the economic provisions for exploiting the advantages of economic backwardness, while necessary, are far from sufficient. The social and organizational requirements for channeling economic activity to allow for some minimum efficiency must have been, and must still be, unsatisfied; and this lack was enough to offset the economic advantages of backwardness and keep the underdeveloped countries at an economic standstill or permit only a slight growth in per capita product, which meant a marked loss in position relative to the developed areas.

Three social concomitants of economic backwardness seem crucial in any consideration of the economic growth problems of underdeveloped countries, whatever the role assigned to population increase. First, the main economic activity of these countries, particularly in agriculture, has been following long-established patterns, only slightly modified by contact with the rest of the world and by the emergence of export-oriented sectors of a more modern type. This long persistence of old patterns of agricultural and related production typical of the large populations

of Asia, most of Africa, and of the indigenous Indian populations in much of Latin America means an entrenched heritage of
economic, political, and social institutions adapted to these patterns of economic activity; and the reduced potential for additional productivity caused by population growth means greater
population pressure *within* the framework of old, traditional
technology. Therefore the advantages of backwardness—reduced economic requirements for the application of modern
technology—can be realized only if changes are introduced into
the old institutional framework to accommodate the new
technology—whether in land distribution and tenure, control
over financing of agriculture, provisions for storage and market-
ing, or in the institutions governing the use of labor in and out
of agriculture to provide productive employment to persons displaced with a rise in agricultural productivity.

Since the old technology has failed, the new techniques must
be used and they require inputs not only of economic capital
but also of social capital, if one may use the term to designate
efforts and costs involved in modifying old established social institutions to provide the indispensable legal, political, and social
conditions for the new technology.[14] Unless these changes are
made, only a few of the more venturesome entrepreneurs, in agriculture or elsewhere, will attempt to apply modern technology
because the risks are excessive; and others will direct their efforts into uses that are easier and safer but least productive in
terms of socially desirable economic growth. The channeling of
savings into hoards of gold and precious ornaments, into layer-
ing of property rights over agricultural land, and into high-rent
urban real estate, are illustrations of the latter that easily come
to mind.

Second, many of the presently underdeveloped countries with
a vast majority of world population have, in the past century or
longer, either been colonies governed by a distant metropolitan
country; or, if sovereign states, have been handicapped by governments either too weak to withstand the aggressive pressures

[14] This need to shift the whole basis of technology and avoid the error of
assuming that gradual adjustments within the traditional technology could
provide an effective basis for economic growth, in agriculture and hence
elsewhere, is the major point made by T. W. Schultz in *Transforming Traditional Agriculture* (New Haven and London: Yale University Press,
1964).

of more developed countries or insufficiently responsive to the country's growth needs in dealing with the interests and pressures of groups inimical to economic modernization. Consequently, the development of a viable political structure that would provide adequate auspices for modern economic growth has been slow. Evolution of a political consensus of the population, or of an effectively trained and committed bureaucracy, has been far too limited for modern economic growth, which requires a modern state able to resolve conflicts usually generated by growth and to provide the necessary economic and social overhead capital. Even in the presently industrialized countries the political requirements of economic growth were often taxing, and many conflicts that growth generated (between agricultural and non-agricultural population, between workers and proprietors, between creditors and debtors, among regions, etc.) could not be resolved by a peaceful consensus of representative central governmental institutions. The Civil War in the United States and the efforts, often laborious and painful, to adjust political sovereignty to underlying community of feeling—illustrated by the separation of Belgium from the Netherlands, and of Norway from Sweden, or by the unification of Germany and of Italy—are partial evidence that political viability sufficient to assure the proper decisions relating to a country's economic growth and to its conditions is not easily attained. The current political turmoil and frequent breakdowns into internal conflicts in so much of the underdeveloped world may be exaggerated by us—since all such events are likely to over-impress the contemporaries. But the minimum political stability and efficiency needed for sustained economic growth seem to be lacking in most underdeveloped countries—from the most populous in Asia to those with apparently greater natural resources per capita in Africa and in Latin America. Political instability, governments too weak to provide the economic and social overhead, divisive tendencies within the population among races, tribes, regions, castes, etc., are all conditions that sharply reduce the economic growth capacity of a country.

Third, the persisting patterns of economic activity and of the social and political institutions of a country are reflected in the general outlook and the scales of values of the population—if only in the sense that all these aspects of human life must be generally consistent. An institution like the caste presumably affects the views of the people involved on the relation of man to man; and the views on which the power of a government rests are different in a traditional land-empire like pre-modern China from those held in a modern developed country with a democratic constitution. A high rate of modern economic growth is compatible with some sets of values and views, and not with others. It is incompatible, in the long run, with significant downgrading of the material welfare of the population; with severe restrictions on the search for and application of new knowledge and technology; with limited freedom to match the capacity of the population, afforded adequate and equitable life and learning, with the productive tasks of society. It is hardly surprising that the general outlook and the scales of values of populations acquired through centuries of traditional organization in the presently underdeveloped areas differ significantly from those associated with and required for a high level of economic performance; and while some small groups in these countries have acquired modern views and have thus become "westernized," they are only a very small minority of the population. Hence, if we gauge economic growth, as we do and must, by the criteria of a modern economic society, and in estimating the national product of India, for example, do not assign any positive values to the psychic income presumably gained from unproductive cattle, or from preservation of monkeys and destructive pests, while deducting the values of the crops that they destroy, traditional views *must* reduce the economic growth potential, as such growth is currently defined and measured.

We can easily add to these social concomitants of economic backwardness, to accentuate the obstacles which they create. Thus, the recent achievement of political sovereignty by so many underdeveloped countries has brought with it not only the responsibility for internal growth, which in the long run is all to the good, but also the responsibility for national security, which involves problems aggravated by the partitions forced through when independence was attained, and by the artificial character of some of the political boundaries drawn. The resulting international frictions have certainly consumed a substantial volume of resources that would otherwise have been available for economic advance. In the present international situation, the danger of backwardness, as well as the increasing contact with the rest of the world, may have made claims upon the government and raised the expectation of significant groups within the population that inhibit the pursuit of an efficient, long-term economic policy, and the maintenance of internal and external peace. Moreover, the exploitation of modern technology requires a sustained conversion of domestic resources and institutions to new uses, and that is not easy. Even on the technical level, it is a matter not only of borrowing and copying but also of modifying and adjusting the prototype to fit the specific structure of domestic resources and needs.

To be sure, the social and political obstacles to economic growth in the underdeveloped countries can be exaggerated, particularly since we cannot estimate the growth that could have taken place if they had been removed. Almost all underdeveloped countries have enjoyed substantial growth in recent years. But in making a broad judgment concerning the major focus of the growth problems in underdeveloped countries— taken as a group and allowing for a range within them—the preceding discussion can be summarized as follows. The underdeveloped countries possess a large potential for economic growth: modern technology provides the needed devices and tools (subject to feasible modifications and innovations to be made by the technicians of the underdeveloped countries themselves); and their economic resources permit absolutely modest but relatively large diversions from current product into capital (broadly defined) that are adequate for substantial growth, given low capital-output ratios as the typical advantage of economic backwardness. The core of the problem seems to lie in the inadequate internal social and political institutions, including some with a dominant economic content, which fail to provide the auspices for effective, sustained exploitation of the advantages of economic backwardness, and which are not easily modified. This difficulty is naturally compounded by international turbulence, partly arising from the recency of the achievement of sovereign status by such a large proportion of the currently underdeveloped areas.

This view bears directly on the question regarding population increase in the underdeveloped countries as an obstacle to a rise in per capita product. Obviously the high rates of population increase, and a rapid acceleration like that of the recent decade or two, resulting from continuing high or even slightly rising birth rates and sharply declining death rates, aggravate the already difficult problems of growth. Channeling more resources into capital formation, broadly defined, is an additional organizational task that would increase the burden of the already overtaxed machinery of the existing economic, political, and social institutions in underdeveloped areas. In particular, since the greatest pressure may be felt in agriculture, the traditional sector and the one most difficult to transform, additional constraints due to rapid population growth may not be easy to bear. And yet, if the preceding discussion correctly describes the balance of factors with respect to the *aggregate* supply of goods per capita, a higher rate of population increase, although an *additional* problem, would probably not be as great an obstacle as the failure to exploit the potential due to delays in adjusting social and political institutions. Given some favorable development within the latter, additional population could be accommodated, even if possibly at the cost of a smaller rise in per capita income than might otherwise occur. Given less favorable development, even if population growth slows down, misery will continue—even though it might be aggravated by population increase. Thus, one could hardly argue that in much of sub-Sahara Africa, Latin America, and even Asia, a reduction of population growth to say a tenth of a per cent from the current annual rate of 2 or more per cent would significantly alleviate the acute growth problems. Indeed, in view of the essential institutional and what might be called the "ideological" framework, the high fertility rates that cause the high rate of population increase may be less important for their direct effects—greater capital requirements, etc.—than as evidence of the population's lack of confidence in, or indifference to, the value of investment in its children by education and training. This lack of confidence or indifference is a reflection of the failure of the existing society to convince the population of the long-term wisdom of restricting the size of the family for the future benefit of its younger members.

The implications of this position for the evaluation of population policies should not be misunderstood. Unquestionably, strenuous efforts at reducing the birth rate in the underdevel-

oped countries are fully warranted, if they do not constitute a
large drain upon economic and organizational resources that
would otherwise be used advantageously to raise per capita
product and indirectly induce a more rational long-term family
planning process in a different and farther-going fashion. After
all, even the partial reduction of additions to what is otherwise
a heavy burden is all to the good. But other inferences may put
policies aimed at direct population control within a better
perspective and prevent placing undue hopes on their effects.
First, even a reasonably successful population-control policy
will not solve the major economic growth problems of the underdeveloped areas: these will remain with a lower rate of population growth or even with no increase in population (and they
may be replaced by other problems if population actually declines rapidly). Second, the short-term effects of current reduction in birth rates are quite limited, short-term in this case
meaning a period of one to two decades, which is fairly long
when we consider strains of economic backwardness. Fewer
births for a number of years mean only a reduction in the proportional numbers in the younger age groups, whose consumption per head is relatively low and whose effects on the distribution of product between consumption and capital formation are
moderate.[15] Since the growth problems of the underdeveloped
countries are far too acute to permit a delay of two to three decades for their resolution, control of population growth, important as it may be for the longer range future, offers little hope
for the immediate present. Third, this implies that the choice
between population control and no population control means
only moderate differences in current per capita product, not a
change from bare sustenance to surfeit. Fourth, a set of policies
directed at the economic, political, and social institutions of the
underdeveloped countries is required for the solution of their
growth problems, i.e., to increase significantly their capacity to
take advantage of their economic backwardness. But this set of

[15] In the calculations in the Coale-Hoover volume, a 50 per cent reduction in the birth rate from 1956 to 1981 leads to a rise in per consumer income of less than 3 per cent in the first 10 years, i.e., to 1966; of less than
7 per cent in the first 15 years, i.e., to 1971; of less than 15 per cent in the
first 20 years, i.e., by 1976 (see Projection 1, Table 38, p. 272). A *minor*
change in the capital-output ratios could either aggravate or more than offset these effects.

policies, if successful, would also indirectly spread population control far enough to make it really effective in the long run. The changes in social and economic structure (and in the international situation) would provide reasonable assurance to future parents that their children will profit from fewer siblings, both in terms of survival and in terms of the effective return on their better education, training, and health. Without these changes, parents see no reason to limit the size of the family but may have many children in the expectation that some will survive and fight their way, on the basis of genetic and other noninvestment endowments, to a fruitful life. Pursuit of a family-planning policy that limits the birth rate and envisages a trained and educated younger generation, most productive in terms of desirable goals of economic growth, would result in a sufficiently moderate rate of population growth, but it requires changes much the same as those required in traditional economic, political, and social institutions to optimize economic growth.

6. Concluding Comments

Our discussion, in the main, emphasized that purely technological and economic factors allow sufficient margins, in most underdeveloped countries, to permit substantial and sustained economic growth, even with a significant rise in population—at least for the proximate future of two to three decades. The difficulties and the problems lie in the limited capacity of the institutions of the underdeveloped countries—political, legal, cultural, and economic—to channel activity so as to exploit the advantages of economic backwardness, in the way of low incremental capital-output ratios, capital being broadly conceived to include economic inputs into education and other human investment.

This conclusion cannot be tested for lack of empirical data on social institutions and organization. However, some interesting statistical associations of growth rates, although of limited value, are revealed by the available statistics for the post-World War II years. The sample in the reference table is limited to non-Communist countries, is affected by the brevity of the period, and is distorted by continuing effects of postwar recovery. But it is the major body of evidence upon which we can draw easily;

and the sixty-three countries cover a wide range of economic development and a wide variety of economic and social institutions.

Three relevant points are suggested by the data. First, the average rate of growth of total product for the entire sample is close to 5 per cent per year; and even if corrected for the inflation due to the inclusion of postwar reconstruction years, it would be well above not only the average but even the higher population growth rates. There is thus capacity for *product* growth at rates significantly higher than population growth; and the rate of increase in *per capita* product of most countries covered in the table is high, even in the recent periods of accelerated growth in population.

Second, for the sample as a whole, correlation between population growth and growth in per capita product is negative (line 19); and the association is statistically significant, although not at demanding levels (which call for an index at least three times its standard deviation). But this negative correlation is due to the difference between the developed and the underdeveloped countries (compare lines 1–18, particularly line 6 for the developed group as a whole, with lines 12 and 18 for Asia-Africa and for Latin America). The question then arises whether a high rate of growth in per capita product is a result or a function of a high level of economic development rather than of a low rate of population growth—in the sense that it is the high level of economic development that yields both the high rate of growth in per capita product and the low rate of population growth, and that the latter are independent of each other.

Third, this last suggestion is denied, at first glance, by the negative association between the rates of growth of population and of per capita product *within* the group of developed countries (line 20) which, if significant, would indicate that even in the developed countries higher rates of population growth impede growth in per capita product. But the negative correlation is due entirely to the contrast between the overseas offshoots of Europe (listed in line 21) whose population grew more rapidly than that of Europe and Japan (partly because of immigration) but whose per capita product grew at lower rates unassociated with population movements. Exclusion of these four countries reduces the association for the developed coun-

I. *Average Rates for Groups of Countries Arrayed in Increasing Order of Rates of Growth of Population* (%)

A. *Developed Countries (Including Japan)*

Groups	Population (1)	Per capita product (2)	Total product (3)
1. 1–4	0.29	3.66	3.96
2. 5–8	0.65	3.60	4.28
3. 9–13	0.94	5.07	6.05
4. 14–17	1.46	3.49	5.00
5. 18–21	2.19	2.02	4.25
6. Average, 21 countries	1.10	3.64	4.77

B. *Asia and Africa (Excluding Israel and South Africa)*

Groups	Population (1)	Per capita product (2)	Total product (3)
7. 1–4	1.81	2.17	4.02
8. 5–8	2.25	2.91	5.23
9. 9–13	2.76	1.28	4.07
10. 14–17	3.05	2.34	5.46
11. 18–21	3.43	2.67	6.19
12. Average, 21 countries	2.66	2.23	4.95

C. *Latin America*

Groups	Population (1)	Per capita product (2)	Total product (3)
13. 1–4	1.56	2.51	4.12
14. 5–8	2.30	0.94	3.26
15. 9–12	2.84	3.24	6.17
16. 12–15	3.05	1.60	4.70
17. 16–19	3.40	2.66	6.15
18. Average, 19 countries	2.61	2.20	4.86

II. *Spearman Indexes of Rank Correlation Between Rates of Growth of Population and of Per Capita Product*

Groups	Number of countries (1)	Index of rank correlation (2)	Standard deviation (3)	Ratio, col. 2 to col. 3 (4)
19. All countries (incl. Israel and South Africa)	63	−0.309	0.1270	2.43
20. Developed countries	21	−0.434	0.2236	1.94
21. Developed countries excl. overseas (Canada, U.S.A., Australia, New Zealand)	17	0.061	0.2500	0.24
22. Asia and Africa (excl. Israel and South Africa)	21	0.079	0.2236	0.35
23. Latin America	19	0.246	0.2357	1.04
24. All underdeveloped (lines 22 and 23)	40	0.111	0.1601	0.69

The underlying data are from *Yearbook of National Accounts Statistics, 1965* (New York: United Nations, 1966), Tables 4A and 4B, pp. 467–73. The rates for total gross domestic product and product per capita, shown for two periods before and after 1960, were combined with due allowance

tries to insignificant levels. Nor is the association significant for
the Asia-Africa group (line 22), for Latin America (line 23), or
for all forty underdeveloped countries on these three continents
(line 24). The implication is that the rate of population growth
among the underdeveloped countries has no uniform effect on
growth in per capita product—a denial of the hypotheses discussed above that assumed that high rates of population growth
would be particularly limiting on the growth of per capita product in the underdeveloped countries, with their lower reserves
and increased pressure of population on economic resources.

The lack of significant association between population growth
and growth of per capita product would only be confirmed if we
were to widen our sample to include the Communist countries,
or extend our review to the long-term trends in the developed
countries back to the mid-nineteenth century (or earlier). Statistical associations do not help us to discriminate clearly among
determining factors, but they should at least serve to exclude
claims to primacy for single factors whose effects do not prove
dominant in the empirical data.

Two sets of qualifications apply to our discussion of the effects of population increase on economic growth; and these must
be explicitly stated in order to place the analysis in proper
perspective. The first set stems from the fact that we confined
our view of economic growth to one index—aggregate output
per capita. We limited our review to the effects on this index
alone of the technological, economic, and social constraints on
the proper response of an economy to higher rates of population
growth. Obviously there are other important and desirable aspects of economic growth. Adequate employment opportunities,

---

for the difference in duration. The population growth rates were calculated
from these.

The averages in lines 1–18 are unweighted arithmetic means of the
growth rates for the countries in the group.

The developed countries are largely in Western Europe (including Greece)
and the overseas countries listed in line 21. Asia and Africa include the
major populous countries, although Indonesia, Nigeria, and Egypt are
omitted for lack of data. The coverage of Latin America is fairly complete.

The formulas for the Spearman index and the standard deviation (for an
n of about 20 or more) can be found in Maurice G. Kendall, *Rank Correlation Methods*, 2nd ed. (London: Charles Griffin & Co. Ltd., 1955), paragraphs 1.14, pp. 8–9, and 4.13 and 4.14, pp. 58–59 (equation 4.7).

minimum equity and stability in the distribution of the product, and, above all, an optimal combination of individual freedom and social responsibility are goals that we would wish economic growth to attain, or at least not contravene. Even if we grant that a high rate of population growth is technologically and economically feasible, conditions are such in many underdeveloped countries that the attempt to divert even the moderate proportion of consumption into the capital formation required by a higher rate of population increase might involve tighter, centralized political controls that would sharply limit individual freedom and adjustment and adversely affect the long-run evolution of a society and economy responsive to the changing needs of its members. Even if growth in per capita product were not impeded by a higher rate of population increase, the latter might create other serious problems of adjustment, e.g., in providing employment for an increasing number of entrants into the labor force, over and above that automatically provided by the increased capital formation assumed to sustain per capita output and its growth. In short, with the several minimum goals that acceptable economic growth should satisfy, a high rate of population increase, while not necessarily having a major and direct effect on the increase in per capita product, may obstruct adequate employment, income equity, individual freedom, and other desiderata in the economic modernization of societies.

The second set of qualifications stems from the fact that we limited the analysis to the *aggregative* aspects of population increase and economic growth, and did not consider the *differential* aspects, i.e., the differences in the rate of population increase among various economic groups within a country. Even if group differentials in the rate of increase in numbers were not *systematically* related to economic and social status, a higher rate of population increase, proportionately the same for all economic and social groups, would be far more serious, and adjustment far more difficult, for the poorer than for the richer groups. Even a moderate proportionate reduction in consumption, required in adjusting to a higher rate of population increase, would be far more difficult for the lower income groups; and if the incomes of both the poor and the rich were reduced (or their gains withheld) by the same fraction, the welfare burdens of income inequality would become heavier.

In many societies and over long periods, fertility and the rate of natural increase have been greater for the poorer and lower social status groups than for the richer and higher social status groups. The evidence is abundant for the developed countries. Birth and fertility rates have differed and still differ, substantially, among various groups within the population of developed countries—among groups distinguished by economic position, occupational status, type of residence (e.g., rural versus urban), and a variety of other social characteristics, including the biological (race) to which social distinctions have been attached.[16] The major problems generated by population increase in the developed countries stemmed from the persistent and far from accidental circumstance that the higher birth and fertility rates characterized those groups whose economic position (and often social status) was lower—the rural rather than the urban; within the urban population, the poorer rather than the richer; the manual workers with little schooling rather than the white-collar workers with professional education; among the races discriminated against, such as non-whites in this country, rather than among the dominant ones. Since these higher birth rates were offset only partly by slightly higher death rates, the rates of natural increase among the economically and socially less favored also tended to be much higher than those of the economically and socially more favored.

The evidence for underdeveloped countries, although scantier, also points to greater fertility, and implicitly to higher rates of natural increase, among the rural, and hence lower-income, groups than among the urban, and hence higher-income, groups. Sample studies show a distinctly negative correlation between fertility and income for families classified by size of income.[17]

[16] For a summary discussion see Gwendolyn Z. Johnson, "Differential Fertility in European Countries," and Clyde V. Kiser, "Differential Fertility in the United States," in Ansley J. Coale, ed., *Demographic and Economic Change in Developed Countries* (Universities—National Bureau of Economic Research Committee, Princeton University Press, 1960).

[17] For a summary of rural-urban fertility differentials for a range of countries, from industrial to agricultural, see *Demographic Yearbook, 1952* (New York: United Nations, 1953), Table F, p. 17, and the discussion on pp. 16–17. Recent evidence on fertility, including economic and social differentials in underdeveloped countries, is given in George W. Roberts, "Fertility," a background paper prepared on behalf of the United Nations, for the 1965 World Popuation Conference (mimeo.).

Since the fertility differentials are too large to be offset by plausible mortality differentials, we may reasonably assume a higher rate of natural increase for the lower income and social status groups than for the higher groups within the underdeveloped countries also.

This negative correlation between birth rates and rates of natural increase, on the one hand, and economic status and per capita economic performance, on the other, raises problems with respect to the economic advance of the poor and generally less favored groups within any society—not only in keeping economic and social inequality from widening because of the greater growth in numbers among the poor and in trying to reduce that inequality as a concomitant of economic advance, but also in providing a sufficient upward economic flow of potential human talent from the surplus at the low economic levels. In the course of growth, the presently developed countries have met these problems by a variety of institutional changes, ranging from provision of free education and other social services to a revolution in the system of matching people to economic jobs to permit relatively free mobility. But even in the developed countries the problems may be accentuated when a rise in the overall rate of population growth means a greater differential between the lower and upper economic and social groups, and acceleration in the growth of the former; or when technological changes, requiring more education and investment in human capital, may impede upward economic and social mobility that in the long run is indispensable to the efficiency of the economic society—if it is to function as a unified and coherent unit rather than as a shaky coalition of two or more "subnations" in continuous conflict with each other.

The problems created by a greater rate of population increase among the lower than among the higher income groups are far more acute in the underdeveloped countries—with their lower overall per capita income and smaller economic reserves. If a high rate of population increase would bring about an even wider income inequality than now exists in the underdeveloped countries, the consequences in the way of misery, failure of unity, and loss of political viability might indeed be dire. For an adequate analysis of these problems our discussion of the relations between higher rates of population increase, capital requirements, dependency ratios, and the like, would have to be extended to cover significantly different economic and social groups *within* the underdeveloped countries, and coupled with the assumption that the higher rate of population increase means particularly high rates for lower income and social groups. The new parameters might show that large groups within these societies could not make the assumed adjustment to a high rate of population increase. And what seemed feasible in aggregative terms might cease to be feasible when the analysis distinguishes the lower economic groups—unless we further assume that drastic changes are made in the social and political structure to prevent what might otherwise be a breakdown resulting from wider economic inequality.

Both the effects of population increase on aspects of economic growth other than aggregate income per capita and the differential impact of population growth on distinct economic groups within a country obviously merit further analysis. Such analysis is essential if we are to approximate the *weights* of the effects of the type only hinted at in the few preceding paragraphs. But at this juncture, we can only note these aspects of the relation between population increase and economic growth as qualifications, with weights to be determined by further exploration, of the narrower analysis articulated more fully in this paper. The latter, by design, concentrated on the aggregative aspects and on per capita product—an approach generally followed in the current, neo-Malthusian, literature, which seemed to require a critical examination.

Economic Capacity and Population Growth

Given the sharp rise in the rate of growth of world population over the last two to three decades and the concentration of this growth in the less-developed countries, we are faced with the question of whether world economic capacity is equal to the strain thus imposed on it. Production of an adequate supply of the required goods, while not the *only* function of the economic system, is surely the first priority goal. Therefore, we concentrate in this paper on the economic capacity to produce enough to satisfy the needs of the rapidly growing population projected for the future.

1. Capacity to Produce (With Special Emphasis on Food)

This review is limited to the period to the year 2000 and emphasizes the requirements for and supply of food. These two limitations are easily justified on grounds of expediency: the authoritative world population projections terminate in 2000, and the easily available analyses of requirements and of the capacities to satisfy them deal largely with food and other natural resource

Reprinted from Richard N. Farmer, John D. Long, and George J. Stolnitz, eds., *World Population—The View Ahead* (Bloomington, Ind.: Bureau of Business Research, Graduate School of Business, Indiana University, 1968), pp. 51–97. The paper was presented at a conference in Bloomington in May, 1967.

industries. There are, however, more illuminating reasons for so circumscribing our review. The time limitation reflects the difficulty inherent in projecting over a longer period the process of technological and institutional change, since the latter moves at a rapid rate, and the cumulative interaction of its effects over a long period is not measurable in tolerably acceptable quantitative terms.[1]

The emphasis on requirements for and supply of food limits our view to only *one* complex of natural resource-based industries, but it is clearly the most important; we can supplement our detailed consideration of this complex with brief reference to other resource industries, largely mineral. At any rate, our discussion must stress the capacity to provide the necessary basic goods rather than dispensable goods (unless for some country or region, under conditions of international division of labor, the dispensable goods can be used to purchase the necessary).

Two sets of estimates of food requirements for the prospectively much larger world population have been published recently by the Food and Agriculture Organization; we will consider these, with special attention to the underdeveloped, low-calorie regions (Table 1). The population projections shown here for the less-developed regions are fairly close to those of the United Nations, being between the "medium" and "high" variants of the latter.[2] The definitions of these variants, which

[1] This rapidity of technological and institutional change is a function of the greatly increased technological power of mankind; the latter also means the increasing control over death, which has led to acceleration in the rate of population increase and thus paradoxically intensified the concern with the adequacy of our productive capacity while making it impossible to gauge such capacity beyond a relatively short span. Were we to pose the same question for the pre-modern centuries, when technology changed at what was relatively a snail's pace, a longer time span could be projected— with the emphasis on the stock of available nonreproducible resources and a barely changing stock of technology.

[2] The decadal rate of growth of the population of the low-calorie regions assumed in Table 1 for the period 1958–2000 is 24.0 per cent for the earlier estimate and 24.4 per cent for the later estimate (see Table 4, line 12, columns 1 and 2). For the period between 1960 and 2000, the decadal rate of growth in the UN population projections, with a rough allowance for the shift of the River Plate countries from Latin America and hence from the underdeveloped regions, works out to 23.5 per cent in the medium projection and to 28.1 per cent in the high projection.

See *World Population Prospects as Assessed in 1963* (New York: United
[*continued on page* 52]

	Food supplies in 1958			Food requirements in 2000		
	Population (mill.) (1)	Food supply per capita (index) (2)	Total food supplies (index) (3)	Projected population (mill.) (4)	Required food per capita (index) (5)	Total food requirements (index) (6)
1. Asia and Far East	1,498	88	1,318	3,639	147	5,349
2. Near East	125	159	199	327	186	608
3. Africa	208	101	210	421	129	543
4. Latin America (excl. River Plate countries)	170	155	264	548	163	893
5. Total, low-calorie regions (Group I)	2,001	100	1,991	4,935	150	7,393
6. Total, high-calorie regions (rest of world, Group II)	858	333	2,857	1,332	333	4,436
7. World	2,859	167	4,848	6,267	189	11,829

Relatives of Projections and Requirements in 2000;
Population and Food Supply in 1958 or 1957–59 = 100

	1961–63 Estimate			1965 Estimate		
	Population (mill.) (1)	Food per capita (2)	Total food (3)	Population (mill.) (4)	Food per capita (5)	Total food (6)
8. Asia and Far East	243	167	406	245	170	417
9. Near East	262	117	307	257	130	334
10. Africa	202	128	259	223	151	337
11. Latin America (excl. River Plate countries)	322	105	338	315	114	359
12. Total, low-calorie regions (Group I)	247	150	371	250	157	393
13. Total, high-calorie regions (Group II)	155	100	155	160	119	191
14. World	219	113	247	223	123	274

Lines 1–7, columns 1 and 4, and lines 8–14, columns 1 and 2: From Freedom from Hunger Campaign, *Possibilities of Increasing World Food Production,* Basic Study No. 10 (Rome: Food and Agriculture Organization, 1963), Table 1, p. 14 and Table 2, pp. 24–25. Near East includes Cyprus, U.A.R., Iran, Iraq, Israel, Jordan, Lebanon, Libya, Sudan, Syria, and Turkey. Asia and the Far East, and Africa correspond to the usual definitions of the two continents, minus the relevant countries listed under Near East. River Plate countries excluded from Latin America and included under the high-calorie regions are Argentina, Uruguay, and Paraguay. The entry in line 6, column 4 is from P. V. Sukhatme, "The World's Hunger and Future Needs in Food Supplies," *Journal of the Royal Statistical Society,* Vol. CXXIV, Series A, General, Part 4, 1961, Table 18, p. 500. All other figures in this paper are identical with those for low-calorie regions in *Possibilities of Increasing World Food Producton,* Basic Study No. 10.

Lines 1–7, column 2: From Freedom from Hunger Campaign, *Third World Food Survey,* Basic Study No. 11 (Rome: Food and Agriculture Organization, 1963), Table 9, p. 20. In this table, percentage distributions among the several regions of world population and world food supplies are given for 1957–59 (which we identified with 1958). From these we derived an

differ largely with respect to the date of the onset of the expected decline in fertility, are given in the original source. Here it suffices to say that "the 'medium' estimates are intended to represent the future population trend that now appears most plausible." [3] Hence the allowances for population growth in the low-calorie regions, made in the FAO estimates of requirements, appear to be adequate—although, as will be indicated in Table 4, the rates are slightly lower than those observed over the last quinquennium.

The detailed discussions of per capita food requirements in the year 2000 in the FAO, Freedom From Hunger Campaign, Basic Studies Nos. 10 and 11, dismiss any need to match the dietary patterns of the high-calorie countries in Group II, in which "the problem is often one of overeating rather than undereating, though malnutrition is still to be found in certain social groups and in certain areas" (Basic Study No. 10, p. 21). No targets are set for Group II countries in Basic Study No. 10, and to complete the picture we assumed per capita food requirements for that group in 2000 equal to per capita supplies in 1958. The later FAO study does allow for increases in food supplies per capita in Group II countries, but they are minor.

---

index of per capita supplies, to the base of an average for all low-calorie regions as 100. The calculations yield an index somewhat less than 100 because the population distribution among regions in Basic Study No. 11 is slightly different from that in Basic Study No. 10.

Lines 1–7, column 5: The product of column 2, lines 1–7 and column 2, lines 8–14 (or summation for lines 5 and 7).

Lines 8–14, columns 4–6: From P. V. Sukhatme, W. Schulte, Z. M. Ahmad, and G. T. Jones, "Demographic Factors Affecting Food Supplies and Agricultural Development," background paper, United Nations World Population Conference, 1965, Table 1, p. 40. We assumed that the absolute totals for 1957–59 were those shown in lines 1–7, columns 1–3. The indexes for year 2000 are given in the source for Group I regions and the world; those for Group II were implicit and calculated by us.

Columns 3 and 6: The product, divided by 100, of columns 1 and 2, and 4 and 5, respectively.

Nations, 1966), Table A3.2, p. 134; Table A3.3, p. 135; and Table A3.8, p. 144. The trends in Tables A3.2 and A3.3 for temperate South America, which includes Chile in addition to the River Plate countries, were applied to the 1960 totals for the latter countries in Table A3.8, and the results were subtracted from the totals for the underdeveloped countries in Tables A3.2 and A3.3.

[3] *World Population Prospects as Assessed in 1963*, p. 6.

The more important task of setting the food requirement levels for the low-calorie countries involves estimating (a) calorie supplies necessary to sustain life and provide for the work energy needs, while allowing for the unavoidable wastage between production and consumption and for some inequalities in distribution; and (b) protein supplies, particularly in animal but also in vegetable form, necessary to assure a minimum quality of diet. In the earlier study, the per capita daily requirements in year 2000 for the four major regions in Group I are put between 2,400 and 2,500 calories, between 42 and 57 grams of vegetable proteins, and at 20 grams of animal proteins (see Basic Study No. 10, Table 2, pp. 24–25). In the second study the calorie requirement remains the same; animal protein requirements vary (among the four regions) between 20 and 25 grams; and vegetable protein requirements are within a more limited range from 46 to 54 grams (see Basic Study No. 11, Table 20, p. 57).

More important than the minor differences between the two sets of estimates is the fact that both fix the food targets in the low-calorie countries in year 2000 at modest levels—at least in comparison with the levels now prevailing in the developed countries in Group II (granted the difference in climatic conditions). In 1958, per capita daily consumption in the developed countries was over 3,000 calories and 134 grams of proteins of which 44 grams were animal (see Basic Study No. 10, Table 1, p. 14). As Table 1 shows, even attainment of the targets would mean an economic value in year 2000 of per capita food consumption less than half that of current per capita food intake in Group II countries. But the requirements are meant to represent a "sufficient" nutritional goal, and if attained would constitute an adequate level of per capita food consumption and one significantly closer to that of the Group II countries than today.

We come now to the main question: are these targets attainable? Are the natural resources and the technological knowledge at hand sufficient to assure the attainment of the required food supply levels—considering that they mean a rise of 67 to 70 per cent in per capita food supplies in the Far East and of between 30 and 50 per cent in Africa and, with the prospective population increases, a tripling or quadrupling of total food supplies (see Table 1, lines 8–11, columns 2, 5, and 6)? The answer in Basic Study No. 10, devoted primarily to this problem, is, on the

whole, in the affirmative; so is the one based on the later estimates, given in the paper presented at the 1965 UN World Population Conference (see notes to Table 1).

In Basic Study No. 10 the answer is given region by region,
rather than for the world as a whole, because "it is unlikely that
imports of food from the wealthier to the less wealthy regions can
ever provide more than a small part of the needs. This would
still remain true even if commercial imports were supplemented
by substantial grants-in-aid through free distribution of surplus
food stuffs" (p. 221). In this consideration by regions, no serious
question arises about Europe, North America, and Oceania.
Here one can repeat what the study says about North America:
"Resources, or future production capacity, are certainly capable
of taking care of any probable requirements, with capacity to
spare" (p. 221). The question then is about the four underdeveloped regions.

> In Latin America and Africa, the physical resources are
> unquestionably ample, without approaching their full utilization,
> to meet the estimated increases required. . . . in the Near East,
> an increase in production in excess of threefold [required; see
> Table 1] would push utilization of resources much closer to the
> limits set by present technical knowledge than would be the case
> in either Latin America or Africa. . . . it is an area in which
> there may be cause for some disquiet from the point of view of
> the natural resources. Water is strictly the limiting factor. . . .
> Of course, all this might be changed by the desalinization of sea
> water at costs which would be economic for irrigation, though
> transportation costs to areas far removed from the coast could
> still remain a problem. . . . In the Far East the balance between
> future food needs and known potentialities for production may
> well prove to be delicate. . . . If governments go about their
> task of planning agricultural development, armed with a clear
> and realistic knowledge of the feasible goals, the chances of
> bringing about a better balance between needs and production
> before it is too late will be considerably enhanced.[4]

The general conclusion is thus to affirm technological feasibility of the food requirements assumed for year 2000. Basic Study
No. 10 concludes by saying that "the existence of large untapped

[4] Freedom From Hunger Campaign, *Possibilities of Increasing World
Food Production*, Basic Study No. 10 (Rome: Food and Agriculture Organization, 1963), pp. 221–23.

resources of nature and knowledge represents a challenge to the ability and good will of man to solve a problem which is capable of solution" (p. 223). And this conclusion is repeated, with reference to somewhat higher food production targets for 2000, in the paper prepared for the 1965 World Population Conference: "It would appear that within the next twenty years (and even up to the end of the century) the technical possibilities for increasing production are more than adequate to meet the full needs of the growing population" (pp. 31–32).

The general grounds for inferring technological feasibility of the food supply targets given above, and the more specific meaning of the feasibility conclusions, will be discussed in the following section. Before doing so, we present a summary of the trends in food production and supplies, total and per capita, observed in the recent past—so that the targets for year 2000 and the rates of growth required to reach them can be viewed against the background of recent growth rates.

Table 2 summarizes the trends in food production since the late 1920's—a period of three and one-half to four decades, the longest for which food and population estimates for the world and the low- and high-calorie regions, are available.[5] Four aspects of the trends merit explicit mention.

---

[5] The League of Nations estimates of "foodstuffs" include "food crops, meat, sea fish, milk, beverages, tobacco, as well as part of the group of oil materials and oils; this group thus includes partly crude foodstuffs ready for consumption and partly raw materials of the food, drink and tobacco industries" (see *World Production and Prices, 1936–37* [Geneva: League of Nations, 1937], Appendix I, p. 98). The index is an aggregative one, using quantities multiplied by "representative 'world' prices ruling in 1930, expressed in terms of gold dollars according to average annual rates of exchange" (p. 98).

The FAO food production indexes include "grains, starchy roots, sugar, pulses, oil crops, nuts, fruit, vegetables, wine, livestock, and livestock products. To avoid double counting, allowances are made for commodities used for livestock feeding; these include products fed as such, and semi-processed feeds such as oilcakes and bran. In addition, to the extent that adequate estimates are possible, allowances are also made for imported feeds, seed, and production waste." See Freedom From Hunger Campaign, *Third World Food Survey*, Basic Study No. 11 (Rome: Food and Agriculture Organization, 1963), p. 80. The indexes are constructed by applying regional weights, based either on 1934–38 or 1952–56 farm price relationships, to the production figures.

Although the League of Nations and the FAO indexes differ somewhat in scope, the former can be used for rough extrapolation of the latter.

Table 2. TRENDS IN FOOD PRODUCTION, TOTAL AND PER CAPITA INDEXES,
1925–29 TO 1962–64
(1934–38 = 100)

	1925–29 (1)	1948–52 (2)	1957–59 (3)	1962–64 (4)	1934–38 Percentage shares in world total and relatives of per capita food production (to world average) (5)
World incl. Mainland China					
Total Food Production					
1. Low-calorie regions	92	109	142	161	43
2. High-calorie regions	93	117	149	167	57 (67)
3. World	93	113	146	164	100
Population					
4. Low-calorie regions	90	120	143	163	68
5. High-calorie regions	92	105	118	126	32 (42)
6. World	91	115	135	150	100
Per Capita Food Production					
7. Low-calorie regions	102	91	99	99	63
8. High-calorie regions	101	111	126	133	178 (160)
9. World	102	98	108	109	100
World excl. Mainland China					
Total Food Production					
10. Low-calorie regions	n.a.	115	148	167	33
11. World	n.a.	116	148	167	100
Population					
12. Low-calorie regions	n.a.	124	147	165	58
13. World	n.a.	116	135	149	100
Per Capita Food Production					
14. Low-calorie regions	n.a.	93	101	101	57
15. World	n.a.	100	110	112	100
Ratio of Per Capita Food Production, High- to Low-Calorie Regions					
16. Incl. Mainland China	2.8	3.5	3.6	3.8	2.8
17. Excl. Mainland China	n.a.	3.4	3.5	3.7	2.8

Rates of Growth per Decade (%)

	1925–29 to 1948–52 (1)	1934–38 to 1948–52 (2)	1948–52 to 1962–64 (3)	1925–29 to 1962–64 (4)	1934–38 to 1962–64 (5)
World incl. Mainland China					
Total Food Production					
18. Low-calorie regions	7.7	6.4	35.0	16.8	19.3
19. High-calorie regions	10.5	11.9	31.5	17.7	20.9
20. World	8.8	9.1	33.2	17.1	20.1

	1925–29 to 1948–52 (1)	1934–38 to 1948–52 (2)	1948–52 to 1962–64 (3)	1925–29 to 1962–64 (4)	1934–38 to 1962–64 (5)
Population					
21. Low-calorie regions	13.3	13.9	26.6	17.9	19.8
22. High-calorie regions	5.9	3.5	15.1	9.1	8.9
23. World	10.7	11.3	20.9	14.9	16.2
Per Capita Food Production					
24. Low-calorie regions	−5.0	−6.6	6.7	−0.9	−0.5
25. High-calorie regions	4.3	8.0	14.3	7.8	11.0
26. World	−1.7	−2.0	10.2	1.9	3.4
World excl. Mainland China					
Total Food Production					
27. Low-calorie regions	n.a.	10.5	33.2	n.a.	20.9
28. World	n.a.	11.2	32.4	n.a.	20.9
Population					
29. Low-calorie regions	n.a.	16.6	24.6	n.a.	20.4
30. World	n.a.	11.2	21.2	n.a.	15.9
Per Capita Food Production					
31. Low-calorie regions	n.a.	−5.2	7.0	n.a.	0.4
32. World	n.a.	0	9.2	n.a.	4.3

n.a.: not available

The estimates for 1934–38 and later years are from P. V. Sukhatme, "The World Food Supplies," *Journal of the Royal Statistical Society,* Vol. CXXIX, Series A, General, Part 2, 1966, Table 6A, p. 234. The note to the table indicates that "these index numbers have been calculated by applying regional weights based on 1952–56 farm price relationships to regional production figures adjusted to allow for quantities used for feed and seed." The table shows indexes for total and per capita food production, and the population indexes were calculated from these. For the composition of the low- and high-calorie groups see notes to Table 1. It is assumed that "prewar" means averages for 1934–38, as is indicated by the use of 1936 as the central year (see "The World Food Supplies," Table 6B, p. 234).

The indexes of total food production were extrapolated back to 1925–29 by means of the League of Nations estimates in *World Production and Prices, 1938–39* (Geneva: League of Nations, 1939), Appendix I, Table 1, p. 87; Table 3, pp. 90–92; Table 5, pp. 97–100. The low-calorie regions here were Asia, Africa, and Latin America; the high-calorie regions were Europe (including the U.S.S.R.), North America, and Oceania. Population figures for these continents (disregarding the minor adjustment for the River Plate countries here and in the case of food production) were interpolated for 1927 and 1936 between the UN estimates for 1920, 1930, and 1940—the latter two from the *Demographic Yearbook, 1965,* Table 1, p. 103, and the first from *World Population Prospects as Assessed in 1963* (New York: United Nations, 1966), Table A3.1, p. 133—along a straight logarithmic line. The rates of growth thus obtained for total food production, population, and per capita food production were applied to the indexes for 1934–38 to estimate the level in 1925–29.

The shares in column 5 for food production are from *Third World Food*

First, for the world as a whole, food production grew rather slowly between 1925–29 and 1948–52, probably as a result of the depression and the war.[6] Indeed, for the world, including Mainland China, the rate of growth of food production, 9 per cent per decade, was lower than that of world population, 10.7 per cent per decade—so that per capita world food output declined almost 2 per cent from 1925–29 to 1948–52 (Table 2, lines 20, 23, 26). In the postwar period growth in world food production accelerated to 33 per cent per decade; thus, despite the marked rise in the rate of growth of world population, per capita food production rose 9 or 10 per cent per decade (column 3). On balance, however, in the full span of some thirty-six years (from 1927 to 1963, the midpoints of the two terminal periods) the growth of world food production per capita was less than 2 per cent per decade (column 4).

Second, while *total* food output grew over the full period at about the same rate in the low-calorie and in the high-calorie regions (16.8 and 17.7 per cent per decade for the longest period, and 19.3 and 20.9 per cent for 1936–63; see lines 18 and 19, columns 4 and 5), population grew at much higher rates in the former than in the latter (18 or 20 per cent per decade and about 9 per cent respectively; see lines 21 and 22, columns 4 and 5). As a result, from 1936 to 1963 food output per capita grew much less in the low-calorie than in the high-calorie group —either declining 0.5 per cent per decade (including Mainland China) or rising 0.4 per cent per decade (excluding Mainland China), compared with a rise of 11 per cent per decade in the high-calorie regions (lines 24, 25, and 31, column 5). But in both groups, the postwar period witnessed a much higher rate of

Survey, Basic Study No. 11, Appendix 2B, p. 85; and for population from the UN data indicated in the paragraph above. The entries in parentheses in lines 2, 5, and 8 are the shares and relatives for the high-calorie group in the world excluding Mainland China. Per capita food production for Mainland China in 1934–38 (which was deducted from the total for low-calorie regions) was assumed to equal that in the low-calorie regions as a whole, excluding China.

[6] The findings for the world and the low-calorie regions including and excluding Mainland China are fairly similar. Mainland China was excluded so that the estimates in Table 2 could be used in conjunction with those in which the four low-calorie regions are distinguished, and in which the Far East omits Mainland China.

growth of total and of per capita food production than the pre-war years.

Third, as a result of these differences in trends in per capita output, the relative disparity in per capita food production between the low- and high-calorie regions widened over time. The ratio of per capita food output in high-calorie to that in low-calorie regions, including Mainland China, rose from 2.8 in 1925–29 to 3.8 in 1962–64 (line 16); in the comparison excluding Mainland China, the ratio rose from 2.8 in 1934–38 to 3.7 in 1962–64 (line 17).

Finally, since the low-calorie, underdeveloped regions are our primary interest, the trends in their per capita food output should be noted particularly. From 1925–29 to 1948–52 this per capita food production dropped about 11 per cent—a decline not quite made up in the next eight years (from 1948–52 to 1957–59)—and in the last observed quinquennium, 1957–59 to 1962–64, it was at a standstill (line 7). In almost four decades per capita food output in the low-calorie regions showed no significant rise.

This discussion relates to observable trends in food production, not in food supplies, and does not distinguish the four major regions within the low-calorie group. We supplement it by distinguishing these four regions and providing estimates of both food supplies and food output (Table 3).

Table 3 is, however, subject to several qualifications. First, we calculated supplies by adjusting domestic production by the net balance of exports and imports—disregarding the possible contribution of net changes in domestic inventories. Second, in deriving the net balance of imports and exports, and hence the shift from output to supplies, for the high-calorie group we relied on weights and indexes for Western Europe, North America, and Oceania—thus omitting Eastern Europe (and the U.S.S.R.)—and included the River Plate countries with Latin America and the low-calorie group. Third, at several steps in the calculations, we had to introduce adjustments to assure conformity of the weighted averages of indexes for the individual regions with the indexes for the low- and high-calorie groups as wholes (from Table 2), and to make the world net balance of exports and imports equal zero. But all these qualifications are minor, because net changes in inventories cannot affect long-

(World and low-calorie regions excl. Mainland China)

	Far East (1)	Near East (2)	Africa (3)	Latin America (4)	Low-calorie regions (5)	High-calorie regions (6)	World (7)
Net Balance of Food Exports ($-$) and Imports ($+$), % of Domestic Production							
1. 1934–38	-2	-1	-14	-25	-10	$+7$	0
2. 1948–52	$+3$	$+3$	-10	-11	-3	$+2$	0
3. 1962–64	$+5$	$+6$	-11	-10	0	0	0

A. Indexes (1934–38 = 100)

	Far East (1)	Near East (2)	Africa (3)	Latin America (4)	Low-calorie regions (5)	High-calorie regions (6)	World (7)
Total Food Production							
4. 1948–52	105	122	127	129	115	117	116
5. 1962–64	151	192	181	185	167	167	167
Total Food Supplies							
6. 1948–52	112	128	133	154	124	112	116
7. 1962–64	165	211	191	227	185	157	167
Population							
8. 1948–52	121	122	121	135	124	105	116
9. 1962–64	155	166	161	187	165	126	149
Per Capita Food Production							
10. 1948–52	87	100	105	96	93	111	100
11. 1962–64	97	116	112	99	101	133	112
Per Capita Food Supplies							
12. 1948–52	93	105	110	114	100	107	100
13. 1962–64	106	127	119	121	112	125	112

B. Rates of Growth per Decade (%)

	Far East (1)	Near East (2)	Africa (3)	Latin America (4)	Low-calorie regions (5)	High-calorie regions (6)	World (7)
Total Food Production							
14. 1934–38 to 1948–52	3.5	15.3	18.6	19.9	10.5	11.9	11.2
15. 1948–52 to 1962–64	32.2	41.7	31.3	32.0	33.2	31.5	32.4
16. 1934–38 to 1962–64	16.5	27.3	24.6	25.6	20.9	20.9	20.9
Total Food Supplies							
17. 1934–38 to 1948–52	8.4	19.3	22.6	36.1	16.6	8.4	11.2
18. 1948–52 to 1962–64	34.7	46.9	32.1	34.8	36.0	29.7	32.4
19. 1934–38 to 1962–64	20.4	31.9	27.1	35.5	25.6	18.2	20.9
Population							
20. 1934–38 to 1948–52	14.6	15.3	14.6	23.9	16.6	3.5	11.2
21. 1948–52 to 1962–64	21.0	26.7	24.6	28.5	24.6	15.1	21.2
22. 1934–38 to 1962–64	17.6	20.6	19.3	26.1	20.4	8.9	15.9

B. Rates of Growth per Decade (%)

	Far East (1)	Near East (2)	Africa (3)	Latin America (4)	Low-calorie regions (5)	High-calorie regions (6)	World (7)
Per Capita Food Production							
23. 1934–38 to 1948–52	−9.6	0	3.5	−3.2	−5.2	8.0	0
24. 1948–52 to 1962–64	9.3	11.8	5.4	2.7	7.0	14.3	9.2
25. 1934–38 to 1962–64	−1.0	5.5	4.4	−0.4	0.4	11.0	4.3
Per Capita Food Supplies							
26. 1934–38 to 1948–52	−5.4	3.5	7.0	9.9	0	4.7	0
27. 1948–52 to 1962–64	11.4	15.9	6.0	4.9	9.2	12.7	9.2
28. 1934–38 to 1962–64	2.3	9.3	6.5	7.4	4.3	8.5	4.3

Lines 1–3: From P. V. Sukhatme, "The World Food Supplies," Table 11, p. 238. The net balance percentages are given for the three dates for each low-calorie region and for Western Europe, North America, and Oceania among the high-calorie regions. We calculated the net balance for the total low-calorie group (column 5) by using the 1934–38 production weights in *Third World Food Survey,* Basic Study No. 11, Appendix 2B; we did likewise for the high-calorie regions, after eliminating the U.S.S.R., the weights for which were derived from *World Production and Prices, 1938–39.* Minor adjustments were made to the algebraic total of the net balances for the regions in order to have the net balance for the world excluding Mainland China equal zero.

Lines 4–5, 8–9, and 10–11: The indexes in columns 5–7 are identical with those in Table 2 and were kept so by design. Consequently, the weighted averages of the indexes for the several regions (the four low-calorie and the three high-calorie—the latter, in fact, did not account fully for the total since the U.S.S.R. and Eastern Europe and the River Plate countries were omitted) had to be adjusted to the over-all indexes used in Table 2 to assure identity.

The regional production indexes were taken from *State of Food and Agriculture, 1966* (Rome: Food and Agriculture Organization, 1966), Annex Tables 2A and 2B, pp. 195–98; and linked with the 1934–38 base by the indexes in the FAO *Production Yearbook, 1958,* Tables 6 and 7, pp. 27–28 (the overlap was for 1954–55 through 1956–57). The FAO indexes are for crop years beginning in the years indicated in the stubs. Indexes are given for both total and per capita food production and those for population were derived from these.

Lines 6–7 and 12–13: Indexes of supplies were calculated by applying the net balances of food exports and imports to the adjusted regional indexes of output, and then further adjusted so that the balance added out to zero for the world on each of the three dates.

All adjustments referred to above, made to reconcile weighted regional indexes with given broader and world totals, are minor and do not affect the results significantly.

Lines 14–28: Calculated directly from lines 4–13.

term trends appreciably, because the weight of Eastern Europe and of the River Plate countries in output and trade of the high-calorie group is limited, and because the conformity adjustments were all small.

The additional detail reveals that it was in the Far East and in Latin America that the per capita food output declined over the full period from 1934–38 to 1962–64 (line 11, columns 1 and 4). In the Far East, marked by the lowest per capita food production in recent years, the decline from 1934–38 to 1948–52 was as much as 13 per cent; and the level in 1962–64 was still 3 per cent below the prewar (lines 10 and 11, column 1). Yet the rate of population growth in the Far East was distinctly below that of the other low-calorie regions.

However, the major new finding in Table 3 relates to the trends in food *supplies,* as distinct from food production. Here we observe that the net export balance of food relative to domestic production, marked in 1934–38 in all the low-calorie regions, either shifted to a net import balance, as in the Far and in the Near East, or declined perceptibly, as in Africa and Latin America (lines 1–3, columns 1–4). Hence for the low-calorie regions as a whole a significant net export balance in 1934–38, 10 per cent of domestic food output, had virtually disappeared by 1962–64; correspondingly, the net import balance in the high-calorie regions declined from 7 per cent of domestic output before the war to zero in 1962–64 (lines 1–3, columns 5–7).

This means that in the low-calorie regions per capita food supply rose more, or declined less, than per capita food production—either because food output for domestic consumption rose more than that designed for exports, or because the ratio of exports to output of foods both consumed domestically and exported declined, or because imports (relative to domestic food output) increased—or for all three reasons. Thus while in the low-calorie regions (excluding Mainland China) food production per capita in 1962–64 was barely above that in 1934–38, food supplies per capita were 12 per cent higher—and even in the Far East the index was 6 per cent above that for 1934–38 (lines 11 and 13). Conversely, in the high-calorie regions per capita food supplies in 1962–64 were 25 per cent above the 1934–38 level whereas per capita food output was 33 per cent higher.

Yet even in terms of per capita food supplies, the rate of growth in the high-calorie regions was almost double that in the low-calorie regions. In 1934–38 the ratio of per capita food supplies in the high-calorie to those in the low-calorie regions was 3.3 to 1, higher than that for output per capita (2.8 to 1) because of net imports of food to the high-calorie and net exports of food from the low-calorie regions. By 1962–64 the ratio of per capita food supplies rose to 3.7.

We may now ask how the rates of growth implicit in the food requirements for the year 2000 compare with those for the recent past. Table 4 shows the rates of growth needed if the food requirements are to be satisfied—for two periods, one to 2000 and the other to 1975, the terminal dates in the presentation of the requirements—and the observed rates for the quinquennium since 1958.

The rates in columns 1–3 are to be viewed largely as required rates of growth in production—as in the analysis of feasibility quoted above, which treated the food production potentials region by region. To be sure, the possibility of trade and transfer of food among regions is not ignored. But it is assumed that they contribute relatively little to the needed growth in domestic supplies. This assumption will be noted in a later section when we deal with what might be called differential aspects of the projections, requirements, and feasibility. For the present, one may be justified in viewing the implicit rates in Table 4 as those in food production—to be compared with the observed growth rates in total food production in Tables 2 and 3.

The results of such a comparison depend largely upon the period in the past used for reference. As Table 4 shows, the required rate of growth in food production is between 37 and 41 per cent per decade for the low-calorie regions, and between 24 and over 27 per cent for the world as a whole (lines 5 and 7, columns 1–3). But per capita food production and supply also depend upon the rate of population increase.

In the observed past, the period favorable to growth of food output was between 1948–52 and 1962–64—to take a time span long enough to warrant use in the comparison. Over that period, world food production grew 33.2 per cent per decade (see Table 2, line 20, column 3). *If* the growth experience of that decade to decade and a half is indicative of the long-term potential to year

Table 4. RATES OF GROWTH IMPLICIT IN FOOD REQUIREMENTS 1958 TO 2000 AND 1958 TO 1975, AND OBSERVED RATES, 1957–59 TO 1962–64

	Rates of Growth per Decade (%)				
	Implicit in Requirements				Fulfill-ment ratio, col. 4 ÷ col. 3 (5)
	1958–2000, early estimate (1)	1958–2000, later estimate (2)	1958–1975, later estimate (3)	Observed 1957–59 to 1962–64 (4)	
Total Food Requirements and Production					
1. Far East	39.6	40.5	42.7	34.7 *	0.81
2. Near East	30.6	33.3	35.2	27.9	0.79
3. Africa	25.4	33.5	33.8	32.4	0.96
4. Latin America	33.6	35.6	39.5	27.7 †	0.70
5. Low-calorie regions	36.6	38.5	40.9	28.6 *†	0.67
6. High-calorie regions	11.0	16.7	16.7	25.6	1.53
7. World	24.0	27.1	27.4	27.3 *	1.00
Population					
8. Far East	23.5	23.8	21.9	24.8 *	1.13
9. Near East	25.8	25.2	23.4	28.6	1.22
10. Africa	18.2	21.0	18.3	26.3	1.44
11. Latin America	32.1	31.4	29.4	31.0 †	1.05
12. Low-calorie regions	24.0	24.4	22.4	27.3 *†	1.22
13. High-calorie regions	11.0	11.8	13.5	12.7	0.94
14. World	20.5	21.0	19.8	22.8 *	1.15
Per Capita Food Requirements and Production					
15. Far East	13.0	13.5	17.1	7.9 *	0.46
16. Near East	3.8	6.4	9.6	−0.6	−0.06
17. Africa	6.1	10.3	13.1	4.9	0.37
18. Latin America	1.2	3.2	7.8	−2.5 †	−0.32
19. Low-calorie regions	10.2	11.4	15.1	0.0 *†	0.00
20. High-calorie regions	0.0	4.3	2.8	11.4	4.07
21. World	2.9	5.0	6.3	3.7 *	0.59

* Excludes Mainland China.
† Includes the River Plate countries.

Columns 1–2: Calculated from the indexes in Table 1, lines 8–14.

Column 3: From P. V. Sukhatme and others, "Demographic Factors Affecting Food Supplies and Agricultural Development," p. 40. The source shows projected population and requirements for both 1975 and 2000 (as indexes to the base 1957–59 = 100), for the four low-calorie regions, the total for them, and the world. Those for high-calorie regions were calculated using the weights for 1957–59 given in *Third World Food Survey*, Basic Study No. 11, Table 9, p. 20.

Column 4: Based on total and per capita indexes in *State of Food and Agriculture, 1966*, Annex Tables 2A and 2B, pp. 195–98, for each low-calorie region; on the indexes in Table 2 for the low- and high-calorie regions and the world. Population indexes were derived from those for total and per capita production.

2000, the growth rates of world food production implied in the requirements (24 to 27 per cent per decade) can apparently be met. But two difficulties emerge. First, the food requirements for the low-calorie regions imply an appreciably higher rate of growth (as high as 41 per cent per decade, if the later estimate of requirements is used) if the need for a higher rate of growth in the earlier phases (that is, from 1957–59 to 1975, compared with 1975 to 2000) is to be recognized, as given in an FAO later projection. Yet the rate of growth of food output for the low-calorie regions even from 1948–52 to 1962–64 was 35 per cent per decade—over a tenth lower. Second, the population projections implicit in the FAO estimates of requirements have been exceeded in all the low-calorie regions in the last observed quinquennium (lines 8–12, column 4). If these higher rates of population growth were to be assumed for reference purposes, total food requirements would have to be raised above the levels in column 3; the excess of these required rates over those observed in the presumably favorable period of 1948–52 to 1962–64 would be even greater.

The high level of the targets for the low-calorie regions, particularly the Far East, generates disturbing doubts which are only compounded by the question of whether the growth experience in the post-World War II decade to decade and a half is a valid reference base for judging the accuracy of the measures of long-term growth potentials. It may be considered too favorable a base, because the slowdown during the depression and the war may have left a backlog of easily tapped sources of growth, which cannot be expected to remain available for the long period ahead to 2000. Some justification of this view emerges when we find that the growth rates in food production for the low-calorie regions as a whole and for the world (both excluding Mainland China) in the last quinquennium are 28.6 and 27.3 per cent (Table 4, column 4)—distinctly lower than those for the full period 1948–52 to 1962–64, 33.2 and 32.4 per cent respectively (Table 3, line 15, columns 5 and 7). An even more telling factor is that the growth of food output in the low-calorie regions depends on expansion of area (or increase in number of cattle), rather than, as in the high-calorie regions, on higher yields per area or per cattle unit. The FAO estimates show that of the growth in the output of nine major food crops between the prewar period and 1962–63 in the low-calorie regions, over seven-tenths were due to expansion in area and less than three-tenths to rise in yield—whereas in the high-calorie regions, the former accounted for less than one-third of total growth and the latter for over two-thirds.[7]

Similar contrasts between the high- and low-calorie regions, although not as wide, are shown regarding the growth of output of cattle products dependent on increases in number of cattle and on the rise in yield per unit. The implication is that, since expansion of land under cultivation in the less-developed areas is not likely to continue in the future, the recent growth of food output in these areas, impressive as it may appear, provides little assurance for the future. On the other hand, it may be argued that in many low-calorie countries the postwar period was still much affected by political changes and uncertainties, which depressed production, and that the realistic potential would be underestimated if no allowance were made for these elements in using the postwar period as guide.

Obviously, past growth rates, particularly those for a period as short and as affected by major disturbances as even the longest time span in our tables, are a rough and uncertain guide to potentials for the future. We summarized the trends in the recent past, not because we expected to find sure guides for the future, but to observe what actually happened—since our interpretation of what might happen if the food targets are or are not met depends largely upon our knowledge of what occurred in the recent "untargeted" past. But while Table 4 suggests that the projections and requirements are *not* unrealistically high when we compare them on a worldwide scale and refer to the relatively favorable post-World War II period, rather substantial excesses and probable shortfalls emerge when comparison is made for individual low-calorie regions. Furthermore, the record of

[7] See P. V. Sukhatme, "The World Food Supplies," *Journal of Royal Statistical Society*, Vol. CXXIX, Series A, General, Part 2, 1966, Table 7, p. 235 (for the food crops) and Table 8, p. 235 (for cattle products). The crops covered include wheat, rye, barley, oats, maize, rice, potatoes, groundnuts, and soybeans. In the case of cattle products, the yield accounted for only one-eleventh of the total rise in the low-calorie regions, and for over four-tenths of the total rise in the developed regions (the products were meat and milk, with one unit of meat converted to 10 units of milk).

the last quinquennium clearly indicates no progress in the low-calorie regions toward higher food production per capita—so that the accumulated shortfall, added to the originally set requirements for 1975 or 2000, raises the targets even further.

2. Technological, Economic, and Social Aspects of Capacity to Produce

Conclusions as to the capacity to provide other natural resource-based products for the population in year 2000 (and even somewhat later) are generally similar to those for food. Thus in a recent review of the supply and demand for natural resources to the year 2000, Joseph L. Fisher and Neal Potter concluded, concerning prospects of the underdeveloped countries, that

> we are not persuaded that the next few decades will see any general or marked deterioration of living levels because of increasing scarcity of raw materials. . . . We venture the view that living levels in most countries can increase over the coming years, with diets improving slowly and energy and mineral use more rapidly. . . . We do not believe that shortages and inadequacies of natural resources and raw materials are likely to make modest improvements in levels of living impossible of achievement.[8]

In a paper prepared for the 1965 UN World Population Conference Joseph J. Spengler stresses the wide potentialities of synthetic substitution for natural mineral resources.[9]

Finally, in an introductory paper for Session B–10 of the World Population Conference, a session that dealt with possible problems in the supply of natural resources, Edward A. Ackerman contrasts the "technological optimism view" (according to which "the potential resources of the earth are so large when man's creativity is applied to them that it is meaningless to set arbitrary limits for future world population for an indefinite period in the future") with the "planned population equilibrium view" (according to which "the world population-resources

[8] Joseph L. Fisher and Neal Potter, *World Prospects for Natural Resources* (Baltimore: The Johns Hopkins Press for the Resources of the Future, Inc., 1964), p. 68.

[9] Joseph J. Spengler, "Population and Natural Resources," Background Paper B.10, United Nations World Population Conference, 1965, p. 31. For the relevant quotation see the first paper in this volume, "Population and Economic Growth," p. 6.

problem must be viewed as one of unstable equilibrium, with the demand of population eventually having the capacity to out-run the supply from resources"). He then writes:

> There can be no doubt that the technological optimism position is correct if we are to consider the world as a whole for . . . about 50 years. The world has the resources to support the pop-ulation which would be attained by a projection of the 2 per cent growth rate that has recently prevailed, and probably at a higher average standard of living than now. . . . The evidence for this conclusion can be drawn from many sources. It is con-sidered to be enough a matter of public record so that no restate-ment or documentation is needed here. However, as we shall see later, the same conclusion is not necessarily applicable to all re-gions of the world, individually considered.[10]

In dealing now with the general grounds for feasibility conclusions for food requirements, we may assume that they are similar to those underlying the parallel conclusions for the pro-duction capacity of other natural resource-based products. The following discussion of the several aspects of these feasibility conclusions must perforce be general, since no economist has the competence to judge these estimates in technical detail—even if all the necessary details were available. Rather, the at-tempt is to define the general bases of the conclusions, to distin-guish as clearly as possible the technological, the economic, and the social aspects of these judgments, and thus be in a position to recognize the questions that arise in a critical scrutiny of these judgments and underlying estimates.

TECHNOLOGICAL ASPECT · The technological content of the con-clusions concerning productive capacity for the future may be put in the following general terms. The known stock of tested technological knowledge relevant to the field (whether it is food or other natural resource-based products) can, with the other production factors (labor, reproducible capital) assumed avail-able, be applied to the known natural resources (used and un-used) to increase the volume of production at a higher rate than the projected rate of population growth, and thus assure a higher output per capita. Given the projected populations and

[10] Edward A. Ackerman in *World Population Conference, 1965*, I, Summary Report (New York: United Nations, 1966), p. 260.

their requirements (targets), this statement clearly implies that we can evaluate the production equivalents of existing technological knowledge (which can be used more extensively than it is currently) and the availability of natural resources (or of their substitutes).

While natural resources and population trends and requirements must obviously be evaluated region by region because they differ so much from area to area, technological knowledge is a worldwide complex presumably available to all. Setting aside for the moment problems of different potentials for individual regions in the world, to be noted in the next section, we shall proceed here with an approach that, while recognizing regional differences in resource and population requirements, summates the production potential for the world, or for the large underdeveloped, low-calorie groups and developed, high-calorie groups.

The emphasis on both the stock of tested technological knowledge and the known natural resources is unique to the analysis of production potentials of natural resource-based products. For goods not directly dependent on these nonreproducible natural resources, we need only know the available stock of technological knowledge; if it permits wider than current use, no further questions arise. Thus if we were considering the capacity to supply a greater volume of barbers' services, or even of those of physicians, all we would need to know is whether the relevant stock of knowledge can be acquired by a larger number of practitioners, or whether the arts involved permit greater efficiency even within the existing stock of knowledge, or both. No question of natural resource availability arises, unless we assume that the services under discussion depend upon some exceptional genetic endowment and that the prospective rise in population will reduce or fail to increase the proportional supply of this limited genetic resource.

How can the existing stock of relevant technological knowledge and the inventories of known natural resources be translated into feasible productive capacity? How can one judge the detailed examination in the FAO, Freedom From Hunger Campaign Basic Study No. 10 of the available but not fully used land and related natural resources; of the ways to increase yield per land unit by seed selection, pesticides, fertilizers, and so on;

of the ways to increase the food supply from fishery resources? As already indicated, examination of technical detail is out of the question. But two characteristics of this and similar evaluations of technological feasibility and potentials may be noted, since they require no technical expertise. First, the data on existing natural resources are almost necessarily incomplete, and the understatement is likely to be especially great in the less-developed countries. Second, the estimates and evaluations relating to a long period ahead are based almost exclusively on the *existing* and tested stock of technical knowledge. In the nature of the case it would be difficult and well-nigh impossible to take account of the additions to the stock of knowledge that will be made in the near future; yet the application of this *new* knowledge may affect the production potentials, if not early then late in the period for which projection is attempted.

Knowledge of available natural resources is perforce incomplete because an up-to-date inventory, conforming to modern technology standards, requires relatively large inputs of capital and highly skilled labor, is beyond the means of the less-developed countries, and is not readily undertaken even by the developed countries, unless it holds out promise of prospective use. Furthermore, since the definition of a resource and its accessibility are both functions of current technology, changes in technology require continuous re-evaluation; even developed countries do not possess up-to-date knowledge of all their natural resources—ranging from the quality of soil to the subsoil wealth in coastal waters or in some backward region. Such omissions are relatively greater in the less-developed countries, since their knowledge and indeed their whole view of natural resources are largely set by their own, rather than by modern, technology— qualified by intervention or assistance of economic units from the developed regions. This situation is amply illustrated by continuous discoveries—once growth quickens or contacts with the developed regions intensify—of natural resource deposits or potentials (for example, oil in Libya and the Arab peninsula, and various export crops in Africa) in many underdeveloped countries formerly assumed to be barren of such wealth.

Given the known resources, ascertaining the productive potential afforded by the existing technology, capable of wider than current use, is even a more complicated matter. The productive potential is essentially derived from comparisons of practices pursued in some parts of the world with those of a more advanced character—tried, tested, and adopted on a substantial scale in the latter. The gaps between current practices and the better practices, let alone the best, are numerous and wide. Such gaps may exist even in the developed countries because current activities may have been the best possible under the older technological knowledge and may have become so entrenched that a shift to a different and more efficient practice, permitted by recent technological change, faces structural obstacles.[11] In the less-developed countries such lags are necessarily greater, since the prevailing technology originated even earlier and was less affected by modernization and industrialization, despite the substantial carry-over value of modern technology evolved and applied in the developed countries—differences in climate and natural resource endowments notwithstanding. Disparities in technological level are marked even *among* the less-developed countries, all of which are employing premodern technology in agriculture, as is evident in a comparison of much of Africa with much of East Asia; traditional intensive agriculture in East Asia reached a high level of efficiency that permitted the emergence and long-term growth of a large and dense population.

But granted these numerous and substantial lags of current behind better practices, which make estimates of large additional productive capacity plausible, the question here relates to the extent to which these estimates take into account *further* developments in technology that may occur within the long span projected, in this case almost forty years. In trying to answer this question, one may usefully distinguish among various probable changes in technology that differ in magnitude, as well as in the time span required for their emergence, testing, and sufficiently wide application to affect productive capacity significantly. Assuming realistically that at any given time a stock exists of probable technological changes, with a full distribution along the scale of magnitude and of duration of the period of maturity to a significantly spread innovation, an evaluation of

[11] See, for example, the discussion of the vast potential of more effective land utilization in Australia in *Possibilities of Increasing World Food Production*, Basic Study No. 10, pp. 52–54 and 75–85.

production potentials over a forty-year span could hardly take full account of those changes whose effects may be realized toward the end of that span. And, indeed, for obvious reasons of caution, evaluation of the type indicated cannot assign significant weights to technological changes as yet untested, let alone those unborn. Those future changes that are explicitly recognized, but are not made the basis for a sanguinely optimistic technologic view, are seen as "escape hatches from any tendency toward increasing scarcity" of natural resources, but their possible effects are not directly included in the evaluation—in an effort to avoid confusing the possible with the conjectural and merely probable.[12]

If, all other conditions being equal, the evaluation of the technologically feasible productive capacity is subject to downward bias because of omissions in the inventory of known natural resources and because of the unavoidable exclusion of future technological changes that are likely to affect capacity *within* the time span of the projection, it would be difficult to attach a reasonably precise weight to the bias. This difficulty is due to lack of knowledge, and could be resolved only if some analogy could be drawn with the past, when similar evaluations may have been understated for the same reasons. No such comparisons are at hand, and the dangers of such analogies are patent. Review of the available literature suggests that there is wide disagreement; all one can safely state is that the downward bias is there, and *may* be significant.

In this connection one speculative observation may be of interest. Table 3 in the preceding section indicates that in some low-calorie areas the long-term rise in per capita supplies of food has been slight. Over the twenty-seven years from 1934–38 to 1962–64, this rise was only 6 per cent for the Far East excluding Mainland China (line 13, column 1); judging by the evidence in Table 2, the same small rise would probably characterize the longer period back to the second half of the 1920's. Yet over the same three and one-half decades the mortality rate in that region dropped sharply, which also suggests a decline in the morbidity rate; *aggregate* output, if not food production, total and per capita, also increased—while inputs of hours per

[12] The term is from *World Prospects for Natural Resources*, footnote 6, pp. 49–51.

head probably declined.[13] If so, with minor rises (and in some areas perhaps even slight declines) in per capita food supply, as measured by the economic weight of food, the countries managed to lengthen the life span, probably reduce morbidity, and achieve a significantly higher product per capita and presumably per unit of effort.

If this finding remains after adjustments for possible biases in the measures of national product, it suggests that the same, slightly greater, or perhaps even slightly smaller, *economic* value of food per capita permits sizable improvements in the life and work that food is supposed to sustain. On the technological level, this suggests a trend toward greater efficiency of food, supplemented perhaps by products and services of modern medical care activities—greater efficiency in that the contribution of food and supplements to health, life, and work per unit of economic cost rose over time. This hypothesis may have significant bearing upon the meaning of food requirements for the future, measured as they are in constant price values; to pursue it further would require analysis of nutrition and health values of different food products compared with their economic weight— which is beyond our competence and the scope of this paper.

ECONOMIC ASPECT · Productive capacity in the field of our concern depends not only on the stock of tested technological knowledge and known natural resources, but also on the input of labor and reproducible capital—which in our formulation of technological feasibility were assumed to be available. But to say that it is technologically possible to provide a larger food output for the larger population in the year 2000 means one thing when labor and capital needed for this task are so large relative to total supply that assurance of food would mean scarcity of other goods; it means a different thing if the technological knowledge available for wider use requires only a mod-

---

[13] Gross domestic product per capita (in constant 1958 prices) in the Far East (East and Southeast Asia, excluding Japan and all the Communist countries) rose 25 per cent from 1950 to 1963; the rise in Latin America over the same period was 30 per cent; and in all non-Communist less-developed countries it was over 35 per cent. See *Yearbook of National Accounts Statistics, 1965* (New York: United Nations, 1966), Table 8B, pp. 488–90. The decline in average hours is characteristic even of moderate industrialization.

erate input of labor and capital, leaving an adequate supply of these resources for sustained growth in other areas of the economy. The problem of scarcity and opportunity costs is clearly economic; we may refer to these costs as the economic aspect of the judgments of productive capacity.

The distinction between technological and economic aspects is, in good part, false, for if the technological possibility of providing food, minerals, or some other limited group of goods can be realized only with a heavy draft upon labor and capital that would starve other important goods categories, it is not likely to be defined as technologically feasible. For technology is distinguished by a positive relevance to the satisfaction of human wants, and a production possibility that satisfies some needs but starves others can be viewed as technologically feasible only in a narrow and misleading sense of that term. Hence, a properly defined technologically feasible situation is necessarily economically feasible in that its requirements in the way of economic resources do not prevent needed and desirable growth elsewhere.

These comments are not made as a semantic exercise, but to emphasize that evaluations of productive capacity of the type already discussed necessarily imply economic feasibility even as they assert technological feasibility. And sometimes the implication is made explicit—as illustrated by the following quotation.

> It would, of course, serve little purpose to consider the technical possibilities for increasing production without bearing in mind that many things which are technically feasible may be uneconomic. . . . Increases in production achieved in this way [uneconomic] would result in the human race growing poorer. Man would be producing more food and other agricultural products only at the expense of other things. The objective of this study is rather to consider the possibilities for raising agricultural production within the framework of, and as part of, a rising standard of living.[14]

In other cases no explicit statement is made, but it is clear from the general context that economic feasibility—in the sense of a sufficient supply of labor and capital for other required and desired results of economic growth—is meant. Indeed, even the

[14] *Possibilities of Increasing World Food Production*, Basic Study No. 10, pp. 7–8.

population projections are based on and imply technical and economic feasibility assumptions. The following statement accompanying the recent UN projections of world population to the year 2000 is revealing: "Continuing substantial progress in economic and social development, however, is implicit in the assumptions on which the estimates are based." [15]

In short, if we ask whether the larger population numbers estimated for the future in the authoritative projections of the UN can be sustained, the answer is bound to be in the affirmative —at least by the authors of these projections; in *that* sense it is predetermined.

Two types of findings are implied if, in general terms, the economic aspect of productive capacity for the future larger population deals with the supply of capital and labor, and if "economically feasible" means that the larger volume of food or minerals calls for inputs of material capital and of labor (of various skills) which the economy can supply over the projected future while still allowing for growth in other areas. The first finding is that the *specific* material capital and the *specific* labor skills required for the greater output of food and so on can be provided by the country's economy or secured in trade (and other intercourse) with the rest of the world. Since these specific

---

[15] *World Population Prospects as Assessed in 1963*, p. 6. An even more explicit statement is made in the *Provisional Report on World Population Projection*, released in 1964: "A three-fold increase in the world population during the last hundred years has been made economically possible by technological inventions, investments in improvement of production equipment and in the use of natural resources, increasing skills, and heightened efficiency of economic organization, including the organization of international co-operation. *It is taken for granted in the projections presented here that developments along these lines will continue and indeed will be accelerated in the future.* [Italics added.] Otherwise even the increases projected on the 'low' variants for some of the most crowded and economically least developed regions might be impossible." [Because of continued high death rates and so on.]

The "high" and "low" variants in this report are thought to be wide enough to accommodate both a moderately optimistic and a moderately pessimistic view in these respects (production possibilities, for example), so far as prospects up to the end of the century are concerned (pp. 7–8).

inputs are only a limited part of total inputs and since their availability in the world is assured because the demand for them was derived, in the technological analysis, from an existing technology, no serious questions attach to this implied finding of economic feasibility.

The second finding—that the capital and labor resources required for larger output of food and so on, combined with those needed for growth elsewhere, do not exceed the capacity of the economy—is a much broader judgment and subject to less certain tests. How does one judge the capacity of an economy (or nation) to generate sufficient material capital formation and to provide sufficient labor force with the skills needed by required economic growth, *including* the growth of output of the particular goods that are of prime concern here? Such judgments are necessarily crude, and rest essentially on analogies with the past. If in the past, several countries with differing historical heritage, natural resources, social and political structures, size, and so on managed to generate material capital formation of, say, 15 to 25 per cent of GNP, and to provide labor with adequate training in needed skills (all of this permitting growth of x per cent per year per capita), it seems plausible to assume that other countries, not too far beyond the range of past experience, could do likewise. This should suffice to satisfy the requirements of the projection. Of course, this type of analysis can easily be refined with respect to the scope and measurement of various kinds and vintages of material capital, skills of labor, and disaggregation of the total product by components.

The intention here is not to deal with the specific aspects of such analysis, but to suggest the general structure of the economic side of the evaluations being discussed. This general structure is particularly important because it points directly to the dependence of the economic aspect of these evaluations upon what, for lack of a better term, may be called the social structure, the social aspect. Clearly, all economic activities and relations depend upon (even though they affect in turn) the political and social structure of society as well as the beliefs and scales of values of its members; the latter affect the capacity to generate savings and capital, the capital-output ratios, the integration of modern education and higher skills, and all that we usually classify as economic.

SOCIAL ASPECT · By social we mean here the political and social framework of the society, including the historically inherited beliefs and scales of values, which set the *conditions* for economic activity and hence for application of technology but are themselves not directly modified by the latter. An attempt at an economic innovation will not immediately and automatically effect changes in the social structure that will assure that innovation's spread and success. Insofar as such a social and ideological framework—one that conditions economic activity and application of technology—does exist, changes in it may constitute necessary requirements for modern economic growth, that is, for growth at a high minimum rate per capita, accompanied by rapid shifts in the industrial allocation of labor, capital, and product.

And, in the present connection, the existence of such a social structure means that the finding of technological and economic feasibility implies the feasibility of the changes in the social framework that are needed to permit economic performance to develop to the full extent that supplies of skilled labor and material capital warrant, given the existing technology and known natural resources. Such necessary and desirable changes in social structure and guiding views may be termed the social aspect of judgments concerning capacity to produce.

Here, too, a sharp line between the economic and social, like that between the technological and economic, is not easily drawn. Some institutions (for example, village credit cooperatives) may seem to be purely economic, yet they may perform governmental functions or may require the support of the central political structure to operate properly. Some government actions, like the fixing of exchange rates or income taxes, are purely economic in intent, yet they imply a specific relation between the government and the governed. Where, in these cases, is the line of division between economic and social? Nevertheless, the distinction appears significant when we deal with the *broad* political and social framework, which channels economic activity and which, by that token, cannot be identified with it.

That social preconditions of technological and economic feasibility exist and do not *automatically* follow from the availability of technological knowledge and economic resources, can hardly be doubted. After all, a viable political framework that assures a minimum of peace and equity in the process of modern economic growth—which like any process of change is provocative of conflicts—is indispensable for sustained growth. And the effects of failure of the political framework are all too obvious in recent experience (in Indonesia and Nigeria, for example) to be stressed. The limiting effects on economic growth of a system of beliefs inherited and adjusted to a preindustrial past, as in India, are also patent. And one must note, particularly, the relevance of international relations in their range from peaceful and planned trade and investment to armed conflict and pressure to divert resources to nonproductive armaments.

Social feasibility *must* be assumed if technological and economic feasibility are to be justified; that assumption would also rest on an analogy with the past, referring to changes in the social and ideological framework of many presently developed countries in the process of their economic growth. But unlike the technological aspect of the analysis (which rests upon tested applicability of devices and processes under specific physical conditions) and unlike the economic aspect (which deals with productive resources and their functional relations that can be at least statistically tested), the social aspect of the analysis is not amenable to measurement and hard tests. In particular, we do not know whether many of the presently underdeveloped countries are so far beyond the range of the social, political, and ideological framework within which modern economic growth could be observed in the past (all among Western European areas and their descendants overseas, with the single exception of Japan) that the lessons of the past, indicating feasibility of the needed social changes, may not apply. Even if we argue, as we should, that no region of the world, no human community, is so unique that lessons from the observable past of a large part of mankind are irrelevant or inapplicable, the *specific* application may still be impossible. We have no tested analysis at hand of the amount of social change that did occur and was needed in connection with various magnitudes of economic growth in the past—in the light of which social feasibility could be explored for the less-developed regions for which technological and economic feasibility were otherwise assumed to warrant prospective growth in productive capacity.

There is, consequently, a question about the social aspect of productive capacity that does not apply with the same force to the technological and economic aspects. Can we gauge the probability that the required social, political and ideological changes will be made? And since technological and economic feasibility will not materialize unless the social changes are made, the question affects the whole judgment regarding productive capacity. In other words, this judgment specifically assures the attainment of this capacity *only* if social and related changes are made—often not fully specifying what these would be since there is no firm basis for doing so. And thus the whole matter is presented as a challenge to mankind—a challenge that is real because the technological and economic potentials are there if only the broad social changes are made.

This interpretation may be illustrated by two quotations from Basic Study No. 10. In discussing Africa and Latin America, for which, as already cited, physical resources are adequate for the required rise in food production, the report adds the caveat: "The outcome will depend primarily upon the establishment of progressive and stable governments that are willing and able to mobilize their own resources and make effective use of foreign aid" (p. 222). And concluding the summary for the world as a whole, the report adds:

> It seems probable that a sustained and satisfactory rate of progress will require the allocation of appreciably greater resources for the education of peoples, for research, for physical investment, and for international leadership and co-ordination than the nations of the world are making available at present. It will also require a greater willingness to move toward the institutional changes which would provide a more generally favorable climate for productive investment and application of technology.[16]

One should add that the weight of the required social changes as conditions of technical and economic feasibility is all the greater because, as suggested earlier, the extensive growth of food output and agriculture in the less-developed regions would have to give way to intensive growth with emphasis on yields. The implied shift in technology requires greater education, different patterns of organization of land and agriculture, and a va-

[16] *Possibilities of Increasing World Food Production,* Basic Study No. 10, p. 223.

riety of changes in both agricultural and nonagricultural institutions that would not be required if the same technology could be pursued broadly with some hope of meeting the targets.[17]

The emphasis on the need for social change is so obvious as to seem tautological; it is important to point out that it is *not*. One can easily imagine a situation in which technological and economic feasibility would be assured *without* any changes in the political and social framework or in the prevailing views of the population—for example, in many presently developed countries with respect to sizable growth in productive capacity. That the less-developed countries are characterized by political, social, and ideological structures that *must* be changed significantly if the technological and economic potentials of greater productive capacity are to be realized is a fact of major importance. To the extent that the technological and economic feasibility of supporting a larger population at a higher standard of living depends on a variety of relatively major changes in the political, social, and ideological cast of many underdeveloped societies or on the evolution and maintenance of a world system of international relations radically different from the present, all statements concerning capacity to provide for larger populations are challenges that may or may not be met. Insofar as such challenges are a matter of decision by individual nations and regions, we must shift from the more aggregative views and consider the *differential* aspects of the feasible trends in productive capacity in response to larger population.

DIFFERENTIAL ASPECTS OF CAPACITY TO PRODUCE AND SUPPLY · The above discussion and quantitative illustrations have treated the major regions, and the low-calorie and the high-calorie groups, as wholes. Consequently, the requirements, as well as past production and supplies, were added for the several countries within each region or group; greater rises or declines

[17] This need to shift to a new technological and hence institutional base is the main thesis in Theodore W. Schultz, *Transforming Traditional Agriculture* (New Haven, Conn.: Yale University Press, 1964). See also Lester Brown, *Increasing World Food Output: Prospects and Problems,* Foreign Agricultural Economic Report No. 25, U.S. Department of Agriculture (Washington: U.S. Gov't. Printing Office, 1965), in which considerable emphasis is placed on educational and institutional changes required for a "take-off" in yields.

in some countries offset lesser rises or declines in others. While such summation is indispensable in economical presentation, the implicit assumption that food production and supplies move easily and at no cost among countries within a region, and that the requirements for them can be added without distinction, is unrealistic. Besides, our conclusion in the preceding section that decisions relating to the broad social aspect are of key importance in validating technological and economic feasibility of production prospects would direct our attention to individual countries. They are the loci of major decisions concerning changes in social, political, and economic institutions, granted the mitigating effects of relations with other members of the concert of nations and various international organizations.

If we distinguish among countries and disaggregate the broad categories used in the preceding discussion, differential aspects of the capacity to produce emerge. These are associated with (1) differences among countries with respect to natural resources, historical heritage, and productive patterns and requirements; (2) differences between long-term trends and projections and short-term fluctuations in production and supply; and (3) the possibility that *within* the individual countries (particularly the larger ones) several areas and several social groups may fare differently with respect to per capita production and supplies; hence, long-term trends in prospects as well as short-term fluctuations may have different impacts on the different areas and population groups within a country.

1. Even when a low-calorie region is defined by a distinctively low-calorie consumption per capita, the several countries within it are likely to differ with respect to food consumption and production, rate of growth projected for population, and magnitude of required growth in food output to meet future requirements. Above all, the likelihood that the projected growth of food production or supplies will be realized is not the same for the several countries, since their capacity to make the needed social and political changes and mobilize the required economic resources is far from uniform. Unless the estimates of requirements and of productive capacity are carefully prepared on the basis of data specific to each country, and unless some account is taken of the relative probability of the required changes being made in each country's institutional framework (a

nearly impossible task) we can hardly assume that growth in each country will conform to the feasibility projections.

Population projections are provided for individual countries, and presumably food requirements and targets can be approximated, but the latter cannot be identified with food *production* targets as was done for the world and the large regions within it. Individual countries need not aim at high food production if they can attain a higher level of other output more economically, and if they can use their comparative advantage to secure food in exchange for other products. Indeed, a productive capacity estimate for an individual country cannot be limited to food, but must include exportable goods for which food can be exchanged. Therefore, the estimate must approximate capacity to generate almost all products, not food alone. Many developed countries could, and did, rely on imports to cover their food deficits, as the data in Table 3 on net balance of food imports and exports suggest. Many underdeveloped countries possess resources other than food in which they have a large and lasting comparative advantage, and on which they can rely for a large and growing volume of food imports (for example, the Arab oil sheikdoms and several ore-rich countries in Africa).

We cannot spell out the food production targets implicit in the food requirements for individual countries, and compare current production records with these targets, country by country. Nor do we have the country production targets in the more general form of some required rate of growth of per capita total product, or of some limited but broad part of it (that is, exportable commodity product). Still, it may be argued that in the larger underdeveloped countries coverage of any substantial food deficit (relative to food requirements) by imports is not likely to be feasible. If food output and requirements at adequate levels amount, say, to 30 per cent of gross product (a not unrealistic figure for an underdeveloped country) and if the deficit is, say, one-sixth, the required food imports would be 5 per cent of gross product.

Given the low foreign trade propensity of large countries, particularly the underdeveloped ones, such a food import requirement might absorb the total import capacity of the country, leaving no resources for other indispensable raw material imports. Even the smaller underdeveloped countries cannot afford a gap between domestic food production and requirements (or a reduction in the excess of the former over the latter) unless they possess another export product or can produce import substitutes without excessive cost. The former usually requires some natural resource other than food as a basis of comparative advantage, and the latter assumes efficiency of industrial production not usually found in the less-developed countries.

However, the main argument here is that distinguishing the many individual countries, disaggregating the analysis, requires many more tests of the capacity to introduce the social, political, and institutional changes needed for the realization of technological and economic potentials—the latter assumed to be broadly given. In some underdeveloped countries, the social and institutional changes required for tapping the technological and economic potentials would have to be radical and far-reaching; the probability of such changes occurring would be low. The ensuing failure may be in food production or in the capacity to export in return for more food, or in the capacity to substitute efficiently for industrial products formerly secured by food exports no longer feasible.

The form of the failure is less important here than the likelihood of its occurrence, although it would be critical in its consequences if it involved a shortfall in food production and supplies in a large underdeveloped country, where food supply and reserves per capita are low to begin with. The point is that attainment of overall food targets for a region does not exclude the likelihood that *within* the region there may be substantial failures to reach production and supply levels, failures that may be the source of continuing crises in a changing list of the less-developed countries.

2. A long-term goal and projection of the type discussed may be reached by a constant rate increase or by an allowance for systematic changes in the rate of growth within the time span of the projections. But whether the rate changes systematically or is constant, the long-term targets do not allow for short-term fluctuations; yet the latter may occur even if the long-term trends are satisfactory. Such fluctuations are particularly common in food and agricultural production, and are often associated with weather and other factors not easily controlled. Pre-modern agriculture, with its low productivity, is particularly

subject to these short-run disturbances by weather and other natural factors; it is in the less-developed, low-calorie countries that such fluctuations may be especially disrupting, since a short-term decline in domestic food output per capita may, because of small reserves, cause a supply crisis.

Table 5, limited to the three low-calorie regions for which continuous indexes of food production per capita are available for a number of countries, provides ample illustration of the susceptibility of food production per capita to short-term fluctuations, particularly in individual countries compared with the total for a larger entity such as a region. First, by comparing column 1, based on three-year averages, with column 2, based on seven-year averages, we can see how much the rate is affected by the brevity of the period. For the region, the effect is small: about a tenth for the Far East (line 1), even less for the Near East (line 13), and relatively sizable only for Latin America (line 20), because the low regional rate reflects a combination of upward and downward trends among the several countries. For the individual countries the shift from three- to seven-year averages results in much greater differences in a preponderant proportion of countries. Second, the average deviation from the straight line fitted by semi-averages, using the seven-year averages employed for column 2, is appreciably larger for each country than for the region of which it is a part (column 3)—a measure of variability which we calculated only for those countries in which per capita food output rose over the full period. This variability means that the upward trend is not at a uniform but at a variable rate, probably including absolute declines. Finally, the number of absolute declines is given in column 4, again for the countries with upward trends; it can be observed that most countries with upward trends were affected by absolute declines at least four times out of a total of twelve possible year-to-year changes, that is, in at least a third of the period.

There is no reason to assume that such short-term variability will vanish in the next two to three decades—even for countries in which the long-term rates of growth will be up to the targets. To be sure, if the rate of growth of per capita output is unusually high, as it was in Israel (line 16), absolute declines are infrequent. But as the evidence in Table 4 (column 3) shows, required rates of growth in per capita food production range, even

Table 5. RATES OF GROWTH AND MEASURES OF VARIABILITY, PER CAPITA FOOD PRODUCTION, INDIVIDUAL LOW-CALORIE COUNTRIES, POSTWAR YEARS

	Rates of growth per decade (%)		Measures of variability (countries showing rise over period in col. 2)	
	1952–54 to 1962–64 (1)	1952–58 to 1958–64 (2)	Absolute average dev. from trend (3)	Number of years of decline (4)
Far East				
1. *Region*	9.2	10.2	1.7	3
2. Burma	5.3	8.1	3.7	7
3. Ceylon	9.7	9.9	4.8	2
4. China (Taiwan)	7.1	4.7	2.9	4
5. India	4.0	6.5	2.4	4
6. Indonesia	−8.9	−7.5	—	—
7. Japan	27.4	21.1	3.8	4
8. South Korea	8.3	6.8	7.8	6
9. Malaya	35.9	36.2	4.5	5
10. Pakistan	0.6	2.9	3.8	6
11. Philippines	−2.0	−3.1	—	—
12. Thailand	20.1	17.8	7.5	4
Near East				
13. *Region*	7.1	6.9	2.3	4
14. Iran	6.8	6.5	4.8	4
15. Iraq	−9.0	−12.0	—	—
16. Israel	68.8	67.6	3.3	1
17. Syria	−6.5	−22.0	—	—
18. Turkey	4.3	9.0	6.5	5
19. U. A. R.	18.1	10.5	3.8	3
Latin America				
20. *Region* (including River Plate countries)	3.0	1.9	1.6	5
21. Brazil	11.5	12.9	1.8	2
22. Chile	−2.9	−3.8	—	—
23. Colombia	−0.7	−3.1	—	—
24. Cuba	−13.1	−8.7	—	—
25. Guatemala	−2.0	−1.0	—	—
26. Honduras	−6.8	−3.3	—	—
27. Mexico	39.0	39.0	3.3	2
28. Panama	4.8	2.1	2.9	4
29. Peru	−11.0	−6.2	—	—
30. Venezuela	21.1	19.2	5.3	4
River Plate Countries				
31. Argentina	1.0	−4.7	—	—
32. Uruguay	−27.2	−33.8	—	—

The calculations are based on the indexes in *State of Food and Agriculture, 1966,* Annex Tables 2A and 2B, pp. 195–98.

The deviations in column 3 are from a straight line fitted to the averages for 1952–58 and 1958–64. The underlying series are indexes with 1952–56 = 100; the averages, for series with upward trends, range from about 100 to less than 125. The average deviations would therefore be roughly the same if taken as percentages of the average level.

Column 4 shows the number of years in which the per capita index of food production declines absolutely (the number of annual changes in the entire period is 12).

in the period from 1957–59 to 1975, from 8 to 17 per cent per decade. Several countries in Table 5, with growth rates in column 2 within that range (Burma, Japan, Thailand, Turkey, and Venezuela) show four or more absolute declines. If experience is any guide, we should expect absolute declines in per capita food output to continue with some frequency in individual countries, even if the long-term projections are approximated.

Short-term declines in food production could, of course, be compensated by special imports or, if the long-term trend is satisfactory, by domestic stockpiling that would help to even out supply over time. But in the latter case—one reason for calculating the measures of variability in Table 5 only for the countries with an upward trend in per capita food production—the additional task requires a long-term policy which in its consistency and even approximate accuracy implies an efficient central government. As has been said, such a government is *not* characteristic of underdeveloped countries. The main point here is that short-term instability in production, even when trends in productive capacity are favorable, constitutes an additional burden and intensifies the need for political and institutional changes that are essential in the long run.

3. Area differences within a country are likely to be particularly wide in natural resource endowment, and hence in agriculture and other natural resource-oriented industries. Within agriculture, other conditions being equal, internal area differentials in long-term trends and particularly in short-term fluctuations would tend to be wider in the less-developed than in the more-developed countries. Thus, the comments above on the frequency of disturbing fluctuations in less-developed, low-calorie countries can be repeated for areas within these countries—with the significant additional suggestion that such disruptions are likely to be more frequent if we consider the impact on any important area within the country rather than that on the country as a whole.

Indeed, in some large underdeveloped countries, the several areas may be so distinct, the means of transportation and communication among them so limited, and the degree of coherence and resulting power of the central government so weak, that a local area crisis cannot be alleviated by domestic resources and may have international repercussions (as has been the case with

India recently). Furthermore, diversity is possible even in long-term trends among the areas, and is only reduced slightly by internal (within the country) flows of resources.

Consequently, conformity for the country as a whole to the food requirement targets (or any other set of production goals) may be accompanied by a long-term lag or failure of some areas within the country that is *not* adequately compensated by the flows between them and the other more prosperous and more rapidly growing areas. While such diversity in internal area trends will eventually be compensated by increased mobility in the process of growth, there may be delays and frequent area crises—particularly if even the more prosperous areas lag behind the countrywide production targets.

In addition to the wider divergence among internal areas in the less-developed countries than in the developed countries in susceptibility to different short-term fluctuations in food production (or production of other natural-resource products) and even to different trends, there is the wider inequality in the distribution of the population among income-size and level-of-living classes. As a result, the countrywide averages of food output or supply per capita may be raised much more by the high level of consumption of the small top income class in the less-developed countries than in the developed.[18] Even though the share of the lowest income groups (say the bottom quartile) is no lower relative to the countrywide average in the less-developed than in the developed countries, the absolute levels are much lower in

[18] See, for example, *Possibilities of Increasing World Food Production*, Basic Study No. 10, pp. 24–25: "The figures . . . are . . . based upon national averages and thus ignore the fact that a proportion of the population already has a diet which exceeds the proposed level, while for the greater part of the population the deficiencies in diet . . . must be greater than indicated by the national averages. . . . This probably applies to Latin America, where there exists quite a large middle and wealthy class, including foreigners as well as indigenous population, whose dietary habits have little in common with the millions of Indians and Mestizos who are found in the rural areas; and to Africa, where in certain areas of the Mediterranean littoral, in East Africa and in South Africa, there exist several million people of European origin, whose consumption of the higher-priced foods must weigh fairly heavily in the regional averages".

See also the discussion of differences among families in calorie supplies per consuming unit in Burma and India and differentials in other Asian countries in P. V. Sukhatme, "The World's Hunger and Future Needs in Food Supplies," *Journal of the Royal Statistical Society*, Vol. CXXIV, Series A, General, Part 4, 1961, 483–88.

the former than in the latter. If we add somewhat higher economic status groups (still not including those at the very top), the share does become a lower relative of the countrywide average in the less-developed countries.

Consequently, absolute declines in production or supply per capita associated with short-term fluctuations, for internal areas or the whole country, and the diversity in the conformity of the trends in individual countries to the required targeted levels have a much greater impact on the numerically dominant groups within the underdeveloped, low-calorie countries than they could have in the more-developed countries with their high supply levels and larger reserves. Even perceptible rises in the countrywide supply of food per capita may not mean a significant increase, or *any* increase, in the per capita supply of the lower economic groups, whose shares in the total may decline.

This last point is of particular importance if the failure to raise per capita food output or supplies also reflects a high rate of population growth. In the underdeveloped countries, as in many developed countries, fertility rates are negatively correlated with income and level of living. Urban population, with its higher per capita income level, has a lower fertility rate than rural population with its lower per capita income, and within urban population, the lower income groups have higher fertility rates.[19] Differentials in fertility and in the rate of natural increase tend to be associated positively, because mortality differentials—which run counter to those in fertility—are too narrow to offset them. This means that if rates of population growth are high, the rate of natural increase of the lower income groups is likely to be higher than that of the upper income groups—and the differential is greater than when planned family limitation or other factors lower the overall rate of population increase. Hence unless changes, by policy design or otherwise, reduce economic inequality within the country, such inequality will tend to be wider with a high than with a low rate of population growth. The impact, under these conditions, of any failure to provide the same or a growing amount of food

[19] See George W. Roberts, "Fertility," Background Paper A.1, United Nations World Population Conference, 1965, pp. 61–62, on rural-urban differentials and p. 66, on income status differentials in fertility, both for the less-developed countries.

per capita is likely to be all the more painful for the lower economic groups, whose shares in total product, for reasons indicated, may decline.

Here again we could list various policies that could be used domestically to assist the lagging areas or the depressed lower socioeconomic groups, policies that have been used and are still being used in the more-developed countries. But the required transfers of resources from the more prosperous areas or groups within the country, and the systematic movement of people from the less to the more rapidly growing internal areas, again imply the existence of an effective central government, of a consensus within the country that would permit such transfers, and of ingenuity in fitting the remedy to the specific conditions of the problem. None of these is easily found in the less-developed countries.

3. Summary Comments

This paper dealt, somewhat discursively, with the question of whether the productive capacity of the world could sustain the prospective growth in population—a question urged by the concern in recent years over the possibly catastrophic consequences of the population explosion. In considering this problem for the limited time span to year 2000 it proved necessary to distinguish the several aspects—technological, economic, and broadly social—of the evaluation of productive capacity; to examine the evidence and reasoning that underlie judgments relating to these aspects; and to emphasize the difference between capacity for the world, or for a large region taken as a whole, and for the individual countries, which currently and in the foreseeable future are the loci of major social and economic decisions. The discussion, particularly the details, related to capacity to produce and requirements for food, but it applies in large part to other natural resource products as well. Much of it is relevant also to the capacity to produce and requirements for any major good viewed as basic rather than as an easily dispensable luxury.

We may now summarize the conclusions, briefly and perhaps dogmatically. The only useful qualification is the obvious one that all the judgments are fairly crude, since they are not based on a relatively complete body of "hard" evidence, properly tested.

1. If we deal with the world, or its large regions, or even with individual countries (excluding those on the fringe of human settlement and in extraordinarily difficult natural surroundings, for example, the Arctic wastes), and with a period extending to year 2000 (or say fifty years ahead), the available and tested technological knowledge and the known natural resources are adequate for sustaining the projected population numbers at moderately rising standards of living. If requirements of natural resource products, like food and minerals, can be satisfied, the potential for goods not directly dependent on limited natural resources is even greater. This appraisal of technological feasibility is subject to a downward bias, since the inventory of known natural resources is necessarily incomplete and any evaluation of existing knowledge does not take account of new knowledge that may emerge and mature within the long projection span.

2. As usually evaluated, technological feasibility implies economic in the sense that the possible increase in food, fuel, and so on is provided by a technology that, when applied to known natural resources, requires a limited input of labor and reproducible capital, and leaves adequate supplies of both productive factors for growth elsewhere. This conclusion as to joint technoeconomic feasibility follows from the assumption that only those technological possibilities that are "economical" of labor and capital are pursued, and from the observation that aggregate requirements for capital, material or invested in labor skills, are not only a moderate proportion of total product, but are also moderate relative to the growth in product that they can generate.

3. It should be emphasized that the technoeconomic feasibility of sustaining a growing population at a moderately rising level of living does not imply that, with a *lower* rate of population increase, higher rates of growth in per capita food supply or per capita product would not become feasible. The judgment is merely that the available technology, natural resources, and economic resources (labor and capital), can preclude the subjection of the expected larger populations to the Malthusian "positive" checks (famine, disease, and so on).

4. The technological-economic potentials can be realized in

many parts of the world, particularly the less-developed, low-calorie regions, *only* if the political, social, and economic institutions are changed, with consequent changes in the scales of values and priorities guiding the population. Land reform, a stable and viable central government responsive to the long-term needs of the community, a pattern of behavior that assigns sufficient weight to material welfare, and possibly other social changes are, in varying degree, indispensable to an effective and economic application of modern technology. Obviously, the variety and depth of these required social changes will be wider and greater if the food or agricultural targets cannot be attained by extension or slight modification of the old and traditional technology, but call for a shift to a different and modern technological base.

5. The capacity for making the required social changes and hence what may be called "social feasibility" cannot be appraised in general and yet testable terms. Whatever the cause and whatever the effect—whether the difficulty of measurement makes for ignorance, or ignorance makes for difficulty of measurement—our present knowledge of the precise social changes required for differing rates of economic and technological advance from different bases is poor. We have no inventory of the known political and social resources and their capacity for change. This aspect of the future is therefore usually presented as a "challenge" in response to the promise extended by the technoeconomic potentials, but one that may or may not be met—with the result that the economic growth potentials may or may not be attained.

6. Since the individual country is the locus of decisions on changes in social, political, and economic institutions, the feasibility problem must be examined not only for the world and major regions, but also for individual countries. Furthermore, a distinction must be drawn between trends and short-term fluctuations. It should be recognized that the several areas within a country and the distinct socioeconomic groups within the population may differ in their growth potential and in their response to population growth.

7. Distinguishing the individual countries increases the number of points at which social and institutional difficulties may limit otherwise satisfactory technological and economic growth

potentials, not only for food but also for other products. A single country may use some of these in international trade to obtain essentials. This means that, even if the world and the broad regions manage to raise output to provide for a growing population, some countries may fail. The loci of the resulting supply crises may shift over time from one country to another.

8. Distinguishing between trends and short-term fluctuations and recognizing the susceptibility of agriculture in the less-developed countries to vagaries of weather and natural calamities, one may expect that, even if the long-term growth trends are satisfactory, absolute declines in per capita production would be frequent. The task of dealing with the crises that would probably result emphasizes the need for a stable and effective central government capable of pursuing a long-term policy aimed at stabilizing supplies over time.

9. The same consideration is suggested by the recognition of the different impact of lagging trends or short-term declines on various areas or socioeconomic groups within a country. Diversities among areas and inequalities in income and levels of living are particularly conspicuous in the less-developed countries. Bridging inter-area differences or relieving the impact of short-term declines on the lower economic groups may prove to be acute problems, since the average level of living is low and the central government is weak—particularly in the larger countries.

The above conclusions indicate that the failure to provide adequately for the prospective population numbers to year 2000 is likely to stem from the inability of society in less-developed countries to introduce the possibly major changes in their social and political organization and in their economic institutions that may be needed to exploit the otherwise adequate techno-economic potentials. Such failure may also stem from the slow pace of improvements in international relations that would optimize the use of resources in furthering economic growth, particularly in the underdeveloped, low-calorie regions. In view of the long-recognized and repeatedly commented upon lag in the adjustment of the social and political structure to the techno-economic potentials, particularly in modern history when technical change and economic innovation are so rapid, such conclusions are neither novel nor surprising.

What they mean in terms of the possibly calamitous consequences of the high rate of population growth projected to year 2000, particularly in the less-developed countries, depends largely upon one's judgment of the capacity of these countries to make the necessary social and political changes. Their meaning also depends on the capacity of the world to minimize wasteful strains in international relations (whether among the developed countries, among the less-developed, or between the two groups) and to further economic growth where it is most needed.

My own judgment is that neither wholesale calamity—widespread starvation and devastating epidemics—in the populous less-developed countries, nor widely successful social and political modernization permitting a rapid and effective exploitation of the large technological and economic potentials which many of them possess, will eventuate. But it is a judgment that does not reflect tested experience in a recognizably explicit fashion. The prospects for change in the social and political structure of the less-developed countries and in the framework of international relations can hardly be explored by the methods of economic and quantitative analysis; they require data and tools that are beyond the scope of this paper.

Economic Aspects of Fertility Trends in the Less-Developed Countries

1. Fertility Patterns

Less-developed countries (LDCs) are defined here as those with a per capita or per worker economic product that is distinctly below some low limit, an indication of substantial failure to exploit the potentials of modern material and social technology. To call these countries "developing" is to mask their problems; and is, moreover, confusing since all countries are (or try to be) developing. Nor would it be fruitful to spend much effort on setting the low limit that separates the LDCs from the developed or, precisely, more-developed countries (DCs).[1] While there is a continuum with respect to per capita or per worker product, students in the field are in general agreement regarding the identity of the LDC group. It includes Asia, except Japan (and Israel with its high per capita income); Africa, except possibly

[1] For more detailed discussion of the LDCs and DCs see a later paper in this volume, entitled "The Gap: Concept, Measurement, Trends."

Reprinted from S. J. Behrman, Leslie Corsa, Jr., and Ronald Freedman, eds., *Fertility and Family Planning: A World View* (Ann Arbor: The University of Michigan Press, 1969), pp. 157–79. The paper was presented at a conference at the University of Michigan in November, 1967.

South Africa (and for certain purposes South Rhodesia); Latin America, except possibly Argentina, Uruguay, Venezuela, and Puerto Rico; and Oceania, other than Australia and New Zealand. There is some question concerning a few countries in Southern Europe (Greece, Albania, Portugal, Spain) and in Eastern Europe (Bulgaria and Romania); but for the present purposes we exclude them from the LDC group. The DC group includes Northern and Western Europe, the U.S.S.R., a few countries in Eastern Europe (East Germany, Czechoslovakia, Hungary), Japan, North America, Australia and New Zealand, and some smaller units.

Given this broad classification, the differences in current fertility levels between the LDCs and the DCs are marked. The average crude birth rate for 1960–64 for the LDCs is about 40 per thousand; for the DCs about half that, over 20 per thousand.[2] And the contrast is even greater for some major subregions within the two groups: thus, for Northern and Western Europe and Japan, the crude birth rate for the quinquennium was between 17 and 18 per thousand; for Africa it was 47 per thousand. Moreover these differences in fertility levels are neither recent nor short-term. United Nations sources reveal that in the late 1930's crude birth rates in Asia (including Japan), Africa, and Latin America (including all countries) ranged well above 40 per thousand, whereas those in North America, Europe including the U.S.S.R., and Oceania (which is dominated by Australia and New Zealand) ranged from 17 to 24 per thousand, and similar differences are found in the 1940's and the 1950's.[3]

These wide differences in level are not the only aspect of the

[2] The calculation is based on *Demographic Yearbook, 1965* (New York: United Nations, 1966) Table 1, p. 103. The 1960–64 birth rates shown there were weighted by the arithmetic means of the 1960 and 1964 populations. The LDC group is the sum of Africa; Asia except Japan; Latin America except temperate South America; and Oceania, other than Australia and New Zealand. The DC group is the sum of Western, Northern, and Eastern Europe, the U.S.S.R., Japan, North America, and Australia and New Zealand. Southern Europe and temperate South America are excluded.

[3] For 1937 see *World Population Trends, 1920–1947* (New York: United Nations, December, 1949), Table 2, p. 10; for 1947 see *The Determinants and Consequences of Population Trends*, Population Studies No. 17 (New York: United Nations, 1953), Table 51, p. 71. For the 1950's see tables in earlier issues of the *Demographic Yearbook* similar to that cited in footnote 2.

fertility patterns in the LDCs and the DCs that should be of interest in an attempt to discern their economic causes and consequences. Several others, for which the underlying evidence relating to the 1950's and early 1960's can be found in the United Nations demographic publications, are stated summarily here.

First, the differences in crude birth rates between the two groups of countries are *not* due to differences in the age structure of women within the childbearing ages, or in the shares of these women in total population. Adjustments for proportions of women and for their age structure have only minor effects: the gross reproduction rates are above 2.0 for almost all the LDCs, and are below 2.0 for all the DCs.[4]

Second, the difference in incidence of marriage (including consensual) is significant only for women under 25 years of age. In these early ages the proportions of married women to all women are distinctly higher in the LDCs than in the DCs, but the differences disappear in the older groups. With a rough allowance for disparities in intramarital fertility (for the 15–19 age class of women assumed to be zero, and for the 20–24 age class assumed to be about half-way between zero and the relative difference in the 25–29 age class), the difference in marriage incidence accounts for about a quarter of the total disparity in crude birth rates between LDCs and DCs—an estimate that is perhaps on the high side.

Third, there are wide differences in intramarital fertility in the two age classes of women that markedly affect the total birth rates—25–29 and 30–34. The differences for these two age classes contribute about one-half of the total difference in crude birth rates between the two groups.

Fourth, the relative, though not the absolute, differences in intramarital fertility continue and rise for older women still in their childbearing period, 35 and over. As much as a quarter of the total difference in crude birth rates between the LDCs and the DCs is accounted for by the continuation of fairly high fertility beyond female age 35 in the former and by the rapid decline of fertility of the older women in the latter.

[4] See *Population Bulletin No. 7, 1963* (New York: United Nations, 1965), which is devoted to fertility trends, summarizes a huge volume of data, and contains much analysis relevant to the central theme of this paper.

Finally, this prevalence of higher fertility in the LDCs associated with earlier marriages, with much higher intramarital fertility in the major childbearing ages below 35, and with the continuation of childbearing to more advanced ages beyond 35 results in distinctive characteristics of both births and parents in the LDCs compared with the DCs. First, the share of higher order births in total births is larger in the LDCs than in the DCs. Indeed, over one-half of the difference in the crude birth rates between the two groups of countries is accounted for by births of fifth or higher order. Second, parents, particularly fathers, of a substantial proportion of new-born children are older in the LDCs. Thus in countries with per capita product below $200 (in 1958), one-fourth of the children born had fathers 38 years old or older, and the birth rate specific to this age group was 120 per thousand; whereas in the high income countries, one-fourth of total births had fathers only 35.7 years old or older, and the specific birth rate was 30 per thousand.[5]

This persistence of higher fertility for a long time span within the family life cycle, which means large household units and many families with young children and fathers advanced in age, is one set of characteristics of the fertility pattern of the LDCs relevant to any explanation of economic causes and effects. The second, only barely touched upon, is the clustering of fertility measures around a high average in the many LDCs, matched by a similar though less concentrated clustering of fertility measures around a low mean in the DCs. Crude birth rates in the LDCs range from the high 30's upward, are mostly above 40 per thousand, and rise to the high 40's, whereas those for the DCs cluster between 16 and 20 for the "older" countries of Europe and Japan, and between the lower and upper 20's for the "young" and open countries like the United States, Canada, and the U.S.S.R. In only a few countries in the world is the crude birth rate between the upper 20's and upper 30's, and the world distribution is distinctly bimodal, with the two modes represent-

[5] See Simon Kuznets, *Modern Economic Growth* (New Haven, Conn.: Yale University Press, 1966), Table 8.2, pp. 438–39. The accompanying discussion covers the demographic patterns in the less-developed countries; but the grouping used in the table is too broad to reveal the full range of differences among countries.

ing the two groups. Gross reproduction rates show the same double clustering.[6]

The contrast between this bimodal distribution of fertility measures and the relatively unimodal distribution of per capita income and other economic and social characteristics is clearly pertinent to our theme. It immediately suggests that the relations between fertility as an effect and social factors as causes are neither simple nor continuous. It reflects the insensitivity of fertility levels to wide differences in economic and social factors despite the marked contrast between the LDCs and the DCs, each taken as a whole, with respect to both social factors and fertility.

2. Causes, Economic and Other

An economic explanation of the differences in fertility rates between the LDCs and the DCs would presumably identify the differences in material and social conditions associated with different per capita products and show how, given these differences, an economic calculus designed to optimize the contribution of children—as consumer and as producer "goods"—to the long-term economic welfare of the deciding unit (presumably the parent family) would yield different estimates of the number of children to be brought into the world. Questions would arise in identifying the relevant economic characteristics associated with different per capita incomes or other indexes of economic performance; in modifying the economic calculus to include responses that have been codified into social customs and prescribed patterns; and in considering the possible gap between decision and execution.

But important as these questions are, we can ignore them in the present connection and observe a variety of economic causes of the high fertility rates of the LDCs. If our comparison is limited to the two groups, each taken as a whole and distinguished initially by per capita product, the variety of associated differences in economic structure, institutions, and practices is wide-ranging from differences in relative shares of productive sectors

---

[6] See *Population Bulletin No. 7*, Chap. IX, pp. 134–51, which emphasizes this bunching and presents some analytical suggestions as to its implication.

(agriculture, manufacturing, etc.) to those in size and structure of economic units (large, small, individually managed, under corporation ownership, etc.), to differences in structure of the economically active population (by employment status, occupation, industrial attachment, education, etc.), to differences in use structure of product (between consumption and capital investment), to those in importance and structure of foreign trade, and so on. All of these reflect different conditions of life under which participation in economic activity—probably the most time-consuming activity of man—and the distribution of its product take place. If we assume that the social unit that decides on births makes such decisions after considering their consequences and if the consequences of births impinge upon the economics of the deciding unit, we may reasonably conclude that the differences in the structure of economic life associated with different per capita products exert a variety of influences on birth decisions. And we could easily prepare a lengthy list of economic causes to "explain" the higher birth rates of the LDCs: the use of young children's labor in agriculture and handicrafts; the reliance on offspring for old age security; the greater value of children in a traditional than in a market-oriented economy; the lack of productive outlets for the female members of the household, most of whose time is spent in bearing and rearing children, etc. And while these hypotheses cannot be proved, neither can they be denied in the simple associations and regressions in the cross-section comparisons that include both groups of countries.[7]

But although the economic factors obviously exert *some* influence on birth rates and make *some* contribution to the explanation of the higher fertility levels in the LDCs, they should not be unduly emphasized—for two reasons. First, even when we deal with the two groups as wholes, many other diverse social and demographic factors—most of them *loosely* associated with, but distinct from, the economic—may be equally, and perhaps even more, important. The most conspicuous of these other factors is the death rate—which for the LDCs averaged, on a crude basis, about 20 per thousand for 1960–64, compared with

[7] In *Population Bulletin No. 7* the correlations for *all* countries between gross reproduction rates and such economic variables as per capita income, the share of non-agriculture in labor force, energy consumption per capita, are all high, negative, and statistically significant (see Table 9.8, p. 148).

less than 9 per thousand for the DCs. If it is the surviving children that are planned for, the difference in death rates alone would account for more than half of the observed difference in crude birth rates.[8] Furthermore, many political and social variables, despite their economic implications, cannot be treated as economic factors. Thus, if the political structure is weak, or if the structure of the economically active population is determined by the extended family, the tribe, the caste, or the clan, rather than by each individual's capacity objectively tested in the market place, the whole economic and social calculus of childbearing is affected. The high fertility levels in the LDCs may therefore be associated more closely with these political and social characteristics than with economic variables (like the share of agriculture or level of per capita income). How do we distinguish the effects of each of these groups of variables— political, social, economic, and even demographic? We have ignored this question by dealing with economic causes alone, but it is clearly most significant for both analysis and policy-making. The answer to it may explain the failure of birth rates to decline in many LDCs despite a substantial long-term rise in per capita income, and may indicate the need for modifications in social institutions and practices before birth rates can be lowered.

[8] The death rates were calculated in the manner indicated for birth rates in footnote 2.

In a highly suggestive paper, "Mortality Level and Desired Family Size" (given at the 1966 meeting of the American Association for the Advancement of Science), David M. Heer and Dean O. Smith, of the Harvard University School of Public Health, present a simulation analysis showing gross reproduction rates (GRR) and intrinsic rates of natural increase based on the assumption that the parents, while having a perfect method of birth control, want "to be highly certain that at least one son will survive to the father's 65th birthday." On the assumption of a 95 per cent probability of attaining the aim, this simulation analysis for several United Nations mortality models of varying expectation of life at birth shows a steady decline in the GRR as expectation of life rises, but an inverted U shape in the intrinsic rate of natural increase, the latter being low at both very high and very low levels of mortality. The GRR at life expectancy (both sexes) of 35 years is 3.6 and the intrinsic rate of increase is 2.72 per cent per year; at life expectancy of 50 years, the GRR declines to 2.4 but the intrinsic rate of increase is still 2.53 per cent; at life expectancy of 71.7, the GRR is 1.27 and the rate of increase is 0.9 per cent. Although the analysis is subject to several modifications, some of which are presented in the paper, it does demonstrate the effect of changing mortality on birth rates and rates of natural increase when the surviving size of family is being planned. The actual cross section of countries by rates of natural increase and mortality (for 1946–63) shows the inverted U shape.

We have no basis for assigning proper weights to the specific effects of economic and other variables on the high birth rates in the LDCs; and, in fact, we may not even have adequate tools for the purpose.[9] My inclination, not too firmly based, would be to assign rather limited weight to the purely economic variables, for several reasons: the decisions on birth rates are long-term; knowledge needed for the economic calculus is limited; and in the less-developed countries the effects of different social institutions and life patterns minimize economic weights relative to sheer survival.

The statement that economic factors, in their possible effects on fertility, are part and parcel of a wider social and technological framework, and may be overshadowed by other components, is supported when we turn to the distinctions within the LDCs. Four subregions are suggested by historical and geographical considerations: Asia, excluding Japan and the Southwest; the Near East, comprising Southwest Asia and Northern Africa; sub-Saharan Africa, including or excluding South Africa (and possibly South Rhodesia); and Latin America, including or ex-

[9] The limited statistical effects of the economic variables, once other variables are included in the regression equations, are suggested in a paper by Irma Adelman, "An Econometric Analysis of Population Growth," *American Economic Review*, Vol. LIII, no. 3, June, 1963, 314–39. A simple regression shows a negative and statistically significant association between age specific (by age of mother) birth rates and per capita income. But a multiple regression equation that includes the share of the labor force employed outside of agriculture, an index of education, and an index of population density, shows that the partial regression coefficient of the age specific birth rates on per capita income is statistically insignificant for all but the two lowest age classes (15–19 and 20–24) and its sign is *positive* (see Table 1, p. 321). On the other hand, the partial regression coefficient for the index of education is consistently negative, large, and statistically significant. But what economic and social variables are represented by the index of education, a combination of a measure of literacy and one of newspaper circulation?

The opaqueness of many of the statistical variables is one persisting limitation of the multivariate statistical analysis so suggestively pursued in the Adelman paper. What is the meaning of the net regression coefficient of the per capita income variable when the effects of an unknown conglomerate represented by an index of education (or of population density) on both the dependent and the other independent variables have presumably been eliminated? Because of this limitation, the analysis and its findings are only barely informative. The unknown interplay of forces reflected in most measurable variables renders such analysis difficult. It would be eased by multiplying the number of variables, which is impractical; or by refining the formulations, which requires the scrutiny of all the statistical measures under widely different social and economic conditions.

cluding Argentina, Uruguay, Venezuela, and Puerto Rico. These four regions differ substantially in population density, historical heritage, per capita income, and related socioeconomic characteristics like industrialization, urbanization, etc. Per capita GDP in 1958 was $70 for sub-Saharan Africa, excluding South Africa and South Rhodesia; about $75 for Asia; about $150 for the Middle East excluding Israel; and about $210 for Latin America, excluding the four high-income countries. Yet the crude birth rates for 1960–64 averaged about 49 per thousand for Africa, 39 for Asia, 42 for the Middle East, and 43 for Latin America.[10] The range in economic and social variables among the four regions is wide, and would be much wider for individual countries in view of the range in their per capita GDP from more than $400 to below $50. The range in birth rates is much narrower, and is not clearly related to per capita product levels. If countries with per capita product as much as eight times as high as that of other countries nevertheless have much the same birth rate, some aspects of society, presumably unrelated to per capita product and other characteristics of economic performance, must account for these fertility levels.

This implication is reinforced by the absence of significant statistical association between fertility and many economic and social variables when the high fertility (closely identified with the LDCs) and low fertility (closely associated with the DC) groups are studied separately. Table 9.8, p. 148 of *Population Bulletin No. 7*, shows the correlations between GRR and 12 indexes (some economic, like per capita income; others social, like urbanization and newspaper circulation; still others demographic, like life expectancy). Only two of these (the correlations with shares of non-agricultural activities in labor force, and with urbanization) are barely significant within the high fertility group; and they are so low that they account for minor fractions of total variance. For the low fertility group not a single association is statistically significant. In other words, the differences among countries in per capita income and the other 11

[10] Per capita GDP is calculated from *Yearbook of National Accounts Statistics, 1965* (New York: United Nations, 1966), Tables 9A and 9B, supplemented by data for the Communist countries in my *Postwar Economic Growth* (Cambridge, Mass.: Harvard University Press, 1964), Table 1, pp. 29–31. The crude birth rates were calculated as indicated in footnote 2.

variables within the LDC group (or within the DC group) do not account for the differences in fertility; and the causes of the latter must be sought elsewhere.

What this means for movement over time is suggested in a recent study of birth rates for Latin America—the region with the highest per capita income in the LDC group—which assembles and adjusts a significant body of demographic data.[11] According to this study, standardized (for age structure of women within the childbearing ages) birth rates hover around high levels or rise in all countries except Argentina, which is outside the LDC group, and Chile, which shows a slight decline (to the high 30's). The period covered goes back to the 1910's or 1920's, when in several countries (e.g., Colombia and Venezuela) death rates and infant mortality declined (even though the decline was most precipitous after World War II) and product per capita was rising, at least since the 1920's, at a rate of 2 or more per cent per year (so that in a country like Colombia, where standardized birth rates rose to the mid-40's in 1955–59, product per worker more than doubled between 1925 and 1953).[12] Similar combinations of constant or rising high birth rates, declining death rates, and sustained and substantial growth in per capita product can be found for several other countries in Latin America.

The use of the "threshold hypothesis"[13] to explain this insensitivity of fertility levels to wide differences in economic and social variables may be suggestive, but as indicated in *Population Bulletin No. 7* it is only that (even though some "threshold" values for several variables are given in Table 9.9, p. 149, implying some analytical and policy significance). The danger is that the hypothesis, by giving the puzzle a suggestive name, will divert

[11] See O. Andrew Collver, *Birth Rates in Latin America* (Berkeley: Institute for International Studies, University of California, 1965).

[12] The product figures, from ECLA, are given in Alexander Ganz, "Problems and Uses of National Wealth Estimates in Latin America," in Raymond Goldsmith and Christopher Saunders, eds., *Income and Wealth, Series VIII* (London, 1959), Table xxviii, p. 260. The death rates and infant mortality are from the Collver monograph.

[13] "According to this hypothesis, in a developing country where fertility is initially high, improving economic and social conditions are likely to have little if any effect on fertility until a certain economic and social level is reached; but once that level is achieved, fertility is likely to enter a decided decline and to continue downward until it is again stabilized on a much lower plane" (*Population Bulletin No. 7*, p. 143).

our attention from the main question posed by the evidence. Why should there be a threshold and what determines its value? Theoretically, a threshold could be found in the response of a given process to variables a, b, c, d . . . only because the process actually responds to variables x, y, and z, which remain constant while a, b, c, etc., change within a wide range. The threshold hypothesis, in and of itself, is merely a reformulation of the insensitivity of a given dependent variable to a given set of independent variables within a given range, rather than an attempt to *identify* the independent factors that are in fact contributing to the level and range of the "insensitive" dependent variable. It may well be that when these relevant independent variables are identified, they will explain much or all of the change beyond the threshold level also—and thus replace the old set of explanatory variables for which a threshold hypothesis had been formulated.

Thus, further analysis of the factors that make for constant or rising birth rates in Latin America, or in the Near East, despite the high and rising incomes and declining death rates, may show that the key determinants (other than the declining but still high death rates) lie in the system of economic and social rewards to the younger generation—a system that may not change despite rising per capita income, and one that will change only under circumstances which will also necessarily mean a higher per capita income beyond a certain threshold value (which may shift significantly with technological or social changes). The important aspects of this reward system, or of alternative determinants, are still to be identified; and they may even turn out to be economic variables, although not the easily available and conventional ones included now. But once identified, they may also help to explain the differences in fertility rates between the LDCs and the DCs taken as wholes; so that the contrast between the inter- and intragroup association will disappear and with it the need for the threshold hypothesis as a crutch. Obviously, whatever the possibility, existing evidence reveals major gaps in our analysis; and the conventional indexes of economic (and possibly other) factors do not cover an important aspect of the social and economic determinants of fertility levels in the LDCs.

3. Economic Effects

In discussing the economic effects of higher fertility rates in the LDCs, we begin with four limitations. First, we shall deal with economic effects of high fertility only when the latter results in a high rate of natural increase of population. In setting this limitation, we are *not* implying that high birth rates combined with high death rates—and therefore, a low rate of population increase—do not produce undesirable economic effects. Obviously they represent not only a huge waste of human resources, but also conditions of life that inhibit the rational long-term planning requisite for economic growth. We are ignoring the economic effects of this demographic pattern precisely because they are negative and no discussion is needed. Naturally, reduction of high death rates is a matter of high priority—for many reasons, among which economic growth prospects are not necessarily the most important. Our problem here is with high fertility rates associated with moderate death rates—in other words, with the economic effects of high rates of population growth.

This stated, we should note that in many LDCs, particularly in Africa, both birth and death rates are high, and the rates of natural increase are as moderate as those in the older developed countries. It is difficult to estimate the size of the population with this pre-modern pattern of high birth and death rates, because the vital statistics, particularly for LDCs, are most unreliable.[14] But the number may be large, and we stress its existence as another indication of the diversity of demographic patterns within the LDCs that is so relevant to any analysis of economic effects. Although we omit this pre-modern pattern from discussion for the reason indicated, we should bear in mind that the pattern is likely to change in the near future into the one with which we deal, i.e., a combination of high birth and moderate death rates.

[14] If net reproduction rates below 1.5 are taken as moderate, and gross reproduction rates over 2 as high, Table 30 of the *Demographic Yearbook, 1965* shows such a combination for at least six African countries (Central African Republic, Chad, both Congos, Gabon, Upper Volta).

Second, we shall consider the economic effects of high rates of population growth for some moderate span of time—say over the next three to four decades—rather than extrapolate population growth further into the future. Much of our concern with population growth, in both LDCs and DCs, stems from the confrontation of the cumulative effect of fixed percentage rates of growth, at observed levels, with the limits, perceived or reasonably extended, of natural resource supplies or of other non-reproducible natural conditions of our universe. We could not deal effectively with this problem if it were projected far into the future—if only because we cannot forecast either technological or social capacity as easily as we can extrapolate simple growth rates (of population). If we confine our view to the period ending in the year 2000, it can be argued that for the present and prospective population growth (with rates as high as those now shown, or in prospect, for the LDCs), an increasing per capita supply of natural resources or their substitutes is technologically and economically feasible—in the sense that we know how to produce it (technological feasibility) and can do so without absorbing so much of capital and other productive resources as to inhibit the growth of total product per capita (economic feasibility).[15] If this argument is accepted, the economic effects of high rates of population growth can be discussed without concern that technological constraints, arising from shortages of natural resources, may overshadow the question of economic advantages and disadvantages. But even though we put the problem aside here, it should be noted that pressures of population on natural resources can be overcome only at some cost; and that technoeconomic feasibility does not mean social feasibility, i.e., the likelihood that the necessary social innovations will be made—a point to which we return in our concluding comments.

Third, if we assume an adequate supply of natural resources, the economic effects of higher rates of population growth should be related to some criteria of adequate economic performance. It will facilitate discussion if only one criterion—sustained increase in product per capita—is used. This is a major limitation because other and quite different criteria—less inequity in dis-

---

[15] For a more detailed discussion see the preceding paper in this volume, "Economic Capacity and Population Growth."

tribution, greater freedom for consumers, a more meaningful connection between economic performance of individuals and the material conditions of their life, and so on—may be equally, if not more, important. Any attempt to trace the effects of a high rate of growth of population on all these aspects of economic growth is almost impossible. Yet we must emphasize that this limitation qualifies our conclusions severely. While a high rate of population growth may prove to have limited effects on growth of per capita product, it may well have more significant consequences for various structural aspects, the "quality" aspects, of economic and social growth.

The economic effects of a high rate of population increase are presumably those on the supply of productive factors, relative to a growing population. But what are the productive factors? The concept of capital may be limited to material investment, or may also include education, etc. The quality of labor may also be emphasized in diverse ways. Consequently we set a fourth limitation on our discussion, and confine our analysis, in the initial stages, to the effects of a high rate of population increase on the supply of productive factors conventionally and narrowly defined, i.e., on material capital formation and on labor supply without regard for quality changes resulting from investment in education, training, and other elements now conventionally included under consumption.

Within the four limitations set, a high rate of population increase has two types of economic effects: (a) on the age structure of the population, and hence on the relation of dependents to active members of the labor force (the dependency ratio); and (b) on the demand for capital equipment to supply the additions to the labor force (which are large because of the high rate of natural increase) with the average capital per worker of the original labor force, and hence on the possibility of *increasing* the average capital and thus the average product per worker (and possibly per capita).

(a) The effect on age structure can be seen easily from recent data on vital rates and the age distribution of the population of countries grouped by per capita product. For some forty countries with per capita GDP of less that $200 in 1958, which clearly belong to the LDCs, the average crude birth rate in 1957–59 was 42.8 per thousand, the crude death rate was 17.6, and the crude rate of natural increase was 25.2, whereas the corresponding rates were 19.8, 9.8, and 10.0 for the twenty countries, with per capita GDP of over $575, in the DC group. The age composition of population around 1960 for a somewhat smaller sample shows that in thirty-four LDCs, the average share of the ages under 15 was 43.3 per cent, of those 15 through 59, 51.3 per cent, and of those 60 and over, 5.4 per cent; the corresponding percentages for nineteen DCs were 27.4, 58.2, and 14.4.[16] The dependency ratio, calculated as the ratio of total population (all population is dependent upon the product) to the population in working ages (defined here as those from 15 through 59), is 1.95 for the LDCs and 1.72 for the DCs. Thus, the former had about 13 per cent more dependents per member of the working age classes than the latter; and on the assumption of the same product per member of the working age classes, the product per capita would be 12 per cent less in the LDCs than in the DCs. Presumably, a shift toward a higher rate of natural increase would, via its effect on age structure, reduce any growth in the per capita product otherwise secured; and a lowering of the per capita product *level* would in turn have constraining effects on further growth of per capita product.

The ratios just calculated both under- and overestimate the effects on a more meaningful ratio of dependents to possible workers. They underestimate them because they disregard the greater proportional engagement of females, ages 15 through 59, in bearing and rearing children in the LDCs than in the DCs. If we assume that this proportion is about half in the LDCs but only a quarter in the DCs, and also assume rough equality of sexes, the dependency ratios become 2.60 for the LDCs and 1.96 for the DCs, with a relative differential of almost one-quarter (of the larger ratio). But these are overestimates because the consumption requirements of the young and the old are not as high (per unit) as those of the adult working ages; and if we set them at 0.6 of those of the adult working ages, the ratios become 2.09 for the LDCs and 1.64 for the DCs. If in the two groups of coun-

[16] These and other data in this paragraph are from Kuznets, *Modern Economic Growth*, Table 8.2, pp. 438–40.

In "Population and Economic Growth," the first paper in this volume, I used a somewhat different set of age classes, assigning the ages 15 through 64 (rather than 15 through 59) to the adult working ages. The results differ little from those shown here.

tries, product *per working member of the adult age group* is assumed the same, the product *per consuming unit* would, according to the last pair of ratios, be 47.8 units for the LDCs and 61.1 units for the DCs, a differential of over a fifth of the latter.

Granted the validity of the orders of magnitude suggested above, we can conclude that, under the conditions assumed and because of differences in age structure, per unit product associated with a high rate of population increase would be about 20 per cent lower than that associated with a low rate of population increase. But what are the consequences, not for the level, but for the *rate of growth* of per capita product? Two may be suggested. First, during the period of *transition* from low to high rates of population increase, the rise in the dependency ratio would, ceteris paribus, lower the rate of growth of per consuming unit product (and the effects are assigned to changes in age structure alone, *not* to the rise in the rate of population increase). The magnitude of this transitional effect depends upon the length of the period of rising rates of population increase and upon the lag in adjustment of the age structure. Thus, if the shift and its age-structure effects take place over 20 years, a 20 per cent differential in per capita product can reduce the rate of growth in per unit product over those two decades markedly. But this is purely a transitional effect, and would cease the moment the age structure completed its response to the rise in the rate of population increase. Second, ceteris paribus, a per consuming unit product that is *persistently* lower (because of age-structure effects) than a relevant alternative, since at any given time another age structure could have yielded a higher per unit product, has an effect on savings, or investment, and consequently on the rate of growth of total product. This effect is persisting if the age-structure implications of a high rate of population increase are compared with those that would have been obtained if the specific age structure associated with a high rate of population increase could have been avoided. The magnitude of this persisting effect can be suggested, at least illustratively. Data for the 1950's indicate that the net savings proportion (net national capital formation as a percentage of net national product) in the LDCs (those with 1958 per capita GDP below $200) was roughly about 8.5 per cent; whereas that for the DCs (with per capita GDP over $575) was about 15.5 per cent—say in the ratio of 1 to 2.[17] If we use a range of 1 to 6 in per capita product between the two groups of countries—a moderate one after allowing for purchasing power adjustments—the income elasticity of savings (i.e., the ratio of the proportional difference in savings to the proportional difference in income, both taken to geometric means as bases) is about 1.48. A differential in per capita income equal to a fifth of the larger, or 22.4 per cent of the geometric mean, would then mean a differential in savings of 33.2 per cent of the geometric mean, or a differential in the savings *proportion* between 100 and 66.8/77.6, or roughly 14 per cent. If the savings proportion determines the capital formation proportion, and if the latter, given a fixed incremental capital-output ratio, sets the rate of growth of total product, a decline of about one-seventh in the savings proportion means an equal drop in the rate of growth of total product—all of this subject to the qualifications that further discussion of the relations between capital formation proportions and rates of growth of product suggests.

Whether or not the effects just indicated—both for the transitional trend caused by a shift to a higher rate of increase of population and for the persistent consequences of a continuing lower than might have been per unit product on savings, and hence on growth rates—are major, they are based on calculations which assume a direct and close relation between the age distribution and active participation in economic production. Yet there may be little basis for assuming such a close connection, particularly in comparing LDCs and DCs, since many differences in economic and social structure, only some of which are connected with differences in birth and natural increase rates, may affect the age-specific economic activity participation rates. In fact, we find (in the source cited in footnote 17) that for thirty-six LDCs (each with per capita income less than $200 in 1958) the proportion of economically active to total population in recent years averaged 40.7 per cent, compared with 44.7 per cent in the twenty DCs (with income over $575 in 1958). The difference is in the expected direction, but it is only a third as wide as the one implied in the calculations above (where, with

[17] See Simon Kuznets, *Modern Economic Growth*, Table 8.1, pp. 402–8.

allowance for the time adult women spend in bearing and rearing children, the implicit percentages of economically active
population were 38.5 for the LDCs and 50.9 for the DCs).
Clearly, the higher proportion of the population economically
active in the LDCs—higher than one would expect on the basis
of the age distribution—is due to engagement of a larger percentage of the young males (particularly those below the age of
20) and of the old group (much less important statistically). In
the LDCs entry into the labor force is at an earlier age and not
delayed by as long a period of education as in the DC group.[18]
On the basis of the proportions of the economically active (and
the lower consumption requirements of the young and old), the
dependency ratios become 1.87 for the LDCs and 1.74 for the
DCs, and income per consuming unit (on the assumption of the
same return per member of the labor force) becomes 53.4 for the
LDCs and 57.4 for the DCs, a difference of about 7 per cent of
the higher figure. Such differentials are of little consequence for
the rate of growth of per unit product in a transition period or
for the more persisting effects of a slightly lower per unit income.

Thus in any comparison of the LDCs and the DCs, the major
effect of the high rate of population increase, via the age structure, is on the rates of participation in the labor force, particularly by the younger males. The factors to which the higher
birth rates may be a response, viz., those that reduce the value
of investment in the younger generation in the way of education, etc., also make for greater participation in economic activity at earlier ages. To the extent that this failure to invest in
human capital influences growth in per capita product, it belongs to the second category of effects, those via pressure on
capital formation. In dealing with age structure proper we can
infer that, because of different labor force participation rates,
the direct economic effects are minor; and that when the participation rates begin to change, and thus lead to higher dependency ratios, the changes will presumably be in response to

[18] On this and other demographic aspects of labor force see Jan L. Sadie,
"Demographic Aspects of Labour Supply and Employment," Background
Paper WPC/WP/84 for Session A.5 of the 1965 UN World Population
Conference at Belgrade.

changes in views on investment in quality of the younger generation, and will also mean changes in the birth rates and rates of natural increase.

(b) High rates of population increase must affect capital requirements if we assume limited substitution of labor for capital, and a minimum level of capital for turning out product. If we assume that the incremental capital-output (c/o) ratio, i.e., the ratio of additions to capital to additions to product, is 3 to 1, and that population grows 3 per cent per year, the *maintenance* of per capita product would require additions to capital, i.e., net capital formation, equivalent to 3 per cent $\times$ 3, or 9 per cent of total product. If the net capital formation capacity of an economy were, say, 15 per cent of total product, this would leave only 6 per cent of total product for capital formation to provide *additions* to product—which would permit total product to grow an additional 2 per cent, and per capita product 1.9 per cent per year (i.e., $105/103 - 1.00$). But if population were growing only 1 per cent per year, net capital formation needed to maintain per capita product would be only 3 per cent of total product, leaving 12 per cent to provide additions to total product of 4 per cent, and per capita product would also grow about 4 per cent per year. If the net capital formation proportion actually realized were to drop to 10 per cent, the residue for increasing per capita product would practically vanish if the rate of population growth was 3 per cent, but would still be substantial if it was 1 per cent.

In any evaluation of the effect on capital requirements of high rates of population increase, two aspects are important: (1) the degree of fixity in the capital requirements; and (2) the level of the c/o ratio. The more fixed the requirement and the higher the c/o ratio, the greater the pressure of high rates of population increase on capital formation, and hence the greater the constraint on the growth of per capita product. While fixity and level are interrelated, it is best to consider them separately.[19]

(1) Although it appears to be a technological measure, the c/o ratio is largely a social magnitude that is variable over time and differs substantially among countries. Even in the production of a *single* commodity by a standardized method, capital

[19] For a more detailed discussion see again the first paper in this volume, "Population and Economic Growth."

can be utilized with different degrees of intensity (ranging from less than 8 to 24 hours a day) and can be expensive (new, or solid and durable) or inexpensive (secondhand, or less solid and less durable). For several products, all relevant to the same need (e.g., various means of transportation, or types of shelter) the capital employed may involve significantly different c/o ratios. For an open economy, i.e., one that can supplement domestic production by imports (in return for exports), the choice is extended to that between domestic output and foreign provenance—for the same range of needs for final products; and the c/o ratios can be modified by reliance on a different structure and volume of exports and imports.

It is, therefore, hardly surprising that the observed incremental c/o ratios change markedly over time—usually rising in the course of economic growth as pressure to economize on capital declines; and, in cross-section comparisons, are usually lower in the less-developed than in the more-developed countries.[20] Of particular interest in the present connection is the evidence for the post-World War II period, for which we have fairly comprehensive estimates at least for the non-Communist world. Gross domestic product (in 1958 prices) for the less-developed non-Communist countries (Latin America, Asia excluding Japan, and Africa excluding South Africa) grew from 1950–52 to 1962–64 at the rate of 4.58 per cent per year; the comparable rate for the developed non-Communist countries (Europe, North America, Australia and New Zealand, Japan, and South Africa) was 4.02 per cent per year.[21] We also know that in the 1950's net capital formation proportions (*domestic*, related to net domestic product, not national as used above) averaged about 10.1 per cent in the LDCs and 15.4 per cent in the DCs (the former being countries with per capita GDP below $200 in 1958; the latter with

[20] For details of these findings see Papers V and VI in the series entitled "Quantitative Aspects of the Economic Growth of Nations," *Economic Development and Cultural Change*, Vol. VIII, no. 4, Part II, July, 1960 and Vol. IX, no. 4, Part II, July, 1961.

[21] These rates are based on the indexes in the United Nations, *Yearbook of National Accounts Statistics, 1965*, Table 8B, pp. 488–92, with the indexes for the less-developed countries brought through 1964 on the basis of data for individual countries in O.E.C.D. Development Center, *National Accounts for Less Developed Countries* (Paris, February, 1967) (preliminary). The capital formation proportions are from Kuznets, *Modern Economic Growth*, Table 8.1.

per capitas above $575). The gross domestic capital formation proportions (related to gross domestic product) were 15.9 and 22.2 per cent respectively. Since net and gross domestic product have approximately the same rate of growth, the incremental net c/o ratios were 2.2 for the LDCs, and 3.8 for the DCs—a difference of more than 40 per cent of the larger figure (the gross c/o ratios were 3.5 and 5.5 respectively).

This seeming lack of fixity in incremental c/o ratios does not mean that the c/o ratio can be extended downward to some virtually insignificant level close to zero. A sizable chunk of capital, not replaceable by labor, is required if a given group of products, even broadly defined, is to be produced. This irreducible capital, which forms the hard core of the c/o ratio, is presumably found at low levels; and in this sense fixity and level are interrelated. But how low is the low, and how much can the c/o ratio be modified? This question is not easily answered—for it requires knowledge of the effect of the economic and social institutions on the efficiency with which capital can be used in order to optimize economic growth. At this point not only the economic, but also several social factors become important, for they can influence the efficiency of capital use, and fairly significantly on a nationwide scale. All one can say here is that the c/o ratio becomes fixed only at low levels and that it has a wide range which is affected by social and political factors that far transcend the economic—so that the economic effects via capital requirements become dependent on the social and political system—a conclusion which will only be reinforced by consideration of the questions bearing on the *level* of the capital formation requirements.

(2) Given fixity of the incremental c/o ratio, its level is clearly important in evaluating the economic effects of a high rate of population increase because it reveals the magnitudes of the adjustments required to *compensate* for the greater capital requirements. Thus, if the relevant c/o ratio is 3 to 1, and we compare the effects of two rates of population increase, 1 and 3 per cent per year, the difference in capital formation is between 3 and 9 per cent of net product respectively; and the additional 6 per cent of national product, if these are to be shifted from consumption to capital formation, are only a slightly larger fraction of government and household consumption, which together

are well over 80 per cent of national product. We can argue that with this c/o ratio, the shift of resources to provide the additional capital formation required seems moderate. But if the c/o ratio is 15 to 1, capital requirements for the same two rates of population increase are 45 and 15 per cent of national product, necessitating a shift of over a third of consumption into capital formation. Such a large shift is formidable, and would require major changes in the institutions that govern the allocation of resources.

In order to ascertain the level of the incremental c/o ratio—which must be done before the effects of a high rate of population increase in the LDCs can be evaluated—we must identify the capital required to increase product per unit of labor (in the DCs) and then accept or adjust the resultant level in application to the LDCs. In attempting this task, we face two distinct, but interrelated, difficulties.

The first, having to do with observation and measurement of the c/o ratio in the past, forces us to define capital. So far we limited ourselves to the narrow, conventional definition, i.e., material investment in construction, equipment, and additions to inventories, and based the ratios on this definition. But the use, in the analysis of economic growth, of capital inputs so defined together with labor inputs (even when the latter are adjusted for differences in compensation and thus implicitly in quality), leaves a large unexplained residual—a rise in output per unit of input—which must be due to other factors. It is because of this finding that economists have turned to education as a possibly important capital factor. And once capital is defined as any input that raises the productivity of "pure" labor (i.e., labor unaffected by an investment in productivity-raising inputs like education, special health provisions, etc.), its scope is widened to include many uses of product now covered under consumption —ranging from better food, shelter, education, and all such "productive" elements of personal consumption to public outlays, not only on education, etc., but also on other services that increase social and, through it, economic efficiency. With this wider concept of capital, the line of distinction between economic and non-economic shifts, at least as far as analysis is concerned. For in order to measure the relevant capital inputs, we must distinguish within all uses of economic product between "pure" consumption and "pure" capital formation components; and we can do this only through analysis of the content of the activity involved in its bearing upon labor productivity. Even if the specific activity or process requires only a minor input of economic resources, it may have a large effect on productivity. And the analysis clearly points to the next stage, viz., a recognition that economic productivity may be vitally affected by social institutions and processes that in themselves require no or few inputs of *economic* resources. Yet the changes in these institutions and processes required to assure adequate economic productivity may be neither easy nor free, even though the costs are not economic.

The second difficulty is that even if we could identify and measure capital, in terms limited to economic inputs, but corresponding to the broader definition just suggested, the observed measures would relate almost necessarily to the DCs—not only because the data are available for them, but also because increases in the product of the LDCs are likely to follow the paths already established for the developed countries. But one may argue that, whatever the definition of capital and whatever the levels of the derived incremental c/o ratios, these levels would have to be changed when applied to the LDCs, since, ceteris paribus, these countries can choose more economically among a wider variety of capital uses than their predecessors could in the past. The difficulty, however, is in approximating the magnitude of this downward adjustment, in identifying the minimum requirement in the way of social institutions and other noneconomic conditions of economic productivity that were satisfied in the past, and deciding how they can be modified in application to the less-developed countries.

These rather general comments should serve to indicate the difficulties we face in suggesting the relevant levels of the c/o ratios—and indeed, in considering the whole question of the effects of a higher rate of population increase in the LDCs on capital requirements. If we limit capital to the narrow, conventional definition, the observed incremental c/o ratios will be fairly low, about 3 to 1 for the net ratios and about 5 to 1 for the gross ratios, and with a further significant reduction in these ratios (which we cannot specify) when applied to the LDCs, the economic effects of the higher rate of population growth are quantitatively minor and do not necessitate a difficult shift in the allocation of resources even in the LDCs. But this answer is due to the narrow definition of capital, and to the disregard of the other conditions of the efficient use of material capital, that may or may not require substantial economic inputs. And this means that in policy uses one cannot assume that satisfaction of the capital requirements in response to higher rates of population increase and for capital narrowly defined would be sufficient to permit a rise (or even maintenance) of per capita product, despite the high rate of population increase.

The other alternative is to consider the broader definition of capital, which is more realistic but far more demanding. Capital would then include some major uses of product now included under consumption, and consequently the incremental capital-output ratio would be substantially higher. The costs of education alone (including foregone income, which reflects the lower labor force participation ratios among the young and thus reintroduces the age-structure effects of the higher rate of population increase) might double both the capital total and the incremental c/o ratio.[22] And the shift of other "capital-like" elements now classified as consumption (e.g., special health services) would raise the c/o ratio even further. But in drawing the line of distinction between consumption and capital formation, and ascertaining the indispensable elements in the latter, we face the problem of "fixity" in an aggravated form; and we would also face the question of the downward adjustment to be made in applying even the hard c/o ratios observed for the past to the LDCs. Do these countries need the resource-consuming educational, etc., provisions of the developed countries to assure fairly efficient use of material capital to increase economic product? In our present state of ignorance, the relevant incremental c/o ratio, based on this wider concept of capital, cannot be measured with any assurance. It would surely be higher than the ratio under the narrower and more conventional definition of capital, but the orders of magnitude cannot be suggested, although I would guess that the level would not be prohibitively high.

As already indicated, this approach suggests that the purely

[22] See in this connection the illustrative calculation in Kuznets, *Modern Economic Growth*, Table 5.2, p. 231 and the accompanying text.

economic resource requirements of a high rate of population growth, reflected in the c/o ratio which relates *economic* inputs to economic product, would be only moderately high. But, more important, it would stress that the variability of even the broader c/o ratios is due to conditioning of economic efficiency by social institutions and by points of view guiding individuals and societies, aspects of social life that have only minor economic *input* implications and are not likely to be reflected in c/o ratios so long as the numerators of these ratios, even with the widest definition of capital, are *economic* inputs. The belief of East Indians in the sacredness of life, which means a large waste of crops (because of destruction by pests), may significantly affect the c/o ratio in Indian agriculture, and any shift in the ratio in response to a high rate of population growth may necessitate a change in beliefs, which in turn may require only a minor input of economic resources but a large input of other resources in order to modify long-implanted beliefs or to change traditional and respected institutions. The major significance of high birth rates and of a high rate of population increase for growth in per capita product may lie, not in the direct economic effects, which may be moderate even with a wider definition of capital, but in the fact that they reflect a system of views and a set of social institutions unfavorable to modern economic growth.

4. Concluding Comments

One main theme of this paper is that economic causes do not adequately explain the high levels of fertility in the less-developed countries, and therefore a more relevant complex of observable and measurable factors than the conventional measures of economic levels or conventional aspects of economic structure (such as per capita income or the share of agriculture) must be sought. A parallel theme is that the economic effects of the high rates of population increase in the LDCs, i.e., greater capital requirements, seem relatively moderate, and emphasis on them oversimplifies the problem. This is because the conventionally measured economic effects overlook other "capital" items required and, in fact, used in the past. This other capital may represent substantial economic inputs, and, if included, would raise the incremental c/o ratio and thus magnify the economic effects of a high rate of population growth by increasing the numerator. On the other hand, it may mean noneconomic inputs (e.g., such aspects of the political structure as loyalty and stability) that have a marked effect on economic productivity; and if neglected, may mean a higher c/o ratio because of the effect on the denominator.

If we disregard these noneconomic elements, we might find that even with the wider definition of capital, the economic effects of a high rate of population growth would not constitute a major obstacle to an increase in per capita product. And this parallels the conclusion, assumed in the course of discussion, of the technological and economic feasibility of providing the growing population with natural resources. But in both cases the conclusions assume social feasibility, i.e., the capacity of societies to change their institutions and beliefs in order to make more effective use of natural resources or of the economic capital involved in the technoeconomic feasibilities. It may well be that social feasibility is more important than the simpler relation of numbers to resources, natural or reproducible; and that if the prospect of changes in social institutions and views is favorable, the less-developed countries can cope with both the economic effects and the ultimate trend of the present demographic patterns.

Two obvious inferences relating to policy should perhaps be explicitly stated. First, growth policy in less-developed countries must be geared to a much broader set of determinants and concepts than is, or can be, provided by current economic analysis; which means also that, for lack of such an established framework, conventional economic analysis should be more critically scrutinized and less readily accepted. Second, too much reliance should not be placed on the favorable economic consequences of a lower rate of population increase, in contrast to the unfavorable results of a higher rate of increase. Obviously, this is not to deny that population control would make a large contribution —relieving current social tensions, offsetting failures to exploit the given technological and economic potentials, and forestalling major acute problems in the longer run (longer than the one considered here). But it does suggest a conservative view of the possible benefits of a lower rate of population growth, if the determinants of economic growth other than the simple relations of numbers to economic resources are not transformed to induce greater exploitation of the technological and economic potentials available to the less-developed countries.

Capital Formation in
Modern Economic Growth

(and some implications for the past)

This paper deals first with quantitative aspects of capital formation in economically developed countries for the long periods over which their growth can be measured.* Several implications and questions concerning capital formation in the pre-industrial and pre-modern past, suggested by the statistical evidence are then treated in what, for lack of firm data, must be speculative fashion. It is hoped that scholars more familiar than the author with the pre-nineteenth century past will be able to pursue the speculative suggestions and questions more effectively than has been done here.

1. Definitions

Domestic capital formation [1] is defined in current national accounts as additions to the stock of material capital goods within

* I am indebted to my colleagues, Professors Alexander Gerschenkron and John R. Meyer, for helpful comments on the original version of this paper.
[1] The term "capital formation" is used in preference to "capital investment" because "the term investment is sometimes used to indicate the pro-

[continued on page 122]

Reprinted from *Third International Conference of Economic History, Munich, 1965* (Paris: Mouton, 1968), pp. 15–53. The paper was presented at the Munich Conference in August, 1965.

a country, obtained by the expenditure of current product—either of the given country or of some other country. National capital formation equals domestic capital formation minus capital imports plus capital exports. National capital formation also equals the total savings of the country, since these savings can find embodiment only as additions either to the stock of material capital goods within the country, or to claims against the rest of the world, via net capital exports.

Several restrictions are placed on the goods that may be included under capital formation. The first stems, of course, from the distinction between capital goods, i.e., those used in production, and all other goods; and the identification of goods as capital depends upon our view of economic production. Without digressing into a topic that deserves prolonged discussion, we merely note here the exclusion of two rather wide groups of commodities: consumers' durables other than dwellings (passenger cars, major appliances, etc.) in the hands of households and military durables (barracks, airfields, munitions, etc.) in the hands of final users. These commodities are excluded because the household is not considered a firm producing services of consumers' durables and the military establishment is not considered a firm producing economic goods. The second restriction limits capital formation to *material* goods, i.e., commodities, except for claims against foreign countries, which must be included in national (but not domestic) capital formation. This means the exclusion of investment (other than buildings and equipment) in education, health, and all other such factors influencing the productivity of human beings; investment in institutional arrangements (e.g., legislation, administration, voluntary organizations, etc.) that may be of cardinal importance in facilitating economic growth; and, in particular, changes in the stock of knowledge, even if limited to current inputs requisite for its sustenance or increase. Finally, only material and tangible capi-

---

cess of spending money capital for the purchase of capital goods, or more generally, to signify the acquisition of securities and other financial claims" ("Concepts and Definitions of Capital Formation," *Statistical Papers*, Series F, no. 3 [New York: United Nations, 1953], p. 7). The emphasis is on additions to real capital and not on purchase, or on acquisition of claims (except against foreign countries).

tal that is derived from economic activity of the type that defines a nation's aggregate product is included. This means the exclusion of all natural resources, although not of any current inputs employed to introduce such resources into productive use —so that a relatively effortless discovery of vast and valuable natural resources, manna from heaven so to speak, cannot be included under capital formation. Nor can capital formation include acquisitions of territory, or even reproducible capital goods, or claims, resulting from war or aggression, since the latter is not accepted as economic production eventuating in aggregate economic product.

The exclusions just noted, based on criteria of function (capital versus other goods), form (material versus non-material), and source (economic production versus nature and noneconomic activity), have obviously been adopted to facilitate economic measurement and analysis. The restrictive definition of economic production to exclude households and much government activity (particularly military), the limitation of capital goods to commodities that, unlike human beings, can be traded and evaluated on the market, and the disregard of natural resources and concentration on what can be produced—all facilitate economic analysis by excluding from capital formation elements of social and individual behavior that are not clearly subject to economic logic, and elements of nature that are irreproducible and hence presumably unaugmentable by economic action. On the other hand, these exclusions greatly restrict the relevance of capital formation, so defined and measured, to economic growth. But it is expedient to use the currently accepted restrictive definition and take advantage of the clarity and supply of information that it permits.

What then does capital formation include? First, it includes additions to fixed (long-lived) capital goods in the hands of their users, i.e., purchases or own-account construction (exclusive of land value before improvement) of new dwellings and major alterations in old; all other buildings, ranging from industrial plants, to government buildings, to farm structures; other construction including harbors, highways, dams, public utility roadbeds and mains, and the like; and equipment, often subdivided into transportation equipment (rolling stock, airplanes, cars, etc.) and other machinery and equipment. This item is designated domestic fixed capital formation in national accounts tables, and is ordinarily shown as a gross figure (i.e., before allowance for current consumption of fixed capital in the process of production). Second, there are changes, valued at current prices, in physical stocks of raw materials, work in process (except in construction and plantations where it is included under fixed capital formation), and finished products—*in the hands of business enterprises* but including government stockpiles. The sum of fixed capital formation and change in inventories is domestic capital formation. The addition of net balances on current international transactions in goods and in factor payments and accruals (i.e., the excess of exports of goods over imports of goods, and of factor receipts and accruals over factor payments and accruals) converts domestic into national capital formation or national savings. Finally, if fixed capital formation is a gross figure, the resulting totals are gross domestic and national capital formation; if fixed capital formation is adjusted for current consumption, the resulting totals are net domestic and national capital formation.

There are consequently four relevant capital formation totals —two relating to gross and net additions to capital goods *within* the country, regardless of their ownership (by residents of the country or by foreigners) and of any claims by residents on the rest of the world; and two relating to gross and net additions to capital goods and claims *owned* by the residents of the country, regardless of the location of goods. These four capital formation totals are properly relatable to a corresponding set of aggregate product totals: gross and net domestic product, i.e., the output of the factors of production (labor and capital) *located within* the country, regardless of their ownership and of ownership claims of residents against other countries; and gross and net national product, i.e., the output of productive factors *owned* by the residents of the country, regardless of the location of these factors. Both sets of totals can be expressed in current and constant prices, making for eight capital formation and eight aggregate product totals; and there is a corresponding multiplicity of the ratios that relate these: the capital formation proportions, i.e., proportions to the aggregate product of which capital formation is appropriately a part; and the incremental capital-output ratios, i.e., ratios of capital formation, viewed as additions to capital stock, to increases in aggregate product.[2]

2. Capital Formation Proportions and Incremental Capital-Output Ratios: Levels and Trends

Having defined our terms, we can summarize the statistical evidence on levels and trends in the capital formation proportions and incremental capital-output ratios. In this summary, we shall deal with all four capital formation proportions, but only with those based on current price values. For some purposes, constant price proportions would be more appropriate, but a shift to constant prices sharply reduces the number of countries with long-term records; and while the evidence suggests some differences in price trends between capital goods and aggregate product, the differences are not so marked as to call for the use of constant prices, especially since the price indexes, particularly for the more complex capital goods, are not too reliable. Consequently no major error is introduced when we treat capital formation proportions based on current price totals as approximations to those based on constant price totals. For the incremental capital-output ratios, i.e., ratios of capital formation proportions to rates of growth of the relevant aggregate product, the latter must, of course, be in constant prices.[3] The evidence is taken primarily from fairly long records for the United Kingdom, Germany, Italy, the three Scandinavian countries, the United States, Canada, Australia, and Japan—but we shall refer occasionally to data for other countries for recent years.[4]

[2] For more detailed definitions and discussion of both capital formation and aggregate product in national accounts see the *Statistical Papers*, Series F, no. 3, entitled: "Concepts and Definitions of Capital Formation" (New York: United Nations, 1953), and *Studies in Methods*, Series F, no. 2, rev. 1, "A System of National Accounts and Supporting Tables" (New York: United Nations, 1960).

[3] If we designate reproducible capital C, and aggregate product Y, then disregarding time subscripts, capital formation is dC (i.e., addition to C); the capital formation proportion is dC/Y; and the rate of growth of aggregate product is dY/Y. Hence $(dC/Y)/(dY/Y) = dC/dY$, i.e., the ratio of the absolute addition to capital to the absolute addition to product or the incremental capital-output ratio.

[4] The statistical summary that follows is based largely on my two papers in the series entitled "Quantitative Aspects of the Economic Growth of Nations," VI: "Long-Term Trends in Capital Formation Proportions," *Eco-*

1. For the long period which extends for most of the ten countries back to the third quarter of the nineteenth century, both the gross *domestic* and the gross *national* capital formation proportions for the different countries range between somewhat over 11 and about 22 per cent of gross product, although the relative position of some countries changes as we shift from domestic to national capital formation. Since there is a perceptible, although limited, upward trend in the capital formation proportions (see below), averages for such long periods are to some extent artificial. But it is nevertheless significant that for most of the presently developed countries, over the long periods extending back to the mid-nineteenth century, gross capital formation proportions are distinctly below a fifth of gross product.

Net capital formation proportions are necessarily much lower, since capital consumption charges are a much larger share of gross capital formation than of gross product. These net proportions for the long periods range among the various countries from a low of 6 to 7 per cent to a high of 14 to 15 per cent. Here too it is significant that, for most of these developed countries, net capital formation proportions, domestic or national, and thus net national savings rates, were distinctly below a seventh of net output and even below a tenth.

2. Whether these capital formation and national savings proportions are judged high or low depends upon the criteria employed. The criteria of particular interest here are connected with inferences concerning the levels of capital formation and national savings proportions in the pre-modern past; and two comments may be made. First, a national savings proportion of less than 15 per cent—when in the course of modern economic growth per capita product rises on the average close to 20 per cent per decade—can scarcely be considered a strenuous and remarkable achievement. In view of the fact that consumption was over 85 per cent of net product and a shift from a 5 to a 15 per cent net national savings rate meant a minor change in the consumption proportion easily offset by the rise in aggregate product per capita, this shift can hardly be regarded as a revo-

---

nomic Development and Cultural Change, Vol. IX, no. 4, Part II, July, 1961, and V: "Capital Formation Proportions: International Comparisons for Recent Years," *Economic Development and Cultural Change,* Vol. VIII, no. 4, Part II, July, 1960.

lutionary and crucial attainment—an indispensable part of the "take-off" in the Rostovian thesis or the major prerequisite in Arthur Lewis's discussion.[5] As a matter of arithmetic, it meant a minor proportional change in consumption, however proportionately large it was for the much smaller base of capital formation.

The other comment bears upon the magnitude of capital formation as a significant addition to the stock of capital goods that are the embodiment of technological change, the major permissive source of modern economic growth. Here it is the structure of domestic capital formation that is relevant. For the developed countries in recent years, over 20 per cent of gross domestic capital formation was accounted for by dwellings, and another 5 to 6 per cent by changes in inventories. These two components, unlike machinery, do not embody the technological change that is a source of the rise in efficiency characterizing modern economic growth; and the same can be said of much of other construction—some of which (e.g., stores, personal service buildings) also serves consumers directly, and some of which is a provision for governmental overhead. We can therefore state that the capital goods that are clearly carriers of technological change—producers' equipment and the construction that serves public utilities, dams, etc.—account for two-thirds, at most, of gross domestic capital formation in recent years; and for a smaller proportion in the earlier decades when the share of producers' equipment tended to be lower (see below). This statement applies with even greater force to net domestic capital formation. Therefore between 8 and 13 per cent of gross, and between 5 and 9 per cent of net domestic product was devoted to gross and net accumulation respectively of the capital goods that were the carriers and embodiments of technological change. If these capital goods were a crucial and sufficient requirement for growth-inducing technological change, a net savings propor-

[5] For the rapid rise in the national savings-investment ratio assumed in the Rostow theory of the "take-off," and the failure of the empirical data to support this assumption, see my "Notes on the Take-Off," in W. W. Rostow, ed., *The Economics of Take-Off into Sustained Growth* (London, 1963), pp. 22–43. Mr. Lewis's position is suggested in the following statement: "The central problem in the theory of economic growth is to understand the process by which a community is converted from being a 5 per cent to a 12 per cent saver—with all the changes in attitudes, in institutions and in techniques which accompany this conversion." (*The Theory of Economic Growth* [London, 1955], pp. 225–26).

tion of about 5 per cent in the earlier decades would have suf-
ficed to supply the capital accumulation required—suggesting
that the proportion of total inputs needed to provide the material envelope of modern technical progress was a minor fraction.[6]

3. The capital formation proportions rose significantly in the
course of modern economic growth in a number of countries—
from about 11–13 to over 20 per cent for the gross proportions
and from 6–7 to about 12–14 per cent for the net. And for several developed countries that were substantial capital borrowers
in the early phases of their growth, the upward trend was more
conspicuous in the *national* capital formation proportions than
in the *domestic*. Of the ten countries in our sample, only three
failed to show such rises—the United Kingdom, the United
States, and Germany; but data for the first two for the periods
preceding the mid-nineteenth century show that the rise occurred in these earlier periods, and this was probably also true
of Germany. The trend was therefore fairly general—and not
unexpected. Economic growth meant large increases in per capita product, and one would expect that the national savings rate
rose; and, with a greater supply of capital funds, and hence a
relatively lower price of capital, one would expect that the domestic capital formation proportions also rose.

This broad association between modern economic growth and
the rise in capital formation proportions for the developed countries must, however, be significantly qualified. In several countries, the relatively low domestic and national capital formation
proportions found at the beginning of period of coverage remain

[6] This observation is supported by the ease with which presently underdeveloped countries can achieve spectacular "showcases" of modern
technology—so long as the knowledge and a few complementary factors are
at hand. An atomic bomb establishment, if one may consider it an example
of advanced technology, demands material capital that is only a fraction of
one per cent of the aggregate product of the United States; and while the
product of Mainland China is probably between a sixth and a tenth of that
of the United States in the aggregate, and between a twentieth and a thir-
tieth on a per capita basis, China's authoritarian government faces no great
barrier to devoting perhaps one per cent of its product to building an
atomic bomb establishment. The illustrations could easily be multiplied,
but the essential point is clear, viz., that the relative magnitude of material
requirements for apparently crucial capital formation does not *in itself* constitute a major factor in, or an obstacle to, modern economic growth.

low for several decades of rapid economic growth—so that the latter occurs despite modest capital investment ratios, and the rising per capita product has little effect on the national savings rate. Thus in Denmark between 1870 and 1900 capital formation proportions were constant (at about 10 per cent gross and 5 per cent net) or declined slightly, while the rate of growth of gross product rose from 2.7 to 3.3 per cent per year; and similar lags are evident in the data for Norway, Sweden, Canada, and Japan. At the other end, in the more recent decades of growth, as per capita product continued to rise at a substantial rate, capital formation proportions ceased to rise—a point already made above in reference to the United Kingdom and United States (and presumably Germany) where the national savings rates failed to rise beyond the third quarter of the nineteenth century. This failure of the proportion to rise is also observed in Canada after World War I and in Australia after the 1890's.

4. The combination of the broad association between economic growth and the rise in capital formation proportions with the significant disparities in timing of the two variables suggests three implications. First, with economic growth bringing high rates of growth of product per capita or per worker, a rise in the capital formation *proportions* suggests, although it does not fully demonstrate, even higher rates of growth in reproducible capital per capita or per worker. This follows if the incremental capital-output ratios at the beginning of the growth period are equal to, higher than, or slightly lower than the *average* (i.e., total) reproducible capital-output ratio at the start—a not unrealistic assumption. It is, of course, the additions to reproducible capital stock per person or per worker that are so impressive in modern economic growth; and we may thus be led to an easy, but perhaps erroneous, assumption that high capital formation proportions are indispensable.

Second, since in several countries high growth rates associated with modern economic growth emerged and were sustained over several decades with relatively low and constant capital formation proportions, we cannot accept unreservedly the notion that high capital formation proportions are *required;* or that there is a relatively short take-off period over which capital formation proportions rise sharply. It is also questionable that domestic or national capital formation proportions were much lower in the periods preceding the initiation of high rates of growth than in the first few decades of such growth in a number of countries. The model of abrupt and timely change in capital formation proportions at the start of the modern growth periods may fit the case of forced industrialization under authoritarian Communist auspices, but it is not applicable to past economic growth in the free societies of the world.

Third, the failure of national savings proportions to rise in later stages of economic growth, while product per capita continues to grow at substantial rates, suggests some constraints or ceilings on capital formation proportions—so that even in the Communist countries, with the utmost pressure exercised, the proportions to aggregate product totals comparable with those of the West do not exceed 20 to 23 per cent over long periods. These constraints may be due partly to effects of changing technology and associated conditions of life on consumption needs, partly to the trends in the size distribution of income, and partly to institutional obstacles to easy conversion of savings into investments. Whatever the reason, the essential point is that even the richest countries of the world today, with a wealth and capacity far beyond the imagination of our forebears even in the late eighteenth or early nineteenth century, raise the capital formation proportions to only moderate levels—indeed to levels that, on the net savings side, many earlier societies might have found not impossible, and perhaps even not too difficult, to attain.

5. Trends in the structure of domestic capital formation by type are not easily established, because data on changes in inventories are particularly weak and classifications within fixed capital formation are not strictly comparable. Yet despite the limitations of the underlying data, the basic trends are fairly clear. First, the share in capital formation of changes in inventories declines—from earlier levels that are in some countries well above 10 per cent to about 5 to 6 per cent in recent decades. Second, within fixed capital formation, and even within total capital formation, the share of construction declines and that of producers' equipment rises. Thus in several countries the share of construction in total capital formation drops from between 55 and 65 per cent to 45 per cent; whereas that of producers' equipment rises from between 20 and 25 per cent to between 40

and 50 per cent. The decline in the share of construction is partly due to a decline in the share of residential housing, but the share of other construction also shows a drop.

These long-term trends in the structure of domestic gross capital formation reflect shifts in the industrial destination of capital formation, e.g., away from agriculture which requires substantial inventories; or, within fixed capital formation, from residential housing and such sectors as the public utilities which, particularly in the initial stages, required much construction for their basic network, to manufacturing and similar sectors in which the proportion of producers' equipment is relatively high. In good part the trends have also been the result of technological changes which in their effect upon transportation and communication reduced the need for inventories as buffers and which, within a number of sectors, created an increasing demand for advanced equipment and less demand for the construction shell. One may note incidentally that the structure of household consumption, including housing services, indicates a similar shift toward consumers' equipment and away from pure shelter and construction needs. And among the various effects of the shifts within domestic capital formation was the one on the ratio of capital consumption to gross capital formation, and indeed, as will be stressed below, on the very meaning of capital consumption: this ratio must be affected by shifts in the relative importance of categories of capital goods with widely differing economic life spans, and hence differing bases of capital consumption or depreciation allowances.

But the most interesting aspect of these trends is the evidence they provide of the increasing emphasis of modern technology on producers' equipment as the embodiment of technological change. For clearly the rising share of equipment is associated with the widening choice of increasingly complex tools reflecting the advances of technology. And the inputs required to supply the material envelope for these tools may, despite their rising share in total product, represent a diminishing share of the total inputs, even material alone, required to produce the ideas, the knowledge basis of the new tools, and the institutional arrangements, often new, essential for their use. The shift from inventories and simple construction to more complex construction, machinery, and transport equipment is a *trend within* modern economic growth that may well be similar to the *shift to* modern economic growth and the technology underlying it from the earlier patterns of economic growth and technology—in that the former, taken as a whole, represents a movement toward a much greater relative use of advanced knowledge than of purely material capital (and inputs of manhours). Consequently, to repeat, while material capital grew and increased relative to product, the capital proportions could be, and were, maintained at moderate levels precisely because the increase in knowledge and greater capacity for institutional adjustments played much more important roles.

6. We come, in concluding the summary of statistical findings, to the incremental capital-output ratios, which have been stressed so much in the recent literature on economic growth. Confining our attention to domestic capital-output ratios, because the national ratios may be affected by differing and changing proportions of capital exports and imports and are thus less relevant in explaining the growth of output, we consider two sets of findings: one relating to international differences in the levels of these ratios among the several developed countries over the long period, and the other relating to the movements of the ratios over time.

The first set of findings is illustrated most clearly if we give greater weight to the period before World War I than to the one that extends from the 1890's through the 1950's and is disturbed by two world wars and the major depression of the 1930's. Omitting Italy, where sustained modern economic growth did not begin until the 1890's, we find that the average incremental capital-output ratio for the first period ranged from a low of 2.9 for Japan to a high of 7.4 for Germany, on a gross basis; and from 1.6 to 4.8 for the same two countries, on a net basis. Even in the second period, this time including Italy (the averages omit the war intervals) the ratios ranged from 4.3 for Japan to 7.3 for Norway, on a gross basis; and from 2.7 for the United States to 5.1 for Norway and 5.0 for Australia, on a net basis.

The statistical source of such wide divergence in long-period incremental capital-output ratios among developed countries can be stated simply, with the first period as an illustration. For that period gross domestic capital formation proportions ranged among different countries from 9 to 22 per cent; the net capital proportions, from 7 to 13 per cent; and the relative range was thus between slightly above or below 2 to 1. Average rates of growth per year in aggregate product (gross or net, domestic or national, which are all close to each other) ranged, excluding Italy again, from 2.0–2.1 to 4.2–4.3 per cent per year (also a range of about 2 to 1). If there were close positive correlations between capital formation proportions and the rates of growth of aggregate product, the capital-output ratios for the different countries could have been quite close to each other, since the variances for the numerator and denominator of the ratio were about the same. It is the absence of such an association that produced the wide diversity among the countries in the long-term capital-output ratios. Thus Japan, with a fairly low gross capital formation proportion of 10.9 per cent and a net of 6.0 per cent, shows one of the highest rates of growth of product (3.8 and 3.7 per cent per year); whereas Germany, with a gross capital formation proportion close to 20 per cent and a net of 13 per cent, shows a relatively low rate of growth of product of 2.7 per cent; and Norway, with a capital formation proportion substantially higher than that for Japan, shows a rate of growth that is little more than half that of Japan.

A substantive explanation as to why higher capital formation proportions did not lead to higher rates of growth of product would take us far afield, and will merely be hinted at after we deal with the trends in the incremental capital-output ratios. The only relevant observation here is that the international differences in the incremental capital-output ratios are *not* reducible to differences in industrial structure, at least in so far as the scanty available data permit such an analysis. In other words, these countrywide capital-output ratios are neither high nor low because of the different weights of sectors that are generally characterized by high or low *sectoral* capital-output ratios.

The second set of findings is that in most of the nine countries (excluding Italy) the incremental capital-output ratios rose from the first to the second period; and in some markedly, e.g., in Japan, from 2.9 to 4.3 for the gross ratio and from 1.6 to 3.1 for the net, and in Sweden from 4.1 and 2.6 to 5.5 and 3.6 respectively. Moreover, these findings are for two periods that overlap (the span from the 1890's to World War I is common to both);

and a sharper distinction of the time periods would accentuate the change. But there are some conspicuous exceptions: in Germany, the ratios declined (although changes in territory affect comparability); in the United States the gross ratio rose (from 5.1 to 6.5) but the net declined (from 3.1 to 2.7); and in Canada there was little change. The statistical reason for the rise in the ratios in most countries is that the rises in capital formation proportions are not accompanied by equally large proportional rises in the rates of growth of product, if the latter rise at all (the rate of growth of product declined in the United Kingdom and Australia and remained about constant in Denmark, but the domestic capital formation proportion rose in the latter two countries).

How can one explain the divergence among countries, all developed, in the long-period incremental capital-output ratios, or the marked trends in these ratios over time? One possible approach lies in examining the reasons for expecting these ratios for countries undergoing modern economic growth to be about the same and stable over time. The expectation presumably is based on the notion that specific sectors and products are characterized by specific capital requirements and their average and incremental capital-output ratios should be the same the world over. In so far as modern economic growth meant emphasis on the same complex of specific sectors, one would expect similar capital-output ratios in the various countries; in so far as intersectoral shifts have only moderate effects on the aggregate, capital-output ratios would move only moderately over time, and would certainly be stable over relatively short periods, aside from fluctuations due to rates of capacity utilization.

If this conjecture is valid, the plausibility of a common level of capital-output ratios, if not of their complete stability over a long period, is associated with some notion of technological requirements, akin to the notion that one cannot run a railroad without track and rolling stock or produce cars without metal shaping and stamping machines. But clearly such technological constraints or requirements, even for specific products or plants, relate to hard-core minima; and the actual capital-output ratios are usually well above such minima. A machine can be run 8 or 24 hours a day; a railroad roadbed can be two streaks of rust in the desert, as was the case with early American railroads, or it can be a well constructed track capable of bearing heavy trains at high speed. Thus even in a highly specific use, the ratio of capital to output can vary a great deal above a low, indispensable minimum. The capital-output ratios are much more elastic when the output basket offers a choice that can satisfy one and the same complex of needs (e.g., railroads or waterways for transportation, natural or synthetic rubber and clothing fabrics, etc.), as far as domestic output is concerned; and a country engaged in international trade has even greater choice for many specific products, between domestic output and imports from abroad. In so far as each choice involves different capital-output ratios, the aggregate ratios may well differ and change substantially, even for relatively satisfactory and not dissimilar baskets of output and for an adequately high rate of growth. In short, the technological factor that may make for generally common and relatively stable capital-output ratios is overlaid with a variety of economic and institutional factors that may produce a wide divergence and substantial trends in these ratios. Differences and changes in the supply of savings for material capital formation; in the supply of major complementary factors such as natural resources, labor, and management; in the capacity to participate in the international division of labor through imports and exports; in the position in the sequence of followers in the spread of modern economic growth from its pioneering beginnings in England in the late eighteenth century, and many other factors that could easily be listed, may be relevant.

This approach to an explanation is supported by the quantitative evidence in several production function studies that attempt to allocate the growth of aggregate product to the growth of various inputs, particularly labor and capital, and derive the effects of changes in efficiency or productivity on the rise of output per fully covered unit of all inputs. We use one of these, made recently for the United States for the period from 1909 to 1957.[7] Of the total growth rate of national income of 2.89 per

[7] See Edward F. Denison, "The Sources of Economic Growth in the United States and the Alternatives Before Us," *Supplementary Paper No. 13* (New York: Committee for Economic Development, 1962), Table 19, p. 148. Similar results can be obtained from the more detailed study by John Kendrick, *Productivity Trends in the United States* (National Bureau of Economic Research, 1961).

cent per year, the growth of capital accounted for only 0.57 per cent, or no more than a fifth (from 1929 to 1957 the two growth rates were 0.45 and 2.93, and the ratio of the former to the latter between a sixth and a seventh). Since the growth of capital accounts for a limited fraction of the growth of product, its ratio to the latter could hardly be expected to be the same among countries or constant over time—if the view is of the production relations proper, i.e., of capital as the cause and product as the effect.[8]

3. Some Implications for the Past

What do the levels and trends of capital formation proportions and capital-output ratios in modern economic growth, summarized above, suggest for capital formation and its relation to growth in earlier periods? Since the records from which we drew our measures relate to "developed" countries, i.e., those that took advantage of the potentials of modern economic growth, our question may be specified further. Assume that before the nineteenth or late eighteenth century, economic growth in the countries of Western Europe—and we prefer to deal with Western Europe because that is where modern economic growth originated—was largely associated with sources different from those that characterized economic development in the last one and a half to two centuries. It was not the spread of modern science and science-based technology to problems of transportation and production (which eventuated in modern industrialization, mechanization, urbanization, rationalization, and the other

[8] This, of course, does not bar the possibility of common or stable elements in the ratios that may reflect the limits on the levels of both the aggregate, countrywide *savings* rates and the long-term aggregate rates of *growth*. If we could argue that for some reason national long-term savings rates must be at least 10 and no more than 15 per cent, and that differences in growth rates for aggregate product of developed countries cannot, in the long run, be more than say from 2.5 to 5 per cent per year, then even with negative correlation between the two variables, the range in the capital-output ratios could not be wider than 2 to 6; with a random relation between savings and growth rates, the range could not be more than between 1.5 and 2 to 1; and with weak but positive association, the range would be even narrower. But in this case the presumptive similarity or temporal stability of the capital-output ratios would be due to the narrow ranges of aggregate savings and growth rates, *not* to the capital formation proportions determining these growth rates.

strands in modern economic growth) but may have been, say between the late fifteenth and mid-eighteenth century, largely the thrust of European countries into the New World, the spread of transoceanic trade mixed with forced colonization and piracy, as well as a beginning of internal liberalization and the spread of domestic trade and of the lighter manufactures. If then for this preceding epoch of merchant capitalism, we identify the countries that took advantage of its growth potential so that they could be characterized as "developed" in these terms, would their capital formation proportions and the capital-output ratios differ much from those associated with the modern period —granted that the major sources of growth and possibly the sectors of capital destination were quite different in the two epochs (e.g., proportionately more investment in transoceanic trade, etc. in the earlier epoch and more in large-scale manufacturing in the later)? Or are the unusually high capital formation proportions a distinctive characteristic of the epoch of modern economic growth, so that one can argue that in the earlier periods economic growth was less rapid because of a lesser capacity to generate savings, relative to total product or income? And, in the same speculative vein, we could ask the same questions about the pre-sixteenth century period of the developed medieval city economy. Were the material capital formation proportions in the developed economic units of that time, the great trading and craft cities of Italy, Germany, and the Low Countries, including the surrounding countryside—areas comparable to modern nations—similar to those in modern economic growth, again granted that the sources of growth and sector destinations and types of capital formation were different?

The formulation of the questions suggests a notion of distinct economic epochs, associated with epochal innovations that are the major sources of growth during each epoch—innovations that are revolutionary enough to require several centuries for exploitation and general enough to affect a number of large societies. Within each epoch, after some passage of time, the areas, nations, or regions that are "developed," i.e., have taken sufficient advantage of the growth potential of the current epochal innovation, emerge; and we can then search for some common characteristics of such growth, e.g., capital formation proportions of more or less similar level, trend, or bearing on rates of growth of product. Although we cannot present here an adequately detailed discussion of the concept of economic epoch, which is but a simple formal statement of periodization practiced in much of the writing at least on Western economic history, it is important to state these notions explicitly in order to specify our questions concerning the implications for the earlier periods of the quantitative characteristics of *modern* economic growth. And even if the questions now apply to Western Europe in a limited stretch of its past, we may find that some of the formal aspects of the answers are common to comparisons with many other parts of the world and many other segments of the past.

If then, coming back to a specific question, we ask whether the material capital formation proportions in the developed countries of the epoch of merchant capitalism—say the Netherlands, France, and England in the sixteenth, seventeenth, and early eighteenth centuries—were significantly below, or different from, the capital formation proportions associated with modern economic growth, I would hesitate to give a definite answer. And the answer would, of course, be even more difficult if the question were applied to the developed areas of Western Europe in the fourteenth and fifteenth centuries. Yet some conjectures are possible, and may be useful if only as leads to further discussion and research.

We start by recognizing one clearly established relevant difference between modern economic growth and growth in the earlier periods in Europe, say before 1750, viz., the much lower rate of population increase in earlier times. From 1850 to 1960, the population in the area of European settlement, excluding Latin America (i.e., Europe including Asiatic Russia, North America, and Oceania), which is fairly inclusive of, and is dominated by, the more developed countries, grew at average rates of about 10 per cent per decade, or 0.95 per cent per year.[9] The rate of population increase for all Europe could be estimated to be 0.09 per cent per year from 1250 to 1500, and 0.17 per cent

---

[9] Based on the Carr-Saunders estimates through 1900 and the United Nations estimates since 1920. The data for 1850–1900 were taken from *The Determinants and Consequences of Population Trends* (New York: United Nations, 1953), Table 2, p. 11; for 1920–60 from *Demographic Yearbook, 1962* (New York: United Nations, 1963), Table 2, p. 124.

per year from 1500 to 1750. For Western Europe excluding Ireland, Russia, Austria-Hungary, and the Balkans, the rates would be 0.08 and 0.17 per cent respectively.[10]

If we accept these estimates (and there is little question as to the much lower rates of population increase in the centuries before 1750 in Europe, even for the countries that were relatively prosperous), and if we can assign some plausible orders of magnitude to the *long-term* rates of growth of product per capita, we can derive plausible rates of increase of aggregate product. For the recent periods of modern economic growth and for the countries that are now developed, the rate of increase in product per capita was, at the lower end of the range, roughly 1.5 per cent per year, which combined with population growth of about 1 per cent, yields a rate of growth of aggregate product of about 2.5 per cent per year. From this low figure the rate ranges up to 4.5 to 5 per cent per year.

Clearly, the rates of increase in per capita product for the pre-1750 past in Europe were not as high. The Deane-Cole study for Great Britain suggests a rate of increase in per capita output (including home industries) between 0.2 and 0.3 per cent per year for the first three-quarters of the eighteenth century; and over a similar period (from 1701 to 1771), the population grew about 0.27 per cent per year, a rate substantially higher than the 0.17 per cent for Western Europe from 1500 to 1750.[11] Given the long-term positive association between population growth and growth in per capita product that may have been due to peaceful, non-calamitous, and technological conditions favoring both, we would be inclined, in extending the results of early eighteenth century growth in Great Britain, to set the possible (and perhaps maximum) long-term rate of growth in per capita product for 1500–1750 in developed countries of Western Europe at about 0.2 per cent per year—which would mean a rise in per capita product from 1500 to 1750 of about 65 per

[10] See B. Ts. Urlanis, *The Growth of the Population of Europe* (in Russian) (Moscow, 1941). The rates are calculated from the summary tables on pp. 414–15. The population estimates are for countries with constant (1914) boundaries.

[11] See Phyllis Deane and W. A. Cole, *British Economic Growth, 1688–1959* (Cambridge, England, 1962). The per capita product growth rates are from Table 20, p. 80; those of population were calculated from Table 2, p. 8.

cent. An assumed growth rate of 0.3 per cent per year would yield a cumulative rise from 1500 to 1750 of 111 per cent. Since the absolute per capita product even in advanced Europe as late as 1750 was low, the *lower* rate of antecedent growth seems much more plausible—although there may be an element of illusion in this choice.

If then we use the lower growth rate—and the purpose here is to illustrate a question rather than provide a fully defensible answer—the rate of growth of aggregate product from 1500 to 1750 would be 0.4 per cent per year, or about a sixth of the lowest aggregate product growth rate in modern economic development. Let us assume now that the incremental capital-output ratios found in modern economic growth—which ranged from 1.6 to 4.8 on a net basis, with a mean of about 3; and from 2.9 to 7.4 on a gross basis, with a mean of about 5—are applicable to the earlier period. By combining them with the aggregate growth rates for 1500–1750, we derive a net capital formation proportion of 1.2 per cent; and a gross capital formation proportion of 2.0 per cent. Similar calculations for the period 1250–1500, with the rates of growth of product set for purposes of illustration at about 0.2 per cent per year (i.e., 0.08 per cent for population and 0.12 per cent for per capita product), yield a net capital formation proportion of 0.6 per cent and a gross capital formation proportion of about 1.0 per cent.

Are such low capital formation proportions plausible for the developed European countries in the seventeenth or early eighteenth century, or for that matter at the peak of the medieval town economy in the fifteenth century? The answer is not easy, if only because the proportions are so low; and given the character of the data, it is hardly possible to choose, in terms of plausibility of rough orders of magnitude, between 1 and 5, or even 10 per cent for the capital formation proportions. And yet the above calculation does indicate that, if the low rates of growth of aggregate product in these earlier centuries are valid, either the capital formation proportions were much lower, or the incremental capital-output ratios were much higher, than in the recent century in developed countries. One of these two implications *must* follow; or perhaps both must share the burden of the difference. But we definitely can exclude the possibility that both the capital formation proportions *and* the incremental capital-output ratios were similar to those in modern economic growth. And with this helpful exclusion, we will extend our speculation further and try to determine whether it is the capital formation proportions that were much lower, or the incremental capital-output ratios that were much higher.

From the viewpoint of the *savings* aspect of the capital formation proportions, we can argue that these proportions need not have been much lower in the earlier periods than in the recent one. Examination of some relevant evidence suggests that inequality in the distribution of income and wealth in these earlier times was quite wide. (A more careful comparison, which would require a more critical review of the basic data and the use of more sophisticated statistical tools might alter this finding, but only in degree.) The well-known distribution by Gregory King for England and Wales in 1688 shows that the top 5 per cent of the population (i.e., the top in families with the highest per person income) accounted for close to 23 per cent of total income —and even this is an underestimate since families in the King distribution include servants, apprentices, etc. And the wealth distributions for a number of German and Swiss cities (sometimes including their countryside) in the fifteenth century are extremely unequal—even after allowance is made for various limitations due largely to gaps in the data.[12]

[12] The Gregory King distribution is given in a basic table which shows the number of families, persons per family, income per person, for a variety of social groups within the country (see *Two Tracts*, George E. Barnett, ed. [Baltimore, 1936], p. 31). The shares are derived from cumulative arrays of population and total income, in descending order of per capita income with a logarithmic interpolation at the top 5 per cent line.

A diversity of data is available on the distribution of wealth in the fifteenth century German and Swiss cities, derived largely from special taxes on wealth (Augsburg, Frankfurt, Heidelberg and countryside, Basel, Zurich, and several others). For a brief bibliography and discussion see Josef Kulischer, *Allgemeine Wirtschaftsgeschichte des Mittelalters und der Neuzeit*, Volume I (Munich and Berlin, 1928), pp. 176 ff. A cursory review indicates wide inequality, in several cases far wider than that observable in the distribution of wealth in modern times. Allowance must be made for non-coverage of wealth exempted from taxation (at lower brackets), inclusion of household goods, differing sizes of family, non-coverage of certain population classes (clergy, sometimes secular nobility, and often the Jews and other alien groups). Yet the broad impression is of persistent and fairly wide inequality (data are available for some cities for a number of years). A careful analysis of these and similar data for other countries, a task not feasible here, might yield valuable results.

The persistence of an unequal distribution, with the identity of people in the top brackets fairly continuous, combined with long-term constancy or slight rise in real product per capita, means that a substantial proportion of the population continues to live, and society is preserved, on a per capita income that is well below the countrywide average. Thus, if the top 5 per cent of the population receive 25 per cent of income, and the composition of the top group remains unchanged, the lower 95 per cent lives fairly continuously on 75 per cent of income—barring significant transfers (charity, etc.) from the top to the lower income group. If 95 per cent of the population manages to live on a per capita income that is on the average less than eight-tenths of the countrywide (i.e., 0.75/0.95), an allowance for the per capita consumption of the top 5 per cent group of three times the average for the lower 95 per cent, means a savings proportion of $25 - (5 \times 2.4)$, or 13 per cent of total product. Even an allowance for per capita consumption of the top group five times as high still leaves a savings proportion of 5 per cent of aggregate product. The point of this illustration is that, given the assumptions, a "reasonable" limit to inequality in per capita *expenditure* could still leave a substantial countrywide savings proportion. Therefore, with such a savings potential, an assumption of extremely low capital formation proportions in the pre-industrial past in Western Europe requires additional proof.

However, other evidence suggests that at least the *net* capital formation proportions must have been quite low. The incremental capital-output ratios, determined partly by the capital formation proportions, cumulated over a long enough period, will yield the *average* capital-output ratio, i.e., the ratio of accumulated net capital stock at the end of the period to the current aggregate income. Thus if the average life span of depreciable capital is about forty years (the weighted life of the various components of capital formation),[13] incremental capital-output

---

[13] The calculation involves a harmonic mean of the life spans of the components of depreciable capital formation with distinctive life spans. Thus, if we assume that the structure of gross capital formation in these earlier periods allows 70 per cent for construction, 20 per cent for equipment, and 10 per cent for net changes in inventories; if we assume, following current practices, a life of 100 years for construction and of 12.5 years for equipment (net changes in inventories have unlimited life span); and for simplicity calculate on a straight line basis, the average capital con-

ratios cumulated over four decades will determine the ratio of total net capital stock at the end of the period to current income. Hence, if the rate of growth of aggregate product was 0.4 per cent per year during the epoch of 1500–1750, an average net capital formation proportion of 5 per cent for the long period would yield a net capital stock in 1750 (and long before that date) that would be in the ratio to current income (at the same prices) of 5/0.4, or 12.5 to 1. In other words, by 1750 and in fact throughout most of the period the net reproducible capital stock-aggregate product ratio would be 12.5.

Were the average reproducible capital-output ratios at this high level at the end or in the course of pre-industrial growth in Western Europe? The only estimate available, to my knowledge, is again the result of Gregory King's work for England and Wales, as carefully reviewed by Phyllis Deane.[14] For 1688, the ratio of reproducible capital, limited to producers' goods and inventories, livestock, and buildings, to national income of that year is 2.3 (Deane-I, p. 353). Since 1688 was a fairly prosperous year (see *ibid.*, p. 354), this ratio may be somewhat on the low side; and for illustrative purposes we raise it to 2.5. However, land is wholly excluded from this figure. In the estimates for 1688, as much as 64 per cent of total productive capital is attributed to land (Deane-II, p. 270); and surely some part of its value represents inputs of resources to bring it into cultivation and maintain its productivity. Land is of major importance even later; it accounts for over 50 per cent of the total national capital of Great Britain as late as 1832 (Deane-II, Table 70, p. 271). If, to take the most extreme case, the *total* value of land is assumed to represent inputs, and thus is viewed as reproducible capital, the net capital-output ratio in 1688 is raised from 2.5 to 2.5/0.36, or roughly 7. The assumption regarding land is ob-

---

sumption charge would be $(0.70 \times 1) + (0.20 \times 8)$, or 2.3 per cent of gross capital formation, or 2.56 per cent of fixed capital. This implies an average life of $100/2.56$ or 39 years. As will be noted below, the life spans for construction and equipment assumed here may be too long for the earlier periods.

[14] See her "Capital Formation in Britain Before the Railway Age," *Economic Development and Cultural Change*, Vol. IX, no. 3, April, 1961, 352–68 (referred to in the text as Deane-I), and the volume, jointly with W. A. Cole (cited in footnote 11), Chapter VII, pp. 278–314 (referred to as Deane-II).

viously extreme. Nevertheless, the resultant average capital-output ratio would, given a growth rate of aggregate product of 0.4 per cent per year, yield an implicit net capital formation proportion of 2.8 per cent, and this is at the upper end of a range that could vary down to 1 per cent.[15]

This single bit of evidence suggests that the average net reproducible capital-output ratios were not exceptionally high in pre-industrial seventeenth century Europe; and consequently the net capital formation proportions must have been appreciably lower than those in the modern period.[16] This impression is

[15] Population in England and Wales grew from 1600 to 1700 at the rate of 0.3 per cent per year (see Urlanis, *op. cit.*, pp. 414–15); and hence the rate of aggregate growth may have been as high as 0.5 per cent per year. If so, the implicit net capital formation proportion suggested by the capital-output ratios in the text would vary from 1.25 to 3.50 per cent, most probably close to the lower figure.

[16] Since average capital-output ratios reflect cumulations of capital formation over long periods, *including* results of wars and other calamities, and since the summary for the modern period explicitly excludes war periods (at least World Wars I and II) from the averages for capital formation proportions and for rates of growth of product, the question arises whether inclusion of these war periods would modify the averages for the modern period sufficiently to affect the comparisons made in the text.

A precise answer would involve reliable estimates of destruction by war of real capital, which, unfortunately, are not available. Two observations can, however, be made. First, the evidence for the pre-World War I period relating to net and gross capital formation proportions and incremental capital-output ratios would remain unaffected. Second, for the period from the 1890's through the 1960's, we have rough estimates for two countries most clearly affected, one by both wars (Germany) and the other by World War II (Japan). For West Germany and Japan for 1955 the ratios of total net reproducible capital stock to national income at factor cost are 2.3 and 2.4 respectively (see International Association for Research in Income and Wealth, *Income and Wealth, Series VIII* [London, 1959], Table VII, p. 32). Taken, as they should be, to national income in market prices, the ratios would drop to roughly 2.1 and 2.2. In "Quantitative Aspects . . ." Paper VI (already cited), the cumulated ratios of net domestic capital formation to net domestic product, for the years since the 1890's but omitting the war periods, were 3.8 for Germany and 3.1 for Japan (Table 5, pp. 17–18). While the comparison is rough, it suggests a reduction in the incremental capital-output ratio, because of the war, of at least three-tenths. The rate of growth of aggregate product also declined, but largely because the growth in per capita product was retarded during the war and immediate postwar years. If we allow a reduction of some 15 per cent in aggregate growth, the implicit net capital formation proportion in the extreme cases of these two countries would be reduced from 1 to (0.7 × 0.85), or roughly four-tenths. In the case of Japan this would mean reducing the net domestic capital formation proportion in the later period from 14.1 to 8.5 per cent (see Paper VI, Table 1, pp. 5–6)—compared with 6.0 per cent in

also supported by the rather moderate average reproducible, or even total capital-output ratios, for several European countries in the nineteenth century before the beginning of their industrialization, as well as in a number of underdeveloped countries.[17]

If the long-term net capital proportions or net savings ratios were, in fact, significantly lower in the pre-industrial periods in Western Europe than in the recent century of modern economic growth, wars included, and despite the persistent inequality in the pre-industrial size distribution of income, various explanations can be suggested. Some of these may be noted because they emphasize interesting differences between the modern and pre-modern economic and social structures. Thus one may ask, first, whether the upper income recipients in the pre-industrial societies felt a greater compulsion to spend proportionately more and to save proportionately less than those in modern societies. If these upper income groups, particularly among the nobility, had to consume at higher per capita levels—to maintain their position and in a sense to defend their status (more than this would be true of the rich traders in the older times, let alone the high income bourgeoisie in modern times)—an equally wide proportional *income* inequality would be accompanied in the earlier periods by a relatively wider proportional *expenditures* inequality. And this, all other conditions being equal, would mean a lower aggregate savings ratio. Or second, one may ask whether, given an adequate supply of money savings generated by the upper income recipients, the opportunities for productive and safe investments were more limited in the earlier periods—so that the savings may have gone into hoards of gold, silver, and plate, or into loans to governments for unproductive purposes; or to finance consumption of some of the

---

the earlier period; and for Germany the proportion would be reduced from 12.7 to about 7.5 per cent, compared with 12.9 per cent in the earlier period. The point is that even in these extreme cases of war-affected developed countries we need not lower the net capital formation proportions to less than 6 per cent. And of course most of the developed countries were not affected to anything approaching the magnitudes above—with the possible exception of the U.S.S.R., which is in a class by itself.

[17] For a brief summary see my paper, "Quantitative Aspects of the Economic Growth of Nations: IV. Distribution of National Income by Factor Shares," *Economic Development and Cultural Change*, Vol. VII, no. 3, Part II, April, 1959, Appendix B, pp. 61–70.

lower income groups in return for whatever few assets they possessed—all of these in greater proportion than in modern times and all of these, of course, flows of personal savings of a given group in the population (in this case the upper income group) that do not result in capital formation and do not constitute national savings as defined in social accounting.[18] Finally, we may ask whether the impact of all the political, war, demographic, and even climatic calamities that beset these earlier societies on the wealth and incomes of the established upper groups was so great and so lasting that one must discount the available evidence on income and wealth inequality as possibly relating to the more prosperous years. Thus, the assumption of sufficient continuity in the upper income positions may have to be severely qualified—with consequent effects on the savings and investment ratios.

If then we can reasonably assume that the long-term net capital formation proportions in the pre-industrial periods were significantly lower than those in the modern period, the reasons lie not in simple differences in savings propensities flowing directly from lower average incomes, but reflect a variety of basic differences in the economic and social structures of the societies; and particularly in their differing capacity to control, and recover from, social and natural calamities. Nevertheless, the possibility of an appreciably different long-term incremental net capital-output ratio is not excluded. Even if the net capital formation proportions were well below 3 per cent, with rates of growth of product well below 0.5 per cent per year, the incremental net capital-output ratios may easily have been as high as 7-10—much higher than in the decades of modern economic growth. If this is important, it is only as a summary indication that various conditions were so different as to make the relation between net material capital additions and growth in aggregate output less favorable.

The possibility that a much higher incremental capital-output ratio characterized the early periods becomes almost a certainty

[18] It is to this possibility that Phyllis Deane may be referring in summarizing her conclusions from the Gregory King data: "The limiting factors to an increase in the rate of capital formation seem to have operated more from the side of investment than from the side of saving" (Deane-II, p. 260).

if we shift from net to gross capital formation and from the net to the gross incremental capital-output ratio—gross of current consumption of fixed depreciable capital. Even if we assume that the *net* capital formation proportions in the earlier periods were so low that they yielded a net incremental capital-output ratio no higher than that in modern times (say 3 to 1), it can be demonstrated that the *gross* capital formation proportion in the earlier periods would *not* be that much lower; and consequently the incremental *gross* capital-output ratio would be much higher than in the decades of modern economic growth.

The relation between net and gross capital formation, i.e., the weight of capital consumption, can be formulated briefly—if we set aside the less important problem of its allocation over the life of the capital good, and assume a simple, straight line basis. The relation of capital consumption to gross capital formation will then depend upon: first, the share in gross capital formation of fixed capital subject to consumption (as distinct from net changes in inventories that have a perpetual life)—designated *a;* second, the length of life of depreciable capital goods—designated *n,* the number of years in the weighted average life; third, the rate of growth of fixed depreciable capital formation, which, if we assume that both *a* and the gross capital formation proportion are constant, equals the rate of growth of gross product—designated *r.* Under these simple assumptions, the proportion of capital consumption to gross capital formation will be larger if *a* is larger and if *n* and *r* are smaller, and will be smaller if *a* is smaller and if *n* and *r* are larger. The differences in the share of net in gross capital formation will be negatively related to *a* and positively related to *n* and *r*.[19]

The value of *a* in the earlier periods depends again upon our treatment of land. If part (or all) of land is included in reproducible capital and hence in capital formation, its classification as depreciable or non-depreciable capital depends upon the capability of the technology of the time to maintain it in full productive use with current maintenance—since for fixed capital

[19] For the algebra underlying these relations see my paper, "International Differences in Capital Formation and Financing," in Moses Abramovitz, ed., *Capital Formation and Economic Growth* (Princeton, N.J.: Princeton University Press, 1956), Appendix B. See also a detailed discussion with a different emphasis in Evsey D. Domar, *Essays on the Theory of Economic Growth* (New York, 1957).

goods, consumption is calculated only if the economic life of the good is terminable with full current maintenance. If, despite full current maintenance, its productivity declines significantly within a reasonably limited period, land is a depreciable asset. Faced with these complicated questions to which I have no answer, I chose to disregard land as a significant part of reproducible capital—clearly a gross oversimplification of the economics of the pre-industrial societies. But the argument that follows remains unaffected even if we include land under reproducible capital—as long as the inclusion does not increase n, the average life of depreciable capital, by a large factor. What we assume in the calculation that follows is that the *average* ratio of inventories (the non-depreciable part of material capital) to net product is a constant moderate fraction (we use 0.5, a sixth of the total net material capital stock assumed to be in the ratio to net product of 3 to 1); and then derive net changes in inventories from assumed changes in net product itself.

With a determined, the ratios of net capital formation and of capital consumption to gross capital formation will be set by n and r. The important point here is that r was certainly much smaller in the pre-industrial periods than in modern economic growth; and it may well be that n was also smaller, i.e., that the economic life of depreciable capital was shorter—a point to be discussed further below. If both n and r were smaller, the ratio of net capital formation to gross capital formation was also much smaller than it is in modern economic growth; and hence, even if the earlier net capital formation proportion was quite low, the gross capital formation proportion could well have been relatively higher—with consequent effects on the incremental *gross* capital-output ratios.

The marked impact on the ratio of net to gross capital formation of the much lower rate of growth of product (and hence of capital formation volumes) in the earlier periods can be seen from the accompanying Exhibit. If we assume that the average life of depreciable capital goods in the earlier periods is about the same as at present, say roughly forty years, that *net* capital formation proportions are determined by a fixed incremental net capital-output ratio of 3 to 1 (also similar to that in modern economic growth), and that net changes in inventories are determined as noted above, when r, the rate of growth of aggregate product, is 0.4 per cent per year the net capital formation proportion is 1.2 per cent but the gross capital formation proportion is 11.7 per cent; whereas when r is 2.5 per cent per year, the net capital formation proportion is 7.5 per cent and the gross capital formation proportion is 16.3 per cent. The spread in the net capital formation proportion is from 1.2 to 7.5 or a range of over 6 to 1; the range in the gross capital formation proportion is only from 11.7 to 16.3, or about 1.4 to 1. Since the rates of growth of gross product and net product do not differ appreciably, and for rough calculations can be assumed to be identical, the *net* incremental capital-output ratio in both cases is 3; but the *gross* incremental capital-output ratio for the case of low growth is 11.7/0.4, or 29.25, and for the case of higher growth it is 16.3/2.5, or 6.5.

The rate of growth of product, r, has strikingly different effects on the net and gross capital formation proportions and hence on the net and gross incremental capital-output ratios so long as n is kept realistically limited—for the relative magnitude of the differential impact of r diminishes as n is increased, and increases as n is reduced. It is for this reason that we stated above that the inclusion of land under reproducible depreciable capital would have little effect on the conclusions unless it raised n by a large factor.

If land were treated as reproducible but completely non-depreciable capital, similar to net changes in inventories, the effect can be easily calculated. Using the Gregory King figures, we would raise the net capital-output ratio to 7 to 1, leaving the net depreciable capital-output ratio at 2.5 to 1. With these ratios, for Case III ($r = 0.4$ per cent per year), the net capital formation proportion (with $n = 40$) would become 2.8 per cent (instead of 1.2) and the gross capital formation proportion 13.1 per cent (instead of 11.7); whereas for Case IV ($r = 2.5$ per cent per year) the net capital formation proportion would become 17.5 per cent (instead of 7.5) and the gross 25.4 per cent (instead of 16.3). Thus even with land included as a reproducible but not depreciable asset, and an undiminished ratio to net product, the spread in the gross capital formation proportion between Cases III and IV is about 2 to 1, and still much narrower than be-

Exhibit

HYPOTHETICAL PROPORTIONS OF GROSS CAPITAL FORMATION TO GROSS PRODUCT (UNDER VARYING ASSUMPTIONS CONCERNING n, NUMBER OF YEARS IN LIFE OF DEPRECIABLE CAPITAL, AND r, RATE OF GROWTH OF GROSS PRODUCT PER YEAR).

	Value of n in years			
	20 (1)	30 (2)	40 (3)	50 (4)
Case I, $r = 0$				
1. Ratio of net capital stock to net product (assumed)	3.0	3.0	3.0	3.0
2. Ratio of inventories to net product (assumed)	0.5	0.5	0.5	0.5
3. Ratio of net stock of depreciable capital to net product	2.5	2.5	2.5	2.5
4. Ratio of gross value of the net stock of depreciable capital to net product (line 3 doubled)	5.0	5.0	5.0	5.0
5. Capital consumption as percentage of net product (line 4 × 100, divided by n)	25.0	16.7	12.5	10.0
6. Ratio of gross product to net product	1.250	1.167	1.125	1.100
7. Gross capital formation proportion (%) (line 5 divided by line 6)	20.0	14.3	11.1	9.1

Assumptions for Cases II–V: incremental c/o ratios, for net depreciable capital stock = 2.5; for inventories = 0.5.

Case II, $r = 0.002$				
8. Net capital formation as % of net product	0.6	0.6	0.6	0.6
9. Net *depreciable* capital formation as % of net product	0.5	0.5	0.5	0.5
10. f—ratio of capital consumption to gross depreciable capital formation (straight line depreciation assumption)	0.9800	0.9700	0.9600	0.9510
11. Gross depreciable capital formation as % of net product (line 9 divided by 1 minus line 10)	25.0	16.7	12.5	10.2
12. Ratio of gross product to net product	1.245	1.162	1.120	1.097
13. Gross capital formation proportion (%) (line 11 plus difference between lines 8 and 9, the sum divided by line 12)	20.2	14.5	11.25	9.4

Case III, $r = 0.004$				
14. Net capital formation as % of net product	1.2	1.2	1.2	1.2
15. Net depreciable capital formation as % of net product	1.0	1.0	1.0	1.0
16. f	0.95875	0.94083	0.9225	0.9045
17. Gross depreciable capital formation as % of net product	24.2	16.9	12.9	10.5
18. Ratio of gross product to net product	1.232	1.159	1.119	1.095
19. Gross capital formation proportion (%)	19.8	14.8	11.7	9.8

Case IV, $r = 0.025$				
20. Net capital formation as % of net product	7.5	7.5	7.5	7.5
21. Net depreciable capital formation as % of net product	6.25	6.25	6.25	6.25
22. f	0.7794	0.6977	0.6276	0.5673
23. Gross depreciable capital formation as % of net product	28.3	20.7	16.8	14.4
24. Ratio of gross product to net product	1.2205	1.1445	1.1055	1.0815
25. Gross capital formation proportion (%)	24.2	19.2	16.3	14.5

	Value of n in years			
	20 (1)	30 (2)	40 (3)	50 (4)
Case V, r = 0.05				
26. Net capital formation as % of net product	15.0	15.0	15.0	15.0
27. Net depreciable capital formation as % of net product	12.5	12.5	12.5	12.5
28. f	0.6231	0.5124	0.4290	0.3651
29. Gross depreciable capital formation as % of net product	33.2	25.6	21.9	19.7
30. Ratio of gross to net product	1.207	1.131	1.094	1.072
31. Gross capital formation proportion (%)	29.6	24.8	22.3	20.7

The f ratio is calculated from the equation:
$$f = [1 - (1 + r)^{-n}] : nr.$$

For the derivation of this equation, which assumes a straight line allocation of capital consumption (i.e., 1/n per year), see "International Differences in Capital Formation and Financing," Appendix B, pp. 76–81, particularly equation (3) on p. 79, modified to omit the a term and so change the ratio to total gross capital formation into a ratio to depreciable capital formation.

tween the net capital formation proportions of about 6 to 1—and the net and gross incremental capital-output ratios differ proportionately.

Similar but not identical results would be derived if land were included under reproducible and depreciable capital, but assigned eternal life. This calculation shows the effects of the inclusion of land on the average life span (n) of depreciable capital. Using the King figures again, assume that total capital stock, net of depreciation, is 7 (this being the ratio to net product), of which inventories are 0.5, land is 4.0, and truly depreciable capital is 2.5. Since the last figure represents *net* depreciable stock, for the calculation of n it should be raised to the gross value. On the assumptions used in deriving f in the Exhibit, i.e., straight line capital depreciation and constant values for n and r, the ratio of gross undepreciated stock to net depreciated stock (for finite n and r above zero) is $fnr - (1-f)$.[20] For $n=40$ and Case III ($r=0.004$), the ratio is 1.905; and for $n=40$ and Case IV

[20] The undepreciated capital stock is the sum of gross capital formation over n years, i.e., the sum of a geometric progression with $(1+r)$ as the multiplier. This sum (using GCF to designate gross capital formation) can be shown to be $(GCF/r) - (GCF)/r(1+r)^n$, which reduces to $(GCF fnr) - r$. According to the derivation on p. 77 or "International Differences . . . ," the net depreciated sum is $GCF/r \times ([nr - 1 + (1+r)^{-n}]nr)$, which reduces to $GCF (1-f) - r$. Division of the first sum by the second yields $fnr - (1-f)$.

($r = 0.025$), the ratio is 1.685. Hence, for Case III, the proportion of undepreciated fixed capital stock to land is 4.76, i.e., (2.5×1.905), to 4; and the new n is ($100 - [2.5 \times (4.76/8.76)]$), or 74 years. A similar calculation for Case IV yields a new n of 78 years. Thus, the inclusion of land under depreciable capital, with eternal life assigned to it, raises the weighted average life of depreciable capital to almost double the original 40 years. With the new values of n at hand, and bearing in mind that the net capital formation proportions are now 2.8 per cent (i.e., 0.004×7) for Case III and 17.5 per cent (i.e., 0.025×7) for Case IV, we can calculate the gross capital formation proportions for the two cases (computing the new values of f, etc.). These calculations, based on 74 and 78 respectively for n, yield a gross capital formation proportion for Case III of 16.6 per cent and for Case IV of 26.8 per cent. Here again, with a range in the net capital formation proportion between the two cases from 17.5 to 2.8, or over 6 to 1, the range for the gross capital formation proportion is only about 1.6 to 1; and while the *net* incremental capital-output ratio is 7 in both cases, the *gross* incremental capital-output ratio is as high as 16.6/0.4, or almost 42 in Case III and 26.8/2.5, or almost 11 in Case IV.

To lend more realism to the illustration and to test the conclusion further, we assume that in Case III, suggestive of pre-industrial periods, land is included under reproducible capital, and as indicated above, the results are a net capital formation proportion of 2.8 and a gross of 16.6 per cent; but in Case IV, suggestive of modern times, we make another extreme assumption, i.e., that land has been reduced to the point of being completely replaced by fixed depreciable capital (construction and equipment) with $n = 40$. On this basis, f for Case IV is 0.6276, as shown in line 22 of the Exhibit, but it is applied to a net depreciable capital formation proportion that is 16.25 per cent (rather than 6.25). The new gross capital formation proportion for Case IV works out to 35.2 per cent (instead of the 26.8 per cent shown in the preceding paragraph). But even with 74 for n in Case III and 40 for n in Case IV, the range in the net capital formation proportion from Case III to Case IV of about 6 to 1 is still associated with a range in the gross capital formation proportion of 35.2 to 16.6 or a little more than 2 to 1 (instead of the 1.6 to 1 derived in the preceding paragraph); and the gross incremental capital-output ratio in Case III of 42 is still contrasted with a gross incremental capital-output ratio in Case IV of 35.2/2.5, or 14, only a third as large.

Similarly, if we assume that the *net* capital formation proportions in Cases III and IV are the same, despite the marked differences in r, so that the net incremental capital-output ratio in Case III is higher than in Case IV by the ratio of 2.5/0.4 or over 6 to 1, the resulting disparity in *gross* incremental capital-output ratios would be much wider. Thus, if with $n = 40$, we assume that the net and net depreciable capital formation proportions in Case III are at the values given for Case IV (i.e., in lines 20 and 21 of the Exhibit), the gross capital formation proportion for Case III would become 46.9 per cent, compared with 16.3 per cent in Case IV; and the gross incremental capital-output ratio for Case III would then be 46.9/0.4 or 117, compared with that for Case IV of 16.3/2.5 or about 6.5—a range of about 18 to 1, instead of the 6 to 1 range for the net incremental capital-output ratios.

It should be clear from the Exhibit and the other illustrations above that differences in the rate of growth of aggregate product, and hence of capital formation on the assumption of constancy over time (but not similarity in level) of the proportion of the latter to product, suggested by Cases III and IV (i.e., between pre-modern and modern times), have a powerful differential impact on the ratio of capital consumption, and hence of net capital formation, to gross capital formation. When the rate of growth of product is low, capital consumption has a relatively greater weight, reducing any disparities that may be shown in net capital formation proportions, introducing disparities in gross incremental capital-output ratios where none exist in net, and accentuating excesses of net incremental capital-output ratios in periods of slow growth over those of faster growth when these are translated into gross incremental capital-output ratios. To put the conclusion into more meaningful terms: such acceleration in the rate of growth in total product as occurred from the pre-industrial to industrial times reduced the relative burden of capital consumption, of replacement of past and consumed capital stock, and thus made a greater *net* capital accumulation possible with the same (or only slightly increased) gross capital formation proportion—just as the rapid growth of national income makes the relative burden of former deadweight debts lighter. Our comparisons between the modern and the pre-modern periods would thus look different as we shift from net to gross capital formation proportions and from net to gross incremental capital-output ratios.

These effects would, of course, be all the greater if, in addition to assuming lower values for r for the earlier periods, we would assume lower values for n, i.e., shorter life periods for fixed depreciable capital—rather than the larger n that we derived in one of the illustrations by including the total land value under depreciable capital in Case III and replacing all of it by construction and equipment in Case IV. But the possibility of differences in the value of n, as well as the importance of the effects of allowing for capital consumption under different assumed rates of aggregate growth, raises a basic question. What does capital consumption represent? Or, in other words, what does the difference between net and gross capital formation mean? This question should be examined with the comparison of modern and pre-modern times as a background, even though much of what we shall say will be purely formal in reference to concepts, or conjectural in reference to presumptive differences in capital technology.

Fixed or durable capital goods are distinguished from others, fully consumed in current production (such as raw materials and semi-fabricates, fuel, etc.) in that, while contributing to current output, they remain intact for a long period, if maintained properly—and such maintenance is assumed and *not* included under capital consumption. The distinguishing features of fixed capital goods are then (a) current maintenance that is a relatively moderate fraction of the full gross value of the good and (b) a fairly long life period, so that annual depreciation is a limited fraction of the full value. If current maintenance is so high as to constitute a large proportion of the full value of the capital good, there is little to distinguish the latter from raw materials, for which current maintenance (replacement) equals the full value. If the capital good has a short life, say a year, there is again little to distinguish it from fully consumable capital goods, in which consumption is also fully completed within a year. The distinctive and, from the standpoint of economic analysis, key feature of a fixed capital good is that, its life being long, in order to secure the good one must commit, at the time it is secured, resources equivalent to say 100 times its current amortization (if $n = 100$), on the presumption that the high productivity that the capital good provides and that justifies the extra saving effort is not offset by too large an outlay on current maintenance.

We may now ask what determines the life of such fixed capital, the value of n, in modern times. The answer is that *economic* life, which is the relevant one here, i.e., life in economic use at a defined minimum level (relatively full), has been determined in modern times largely by economic obsolescence, *not* by the much longer physical life, i.e., survival intact. The former is a loss in value—in money units of constant general purchasing power—of a capital good, due to technological changes that affect either the capital good itself (by providing better substitutes) or the demand for it through changes in tastes. In the United States business firms are allowed by the Internal Revenue Bureau to charge off annually from 8 to 10 per cent of the cost of equipment, and the firms themselves in their own accounting may use even a higher depreciation rate, but not because the machines fall apart at the end of ten or 12.5 years of use. In fact, properly maintained, modern machinery lasts and performs with the same *absolute* efficiency for several decades; and some of it is often used after passing through second, third, and further hands. The depreciation rate is rather due to the fact that for the same amount of constant dollars—i.e., with the same general purchasing power—one can, because of technical progress, buy in 1965 an item of equipment that, when the services are properly discounted over the future, will be 8 to 10 per cent more effective (more economical, etc.) than a similar item bought and installed in 1964. An apartment building may be assigned a life of between 50 and 100 years, not because, with proper maintenance and barring such catastrophes as war bombing and earthquakes, it will not be intact at the end of a century, or even several centuries; but because tastes in housing and in neighborhoods change—largely as a result of technological shifts and their effects on location and jobs of people—so that many such houses, after five or six decades, may become available to lower (relative) income groups and eventually become slum housing. And, to use an example of consumers' durables, in the United States a passenger car is used for three to five years by its original purchaser and then turned in for a new one, not because the old car no longer provides perfectly good transportation at low cost; but because new style features, partly introduced by car manufacturers to induce *economic* obsolescence, have changed consumers' tastes so that the old car is less desirable.[21]

This combination of long physical and short economic life, of a low rate of physical wear-and-tear with a high rate of economic obsolescence, is a distinctive characteristic of the modern economic epoch. It is the modern advanced technology that permits the use of steel, cement, and similarly durable materials on a wide and increasing scale, with physical durability continually rising, even despite increased intensity of utilization. And it is the high rate of technological change associated with modern economic growth that induces a high rate of growth of per capita income and a high rate of structural shifts in the economy. And all these contribute to a high rate of economic obsolescence, partly as a direct consequence of continuous improvements in capital goods, partly as a consequence of shifts in physical and economic location of consumers, partly as a result of induced changes in taste to which high income consumers are most susceptible.

These comments obviously bear upon the meaning of capital consumption in modern times, particularly that of producers' equipment. If physical deterioration is minimal, and the predominant part of the depreciation charge represents an offset for economic obsolescence that is due to current technological improvements, replacement of capital means that the capacity of the existing stock will *rise* to the higher productivity levels warranted by the current year's improvements; and even *zero* net capital formation means a substantial *rise* in the productive capacity of the capital stock whose value will be shown unchanged. With this interpretation, it is *gross* producers' equipment rather than *net* capital formation that measures the *net* additions to productive capacity of capital.

[21] Of course, once this pattern of short-term changes in consumer taste emerges, producers of cars (or other consumer durables) may, in fact, build cars that are *physically* short-lived—in the sense of requiring significantly higher repair and maintenance charges after a few years of use. But here the short physical life is a consequence of short economic life, rather than the other way around.

The same argument would apply to those components of fixed capital that are subject to economic obsolescence because of changes in tastes, but only on condition that we hold tastes constant. This limiting condition leads to difficulties concerning the price weights and hence the taste structure assumed in the measurement of aggregate product itself. Since we must allow for changes in taste in measuring product, if the latter is to have meaning, we would be inconsistent if we ignored capital obsolescence due to changes in tastes. But we should recognize that under some short-term pressures, when tastes do not change or change slowly, the physical durability of the fixed capital needed for the goods involved assures a reserve stock of immense capacity. To illustrate we need only cite the experience of the United States during World War II. A large stock of housing and durable consumer capital (such as passenger cars) continued in use long beyond its usual economic life—so that, in a sense, capital consumption, previously associated with continuous changes in tastes, was "rolled back" by the pressure of war conditions. Naturally, after the war was over and peacetype production was resumed, the rate of this type of consumption was accelerated. But one reason for the extraordinary capacity of modern economies to recover quickly from devastating wars lies in these large reserves of physically durable capital goods, "depreciated" or "consumed" down to zero in the private and social accounts but still physically intact and capable of providing a large volume of additional services.

What about physical and economic obsolescence in the pre-modern periods? Obviously, some capital goods of earlier times had a long physical life—as is evident in the existing cathedrals, castles, and similar monuments, not to mention the pyramids of Egypt. But these examples of physical durability are the exceptional products of collective arts and crafts inspired by religious, political, or military drives; and little else of the capital formation of pre-modern times may be considered durable. Producers' equipment used metal sparingly because it was expensive, and the quality of the metal that was used was quite poor, so that the producers' equipment was far less durable than the producers' equipment required and made possible by modern production methods. Thus, one could argue that the physical life of producers' equipment, even when currently maintained at high cost, was relatively short. This argument applies also to much non-residential construction, e.g., the earth dams and irrigation channels, roads, bridges, etc., that were much less durable physically than the great modern installations; and, in some cases, required large annual restorations—which, in fact, amounted to a short physical life. Residential and other buildings were subject to weather and fire hazards that have been minimized in modern times by the use of more durable and fire-resistant materials. In short, it can be said that, except for the "monuments" (and even they were subject to changes in tastes and indeed were partially destroyed during revolutions, civil wars, etc.) and some other construction, the physical life of capital goods in pre-modern times was relatively short since they were subject to devastation by fire or other natural hazards, or required large annual replacements or maintenance to survive, or deteriorated rapidly in the process of use even with full current maintenance.

Indeed, at the danger of exaggeration, one may ask whether there was *any* fixed, durable capital formation, except for the "monuments," in pre-modern times, whether there was any significant accumulation of capital goods with a long physical life that did not require current maintenance (or replacement) amounting to a high proportion of the original full value. If most equipment lasted no more than five or six years, if most land improvements had to be maintained by continuous rebuilding amounting to something like a fifth of the total value per year, and if most buildings were destroyed at a rate cumulating to fairly complete destruction over a period from 25 to 50 years, then there was little that could be classified as durable capital. And unless available empirical evidence on the physical life and the vicissitudes of capital goods in pre-modern periods runs counter to the above argument, it suggests that the whole concept of *fixed* capital may be a unique product of the modern economic epoch and of modern technology—and somewhat foreign to the economics of earlier times. To be sure, economic obsolescence was much less important in the earlier centuries; but if the physical life was quite short, economic obsolescence could not have played a major role—at least on a broad and aggregative basis.

We do not have the data to test this comparison between modern and pre-modern times with respect to the physical durability and economic obsolescence of capital goods, and the resulting relative weights of capital consumption and current maintenance. Nor do we know whether the economic life of capital goods in earlier times, determined by physical deterioration rather than by obsolescence, was significantly shorter than the economic life of capital goods in modern times, determined by obsolescence rather than by physical deterioration. Also, the life in use of equipment, that did not have to be exposed to weather and could be better protected against fire, may have been quite long in earlier centuries—if only because technical progress introducing economic obsolescence was at a lower rate. Let us, however, proceed by assuming that the economic life of capital was shorter in earlier centuries—which means that n was smaller and the ratio of current maintenance to full value of capital was larger—and continue our illustrative calculations, based on the Exhibit above, not so much to provide answers as to demonstrate the consequences of the assumptions and the importance of the underlying questions. In the following calculations we deal with reproducible capital, excluding land, although inclusion of part of the land value under reproducible capital would not change the conclusions materially.

1. Taking Case V of the Exhibit, with a rate of growth of product of 5 per cent per year and $n=40$, to represent modern times, we assume that of the total capital depreciation of 9.4 per cent of net product (column 3, line 29 minus line 27) about 5 percentage points represent depreciation of producers' equipment and of elements in construction in which economic obsolescence is the overwhelming factor in depreciation—a not unrealistic assumption, since the rate of depreciation charges on producers' equipment alone is much higher than that on construction. These 5 percentage points then represent additions to the productive capacity of capital, and should for purposes of comparison with the past be added to *net* capital formation. The net capital formation proportion becomes 20.0/1.05, or 19.0 per cent, rather than 15 per cent (line 26, col. 3), of which 2.5 is inventories and the rest fixed capital. The gross capital formation proportion, however, remains 22.3 per cent (line 31, col. 3).

2. Again for Case V, we assume that current maintenance charges—of major importance for fixed depreciable capital alone—amount to about 1 per cent of the full gross value of capital. If net capital stock (defined in a standard way) is in the

ratio of 2.5 to 1 to net product, its full value, including the accumulated depreciation, can be obtained by multiplying by the ratio derived from the formula cited above, $fnr/(1-f)$, which works out to 1.5–so that the ratio of the full value of depreciable capital to *net product* becomes 3.75 to 1. Thus, current maintenance charges are 3.75 per cent of net product, and 3.75/1.094, or 3.4 per cent, of gross product. The proportion of gross capital formation, including current maintenance, to "gross-gross" product (i.e., gross product, including both capital consumption and current maintenance) becomes $(22.3+3.4)/1.034$, or 24.9 per cent.

3. Taking Case III to represent the earlier pre-modern times, we make three assumptions. The first is that n, the economic life of fixed capital, is shorter than that for Case V; and we set it at 30 years. The second is that capital consumption does not represent economic obsolescence, but is physical deterioration, with a resulting loss in capacity that must be replaced to restore the *status quo ante*. The third is that even with the lower n, current maintenance is a larger share of the original value of depreciable capital than in modern times, amounting to 2 per cent. Needless to say, these assumptions are but illustrative conjectures, subject to further change.

In Case III with $n=30$, the net capital formation proportion is 1.2 per cent (of which 0.2 is inventories) and the gross capital formation proportion is 14.8 per cent. To allow for current maintenance charges, we derive the ratio of full to depreciated value which works out to 1.91; the ratio of gross value of depreciable capital to net product is then (2.5×1.91), or 4.775 to 1; and a 2 per cent maintenance charge amounts to 9.6 per cent of net product, or 9.6/1.159, or 8.3 per cent of gross product. Hence, the proportion of gross capital formation, including current maintenance, to "gross-gross" product is $(14.8+8.3)/1.083$, or 21.3 per cent. Thus, the comparison so far shows that while the net capital formation proportion in Case III, 1.2 per cent, is less than a fifteenth of the net capital formation proportion in Case V, 19 per cent, the gross capital formation, including current maintenance, is 21.3 per cent in Case III—not much below the 24.9 per cent in Case V.

4. But the results are even more striking. In the comparison just drawn, we used depreciable net capital formation proportions of 1.0 per cent for Case III and 16.5 per cent for Case V

implying net depreciable capital-output ratios of 2.5 and 3.3 respectively. But since we have no reason to assume higher net incremental capital-output ratios in modern times, we substitute 3.3 for 2.5 in Case III. For $n=30$, the depreciable net capital formation proportion becomes 1.32 per cent (i.e., 0.004×3.3) and the gross capital formation proportion becomes 18.6 per cent (instead of 14.8 per cent, now in line 19, col. 2). Current maintenance charges, now applied to a larger gross capital stock, become 10.4 per cent of gross product; and the proportion of gross capital formation, including current maintenance, to "gross-gross" product becomes 29.0/110.4, or 26.3 per cent. Thus Case III, with a net capital formation proportion of 1.52 per cent compared with 19 per cent for Case V, has a gross capital formation proportion, including current maintenance, of about 26 per cent, *higher* than the gross capital formation proportion, including current maintenance, for Case V, 24.9 per cent.

The implication of all these illustrative calculations is clear. If they are at all valid, or point in the proper direction, a low net capital formation or net savings proportion in earlier times was associated with a high proportion of gross capital formation, including current maintenance; whereas the very much larger net capital formation shares in modern times were attained with gross capital formation proportions, and hence gross savings ratios, that were not much higher than in the pre-modern past. Needless to say, both capital consumption and current maintenance, which keep the productive capacity of capital from deteriorating absolutely, are uses of real resources that might otherwise be available for the production of finished goods. In that sense gross capital formation, including current maintenance, represents gross savings, i.e., withdrawals from current output, uses of resources *not* directly contributing to additional output of either finished consumer goods or finished net new capital. And the illustrations show that in the pre-modern times it took a large gross savings or withdrawal proportion to secure a small net capital formation proportion or a small net savings quota.

4. Summary Comments

The discussion in the preceding section may seem to be an over-elaborate construction of conjectural numbers on a foundation of a few items of tested evidence; but it is not without validity. The major item of tested evidence is the much lower rate of growth of total product in the pre-modern past, associated with a much lower rate of growth of population. If this finding is accepted, several conclusions follow, based on assumptions that are at least plausible; and if the conclusions seem unacceptable, several interesting analytical problems arise and empirical research must be directed toward testing the conclusions.

These conclusions or implications may be listed *seriatim.*

First, *if* the net incremental capital-output ratio can be assumed to be not much higher in the past than in modern times, the low rate of growth of total product implies very low shares of net capital formation, or net savings, in net product (say shares of less than 2 per cent). Given the absolute level of per capita income, its assumed rise (even if gradual), and the marked inequalities in the income distribution, potential savings should be large and the generation of such *low* rates of net savings and net capital formation must be explained. Conversely, if the net capital formation proportion was distinctly higher than the low level suggested and thus the net incremental capital-output ratio in the pre-modern past was distinctly higher than in modern economic growth, this particular difference would have to be explained—especially since the greater relative supplies of labor and natural resources in the earlier times would lead us to expect a higher rather than lower marginal yield on capital, and hence a lower rather than higher net incremental capital-output ratio.

Second, assuming that the economic life of fixed capital goods was no shorter in the past than in modern times (with current maintenance at the required "normal" level), and that capital formation was a relatively constant proportion of product (over time, but not the same for the past and present epochs), the very low rate of growth of aggregate product in the past would in and of itself make for a much higher ratio of capital consumption, and hence of gross capital formation, to net capital formation. This means that even much lower *net* capital formation proportions in the pre-modern past, than in modern economic growth, would imply relatively *high gross* capital formation proportions that would be much closer to modern gross capital formation proportions. Thus, even if in the pre-modern past net capital formation proportions were as low as warranted by a net incremental capital-output ratio equal to that in modern times (say 3 to 1), gross capital formation proportions would be "too high," i.e., the *gross* incremental capital-output ratios would be far higher in the past than they are in modern economic growth.

Third, these contrasts between net and gross capital formation, net and gross savings, and net and gross incremental capital-output ratios are accentuated if we recognize that in modern times capital consumption is in large part an allowance for economic obsolescence due to technical progress—not for replacement for physical deterioration or any absolute loss in productive capacity; whereas in the past, physical deterioration was dominant—the physical life of the durable good was relatively short, and the weight of current maintenance to assure this shorter life was relatively great. Using assumptions concerning these differences in life and relative weight of current maintenance in disfavor of earlier periods, we can show that very low net capital formation proportions in the past were associated, and indeed required, gross capital formation proportions, including current maintenance, that were almost as large as or larger than the high gross capital formation proportions in modern economically developed countries.

Fourth, it follows from the above that the net capital formation proportions may have been so low in the past because the gross capital formation proportions, the gross withdrawals of resources needed merely to keep capital intact without reducing its productivity, had to be proportionately so high. But it does not necessarily follow that this high level of capital consumption and maintenance, due partly to the low rate of growth of aggregate product and partly to the low level of efficiency in maintaining fixed capital, is more important in explaining the low net capital formation proportions in the past than many other, already familiar, institutional and economic factors.

While the major conclusions follow from the Exhibit almost automatically if we accept the much lower rate of growth of aggregate product in the past, more quantitative and related information is needed to test the alternative assumptions consistent with the major conclusions (i.e., low level of net capital formation proportions versus higher net incremental capital-output ratios) and to specify more carefully the orders of magnitude involved. Thus more data on aggregate, or per capita, product and particularly on net accumulated capital for pre-modern times would provide better evidence on the low level of the net capital formation proportions and might indicate whether the net incremental capital-output ratios were high or as low as they are in modern economic growth. Data on wealth, income, and expenditures for various groups in the population, again for pre-modern times, would help to show whether the money-savings flows or the investment opportunities were the limiting factor in net and gross capital formation proportions. Information on the physical life of fixed capital goods in pre-modern centuries—even if only rough indexes like frequency of fires, magnitude of labor inputs into maintenance compared with that into original production, frequency of major repairs, and the like—would help us specify the value of n and the relative weight of current maintenance in pre-modern compared with modern times. In short, the exercise in quantitative conjectures presented above is useful if only because it indicates the relevant data needed to provide acceptable answers to important questions.

Whether the questions are important depends, of course, upon our evaluation of the rather narrowly defined concepts of capital formation and quantitative approximations, used so much in the analysis of recent economic growth. Despite the qualifications suggested at the outset in discussing the three sets of limiting criteria involved in the currently standard definition of capital formation, and despite the emphasis in the discussion above on some basic differences in technology and institutions between modern and earlier times, I feel that the attempt to quantify, on the basis of these narrow but sharply defined concepts, is valuable. Granted that other factors complementing the use of material capital may vary its effect over time and indeed affect the very meaning of its components, material capital, conceived as a clearly defined part of aggregate product, provides a firm conceptual framework with which to start. And the latter must be quantified, at least in terms of rough orders of magnitude, so that the relations built into the framework can be traced and any significant changes or differences in magnitudes can be taken as signals for further analytical exploration of the underlying factors.

Modern Economic Growth:
Findings and Reflections

1. Definitions

A country's economic growth may be defined as a long-term rise in capacity to supply increasingly diverse economic goods to its population, this growing capacity based on advancing technology and the institutional and ideological adjustments that it demands. All three components of the definition are important. The sustained rise in the supply of goods is the *result* of economic growth, by which it is identified. Some small countries can provide increasing income to their populations because they happen to possess a resource (minerals, location, etc.) exploitable by more developed nations, that yields a large and increasing rent. Despite intriguing analytical problems that these few fortunate countries raise, we are interested here only in the nations that derive abundance by using advanced contemporary technology—not by selling fortuitous gifts of nature to others. Advancing technology is the *permissive* source of economic growth, but it is only a potential, a necessary condition, in itself not sufficient. If technology is to be employed efficiently and widely, and, indeed, if its own progress is to be stimulated by such use, institutional and ideological adjustments must be made to effect the proper use of innovations generated by the

Nobel Memorial Lecture, December 11, 1971. Reprinted from *Les Prix Nobel en 1971* (Stockholm, 1972), pp. 313–26.

advancing stock of human knowledge. To cite examples from modern economic growth: steam and electric power and the large-scale plants needed to exploit them are not compatible with family enterprise, illiteracy, or slavery—all of which prevailed in earlier times over much of even the developed world, and had to be replaced by more appropriate institutions and social views. Nor is modern technology compatible with the rural mode of life, the large and extended family pattern, and veneration of undisturbed nature.

The source of technological progress, the particular production sectors that it affected most, and the pace at which it and economic growth advanced, differed over centuries and among regions of the world; and so did the institutional and ideological adjustments in their interplay with the technological changes introduced into and diffused through the growing economies. The major breakthroughs in the advance of human knowledge, those that constituted dominant sources of sustained growth over long periods and spread to a substantial part of the world, may be termed epochal innovations. And the changing course of economic history can perhaps be subdivided into economic epochs, each identified by the epochal innovation with the distinctive characteristics of growth that it generated.[1] Without considering the feasibility of identifying and dating such economic epochs, we may proceed on the working assumption that modern economic growth represents such a distinct epoch—growth dating back to the late eighteenth century and limited (except in significant *partial* effects) to economically developed countries. These countries, so classified because they have managed to take adequate advantage of the potential of modern technology, include most of Europe, the overseas offshoots of Western Europe, and Japan—barely one-quarter of world population.[2] This paper will focus on modern economic growth, but with obviously needed attention to its worldwide impact.

[1] For a discussion of the economic epoch concept see Simon Kuznets, *Modern Economic Growth: Rate, Structure, and Spread* (New Haven, Conn.: Yale University Press, 1966), pp. 1–16.

[2] For a recent classification identifying the non-Communist developed countries see *Yearbook of National Accounts Statistics, 1969*, Vol. II, *International Tables* (New York: United Nations, 1970), notes to Table 5, p. 156. These classifications vary from time to time, and differ somewhat from those of other international agencies.

Limitations of space prevent the presentation of a documented summary of the quantitative characteristics commonly observed in the growth of the presently developed countries, characteristics different from those of economic growth in earlier epochs. However, some of them are listed, because they contribute to our understanding of the distinctive problems of economic life in the world today. While the list is selective and is open to charges of omission, it includes those observed and empirically testable characteristics that lead back to some basic factors and conditions, which can only be glimpsed and conjectured, and forward to some implications that have so far eluded measurement.

2. The Six Characteristics

Six characteristics of modern economic growth have emerged in the analysis based on conventional measures of national product and its components, population, labor force, and the like. First and most obvious are the high rates of growth of per capita product and of population in the developed countries—both large multiples of the previous rates observable in these countries and of those in the rest of the world, at least until the recent decade or two.[3] Second, the rate of rise in productivity, i.e., of output per unit of all inputs, is high, even when we include among inputs other factors in addition to labor, the major productive factor—and here too the rate is a large multiple of the rate in

---

[3] For the non-Communist developed countries, the rates of growth per year over the period of modern economic growth, were almost 2 per cent for product per capita, 1 per cent for population, and 3 per cent for total product. These rates—which mean roughly a multiplication over a century by five for product per capita, by three for population, and by more than fifteen for total product—were far greater than pre-modern rates. The latter can only be conjectured, but reasonable estimates for Western Europe over the long period from the early Middle Ages to the mid-nineteenth century suggest that the modern rate of growth is about ten times as high for product per capita (see Simon Kuznets, *Economic Growth of Nations: Total Output and Production Structure* [Cambridge, Mass.: Harvard University Press, 1971], pp. 10–27). A similar comparison for population, either for Europe or for the area of European settlement (i.e., Europe, the Americas, and Oceania), relating to 1850–1960, as compared with 1000–1850, suggests a multiple of 4 or 5 to 1 (see Simon Kuznets, *Modern Economic Growth: Rate, Structure, and Spread* [New Haven, Conn.: Yale University Press, 1966], Tables 2.1 and 2.2, pp. 35 and 38). The implied acceleration in the growth rate of total product is between forty and fifty times.

the past.[4] Third, the rate of structural transformation of the economy is high. Major aspects of structural change include the shift away from agriculture to non-agricultural pursuits and, recently, away from industry to services; a change in the scale of productive units, and a related shift from personal enterprise to impersonal organization of economic firms, with a corresponding change in the occupational status of labor.[5] Shifts in several other aspects of economic structure could be added (in the structure of consumption, in the relative shares of domestic and foreign supplies, etc.). Fourth, the closely related and extremely important structures of society and its ideology have also changed rapidly. Urbanization and secularization come easily to mind as components of what sociologists term the process of modernization. Fifth, the economically developed countries, by means of the increased power of technology, particularly in transport and communication (both peaceful and warlike), have the propensity to reach out to the rest of the world—thus making for one world in the sense in which this was not true in any pre-modern epoch.[6] Sixth, the spread of modern economic

[4] Using the conventional national economic accounts, we find that the rate of increase in productivity is large enough to account (in the statistical sense) for almost the entire growth of product per capita. Even with adjustments to allow for hidden costs and inputs, growth in productivity accounts for over half of the growth in product per capita (see Simon Kuznets, *Economic Growth of Nations: Total Output and Production Structure* [Cambridge, Mass.: Harvard University Press, 1971], pp. 51–75, particularly Table 9, p. 74, and Table 11, p. 93).

[5] The rapidity of structural shifts in modern times can be easily illustrated by the changes in the distribution of the labor force between agriculture (and related industries) and the non-agricultural production sectors. In the United States, the share of labor force attached to the agricultural sector was still 53.5 per cent in 1870 and declined to less than 7 per cent in 1960. In an old European country like Belgium, the share of agriculture in the labor force, 51 per cent in 1846, dropped to 12.5 per cent in 1947 and further to 7.5 per cent in 1961 (see P. Bairoch and others, *The Working Population and Its Structure, International Historical Statistics, Vol. I* [Brussels: Institut de Sociologie, Université Libre de Bruxelles, 1968], Tables D-4 and C-4). Considering that it took centuries for the share of the agricultural sector in the labor force to decline to 50 per cent in any sizable country (i.e., excluding small "city enclaves"), a drop of 30 to 40 percentage points in the course of a single century is a strikingly fast structural change.

[6] The outward expansion of developed countries, with their European origin, goes back to long before modern economic growth, indeed, back to the Crusades. But the much augmented transportation and communication power of developed countries in the nineteenth century permitted a much

growth, despite its worldwide partial effects, is limited in that the economic performance in countries accounting for three-quarters of world population still falls far short of the minimum levels feasible with the potential of modern technology.[7]

This brief summary of two quantitative characteristics of modern economic growth that relate to aggregate rates, two that relate to structural transformation, and two that relate to international spread, supports our working assumption that modern economic growth marks a distinct economic epoch. If the rates of aggregate growth and the speed of structural transformation in the economic, institutional, and perhaps even in the ideological, framework are so much higher than in the past as to represent a revolutionary acceleration, and if the various regions of the world are for the first time in history so closely interrelated as to be one, some new major growth source, some new epochal innovation, must have generated these radically different patterns. And one may argue that this source is the emergence of modern science as the basis of advancing technology—a breakthrough in the evolution of science that produced a potential for technology far greater than existed previously.

Yet modern growth continues many older trends, if in greatly accelerated form. This continuity is important particularly when we find that, except for Japan and possibly Russia, all presently developed countries were well in advance of the rest of the world before their modern growth and industrialization began, enjoying a comparative advantage produced by pre-modern trends. It is also important because it emphasizes that distinction among economic epochs is a complicated intellectual choice and that the continuation of past trends and their changing patterns over time are subjects deserving the closest attention. Does the acceleration in growth of product and productivity in many developed countries in the last two decades reflect a major change in the potential provided by science-oriented technology, or a major change in the capacity of societies to catch up with that potential? Is it a way of recouping the loss in

---

greater and more direct political dominance over the colonies, the "opening up" of previously closed areas (such as Japan), and the "partition" of previously undivided areas (such as sub-Saharan Africa).

[7] For further discussion see Section 4 below, which deals with the less-developed countries.

standing, relative to such a leader as the United States, that was incurred during the depression of the thirties and World War II? Or, finally, is it merely a reflection of the temporarily favorable climate of the U.S. international policies? Is the expansion into space a continuation of the old trend of reaching out by the developed countries, or is it a precursor of a new economic epoch? These questions are clearly illustrative, but they hint at broader analytical problems suggested by the observation of modern economic growth as a distinct epoch.

The six characteristics noted are interrelated, and the interrelations among them are most significant. With the rather stable ratio of labor force to total population, a high rate of increase in per capita product means a high rate of increase in product per worker; and, with average hours of work declining, it means still higher growth rates in product per manhour. Even if we allow for the impressive accumulation of capital, in its widest sense, the growth rate of productivity is high, and, indeed, mirrors the great rise in per capita product and in per capita pure consumption. Since the latter reflects the realized effects of advancing technology, rapid changes in production structure are inevitable —given the differential impact of technological innovations on the several production sectors, the differing income elasticity of domestic demand for various consumer goods, and the changing comparative advantage in foreign trade. As already indicated, advancing technology changes the scale of production plants and the character of the economic enterprise units. Consequently, effective participation in the modern economic system by the labor force necessitates rapid changes in its location and structure, in the relations among occupational status groups, and even in the relations between labor force and total population (the last, however, within narrow overall limits). Thus, not only are high aggregate growth rates associated with rapid changes in economic structure, but the latter are also associated with rapid changes in other aspects of society—in family formation, in urbanization, in man's views on his role and the measure of his achievement in society. The dynamic drives of modern economic growth, in the countries that entered the process ahead of others, meant a reaching out geographically; and the sequential spread of the process, facilitated by major changes in transport and communication, meant a continuous expansion to the less-developed areas. At the same time, the difficulty of making the institutional and ideological transformations needed to convert the new large potential of modern technology into economic growth in the relatively short period since the late eighteenth century limited the spread of the system. Moreover, obstacles to such transformation were, and still are being, imposed on the less-developed regions by the policies of the developed countries.

If the characteristics of modern economic growth are interrelated, in that one induces another in a cause and effect sequence or all are concurrent effects of a common set of underlying factors, another plausible and significant link should be noted. Mass application of technological innovations, which constitutes much of the distinctive substance of modern economic growth, is closely connected with the further progress of science, in its turn the basis for additional advance in technology. While this topic is still to be studied in depth, it seems fairly clear that mass uses of technical innovations (many based on recent scientific discoveries) provide a positive feedback. Not only do they provide a larger economic surplus for basic and applied research with long time leads and heavy capital demands, but, more specifically, they permit the development of new efficient tools for scientific use and supply new data on the behavior of natural processes under the stress of modification in economic production. In other words, many production plants in developed countries can be viewed as laboratories for the exploration of natural processes and as centers of research on new tools, both of which are of immense service to basic and applied research in science and technology. It is no accident that the last two centuries were also periods of enormous acceleration in the contribution to the stock of useful knowledge by basic and applied research—which provided additional stimuli to new technological innovations. Thus, modern economic growth reflects an interrelation that sustains the high rate of advance through the feedback from mass applications to further knowledge. And unless some obstacles intervene, it provides a mechanism for self-sustaining technological advance, to which, given the wide expanse of the universe (relative to mankind on this planet), there are no obvious proximate limits.

3. Some Implications [8]

I turn now to a brief discussion of some social implications, of some effects of modern economic growth on conditions of life of various population groups in the countries affected. Many of these effects are of particular interest because they are not re-flected in the current measures of economic growth; and the in-creasing realization of this shortcoming of the measures has stimulated lively discussion of the limits and limitations of eco-nomic measurement of economic growth.

The effects on conditions of life stem partly from the major role of technological innovations in modern economic growth, and partly from the rapid shifts in the underlying production structure. To begin with the latter, the major effects of which, e.g., urbanization, internal migration, shift to employee status, and what might be called the merit basis of job choice, have al-ready been noted as characteristics of modern economic growth. Two important groups of effects of this rapid transformation of economic structure deserve explicit reference.

First, the changes in conditions of life suggested by "urbaniza-tion" clearly involved a variety of costs and returns that are not now included in economic measurement, and some of which may never be susceptible to measurement. Internal migration, from the countryside to the cities (within a country, and often international) represented substantial costs in the pulling up of roots and the adjustment to the anonymity and higher costs of urban living. The learning of new skills and the declining value of previously acquired skills was clearly a costly process—to both the individuals and to society. But if such costs were omit-ted from measurement, as they still are in conventional ac-counts, so were some returns. Urban life, with its denser popula-tion, provided amenities and spiritual goods that were not available in the "dull and brutish" life of the countryside; and the new skills, once learned, were often a more adequate basis

[8] Many of the points touched upon in this section are discussed in greater detail in Simon Kuznets, *Economic Growth of Nations: Total Out-put and Production Structure* (Cambridge, Mass.: Harvard University Press, 1971), particularly in Chapter II (pp. 75–98), which deals with the non-conventional costs of economic growth, and Chapter VII (pp. 314–54), which deals with various interrelations between aggregate change and structural shifts in economic and other aspects of social structure.

for a richer life than the old. This comment on the hidden costs and returns involved in the shift toward urban life may apply to many other costs and returns involved in other shifts imposed by economic growth, e.g., in the character of participation in economic activity, in the social values, and in the new pressures on deviant members of society.

The second intriguing aspect of structural change is that it represents shifts in the relative shares in the economy of the specific population groups attached to particular production sectors. Since economic engagement represents a dominant influence in the life of people, the shift in the share of a specific sector, with its distinctive characteristics and even mode of life, affects the population group engaged in it. Economic growth perforce brings about a decline in the relative position of one group after another—of farmers, of small-scale producers, of landowners—a change not easily accepted, and, in fact, as history teaches us, often resisted. The continuous disturbance of pre-existing *relative* position of the several economic groups is pregnant with conflict—despite the rises in absolute income or product common to all groups. In some cases, these conflicts did break out into overt civil war, the Civil War in the United States being a conspicuous example. Other examples, in the early periods of industrialization among the currently developed countries, or, for that matter, more recently within some less-developed countries, are not lacking.

Only if such conflicts are resolved without excessive costs, and certainly without a long-term weakening of the political fabric of the society, is modern economic growth possible. The sovereign state, with authority based on loyalty and on a community of feeling—in short, the modern national state—plays a crucial role in peacefully resolving such growth-induced conflicts. But this and other services of the national state may be costly in various ways, of which intensified nationalism is one, and other effects are too familiar to mention. The records of many developed countries reveal examples of resolutions of growth conflicts, of payments for overcoming resistance and obstacles to growth, that left burdensome heritages for the following generations (notably in Germany and Japan). Of course, this is not the only economic function of the state: it can also stimulate growth and structural change. And, to mention a closely related service, it can referee, select, or discard legal and institutional innovations that are proposed in the attempt to organize and channel effectively the new production potentialities. This, too, is a matter that may generate conflicts, since different legal and institutional arrangements may have different effects on the several economic groups in society.

In that modern economic growth has to contend with the resolution of incipient conflicts continuously generated by rapid changes in economic and social structure, it may be described as a process of controlled revolution. The succession of technological innovations characteristic of modern economic growth and the social innovations that provide the needed adjustments are major factors affecting economic and social structure. But these innovations have other effects that deserve explicit mention; and while these are discussed below in terms of effects of technological innovations, the conclusions apply *pari passu* to innovations in legal forms, in institutional structure, and even in ideology.

A technological innovation, particularly one based on a recent major invention, represents a venture into the partly unknown, something not fully known until the mass spread of the innovation reveals the full range of direct and related effects. An invention is a major one if it provides the basis for extensive applications and improvements (e.g., the stationary steam engine in the form attributable mostly to James Watt). Its cumulative effects, all new, extend over a long period and result in an enormous transformation of economic production and of production relations. But these new effects can hardly be fully anticipated or properly evaluated in advance (and sometimes not even post facto). This is true also of electric power, the internal combustion engine, atomic energy, the application of short rays to communication and computation, the inventions resulting in such new industrial materials as steel, aluminum, and plastics, and so on through a long list that marked modern economic growth. Even when the technological innovation is an adaptation of a known technique by a follower country, the results may not be fully foreseeable, for they represent the combination of something known, the technology, with something new, an institutional and ideological framework with which it has not previously been combined. Needless to say, the element of the uniquely new, of exploration into the unknown, was also prominent in pre-modern times, since innovations in knowledge and technology are the prerequisites for any significant growth. But the *rate* of succession of such innovations was clearly more rapid in modern economic growth, and provided the base for a higher rate of aggregate growth.

The effects of such ventures into the new and partly unknown are numerous. Those of most interest here are the *surprises,* the unexpected results, which may be positive or negative. An invention or innovation may prove far more productive, and induce a far wider mass application and many more cumulative improvements than were dreamed of by the inventor and the pioneer group of entrepreneurs. Or the mass application of a major invention may produce unexpected dis-economies of a scale that could hardly be foreseen in the early phases of its diffusion. Examples of both positive and negative surprises abound. Many Schumpeterian entrepreneurs failed to grasp, by a wide margin, the full scope and significance of the innovations that they were promoting and that eventually brought them fame and fortune. And most of us can point at the unexpected negative effects of some technological or social invention that first appeared to be an unlimited blessing.

The significant aspect here is that the surprises cannot be viewed as accidents; they are inherent in the process of technological (and social) innovation in that it contains an element of the unknown. Furthermore, the diffusion of a major innovation is a long and complicated sequence that cannot be accurately forecast, with an initial economic effect that may generate responses in other processes. These will, in turn, change the conditions under which the innovation exercises its effect on human welfare, and raise further problems of adjustment. To illustrate: we can today follow easily the sequence from the introduction of the passenger car as a mass means of transportation, to the growth of the suburbs, to the movement of the more affluent from the city centers, to the concentration of lower income recipients and unemployed immigrants in the slums of the inner city core, to the acute urban problems, financial and other, and to the trend toward metropolitan consolidation. But the nature and implications of this sequence were certainly not apparent in the 1920's, when passenger cars began their mass service function in the United States.

Indeed, to push this speculative line further, one can argue that all economic growth brings *some* unexpected results in its wake, positive as well as negative, with the latter taking on greater importance as the mass effects of major innovations are felt and the needs that they are meant to satisfy are met. If the argument is valid, modern economic growth, with the rapid succession of innovations and shortening period of their mass diffusion, must be accompanied by a relatively high incidence of negative effects. Yet one must not forget that pre-modern economic growth had similar problems, which, with the weaker technology, may have loomed even larger. Even if we disregard the threatening exhaustion of natural resources, a problem that so concerned Classical (and implicitly even Marxian) economics, and consider only early urbanization, one major negative effect was the significant rise in death rates as population moved from the more salubrious countryside to the infection-prone denser conditions of unsanitary cities. Two points are relevant here. First, the negative effects of growth have never been viewed as so far outweighing its positive contribution as to lead to its renunciation—no matter how crude the underlying calculus may have been. Second, one may assume that once an unexpected negative result of growth emerges, the potential of material and social technology is aimed at its reduction or removal. In many cases these negative results were allowed to accumulate and to become serious technological or social problems because it was so difficult to foresee them early enough in the process to take effective preventive or ameliorative action. Even when such action was initiated, there may have been delay in the effective technological or policy solution. Still, one may justifiably argue, in the light of the history of economic growth, in which a succession of such unexpected negative results has been overcome, that any specific problem so generated will be temporary—although we shall never be free of them, no matter what economic development is attained.

4. *The Less-Developed Countries*

Two major groups of factors appear to have limited the spread of modern economic growth. First, as already suggested, such growth demands a stable, but flexible, political and social framework, capable of accommodating rapid structural change and resolving the conflicts that it generates, while encouraging the growth-promoting groups in society. Such a framework is not easily or rapidly attained, as evidenced by the long struggles toward it even in some of the presently developed countries in the nineteenth and early twentieth centuries. Japan is the only nation outside of those rooted in European civilization that has joined the group of developed countries so far. Emergence of a modern framework for economic growth may be especially difficult if it involves elements peculiar to European civilization for which substitutes are not easily found. Second, the increasingly national cast of organization in developed countries made for policies toward other parts of the world that, while introducing some modern economic and social elements, were, in many areas, clearly inhibiting. These policies ranged from the imposition of colonial status to other limitations on political freedom, and, as a result, political independence and removal of the inferior status of the native members of the community, rather than economic advance, were given top priority.

Whatever the weight of the several factors in explaining the failure of the less-developed countries to take advantage of the potential of modern economic growth, a topic that, in its range from imperialist exploitation to backwardness of the native economic and social framework, lends itself to passionate and biased polemic, the factual findings are clear. At present, about two-thirds or more of world population is in the economically less-developed group. Even more significant is the concentration of the population at the low end of the product per capita range. In 1965, the last year for which we have worldwide comparable product estimates, the per capita GDP (at market prices) of 1.72 billion out of a world population of 3.27 billion, was less than $120, whereas 0.86 billion in economically developed countries had a per capita product of some $1,900. Even with this narrow definition of less-developed countries, the intermediate group was less than 0.7 billion, or less than 20 per cent of the world total.[9] The preponderant population was thus di-

[9] The underlying data are from Everett E. Hagen and Oli Hawrylyshyn, "Analysis of World Income and Growth, 1955–1965," *Economic Development and Cultural Change*, Vol. 18, no. 1, Part II, October, 1969. These are primarily from United Nations publications, supplemented by some auxiliary sources (mostly for the Communist countries), and use conven-

vided between the very low and the rather high level of per capita economic performance. Obviously, this aspect of modern economic growth deserves our greatest attention, and the fact that the quantitative data and our knowledge of the institutional structures of the less-developed countries are, at the moment, far more limited than our knowledge of the developed areas, is not reason enough for us to ignore it.

Several preliminary findings, or rather plausible impressions, may be noted. First, the group of less-developed countries, particularly if we widen it (as we should) to include those with a per capita product somewhat larger than $120 (in 1965 prices), covers an extremely wide range in size, in the relation between population and natural resources, in major inherited institutions, and in the past impact upon them of the developed countries (coming as it did at different times and from different sources). There is a striking contrast, for example, in terms of population size, between the giants like Mainland China and India, on the one hand, and the scores of tiny states in Africa and Latin America; as there is between the timing of direct Western impact on Africa and of that on many countries in Latin America. Furthermore, the remarkable institutions by which the Sinic and East Indian civilizations produced the unified, huge societies that dwarfed in size any that originated in Europe until recently, bore little resemblance to those that structured the American Indian societies or those that fashioned the numerous tribal societies of Africa.

Generalizations about less-developed countries must be carefully and critically scrutinized in the light of this wide variety of conditions and institutions. To be sure, their common failure to exploit the potential of modern economic growth means several specific common features: a low per capita product, a large share of agriculture or other extractive industries, a generally

tional conversion rates to U.S. dollars in 1965. The estimates for the Communist countries have been adjusted to conform to the international GDP concept.

The developed countries include most countries with per capita GDP of $1,000 or more and Japan, but exclude those small countries with a high GDP per capita that is due to exceptional natural endowments (e.g., Netherlands Antilles, Puerto Rico, Kuwait, and Qatar).

For more detailed comparison between the developed and less-developed countries, see a later article in this volume, "The Gap: Concept, Measurement, Trends."

small scale of production. But the specific parameters differ widely, and because the obstacles to growth may differ critically in their substance, they may suggest different policy directions.

Second, the growth position of the less-developed countries today is significantly different, in many respects, from that of the presently developed countries on the eve of their entry into modern economic growth (with the possible exception of Japan, and one cannot be sure even of that). The less-developed areas that account for the largest part of the world population today are at much lower per capita product levels than were the developed countries just before their industrialization; and the latter at that time were economically in advance of the rest of the world, not at the low end of the per capita product range. The very magnitudes, as well as some of the basic conditions, are quite different: no country that entered modern economic growth (except Russia) approached the size of India or China, or even of Pakistan and Indonesia; and no currently developed country had to adjust to the very high rates of natural increase of population that have characterized many less-developed countries over the last two or three decades. Particularly before World War I, the older European countries, and to some extent even Japan, relieved some strains of industrialization by substantial emigration of the displaced population to areas with more favorable opportunities—an avenue closed to the populous less-developed countries today. Of course, the stock of material and social technology that can be tapped by less-developed countries today is enormously larger than that available in the nineteenth and even early twentieth centuries. But it is precisely this combination of greater backwardness and seemingly greater backlog of technology that makes for the significant differences between the growth position of the less-developed countries today and that of the developed countries when they were entering the modern economic growth process.

Finally, it may well be that, despite the tremendous accumulation of material and social technology, the stock of innovations most suitable to the needs of the less-developed countries is not too abundant. Even if one were to argue that progress in basic science may not be closely tied to the technological needs of the country of origin (and even that may be disputed), unquestionably the applied advances, the inventions and tools, are a response to the specific needs of the country within which they originate. This was certainly true of several major inventions associated with the Industrial Revolution in England, and illustrations abound of necessity as the mother of invention. To the extent that this is true, and that the conditions of production in the developed countries differed greatly from those in the populous less-developed countries today, the material technology evolved in the developed countries may not supply the needed innovations. Nor is the social technology that evolved in the developed countries likely to provide models of institutions or arrangements suitable to the diverse institutional and population-size backgrounds of many less-developed countries. Thus, modern technology with its emphasis on labor-saving inventions may not be suited to countries with a plethora of labor but a scarcity of other factors, such as land and water; and modern institutions, with their emphasis on personal responsibility and pursuit of economic interest, may not be suited to the more traditional life patterns of the agricultural communities that predominate in many less-developed countries. These comments should not be interpreted as denying the value of many transferable parts of modern technology; they are merely intended to stress the possible shortage of material and social tools specifically fitted to the different needs of the less-developed countries.

If the observations just made are valid, several implications for the growth problems of the less-developed countries follow. I hesitate to formulate them explicitly, since the data and the stock of knowledge on which the observations rest are limited. But at least one implication is sufficiently intriguing, and seems to be illuminating of many recent events in the field, to warrant a brief note. It is that a substantial economic advance in the less-developed countries may require modifications in the available stock of material technology, and probably even greater innovations in political and social structure. It will not be a matter of merely borrowing existing tools, material and social, or of directly applying past patterns of growth, merely allowing for the difference in parameters.

The innovational requirements are likely to be particularly great in the social and political structures. The rather violent changes in these structures that occurred in those countries that have forged ahead with highly forced industrialization under

Communist auspices, the pioneer entry going back over forty years (beginning with the first Five-Year Plan in the U.S.S.R.), are conspicuous illustrations of the kind of social invention and innovation that may be involved. And the variants even of Communist organization, let alone those of democracy and of non-Communist authoritarianism, are familiar. It would be an over-simplification to argue that these innovations in the social and political structures were made primarily in response to the strain between economic backwardness and the potential of modern economic growth or to claim that they were inexorable effects of antecedent history. But to whatever the struggle for political and social organization is a response, once it has been resolved, the results shape significantly the conditions under which economic growth can occur. It seems highly probable that a long period of experimentation and struggle toward a viable political framework compatible with adequate economic growth lies ahead for most less-developed countries of today; and this process will become more intensive and acute as the *perceived* gap widens between what has been attained and what is attainable with modern economic growth. While an economist can argue that some aspects of growth must be present because they are indispensable components (i.e., industrialization, large scale of production, etc.), even their parameters are bound to be variable; and many specific characteristics will be so dependent upon the outcome of the social and political innovations that extrapolation from the past is extremely hazardous.

5. *Concluding Comments*

The aim of the discussion was to sketch the major characteristics of modern economic growth, and to note some of the implications that the empirical study of economic growth of nations suggests. This study goes back to the beginning of our discipline, as indicated by the title of Adam Smith's founding treatise, *Wealth of Nations*, which could as well have been called the Economic Growth of Nations. But the quantitative base and interest in economic growth have widened greatly in the last three to four decades, and the accumulated results of past study of economic history and of past economic analysis could be combined with the richer stock of quantitative data to advance the empirical study of the process. The sketch above draws upon the results of many and widely varied studies in many countries, most of them economically developed; and the discussion reflects a wide collective effort, however individual some of my interpretations may be.

The most distinctive feature of modern economic growth is the combination of a high rate of aggregate growth with disrupting effects and new "problems." The high rate of growth is sustained by the interplay between mass applications of technological innovations based on additions to the stock of knowledge and further additions to that stock. The disrupting effects are those imposed by the rapid rate of change in economic and social structure. The problems are the unexpected and unforeseeable results of the spread of innovations (with emphasis on the new and unknown indicated by that term). Added to this is the range of problems raised by the slow spread of economic growth to the less-developed countries, all of which have a long history, separate and relatively isolated from the areas within which modern economic growth originated. Thus, concurrent with the remarkable positive achievements of modern economic growth are unexpected negative results even within the developed countries, while the less-developed countries are struggling in the attempt to use the large potential of modern technology in order to assume an adequate role in the one and interdependent world (from which they cannot withdraw even if they wished to do so).

We have stressed the problem aspects of modern economic growth because they indicate the directions of further research in the field. These aspects, the "surprises" and the implicit explanatory "puzzles," are problems not only in the sense of departures from the desirable (that may call for policy amelioration) but also in the sense that our quantitative data and particularly our analytical hypotheses do not provide us with a full view and explanation. As already noted, the conventional measures of national product and its components do not reflect many costs of adjustment in the economic and social structures to the channeling of major technological innovations; and, indeed, also omit some positive returns. The earlier theory that underlies these measures defined the productive factors in a relatively narrow way, and left the rise in productivity as an unexplained gap, as a measure of our ignorance. This shortcoming of the theory in confrontation with the new findings, has led to a lively discussion in the field in recent years, and to attempts to expand the national accounting framework to encompass the so far hidden but clearly important costs, for example, in education as capital investment, in the shift to urban life, or in the pollution and other negative results of mass production. These efforts will also uncover some so far unmeasured positive returns—in the way of greater health and longevity, greater mobility, more leisure, less income inequality, and the like. The related efforts to include the additions to knowledge in the framework of economic analysis, the greater attention to the uses of time and to the household as the focus of economic decision not only on consumption but also on investment, are steps in the same direction. It seems fairly clear that a number of analytical and measurement problems remain in the theory and in the evaluation of economic growth in the developed countries themselves and that one may look forward to major changes in some aspects of the analysis, in national economic accounting, and in the stock of empirical findings, which will occupy economists in the developed countries in the years ahead.

For the less-developed countries the tasks of economic research are somewhat different: the great need is for a wider supply of tested data, which means essentially data that have been scrutinized in the process of use for economic analysis. As already noted, the stock of data and of economic analysis is far poorer for these countries than that for the developed countries —a parallel to the smaller relative supply of material capital. Yet in recent years there has been rapid accumulation of data for many less-developed areas, other than those that, like Mainland China, view data as information useful to their enemies (external or internal) and are therefore either not revealed by government or possibly not even collected. The lag has been in the analysis of these data by economists and other social science scholars, because of the scarcity of such scholars, who cannot be spared for research within the less-developed countries themselves, and because of the natural preoccupation of economists in the developed countries with the problems of their own countries. One may hope, but with limited expectations, that the task of refining analysis and measurement in the developed countries will not be pursued to the exclusion or neglect of badly needed studies of the less-developed countries, studies that would deal with the quantitative bases and institutional conditions of their performance, in addition to those concentrating on what appear to be their major bottlenecks and the seemingly optimal policy prescriptions.

Innovations and Adjustments
in Economic Growth

1. Introduction

Innovation may be defined as application of a new way of attaining a useful end. All three characteristics are important. It must be a *new* way. It must be for some *positive* end. It must be an *application*, distinct from an idea, or theory, or design. Since application implies relation to some positive end, differences among these ends, with inferrable differences in the methods of attaining them, allow us to distinguish economic from other innovations; or technological from social innovations.

We focus our discussion on technological innovations, although consideration of some of their contributions will also involve adjustments that represent institutional and even ideological changes. We concentrate on the technological innovations because they are a major permissive factor in modern economic growth, and because they stand out so clearly and conspicuously as we look back at the history of the economically developed countries.

To quote Professor Nathan Rosenberg, technology refers to "man's capacity to control and to manipulate the natural envi-

Expanded version of a lecture in May, 1972, in the Davidson Lecture Series, The Whittemore School of Business and Economics, University of New Hampshire. Reprinted from *The Swedish Journal of Economics*, Vol. 74, no. 4, December, 1972, 431–51.

ronment in the fulfillment of human goals, and to make the environment more responsive to human needs." [1] Particularly relevant here are the needs and goals satisfied by economic goods. It may be helpful to think of technology as knowledge relevant to man's capacity to control the natural environment for the production of the economic goods that enter final product in national economic accounting. The definition excludes new arrangements among human beings themselves (except as part of nature in medical treatment), and thus omits important sources of increased productivity. But much of what we shall be saying of innovations in the material technique of production of economic goods involving manipulation of the natural environment will also bear upon innovations in economic and social institutions and practices.

Even with this narrow definition of technology and technological innovations, a variety of classifications of the latter can be suggested as helpful in understanding their impact on economic growth and the problems of adjustment. In the next section of the paper, we present preliminary classifications of technological innovation, with cursory illustrations from the experience of modern economic growth. In the following section we attempt to outline the types of adjustment that the technological innovations call for. As will become apparent our meager knowledge of the field permits only tentative classifications and conjectural statements—but even these should prove useful, given the recent interest in some of the negative consequences of technological progress and modern economic growth.

2. Classifications of Technological Innovations

The classifications below are mostly dichotomies, and have not been tested by application to empirical evidence. While they may prove fuzzy in actual use, they provide the framework for later consideration of adjustments to innovations, which are as inherent in the process of economic growth as the exploitation of innovations for greater productivity and higher product per capita.

[1] See his *Technology and American Economic Growth* (New York: Harper & Row, 1972), p. 18. In a footnote the author stresses that this definition is based on a view of man and environment that omits some important aspects of modern technology.

Cost-Reducing and Demand-Creating · The first of these two classes comprises innovations which reduce the real costs of production but leave the product basically the same, except for possibly minor changes in quality. The second class comprises innovations that create new products, and thus new demand—new in the sense that the demand was previously non-existent because the good was not available. The first type of technological innovation shifts the existing cost curve downwards; the second creates an entirely new production function, corresponding to the new product.

Setting aside the difficulties that may be involved in drawing the line between a new product and quality changes of an old one, two comments should be made about the dichotomy, which takes on greater significance as we deal with other classifications with which it can be combined. First, the distinction depends upon specificity in the definition of the product. If we conceive of a product as much wider than a given consumer commodity and, for example, think in terms of light washable fabrics rather than of cotton clothing, the invention of a synthetic material like nylon appears to be an innovation that substantially reduced the real cost of the known product, not one that created a distinctly new product. Likewise one can argue that air transportation brought a reduction in the cost of rapid transport, or that the telephone merely reduced the costs of communication (presumably feasible earlier by rapid couriers or long distance signalling devices). But this wider view of need categories, while important for and relevant to the possible competition between old and new products satisfying closely related or similar needs, must not obliterate real differences between old and new products—in their technological bases, in their time and space location within the economy, and in the significant changes in consumption and investment patterns involved. A tractor is only another version of a workhorse, but it does not originate in the agricultural sector; its production is subject to constraints unlike those of the production of workhorses, and its performance is vastly different. The same can be said of vacuum cleaners, modern washing machines and dishwashers, when compared with the services of domestic servants or housewives. The demand-creating, new-product type of technological innovation has a far wider range than the definition of a few broad groups of human needs suggests.

Secondly, one and the same technological innovation may fall in the cost-reducing class with respect to one product, and in the demand-creating class with respect to another. Thus, in the case of tractors, the innovation is clearly cost-reducing as far as agricultural crops and food products are concerned—since they are not used to produce new *types* of *foods*. But they are a new type of *fixed capital* in agriculture, compared with older types like horses, mules, and oxen. In general, since the output of one production process can function as the input of another, a new capital good or raw material can be viewed as a demand-creating technological innovation at one level and a cost-reducing innovation at the level of the old finished product to which the new input is being applied. It is only when the new capital good or new material permits, for the first time, the production of a new final consumer good, that the technological innovation belongs solely to the demand-creating, new-product class.

CONSUMER GOODS AND PRODUCTION INPUTS · This distinction has been suggested by the comment just made. The consumer goods class covers the new-product, demand-creating innovations; the production input class covers those that affect consumer goods only by cutting their production costs. In a sense, all technological innovations affect consumer goods, but only some involve new types of consumer goods.

This rather uneven dichotomy—one part containing only a component of the demand-creating innovations, the other containing its remaining component and all the cost-reducing innovations—is justified by two arguments. First, the decisions regarding consumer goods innovations, creations of previously unknown consumer goods, are responses made by ultimate consumers, in their individual and household capacity, or through their collective agencies (e.g., government demonstrating demand for final goods beneficial to its citizens). The other group of technological innovations, whether they represent cost-reductions of consumer or other goods, or new types of capital goods and raw materials, is subject primarily to entrepreneurial decisions of private and public entrepreneurs. The factors involved in their choices, the economic rationales underlying them, are presumably different from those that govern the choices of ultimate consumers with respect to new consumer goods—even though, in many cases, the entrepreneurs try to forecast the latter. This comment reflects the working hypothesis that choices by consumers with respect to new consumer goods (excluding minor and frivolous types) are not much influenced by advertising or by other strenuous efforts by business entrepreneurs to influence the structure of consumer tastes. It is the consumers who have made the major choices with respect to the new consumer goods that have emerged in the course of modern economic growth—in food, clothing, shelter, household equipment, transportation, health, and recreation—sometimes to the pleasant surprise and sometimes to the unexpected dismay of the pioneering entrepreneurs. And in observing the spread of consumer tastes from the free developed countries to others, where neither advertising nor consumer sovereignty is significant, we find a similarity of choices. Consumers even in the Communist countries are evincing a desire for passenger cars, television sets, household electrical equipment, organized recreation, and foreign travel. The point is of some importance in any consideration of control or guidance of technological innovations—which, for the first class means control over ultimate consumers, and for the second, control over entrepreneurs, private or public.

Another argument for the dichotomy is to indicate that much of technological progress in modern economic growth is concentrated in the creation of new consumer goods, not of better machinery and raw materials for producing the old goods. This concentration is apparent in the structure of household consumption (or, more accurately, purchases of consumer goods by households) in the economically developed countries, in the direct service components of government consumption (in the health, education, and recreation fields), and even in the residential construction component of capital formation. So much of it is associated with new types of goods and industries that did not exist or were not known, say 50 to 100 years ago. The complexes of consumer goods related to the motor car, airplane, public utilities, electric household appliances, moving pictures, radio, and television—and for that matter the educational and health services with relatively new and sophisticated procedures—are in that group. It is hardly an accident that much of technological invention was devoted to final consumer goods, and was directed at the creation of new types in addition to the reduction in the real cost of the old. Given the low price elasticity of demand for the old final consumer goods, e.g., food and clothing, once technology had brought their unit costs down to low levels, the large potential lay in tapping the demand for a distinctly new type of service.[2] Telephones provided consumer service for which no really close counterpart had existed in the past, no matter how much effort might have been expended; and this is true of much of the complex electrical and electronic household equipment.

DIFFERENCES IN MAGNITUDE · Whether cost-reducing or demand-creating, whether resulting in new consumer goods or directly affecting only production inputs, technological innovations differ widely in magnitude, viewed in terms of larger final output, i.e., final consumption supplemented by capital investment; or, perhaps even in the more clearly positive aspects of economic growth, in terms of increasing ultimate consumption and its structural changes. We have no measures of these effects of *individual* technological innovations, and to obtain them we would have to resolve several difficult problems. There is the obvious problem of defining the unit. Should the introduction of steam power be defined as a single innovation, or should Watt's stationary steam engine be defined as one, its application to internal water transport as another, and its application to land transportation as a third, or should one subdivide even further? There is the problem of identifying the time and place in which the effects are felt. Should it be, for Watt's stationary engine, the first two or three decades upon introduction in the United Kingdom, or the next century the world over? There is the problem of distinguishing between the first order of direct effects and the next orders of indirect or linkage effects—in the way of stimulating complementary services and innovations. But while such problems abound, and no relevant measures are available, some reasonable judgments can be made of magnitudes in terms of the effects on final household consumption. Thus, over the longer period of growth, Watt's stationary steam engine appears

[2] For a major analysis of the central role of demand, final and derived, in determining the focus and volume of technological invention and change, see Jacob Schmookler, *Invention and Economic Growth* (Cambridge, Mass.: Harvard University Press, 1966).

to be a technological innovation far greater in magnitude than, say, the chemical bleaching of cotton cloth; or, to use a more recent illustration, the passenger car seems to be an innovation of greater magnitude than the quick-freezing of foods. One may then ask what general factors, missing from lesser innovations, render some technological innovations major.

Several tentative answers can be given. First, a technological innovation that results in a new, common, and basic production input—such as power—would presumably have widespread effects that would eventually change the size and structure of ultimate household consumption. Each new type of power or energy that emerged in the course of modern economic growth—steam power, electricity, the internal combustion engine, short waves, and most recently atomic energy—if this be a proper listing—displays unique characteristics and is potentially more useful than others for a variety of applications. Once it has found the proper envelopes and has, in the course of increasing use, been understood sufficiently to permit effective utilization, it affects final product in many cost-reducing and new-goods-creating ways. The same is true of new types of widely used industrial materials—steel, copper, aluminum, plastics, etc.—which often have to be introduced to serve as the most effective envelopes for the new types of power; as materials for the new types of tools that are capable of operating at the high speeds or at the high pressures possible with the new sources of power. An innovation involving a new type of power, or a new type of industrial material, or a new type of mechanism for transmitting power is a basic component in the production system of many industrial branches, either already or soon to be operating. It is obviously of much greater magnitude than an innovation affecting a relatively limited, specialized branch of production, with a rather specialized type of process.

Second, a major technological innovation that affects the basic characteristics of the production process, through changes in sources of power, materials, or major tools, increases overall productivity markedly and permits a larger final output with the same or a lesser input of resources. But it has an additional major effect on the structure, and possibly the volume of ultimate consumption, through changes in conditions of participation of man in the production process. If more advanced types of industrial power make for greater economies of scale, and if the scale of plant and firm increases in response (the latter made feasible also by complementary innovations in communication), the role of the human agent participating in the larger firm and plant also changes, as do the conditions of his life, in so far as it is affected by the employment and income pattern. Thus, a major technological innovation with direct effect in greatly reducing the costs of known types of consumer goods may have another major influence through radically transforming the mode of participation of men in production, and changing the size and nature of the communities in which they live. This is a form of demand-creation not associated with the invention of new consumer goods but with changes in conditions of life and work imposed by the transformation of the production system by the major technological innovation. It may be defined as demand-imposition rather than demand-creation; although the former term carries too negative a connotation, suggesting that the new patterns of life and work are distinctly less desirable than the old. This is not necessarily the case, as our discussion of adjustments in the next section suggests. All that the term is intended to convey is that the new type of demand may be said to have originated in the transformation of life and work conditions, not autonomously from innovations that yielded new consumer goods.

Finally, even the technological innovations that specifically create new consumer goods differ substantially in magnitude, depending on the weight of the consumption component and the elasticity of its response. Thus innovations that determine the location of ultimate consumers on the land affect the demand for housing and all the related equipment, a substantial category within total consumption outlay; and they may lead to complementary changes in the services needed to maintain residences and household equipment. By contrast, even technologically sophisticated changes in the chemical provenance of clothing materials, while leading to expansion of synthetic fabrics at the expense of cotton and other vegetable fiber textiles, will hardly have repercussions that substantially transform the structure, or perceptibly augment the volume, of household consumption as measured in the national economic accounts. In general, if a significantly large component of household consumption is comprised of low-cost, efficiently produced goods, with a low price elasticity of demand, even technically significant changes in it are not likely to have much economic effect. In a sense, the effects of innovations related to location of households are large because of the high price and quality elasticity of demand for the characteristics of housing and environment, and for ease of mobility to optimize the adjustments to conflicts between work and living. These may be contrasted with the low price elasticity of response of foods, clothing, or the simpler aspects of shelter (such as fuel, illumination, and the like).

These factors which make some innovations major strongly suggest other characteristics which presumably are not found (or occur infrequently) in lesser innovations.[3] The most important such characteristic is that a major technological innovation requires a long period of sustained improvement and many significant complementary innovations (some of them also major, but derivative) before its ramified and significant effects on the economy in general and on the volume and structure of household consumption in particular are realized.

Consider, for example, a single major innovation like Watt's stationary steam engine. To be at all feasible, it required major modifications in the production of boilers, pistons, and cylinders; and then complementary inventions were necessary for the evolution of the different forms of transmission of work energy through beams, cranks, shafts, etc. Originally, it was essentially a skeleton that had to be fleshed out with many subsidiary inventions, continuous improvements, etc., in order to achieve its efficiency—merely as a stationary engine. Indeed, an invention is major precisely because it is a skeleton on which a number of potentialities for far-reaching improvements are overlaid in the course of time. And some of these in our illustration required better metal machining and better industrial materials to contain the higher steam pressures—thus giving rise to a host of complementary inventions and innovations, many with a transfer value but all indispensable for realizing the great potentials

---

[3] It is difficult to confine ourselves here to a dichotomy, since volume and structure of ultimate consumption may be affected by a *continuum* of technological innovations, once the unit of innovation has been properly defined. The classification into major and minor innovations is thus a crude oversimplification.

of Watt's engine. This provision of a framework for a vast variety of internal improvements and complementary innovations is
found when we consider the effects of modern power sources
that make for economies of large-scale plants; or those of the
passenger car with its demands for a network of highways, a
supply of tires and tire materials, and not least, the numerous
servicing activities, many of which in turn require new tools and
new inventions to make them reasonably economical.

But one may go further and point out that one major technological innovation, like Watt's stationary steam engine, may be
the first in a series of innovations, all exploiting a single source
in nature—so that the technological and economic success of
one application makes it feasible and attractive to extend the
exploitation of that source to other uses. Several examples are
the familiar successions in the use of steam power that ended
with ocean transportation; in the use of electric power that
moved from illumination and industrial power to the fractional
motors in household appliances; and in the use of the internal
combustion engine that moved from tractors, passenger cars,
and trucks, to airplanes. In the case of new industrial materials,
enthusiastic extensions have been made in the uses of cast and
bar iron in eighteenth-century England (often inappropriate
uses and later abandoned); [4] and similarly in the movement of
steel from industrial purposes to residential construction and
small-scale bottling and packaging material. The important
point here is that many major technological innovations are applications of new major sources of power, or new chemical combinations of distinctive quality, and make up a connected series
that adds to the potentials of each application the much wider
potentials of all the other applications of the same source.

Given these characteristics of major technological innovations,
it is obvious that a long time is required for the full exploitation
of their potentials in raising productivity, augmenting final
product, and changing its composition. It took about a century
for steam power to evolve from the revolutionary breakthrough
in the 1770's to the final domination of ocean transportation and

---

[4] See T. S. Ashton, *Iron and Steel in the Industrial Revolution*, 2nd ed.
(Manchester: Manchester University Press, 1951), Chapter II, pp. 25–60,
particularly on the competition for alternative uses between cast iron and
wrought iron.

the completion of the basic railroad network in the economically developed countries in the third quarter of the nineteenth century. It has taken almost as long for electric power to move from the power stations of the 1880's into households in the recent decades. It has taken the internal combustion engine in cars over half a century to evolve from a useful capital good on U.S. farms at the beginning of World War I to a mass consumption durable good affecting residential housing and life in general well after World War II. One may speculate on the time it will take before atomic energy works its way through the successive developments to tap its full potentials—not too clear even today, over a quarter of a century since its first major application for war purposes. The long periods of development following gestation are particularly relevant to the consideration of the adjustments to be discussed in the next section. These adjustments partly explain the long development periods and can be understood only if we abandon the romantic notion of sudden and rapid breakthroughs that produce major results within a few years.

Another implication, not closely related to our theme since we are concentrating here on *results* of technological innovations, not on their *sources,* may nevertheless be noted. Clearly, the major technological innovations are closely tied to fundamental aspects of the natural environment upon which basic research in the natural sciences has a direct bearing. The *major* character of the single technological innovation, and even more of the series originating in a single source, is closely correlated with the *central* place that the underlying source (whether it be energy, in various manifestations, or chemical structure, or transmission mechanism) occupies in the concern of the relevant scientific discipline. The capacity to identify and understand the basic aspects of our natural environment is, in a way, a precondition that makes major technological innovations possible; while their applications, once made, and the realization of their full potential over a longer period provide a positive feedback to our understanding of these basic aspects. This dependence upon contributions of pure science and research is obvious in the cases of steam, electric energy, electronics, and atomic energy, and of the chemistry of industrial and related materials. And in recent years the biological sciences have yielded insight into the reproductive mechanisms upon which vegetable and animal products depend. Thus many technological innovations are major because they exploit the basic natural forces that are the concern of the scientific disciplines; and in the course of this exploitation they continue, for a long while, to enrich our knowledge of these forces sufficiently to provide the foundation for additional applications and improvements. One interesting consequence of this interplay, which extends over long periods, is the difficulty of realizing early in the process the full potentials of a major innovation, or a connected series of them. It is doubtful, for example, that the full potentials of atomic energy or space exploration are clearly perceptible even today—both in the way of positive contributions and of undesirable spill-offs.

3. Groups of Adjustments

In suggesting classes of technological innovation we had in mind their contributions to increased volume and changing structure of final consumption—the latter taken as the simplest and least equivocal single index of the positive aspect of economic growth. We come now to other consequences of technological innovation, viewed here as adjustments by man and society in the attempt to take full advantage of these innovations on the one hand, and to overcome any dislocative and undesirable effects on the other. The task of mapping out established consequences, positive or negative, of technological innovations, other than their contribution to greater productivity and greater consumption, is an ambitious one. The interrelations are complex; the sequences in which a consequence later appears as a cause are long; and the separation of effects of technology from those of other factors, in both economic growth and its costs, is difficult. We can only suggest preliminary groupings of such consequences viewed as adjustments and order the discussion around three such groupings. The first comprises institutional and related ideological changes, which may be viewed as complementary adjustments, needed to permit adequate exploitation of the potentials of technological innovations. The second deals with the dislocative effects of these innovations—those that reduce adequate economic opportunities to some sectors or groups in the economy that suffer from the competitive effects of the new methods or goods, or from the reduced employment that often follows. The third grouping comprises such negative consequences of technological innovations as the depletion of natural resources and pollution. These three groups still exclude some major consequences of technological innovations of the second and higher order of remove; but pursuing these higher order consequences would take us too far afield.

COMPLEMENTARY ADJUSTMENTS · Technological innovations are subject to constraints, in the sense that their economical use requires a certain scale of operation, an adequate input of fixed capital and skilled or disciplined labor, and a variety of other conditions. Most important, these requirements for efficient and economical operation, in the case of major innovations, are likely to differ from those characterizing the older and established technology. Where these requirements involve further complementary technological changes, the given innovation will spark them—a point touched upon in the discussion above. But here we are concerned with requirements that involve changes in institutions, and in the responses of participants in the production processes—changes needed to provide the proper institutional channels and forms for the new technology and to supply the workers and entrepreneurs to man it. These changes are called for because the old institutional channels are geared to an older technology and are not suitable for the new; and because the supply of participants is distributed in response to the older production arrangements and does not fit the needs of the technological innovation.

An enormously wide variety of such complementary adjustments in social and legal institutions, in the distribution and equipment of participants, and in the very governing notions of society has been made in continuous response to the stream of technological innovations. Each new institution, view, or pattern of living and work of the participants, once introduced, assumed a life and effect of its own. There has been, among these adjustments, a series of legal and social innovations, new ways of organizing economic units and establishing the relations within them of the cooperating parts; while the increase in the productive power of man, based on and coupled with a revolutionary extension of man's knowledge of the universe in which he lives, has changed his outlook on nature and society. Thus, in addition to the purely economic responses, there have been a number of responses in the institutional and social framework within which economic processes took place, and in the structure and scales of values by which men were guided.

In the present connection, we make three broad comments on this wide range of complementary adjustments to technological innovations in the course of modern economic growth. First, the emergence of the legal and social innovations required by the major technological innovations was a slow process for two reasons: the experience was new and, usually, alternative and conflicting ways of attaining the desired end had to be weighed. Thus, when the steam railroads emerged as enterprises requiring enormous amounts of fixed capital investment and a new organization to replace the individual or family firm prevalent theretofore, some time elapsed before the modern corporation emerged as a legal innovation; and even more time elapsed before it was realized that such monopolistic corporations required close supervision and regulation by the state to prevent abuses. When wage employment became prevalent and self-employed workers ceased to be the dominant group in the labor force, it took some time before workers' unions attained a legal existence and could play their proper role within the economic structure. The spread of some major technological innovations was slow partly because of the time required to mobilize capital and labor, and particularly because of the time needed to formulate acceptable legal and institutional changes. The same may be said of other major complementary adjustments, for example, the shift in the employment system from the assignment of people to jobs on the traditional basis of personal knowledge or family affiliation to the modern basis of relatively objective tests of qualification for the job. This important shift must have taken a long time to become established and effective. It is in the interplay of technological and social changes that the key to the process of economic growth lies; and it is this interplay that accounts for the length of time that passes before full integration of a major technological innovation into the productive and social system is attained.

Second, in the course of the development of the legal and social innovations required to channel technological innovations effectively, the government plays a major role. It is the authority that makes the overriding decisions concerning some of the new adjustments needed. This has been a continuing function, manifested recently in legislation covering atomic energy. Even if the sovereign state had not had other responsibilities in connection with the dislocative and negative consequences of technological innovations (to be noted below), the need to referee and encourage the legal and institutional innovations for the more efficient channeling of technological innovations would, in itself, have greatly expanded its functions and increased its importance. Furthermore, disparities between social and private returns, so often found in the fields of research and education, as well as in some large and venturesome capital investments, imposed an additional responsibility on the central government in a market economy—one, in fact, greatly augmented by the scientific basis of many major technological innovations in modern economic growth; and by the enormous capital investment that they required, under conditions of limited knowledge of the potentials and prospects that made the ventures too risky for private enterprise.

Third, the numerous and varied adjustments by individual participants in the economic process represented a major transformation of their pattern of living. They involved changes in location, shifts in labor force status to that of employees, more schooling and training in order to satisfy objective criteria of competence, participation in highly organized large plants and enterprises, and so on. Urbanization, membership in large impersonal organizations, higher levels of education and consumption, different patterns of family life, and increasing secularization have all, to varying extent, been responses to the requirements imposed by the exploitation of the successive technological innovations. And this transformation, of both the economic and noneconomic conditions of life and work, was so far-reaching that it may not be possible to establish an adequate calculus of costs and returns for comparison with the pre-existing patterns of life and work.

This does not mean that none of the components involved can be measured and compared. One can, and I have tried to do so elsewhere, estimate the comparative costs of living in the countryside and the cities in an attempt to correct the present measures of growth for the effect of the shift of population to the more expensive urban agglomerations. One can, and this has been the increasing concern of many economists, treat education as capital investment, and recalculate consumption and capital investment in a system that recognizes education as a requirement of modern economic growth and of the higher technical level of the current production system. One can also revise our current national product estimates by treating much of government consumption as intermediate product, on the proper ground that such outlays are for the purpose of lubricating the wheels of our complicated production system and represent adjustments imposed by the complexities and some defects of the latter when left to the unrestrained play of market forces.[5] But while these are useful experiments that would yield estimates of greater relevance and insight than those in our conventional economic accounting, many major incomparable elements will remain for which no acceptable estimate can be devised. To use a simple example: the transformation that produces a structure of the consumption of a modern urban worker so different from that of a traditional farm worker of the past presents a major index number problem, with different results arrived at depending upon whether the quantity or price pattern of one group or the other is used. But this difficulty is minor compared with problems in attempting to measure the advantages of an objective criterion for employment rather than the traditional nepotism of blood and family ties; or in weighing the comparative disadvantages of being a cog in a big but efficient machine and of being an independent worker with low productivity and subject to the vagaries of a market and the possible exploitation by powerful market intermediaries. The adjustments to the new patterns of life and work emerging in response to the potentials of modern technology are so far-reaching that no simple, single valued measure, or even a battery of quantitative tests, would

[5] Illustrative calculations dealing with these "hidden" costs of economic growth (and hence of technological innovation) can be found in my *Economic Growth of Nations: Total Output and Production Structure* (Cambridge, Mass.: Harvard University Press, 1971), Chapter II, pp. 75–98. A more recent recalculation of conventional gross national product for the United States, to approximate an index of welfare, is given in William D. Nordhaus and James Tobin, "Is Growth Obsolete?" in *Economic Research: Retrospect and Prospect*, The 50th Anniversary Colloquia Series, Vol. V (New York: National Bureau of Economic Research, 1972).

yield a fully meaningful comparison. One must rely on a number of quantitative and qualitative analyses which enrich the comparison but cannot be reduced to a simple measure of more or less—unless one limits oneself to measurable goods and such simple gauges of inputs as manhours of work and values of material capital investment.

Because the differences produced by the complementary adjustments to modern technology are many-faceted, discussion of the problems is usually biased, stressing one or another feature and ignoring the many corollaries. It is all too easy to expatiate on the evils of alienation attendant in work in the modern plants without recognizing the brutal conditions of hard and inefficient work in pre-industrial times; or to discuss exploitation of labor in modern times without recognizing that the modern system of recruitment on the basis of objective criteria of merit represents a milder and less brutal form of exploitation than that prevailing in the older status societies with rank based on blood lines and family ties. By contrast it is all too easy to hold forth on the great achievements of modern technology and high levels of consumption without taking into account the costs of transformation, and the burdens that a powerful economic society may impose on its deviant members who put less value on material achievement and more value on non-material goods. In the light of this discussion, it is obvious that the currently accepted, conventional economic accounts represent one rather specifically defined system of valuation and selection that omits many costs, as well as many returns; and much of the current criticism of the system is, in turn, a biased selection of many omitted costs, without adequate attempt to balance them by omitted returns.[6]

[6] It may be unnecessary but prudent to add that the comments on the limitations of conventional national economic accounting and the biases in the current criticism of the measures of economic growth should not be taken as a denial of the value of the conventional measures for many uses, or of the criticism as a stimulus for more extended and relevant measurement. They are meant to emphasize the frequent failure to recognize the limiting definitions and assumptions that underlie the conventional national accounting measures; and the biased concentration of the criticisms on the omitted costs to the exclusion of omitted returns. The discussion implies the need for more sophisticated treatment of conventional measures and of their possible extension; and for the combination of the concentrated attention to what appear to be current problems and deficiencies with a longer historical perspective in which the technological and other innovations that led to the problems become apparent, and in which the solutions to similar problems that emerged in the past are brought to light.

DISLOCATION EFFECTS · Technological innovations may dislocate the productive factors, whether natural resources, reproducible capital, or labor. If the innovation lessens the real costs of existing goods by sharply reducing labor input, and if these goods are subject to price inelastic demand (both domestic and foreign), a substantial part of the previously employed labor force will be forced to seek alternative employment. Or if the innovation introduces a new type of capital or consumer good, superior to the older types serving similar uses, it renders all productive factors involved in the older goods obsolete (e.g., the replacement of horses by tractors in agriculture and of handicraft products by machine-produced textiles). In such cases labor, reproducible capital, and land become unwanted in the older uses; and are forced to seek economically warranted use elsewhere. Or, what is less frequent, the technological innovation may bid resources away from some older industries, forcing them to adjust to a greater scarcity of production inputs than had prevailed theretofore.

There is nothing accidental about the first two types of dislocation, the obsolescence of some older resources and the unemployment of others. They are the effects of competition by the cost-reducing or demand-creating new technological process. The technologies of all sectors of production are interrelated, which means that a technological innovation that has emerged in response to some specific need in sector A may have cost-reducing effects in sector B; and that no sector characterized by older technology is free from the possible effects of technological innovation elsewhere. The internal combustion engine, applied in its early stages to local transportation, was envisaged as a source of mechanized energy in agriculture, and before long the necessary complementary inventions were made. The mechanization of spinning and weaving, originally applied to one textile material, cotton, was bound to spread to other textiles. In general, the forward movement of technology in one major production sector creates pressures to spread the advance to other originally unaffected branches. Only some service activities, in which mass production is impossible, are free from such pressures of purely technological progress; but they, for that very reason, are subject to pressures of progress in knowledge, which they apply or spread (as in the case of the medical, educational, legal, and other professional services).

The problems created by these dislocations lie, of course, in the costs and difficulty of moving from established uses, that have become obsolete, to new uses. The specific characteristics of material capital, whether natural resources or existing reproducible capital, may limit mobility to alternative uses. Pasture land may not be good for anything else, and decreasing demand for horses cannot be successfully adjusted to, given the stocks of horses for which no alternative economically adequate uses are available. In the case of labor, the costs of movement, particularly for older members in established occupations, may be extremely high—much higher than for younger and recent entrants into the labor force. These obsolescence- and unemployment-inducing effects of technological innovation are continuous in modern economic growth. In its earlier stages they affected primarily labor and capital in agriculture and in the handicrafts; in the later stages they affected capital and labor in the lagging industries (which had previously been among the growth industries) such as cotton textiles, coal mining, or simpler types of furniture, clothing, and leather manufacturing. In other words, the problem of obsolescent and unemployed productive resources is a constant accompaniment of the continuous sequence of technological innovations in modern economic growth.

A somewhat milder, but even more pervasive type of dislocation generated by technological innovations is the inequality in returns to various groups and sectors, depending upon their relative benefits from current technological progress. Even if the resources in the older sectors remain fully employed, the sectors profiting from current technological innovations, the so-called growth sectors, will tend to yield higher returns to capital and labor than the others—a reflection of the greater quasi-rent opportunities within them represented by their rapid technological advance and of the use of the market mechanism to enlarge the flow of productive resources to them. This set of income inequalities is built into the mechanism of modern economic growth, and reflects the concentration of technological change in some sectors and the differing lag and obsolescence of others. Here, too, reduction of such inequalities through the movement of capital and labor from the lower-paying sectors and occupations to the higher-paying faces obstacles to mobility. The particular locus of such inequalities is continuously shifting, but they are always present so long as growth occurs, because technological changes have an unequal impact within the economy and society.

Adjustment to the dislocations—obsolescence, unemployment, and income differentials—caused by technological innovations, is commonly made by the movement of labor force and capital away from the affected fields. But for obvious reasons mobility for some factors is limited; and, as already indicated, the shift itself is costly and uncertain. Where economic adjustments cause prolonged unemployment, losses, and persistent income inferiority, political and other pressures are exercised to reduce the competitive effects of technological innovations on the older sectors, to protect them by limiting the application of innovations, or to assist them by the transfer of extra resources, usually under the auspices of the government—the agency expected to deal with such economic and social problems. These resistances to the competitive and destructive effects of technological innovations and to the economic growth that they generate are a common feature of the history of economically developed countries. I cannot deal with this aspect of the growth process in detail, but must stress two general implications. First, because of such resistance, economic growth is far from a self-sustaining and automatic process. There may be and there have been cases where the resistance was so great, and the price of overcoming it so high, that economic growth did not proceed at an adequate pace. Second, it is the sovereign government that is subjected to the pressures by a given group for protection from the possibly negative effects of technological innovation and economic growth. One of its major tasks is to try to shape some consensus, to reduce these pressures so that the technological innovations needed for further economic growth are not too costly in terms of dislocation of the older sectors and of widened economic inequalities. Governmental policies aimed on the one hand at facilitating mobility through provision of greater educational and other opportunities and on the other hand at reducing the negative impact of growth by subsidies and protection, have been varied, continuous, and numerous. It must be kept in mind that the dislocating effects of technological innovations are pregnant with potential conflict and require continuous adjustments to offset the obsolescence, unemployment, and relative deterioration in income position of some groups in economic society. The "creative destruction" of which Schumpeter wrote so illuminatingly and eloquently was not only innovative creation by entrepreneurs, but also *destruction*—and it is the latter and the adjustments and resistances to it that are emphasized here.[7]

DEPLETION AND ENRICHMENT OF ENVIRONMENT · Since technology, as defined above, is manipulation of the natural environment for the benefit of man (and, in our terms, for economic production), there has always been a concern as to the limits of the finite environment, the supply of irreproducible natural resources. This concern was stated most strikingly in the first edition of Malthus's *Essay on Population*. It persisted through the decades of the Classical and Marxian schools to the second half of the nineteenth century but became muted because experience showed that the initial assumption that technological progress could not compensate for possible exhaustion of natural resources was unrealistic. But this fear of the natural limits has always been present, while dormant at times; and has grown recently with the observation of negative effects of economic growth—not on the supply of natural resources necessary for direct economic goods (such as productive land, mineral deposits, water, etc.), but on the general environment in the way of pollution, crowding, noise and the like. In so far as technological innovations had these potentially negative effects—not only depletion of economically limited natural resources but also deterioration of the general and vital environment—some adjustments were presumably required; and, indeed, continuous adjustments have been made in the course of technological innovation and economic growth. Such adjustments will continue to be made as additional negative effects become manifest; or as

[7] The discussion of these dislocative effects of technological innovation is necessarily limited. If complete, it would involve a wide range of aspects of income inequality and mobility of productive resources. In the latter connection, it should be noted that, like the recent entrants into the labor force, recent inflows of savings into investment are the most mobile. The devices for mobilizing capital for new major technological breakthroughs would have to be considered, together with the institutional channels for better allocation of labor resources and changes in their quality. In the text we noted only those aspects of the adjustments that suggest the serious problems generated by displacement effects of technological innovations, and the acute conflicts and resistance that may follow.

the developments in basic science and technology lead autonomously to an enrichment of the environment, thus eliminating the drafts upon it that may have been needed earlier.

Within the limits of this discussion, one can make only a few general comments. First, all technology involves drafts upon the finite components of the natural environment and hence disturbs what would be considered ecological equilibrium. But if such interference by human manipulation may deplete or worsen the environment, this technology can also enrich it. Resources are a function of technology, and technological advance can, for example, move to oil from coal or to atomic energy from oil long before the supplies of coal and oil are exhausted. Admittedly, the environment within which man operates is finite, but its limits are a function of technology, i.e., of the capacity to penetrate further into the oceans, the earth, and space. While every technological advance must eventually have some undesirable effects, it is reasonable to assume that when the latter emerge, man's capacity to deal with them will be no less than it was in the past. The net balance is unlikely to be so negative that the original technological innovation that produced these undesirable effects will be abandoned.

Second, the long time involved in major technological innovations and their novelty make it almost impossible to predict and prepare for the ultimate effects, both positive and negative. This failure to foresee and prepare is of greater concern with reference to the negative than to the positive effects. Thus, the rapid spread to mass use of suburban railroads and passenger cars—new durable goods that affected location and residence patterns—had the positive result (hardly foreseen even by the pioneering entrepreneurs) of permitting population with job attachments in the cities to reside in the more comfortable dormitory suburbs, but they also had the negative effect of reducing the financial viability and worsening living conditions in the central city. This process took a great deal of time; and it would have been difficult, perhaps impossible, to foresee and prepare for its consequences in the early stages. Nor, to shift to the natural environment problems, was it possible to forecast and guard against the full impact of pollution and crowding produced by the mass use of the automobile—which, in other ways, was such a boon to the population. Given the sluggishness in policy response to uncertain future consequences, there is a long delay in adjustments to the negative impacts of major technological innovations on the natural environment.

Third, economic growth in the past and the technological innovations that underlay it involved major deteriorations in the broader environment, which were eventually overcome even if with difficulty. Thus, as recently as the middle of the nineteenth century, when industrialization and urbanization proceeded at a high rate in many Western European countries, the movement into the cities meant, under the existing conditions of medical and public health services, that an increasing proportion of the population was subject to much higher rates of mortality and morbidity than those prevailing in the countryside. It took a revolution in our understanding of infectious diseases and a half century of struggle to reform sanitation and health conditions in the cities as well as a program of substantial capital investment to adjust to, and offset, this deterioration of the environment for the population of the developed countries. Further back in history, the environment of the European countries that eventually became the pioneers of modern technology deteriorated markedly, partly because the cities with their much higher death rates were beginning to be formed, and partly because their populations were exposed to sweeping epidemics of cholera, plague, and smallpox which resulted from the increased contact with the East. This deterioration of environment in the medieval times, like that of the nineteenth century, was a major, almost catastrophic negative effect, compared with which the recent urban troubles of pollution and crowding seem minor indeed. The challenges of technical innovation and economic growth were faced despite these negative effects, and the latter were overcome, if with great difficulty because of the inadequacy of the existing technology and relevant knowledge. Technology and knowledge are far more powerful now, even if resistances within the economic and social framework persist.

Fourth, we can assume from past experience that, with the knowledge and technology at our disposal, adjustments will be made to the negative effects of technological innovation in the way of depletion of resources and deterioration of the environment. We must also recognize that the response to such negative effects, particularly the one on the general environment, is slow partly because it is difficult to foresee their magnitude in the early stages of the application of an innovation, and, in many cases, the economic incentives to provide the adjustment are not existent. Consequently our current estimates of the magnitude of the deterioration and particularly of the costs of overcoming it are not likely to be realistic. The danger is that these costs are exaggerated because of the absence of what might be called technological attention to and hence experience with the problem. We have scant basis for estimating the economic costs of an *efficient* technology to deal with the problem. Nor, for lack of experience, do we have adequate knowledge of the legal and social change that would yield optimal results—just as the regulation of health and sanitary conditions in the cities that developed by the early twentieth century could hardly have been foreseen in the mid-nineteenth century. All one can argue legitimately now is that the deterioration of the environment has been neglected and calls for prompt corrective technological, and complementary social and institutional innovations. But it is unwarranted to assume that the problems are beyond the capacities of modern knowledge and technology. Indeed, they may be due to the failure of our social, political, and economic institutions to respond promptly and effectively because of the usual conflict of interests—between producers and consumers, among regions, and even among nations (in so far as the problems are worldwide). It is the social and political obstacles that are likely to be more serious than our technological capacity. Assuming that the growing impact of pollution and other negative effects force a needed social and political consensus, the adjustment is likely to come and prove as effective as past adjustments to far more critical cases of such deterioration and depletion.

4. Concluding Comments

The discussion dealt with the effects of technological innovations on productivity and final consumption and the various adjustments to them, but did not deal with the sources of these innovations (except when they were inherent in the very effects). In classifying these innovations, i.e., applications of new ways of producing economic goods, we distinguished between those that were cost-reducing without involving new goods (producer or

consumer) and those that introduced new goods—with the latter extending the variety of goods and modifying the structure
of production and consumption more directly than the former.
We distinguished between innovations that create new consumer goods and all others, because in the former class, it is
consumers, in their individual and collective capacity, who
make the choices, not the entrepreneurs who, rather, make decisions on innovations affecting production inputs. There are important autonomous factors in the choices and decisions of final consumers that are not present in those of entrepreneurs.
Finally, we distinguished between major innovations and others,
emphasizing that technological change cannot be viewed as a
series of minor steps that are grouped randomly: they come in
clusters, with a variety of complementary inventions and improvements grouped around a central major innovation. Several
important consequences follow from the emergence of such
major innovations, not the least of which is that they involve
significant complementary adjustments, transformations in the
patterns of work and living. One other consequence not stressed
in the discussion is the continuous shift of focus of the major innovations from one production sector in the economy to another.   .

The effects of innovations on the volume and changing structure of final consumption, the most acceptable index of the
positive contribution of economic growth, are familiar. Several
periods of modern economic growth can be identified with specific major innovations and the related "growth" industries or
sectors. Evidence is available on the large share of "new" goods,
new in the sense of having been generated by technological innovations within the modern period (or at varying distances in
the past), in consumer expenditures (grouped largely around the
modern public utilities, household equipment, the passenger car,
public transportation, education, and health). The discussion
dwelt rather on other effects of technological innovations—
particularly of the major ones. First, there were the institutional
and ideological changes required to channel the new technology
to effective use—a series of political, legal, and social innovations that complemented the technological change—as well as
the adaptation of the active members of society, who had to
man the new technology under the new conditions. Second, there

were the dislocations caused by innovation in the employment of resources for uses rendered obsolete by the new goods or new production methods—resources for which alternative employment at adequate economic levels is not always readily available, and whose loss or unemployment may constitute a grave economic and social problem. A similar and more pervasive impact—income inequalities between old and new sectors—is generated by technological innovations since they are generally concentrated at a given time in a few sectors and do not benefit all sectors equally. Finally, we discussed the possible depletion of, and loss in, the natural environment which may be inherent in technological innovations, since they do disturb the balance of nature for the benefit of man; and disturbance of this natural balance may carry some penalties with it. But our discussion also stressed the enrichment of the natural environment—a major contribution of technological progress—and the past, and growing, capacity of technology to overcome the negative effects of past innovations. This implies that the elimination of these effects lies in the province of the social structure. Since conflicts of interests are never ending, society is limited in effectively setting up the conditions under which the full capacity of technological power can be exercised for only desirable ends.

Limitations of knowledge prevent me from weaving the positive and negative consequences of technological innovations into a time pattern, a life-cycle model of a major innovation in which the time sequence of effects could be outlined. Such a model, if realistic, would be of great interest, and would help us to establish the relative timing and magnitude of the several effects. Thus, the positive contribution of an innovation to a country's economic growth is greatest not in its early period, when, starting from almost nothing, an innovation expands at extremely high percentage rates and shows a remarkably high rate of technological improvement—but in a later period when the resource and output base of the innovation is already sizable, while its growth rate is still substantially above that of the rest of the economy. It is also clear that the dislocation effects of an innovation assume importance in this later phase, well *after* the initial period of turbulent growth from low bases. Furthermore, it is clear that the complementary legal and social innovations emerge at some period *after* the initial phases—and the timing of these adjustments would be a matter of considerable interest. By contrast, the negative effects on the environment of a major technological innovation would, probably, come quite late in its development—after it has grown to giant magnitudes within the economy and society, and created a mass product that makes a detrimental impact on the environment, scarcely perceptible at first but increasingly formidable. These rather tentative comments suggest that the fuller meaning of the effects of technological innovation discussed above would be revealed only if we could establish a time sequence for them, with attention to their changing magnitude. Such a life-cycle model would probably indicate that the concern with depletion of environment usually comes quite late in the development of an innovation (except when its dangerous potentials are evident immediately)—when its positive contributions have become part of everyday life, and are accepted without thought for the past problems to which it was a solution.

But this type of analysis would require a discussion of the causes and sources of technological innovation. We have touched upon them above only when they were seen to be complementary changes needed for the effective exploitation of the potential of a major innovation. The innovations in response to potentials and problems created by earlier innovations are indeed an important group in the total. But other sources of innovation have not been mentioned; and any account of the life cycle of an innovation must include full discussion of its origins —a major topic that could not be covered here.

Notes on Stage
of Economic Growth
as a System Determinant

1. Elements in a Stage Theory

A stage theory of long-term economic change implies: 1) distinct time segments, characterized by different sources and patterns of economic change; 2) a specific succession of these segments, so that *b* cannot occur before *a*, or *c* before *b;* and 3) a common matrix, in that the successive segments are stages in one broad process—usually one of development and growth rather than of devolution and shrinkage.[1]

These three elements—differentiation, sequence, and commu-

[1] "*Development* is any change which has a continuous *direction* and which culminates in a phase that is qualitatively *new*. The term 'development' should be used to characterize any series of events in thought, action or institutional arrangements which exhibits a directional cumulative change that either terminates in an event marked off by recognized qualitative novelty or exhibits in its course a perceptible pattern of growth" (see "Theory and Practice in Historical Study: A Report of the Committee on Historiography," *Social Science Research Council, Bulletin 54* [New York: Social Science Research Council, 1946], p. 117). Devolution is develop-

Reprinted from Alexander Eckstein, ed., *Comparison of Economic Systems: Theoretical and Methodological Approaches* (Berkeley: University of California Press, 1971), pp. 243–67. The paper was presented at a conference at the University of Michigan in November, 1968.

nity within a broad process—seem to constitute the minimum in a stage theory of historical change; or for that matter in a stage theory of many physical and biological growth processes.

How can such a simple design be a summary description or analytic classification of a vast and diverse field of historical change sufficiently plausible to warrant the formulation and persistence of many variants? The answer, at least for economic history, is suggested if we look at the past. We find that, first, the tools that raise economic productivity do not become available before a specific date, say, the late eighteenth century for the steam engine. If this and similar technological and social innovations are of major importance for long-term economic change, the period *before* the innovation is distinguished from the one *after;* and a minimum of two stages, one closed (before) and the other still open (after), is indicated. Second, the technological (or social, or any other relevant) innovation that makes for differentiation (before and after) also introduces a specific, irreversible sequence. To use the same example, the period before the late eighteenth century cannot be classified as a stage *following* the steam engine, and the period after the late eighteenth century cannot be designated as a stage *preceding* the steam engine. The sequence is fixed and unchangeable. Finally, the steam engine is seen to add significantly to economic productivity; and its innovative application appears as part of a longer process in which similar innovations have added to productivity previously and others are expected to add to it in the future—not only to aggregate economic productivity, but, more specifically in this illustration, to the long-term growth of mechanical energy for production purposes. This view leads to the assumption that the period marked by the steam engine must *terminate* when another innovation replaces it as the major source of growth in mechanical energy for production purposes. Thus a single major innovation, viewed as part of a continuous process, sets up a sequence of three distinct stages—before, dur-

---

ment in reverse. Growth and shrinkage emphasize the quantitative rise or decline but also include greater or lesser diversification.

Stage theory is most closely associated with a uni-directional rather than cyclic view of history. In the cyclic view the stages are recurrent; in a uni-directional view, a stage materializes, runs its course, and never recurs. Even in the process of devolution and decline, the return to a level experienced previously is not viewed as a recurrence of the earlier stage.

ing, and after—a sequence that is irreversible, contains these differentiated stages, and is part, necessarily, of a longer process. Although two of these three phases, *before* and *after,* are defined negatively and need additional content to indicate the source of growth that dominates them, they still serve to specify that the major innovation defining a stage positively grows out of a matrix of the longer growth process, and is brought to an end by some factors within the latter. Clearly, this view of combined effects of major innovations and the cumulative process of relevant economic change is at the base of many past stage theories—whether the innovation be in the organizing means of exchange (barter, money, credit); or in the size of the market and hence the character of the organizing institutions (household, city, nation); or a combination of methods of production and control over production resources (slavery, feudalism and serfdom, class society, classless society).[2]

But a stage sequence is suggested not only by the "before," "during,"and "after" periods of one innovation; or, what is the same, the "during" periods of several innovations viewed as parts of one larger process. It is also suggested by the spread of a *single* innovation within the "during" period; and in that sense there are several substages within one stage of a broader sequence. Thus the emergence of economical steam power in the late eighteenth century was only the beginning of a long process, which at the several levels at which it can be observed— spread to various applications of the stationary engine, to internal water transport, land transport, and ocean transport; increasing efficiency within and among these applications; spread first to the more-developed, then to the less-developed countries—also reveals distinct patterns in a specified sequence largely determined by time distance from the initial breakthrough. The process was cumulative in character, with changes in the level and pattern of its growth parameters as in the course of time the easy opportunities of initial spread were exhausted and newly emerging competing innovations (e.g., electric power and internal combustion engines) exerted their constraining influence. Here we have the minimum framework of

[2] For a recent review see Bert F. Hoselitz, "Theories of Stages of Economic Growth," in Bert F. Hoselitz, ed., *Theories of Economic Growth* (New York: Glencoe, 1960), pp. 193–238.

distinctive stages, in a specified sequence, and part of the same continuous process, provided by the changes in potential with increasing distance from the date of introduction; the requirement of earlier improvements to permit further increases in efficiency; and the limitation of the cumulative process to one innovation, assuring a common base for sequential stages. This intra-stage phase sequence is typical of many classifications of early, middle, and late capitalism; and of the Rostovian stages within modern economic growth, if we start the sequence with take-off and omit the pre-take-off segment (which is not actually a stage).

Indeed, such a sequence *within* each stage may be considered an indispensable part of a complete stage theory, because the latter covers several separate stages that emerge and then eventually disappear. Hence, it is difficult to conceive of a stage as static, as part of a process in which its emergence and eventual disappearance are the only relevant and major changes. Internal dynamics is implicit in a stage; and therefore it is likely, if not logically necessary, that a stage follows a sequence of its own from emergence to decline as a major source of growth. We call this sequence of changes integration, as contrasted with the sequence of different innovations marking off distinct stages. *Innovation* and *integration* are then the basic conceptual counters in the game of designing stages—and this is hardly surprising. By definition, innovation represents something *new* that differentiates one historical segment from another; and integration represents the movement of this new (so long as it is effectively new) in its interaction with the *old*. In combination, these two counters portray the continuous process of long-term growth as a succession of major innovations, each denoting a stage and each subject to its own phase pattern of spread (or interaction with the old) that helps to fill the canvas between one major innovational breakthrough and the next.

2. *The Scope of Stage-Setting Innovations*

Innovations can differ widely in their economic magnitude and in the aspects relevant to economic growth. Large and complex innovations may contain sub-innovations that may contain sub-sub-innovations, and so on down to the narrowest significant innovation. Hence, what are inter-innovational stages at one level may become stages in intra-innovational integration at another. One can easily envisage a vast hierarchy of innovations, corresponding sets of stages, and relevant lines of economic growth within which these innovations, stages, and phases of spread loom large. Within such a hierarchy we must choose those innovations and corresponding stages that affect the systems in which economic societies are organized.

The choice should be governed by the desire to use the stage approach in classifying, with intellectual economy, the largest volume of historical data related to the economic growth processes in which we are interested, and which are eventually to be explained; and the intellectual economy means the least loss of detail on major factors that determine economic growth in return for the clearest view of them. The choice is therefore governed by hypotheses identifying the important factors that determine the economic growth process—the latter observed in its most significant manifestations in economic study. Although a stage sequence is not a theory, it is based on preliminary notions concerning the major growth factors and their changing succession, and it is used to organize the data in the light of these notions for the greatest insight into the relevant factors. It should thus clear the way for the next round of richer and more testable hypotheses.

The following discussion of stage of economic growth as system determinant is based upon one guiding notion, the economic epoch. Judging at least by the economic history of Western European peoples (and their offshoots overseas) and possibly by the economic history of other parts of the world, we can distinguish economic epochs—long historical periods, extending over several centuries, during which economic growth appears to have been dominated by a major source that can be identified as the epochal innovation.[3] Within broad historical limits, several successive economic epochs can be viewed as stages within one long uni-directional process of growth. For ex-

[3] For a brief discussion, see my *Modern Economic Growth* (New Haven, Conn.: Yale University Press, 1966), pp. 1–16.

The technological innovations discussed in some detail in the preceding paper in this volume, "Innovations and Adjustments in Economic Growth," are sub-units within the much broader concept of epochal innovations, stressed here.

ample, we can set up a succession from the "pure" (pre-city) feudal epoch of Western Europe of the ninth to eleventh centuries; to the medieval city economy of the eleventh through the fifteenth centuries; to the epoch of overseas expansion and merchant capitalism, extending from the sixteenth through the late eighteenth centuries; and finally to the modern economic epoch, which began in the late eighteenth century and is still going on. But this sequence of economic epochs which can be viewed as stages in a cumulative process of economic growth, cannot be assumed to extend over the full span of economic history, even if it is limited to part of the world community. That history cannot be usefully conceived as a single uni-directional trend, the basic assumption of grand-stage theories claiming universality and complete coverage of the historical canvas. Even if a wider view, which I am incompetent to present, were to reveal a broad upward trend in economic magnitudes over the millennia since the emergence of human societies, the major breakdowns in time and scope within the closer range of the historical past (as distinct from pre-history) could not be neglected in a simplifying assumption of a continuous upward sweep.

These economic epochs, easily distinguishable in the accepted surveys of economic history, which form stages in a continuous process of economic growth only over a limited part of the historical past, fail to satisfy another aspect of the criterion of universality. Although, during any historical period (say a century), a given epoch may characterize the economic growth of several human societies in the world, it does not follow that it characterizes *all* human societies. Although we have boldly referred to the economic history of Western Europe (and its offshoots overseas), we cannot precisely define the group of economic societies involved. Some Mediterranean countries, Spain and Portugal for example, participated vigorously in the overseas expansion that introduced the epoch of merchant capitalism but have only recently entered the modern economic epoch; and others, like those on the Italian peninsula, were never dominated by "pure" feudalism. But even if we disregard the difficulties involved in identifying the economic societies whose history from the ninth century to the present could be viewed as a succession of several economic epoch-stages, we have no basis for assuming that the economic epochs distinguished in European history were worldwide, especially since many human societies have been separate and relatively isolated until as late as a century ago. Many groups of societies lived for centuries with little contact with, and little effective knowledge of, each other—for example, the European societies and those in the Americas, which the former "discovered" only in the late fifteenth century and continued to "discover" thereafter; or the African and Asiatic societies, whose contacts with the European societies were extremely limited. Each of these separate complexes of societies was responding to its own natural environment, was undergoing a historical process that had its own roots, and was removed from significant contact with the other groups of societies. Why should we expect them to experience economic epochs similar in content to, and roughly identical in timing with, those found, say, in the economic history of Western Europe? For all we know, for the 600 years from the mid-fourteenth to the mid-twentieth century China, the one society that incidentally had through this long period a much larger population than all Europe combined, may have experienced only one economic epoch, with the economy dominated by ever-expanding intensive agriculture which constituted the major growth industry while, during the same period, Western Europe went through at least three successive epochs (although two of them were incomplete).[4]

Although economic epochs cannot be generally viewed as stages in a comprehensive and universal sequence, or perhaps because they are not advanced as such stages, the construct is useful in reformulating our topic. Some characteristics of the two concepts—the economic epoch and the epochal innovation—are relevant to this purpose; and in presenting them, we can restate the topic and raise the questions that will govern the discussion in the rest of this paper.

a. The magnitude of an epochal innovation—its capacity to affect the growth of a number of societies over a relatively long period—implies that it also affects several aspects of society. If the major innovation originates in the sphere of material pro-

[4] This observation follows from my reading of Dwight Perkins's monograph, *Agricultural Development in China, 1368–1968* (Chicago: Aldine Publishing Co., 1969). Professor Perkins is not responsible for this broad interpretation of his findings.

duction, as it seems to in the modern economic epoch with the application of science to problems of economic production, the magnitude of the impact necessarily involves institutional and cultural adjustments—changes in the economic, political, and cultural framework essential for the proper use of the greatly expanded power of the production structure. Radically changed production forces could no more be organized under the old institutions than a large railroad or airline could be operated within the institutional framework of a personal or family firm. This is equally true of the more remote realm of ideology, for if an epochal innovation in material technology is, as it must be, a major addition to the stock of knowledge shared by at least a part of mankind, that addition must modify the earlier conceptions of man and nature shared by the societies in which the epochal innovation occurs. On the other hand, if the epochal innovation originates at the institutional level, e.g., in the formation of cities (or in the case of the Roman Empire, in the organization of a would-be universal state, with the major growth factor being the extension of sovereignty by which previously isolated and politically disturbed regions are joined and assured of stability), it does not become the base of an economic epoch until and unless it succeeds in radically affecting economic output and activity.

If economic epochs are complexes of major innovations in material technology, institutional organization, and ideology, the question implicit in our topic can be answered simply. Stages of growth, in so far as they are economic epochs and the latter, whether or not they are stages in the process of growth, are system determinants *by definition*.[5] For if "system" refers to the long-term arrangements by which various units within an economic society are induced to cooperate in production, distribution, and use of the aggregate product—including means of control over productive factors, freedom or constraint on individual units in the existing factor or goods markets, and so forth—then clearly the vast differences in economic technology represented

[5] This applies even more clearly to sequences of stages in the grand theories of the Historical school and some of its later followers, in which stages were almost completely identified with the different modes of organization of economic activity, i.e., with the different economic systems in the usual meaning of that term.

by the several economic epochs imply sufficiently marked differences in the size and character of the economic systems prevalent in the participating economic societies to constitute distinct systems. If this were a promising approach, our discussion would have to emphasize the different economic systems associated with different economic epochs whether or not they are stages in a continuous process of economic growth.

But such a direction for our discussion is not promising; nor would it contribute much or be relevant to the problems of comparability of economic systems as I infer them from the outline for this conference. Study of economic systems with vast differences in technology, in the stock of useful knowledge, and in other major components of economic epochs, would not contribute to an understanding of the differences between economies in which the comparative analysis of systems per se is of primary importance. Is a comparison of the economic system of a tribe in the isolated wilderness of the Amazon with that of an advanced economy like Sweden, or for that matter, of the *oikos* economy of some early Greek settlement with that of a city-state in the Hanseatic League, of real interest for the theme of this volume?

The very definition of economic epochs, which implies radically different bases of economic life and growth, renders that inter-epochal sequence—whether or not it is a stage difference or sequence—inappropriate for our purposes. Perhaps a more appropriate comparison would be that of different economic systems *within* a single economic epoch—of systems in which, despite their differences, the dynamic source of the epoch is a common factor. The appropriate stages would then be those that develop with the integration of the epochal innovation, as a single economic epoch unfolds.

b. I shift now to phases of growth *within* an economic epoch and, more specifically, within the modern economic epoch, extending back to the late eighteenth century; and reformulate our topic to ask how the sequence of phases in the development and spread of the modern economic epoch determines the system that characterizes the world's economic societies. Several aspects of this reformulation ought to be noted.

First, the modern economic epoch is best observed in terms of nation-states, i.e., societies in which political power sets the arrangements for internal mobility, interdependence, and cooperation of domestic economic resources, which permit the economy to operate as a relatively self-sufficient unit—granted that these nation-units can still interact in both peaceful international flow of resources and armed conflict. In the observation of modern economic growth this unit—rather than firms, industries, class groups, tribes, religious communities, and so forth—is chosen, because political power is basic for decisions that channel economic growth, given the transnational potential of the stock of useful knowledge, of material and social technology, available to all. And this choice of unit is all the more relevant here, since our topic is the relation to economic systems, whose concrete, observable applications are within the political units that comprise diverse resources and complex interrelations among them, or among the various branches of the production structure. But in observing the modern economic epoch, we combine the nation-state with the major transnational source of modern economic growth, the underlying epochal innovation that is universal in its potential availability and, in many respects, in actual impact. It therefore follows that the sequence of changes within the modern economic epoch comprises phases not only of internal growth of any participating nation-state, but also of the spread of modern economic growth to other nation-states. The international spread then has further effects on the connections between modern economic growth and the elements of the system within the participating (or otherwise involved) nation-states.

Second, the modern economic epoch is the first in human history which has had worldwide impact—in the sense that the countries that shared in the epochal innovation developed the capacity, at least by the second half of the nineteenth century, to reach effectively and significantly any and all parts of the world. Previously, as already indicated, groups of communities could live apart from and even without any knowledge of each other. But this breakthrough to a potentially universal economic epoch means the coexistence of, and significant contact among, nations and communities following a sequence of growth stages that in the long-term past may have been quite different from the sequence in which modern economic growth is the most recent stage.

Given these broad features of the modern economic epoch—

the variety of phases internal to the participating nation-states and distinguishable in the sequential spread of modern economic growth to an increasing number of these units, as well as the significant universality of international interaction—the relations between these phases (or stages) of modern economic growth and economic systems can be numerous. The discussion that follows deals with four examples of such relations: i) the effect of major phases in the development of modern economic growth within the older developed countries; ii) the effect of coexistence on the economic structure and system of the less-developed countries; iii) the possible connection between system-deviation and delayed entry into modern economic growth; iv) the possible convergence in system-organization in the catching up process after successful, if delayed, entry. What I take to be the main theme of this volume, the problem of comparability between the Communist-party-state system and the free-market-economy system of developed countries, is involved significantly only under points iii) and iv). But since our purpose is to outline more fully the problems of international comparability of economic organization, it seemed useful to extend the view beyond the confines of a Communist-non-Communist dichotomy.

3. The Older Developed Countries

The possible connection between phases in modern economic growth and an economic system can best be brought out by an imaginary but realistic illustration. Assume that 100 to 125 years ago country A, a developed and free-market economy, had an efficient small-scale agricultural sector which dominated its output and accounted for three-quarters of its labor force and, in addition, had some few handicrafts and manufacturing industries and a relatively adequate (for the time) infrastructure in the way of canals, roads, railroads, harbors, shipping, and so forth. Assume also that the state was important, but that its function was primarily to resolve the conflicts that usually arise in economic growth—treatment of public domain, control of currency and credit, freedom of labor markets—and that it was not directly involved in production or in the control of the material assets of the country. Assume that today this country is developed and industrialized, with the agricultural sector producing less than 10 per cent of total output and employing an even smaller share of the labor force, but that it is plentifully supplied with, and has a large export capacity in, agricultural products. Further, assume that in addition to agriculture, which is dominated by a few large farms, some twenty-five huge, billion-dollar corporations dominate about a dozen crucial sectors (manufacturing, transport, construction, electric light and power, and so forth), a variety of nonprofit nongovernmental organizations provide education, health, and similar services, and the government sector is directly engaged in a large volume of economic activity (e.g., high-energy atomic production), because of the danger of entrusting it to private hands or because of the security problems in the international turbulence of the mid-twentieth century. Finally, assume that during this long span, within which we could presumably distinguish phases or stages if we had the data, time, and patience, there were free markets, liberty for anyone to engage in all activities except those considered dangerous by the society, full rights of private property —in short practically all of the appurtenances of a free-market economy. Are the arrangements in this country at both terminal dates one and the same economic system?

The point of this question is whether, with its focus on the principle of internal organization, the definition of an economic system can be independent of the number and size of the parts that are organized into a system. The dictionary definition of the term, from the Greek *syn + histanai*, to place together, is, in its broadest sense, "an aggregation or assemblage of objects (or ideas, or activities) united by some form of regular interaction or interdependence" (*Webster's New International Dictionary*, unabridged, 2nd edition); and it has two components—the principle of organization and the objects that are being organized. Both the principles and the particular objects can differ, but the former is not fully independent of the latter. Thus in an economic system, one type of organization can be based on thousands of small, individual producing units or on a score of giant, nonpersonal corporations, private, public, or a mixture of both. Unless the principle of organization is so specified that the free-market mechanism operates in the same way for all the producing units, an economy may retain the principle of organization, but may change markedly because different assemblages of basic producing units are organized at different times.

This issue can perhaps be seen more clearly if we view the

economy of any country as so many groups of production units, each differing from the others with respect to economic behavior and hence with respect to the application of any of the several principles of organization of the economic system. Examples of such groups are general government, government-owned and operated enterprises, private nonprofit institutions, government-regulated private enterprises (such as public utilities), large private corporations which are in effect public because their actions affect the public interest, small corporations, and personal firms. No observable economy, particularly among the developed countries, consists exclusively of one such group. Hence no economy can be a pure example of a system if the latter is defined by one principle of organization. Even the Soviet economy has always had a small component of private enterprise—individual plots cultivated by peasants, and, I assume, some individual handicraft shops. In the non-Communist developed countries, however, the distribution of total output, labor force, and capital among such groups has changed significantly in the course of modern economic growth; and differences may still exist among various developed countries, all of them in the free-market category or system. If such changes over time or differences in space are classified as "variants" of one and the same economic system, any comparison of systems defined as abstractions may have limited analytical interest, unless it is supplemented by specific consideration of these major variants.

Four complexes of long-term changes in modern economic growth appear to have contributed markedly to the rapid shifts in the size and character of the several parts of the economic system of the older developed countries, and hence in the character of the system itself. First, shifts in the structure of production and in the underlying technology led to much larger optimum or minimum scales of plant and enterprise—with a tendency toward monopoly which led to regulation, or toward quasi-public status of the enterprise. This familiar aspect of industrialization has been discussed at length in an enormous literature. Second, the turbulence of the last half century—the increased international tension and greater tendency toward major conflicts associated with the spread of modern economic growth to more nation-states, particularly the larger ones—stands in sharp contrast to the century before World War I, with its Pax Britannica which is implicitly credited to the effective limitation of economic development to Great Britain and its natural allies (like the United States). Third, a complex of trends, not unconnected with the first two, stems from the increasing recognition of the responsibility of the modern state (and hence of the economy) not only for the juridical and political equality of all its citizens, but also for the equality of economic opportunity—and most recently also for a minimum economic base. These trends clearly lead to the provision of public facilities to implement this purpose when and if the free-market private sector fails to do so. Obviously, the extension of collective action to provide health and education services, to supplement income, and so forth, has marked effects on the distribution of production among different groups of producing units. Finally, a new set of trends has become evident recently, and it stems from the scientific field as an increasing source of economic growth in the most advanced countries. The effects of this source of economic growth on the fate of man are so far-reaching and potentially overpowering that society is reluctant to allow profit-oriented, private enterprise to develop it—at least in the early stages and even later only under specific conditions and limits. The development of atomic energy is one example; another is the current expansion of space exploration; and DNA is a potential third, if and when further research reaches the possibility of control over the hereditary structure and endowments of man.

These four sets of trends, leading to the new industrial state, the new military state, the new welfare state, and the new scientific state—to coin convenient terms—are clearly significant variants of the free-market, individual enterprise state. The mixture of these variants may differ among the presently developed countries—outside of the Communist system and to some extent also within the latter. It would be intriguing to investigate these different mixtures as exemplified by various developed countries, but this would take us too far afield. The discussion so far should suffice to illustrate the main point. Phases of growth in the older developed countries brought about major transformations of the economic system that characterized them originally; and these changes may have differed in the different countries or groups of countries even among the non-Communist developed countries. Comparative analysis of economic systems should perhaps take account of these variants.

4. The Underdeveloped Countries

Offhand, the less-developed countries of today, particularly the non-Communist, might be viewed as societies at the same stage of growth, and characterized by the same economic system, as the presently developed countries at their point of entry into modern economic growth. If this were so, much of the preceding discussion of the stages of growth within the current economic epoch with reference to the older developed countries could be applied here. It could be assumed that the underdeveloped countries are at that early point of the initial phase in which the free-market, individual-enterprise system is beginning to be transformed by industrialization, increase in scale, and greatly widened role and responsibility of the state. Indeed, much of the current analysis of economic growth which relies on cross-section comparison among developed, intermediate, and under-developed countries, assumes this similarity—in a sense equating the less-developed countries to the early stages of the presently developed countries. This assumption may be questioned; and we mention three major considerations that point up the lack of similarity between the economic system of the under-developed countries and the initial phases of the presently developed countries.

First, there is the marked difference at the aggregative level of economic activity. Output per capita is much lower in the underdeveloped countries today than it was in the presently developed countries at the date of entry—a period rather than a point of time—into modern economic growth, i.e., when growth of per capita product (with an already high rate of population growth) began to accelerate, the shift toward nonagricultural sectors occurred, modern technology (modern by the times) was adopted, and so forth. However difficult the comparison of per capita gross product at such distances of time and space, the weight of the evidence clearly suggests that, with the single and significant exception of Japan (the records for which are still to be fully tested), the pre-industrialization per capita product in the presently developed countries, at least $200 in 1958 prices (and significantly more, in the offshoots overseas), was appreciably higher than per capita product in underdeveloped countries in the late 1950's—certainly in most of Asia and Africa, and in a good part of Latin America.

Yet this statistical difference in aggregate output per capita is less important than what it represents. It implies that even today these underdeveloped countries still have such a low product per capita that they are not at the same stage as the presently developed countries were at their initial stage of modern economic growth. This seems to be the case despite access to modern technology and despite the existence of a modern sector within these countries (no matter how small). These underdeveloped countries are either at some earlier stage within the long-term trend of the presently developed countries—in terms of the Western European sequence perhaps at the period of city formation in the early Middle Ages. Or, what is far more defensible, they are at some stage in a sequence of long-term growth separate and distinct from that of the Western European cradle of the modern economic epoch and are following a time and phase sequence that may be quite different.

Only a scholar familiar with the long history of the Asian, African, and Western Hemisphere native communities would be competent to spell out the sequence of which the presently underdeveloped countries are the terminal products. Even then, some allowance would have to be made for the effect on this sequence of adverse contact with the developed West in recent centuries (of which more below). China, for instance, built an empire on intensive agriculture, with central political controls through irrigation, canals, and a literate bureaucracy; and it relied upon a common system of quasi-religious mores and an extended family as the basic unit of social organization. It does seem to me, with only superficial knowledge, that the stage and the corresponding organizational structure represented by this agricultural empire has no close parallel in the sequence of growth stages in Western Europe, certainly not back to the early Middle Ages, and to the Roman Empire or Hellenistic times. Some tribal economies in Africa may have reached their present stage by types of growth and organization for which there are also no effective parallels within the historical past of Western European societies. In short, one major component in the structure and system of underdeveloped countries today is an inheritance from a past that developed along lines that were either quite different from those of the Western European societies in which modern economic growth originated; or, if similar, correspond to a stage of growth in the latter that long preceded the stage just before entry into modern industrialization.

The second relevant consideration is that the presently developed countries (again with the single exception of Japan) were, even before their industrialization, among the more-developed, economically advanced parts of the world. This does not mean that even in the late eighteenth century those countries that eventually became the developed group were in advance of the rest of the world in all sectors of productive activity. But by and large any substantial economic inferiority was a matter of the longer past; and the pioneers or the early followers were the economic leaders of the world even before industrialization (with the possible exception of the Netherlands, which despite an apparently high per capita product in the eighteenth century, was slow to take advantage of modern industrialization). It is a crucial characteristic of the presently underdeveloped countries that they *are* underdeveloped while others are much more developed—and this situation has lasted a long enough time to affect markedly the structure of the underdeveloped countries; and also to cover several phases in the changing impact of the developed upon the underdeveloped parts of the world.

This impact, in the broadest terms, is the introduction of a modern component into the structure of the otherwise traditional underdeveloped countries. The magnitude of this component, its specific economic content, and the way in which it was introduced, confined, or encouraged, could and did vary widely. In a territory with colonial status a substantial modern sector often emerged but was organized by Western entrepreneurs of the metropolitan country. In a politically independent underdeveloped country with an export sector oriented toward the developed countries' markets the economic organization was and is quite different from that in a country with domestically oriented agriculture or industry. And in some others, a few members of the native elite educated in some Western lore are participating in administration and attempting to introduce Western elements into what may still be a purely traditional economic society.

Obviously, in the countries that are still underdeveloped, this modern component, even if in existence for a long period, has not expanded sufficiently to shift the country to developed status, and in most cases has not even raised its per capita product to an intermediate level. Given the long coexistence of developed and underdeveloped economies, it is no exaggeration to argue that a major result of such coexistence in the underdeveloped economies is their dual structure. There are two distinct components, the modern and the traditional; and in marked contrast with the past record of the presently developed countries, the two components continue to perform without the modern one, despite its greater productivity, rapidly outpacing the other. It is the *persistence* of the dual structure and the confinement or limitation of the modern sector that are crucial, for the two have operated simultaneously but for a shorter period in the developed countries also.

Third, while the presently developed countries had begun to reach out to other parts of the world long before the modern economic epoch, this contact was still incomplete in the late eighteenth century. Since that time major changes have taken place in technology, in scope, and even in the leading views affecting the relations between the developed and underdeveloped countries.

Because of these sequential changes in technology, economics, and political philosophy, the scope and character of the impact of developed countries on the various underdeveloped regions of the world also differed. For example, some countries in Latin America, after a long period of colonial status, became politically independent early in the modern economic epoch—so that the dual structure that remained was the result of domestic forces rather than of persistent colonial status. Others, like many in sub-Saharan Africa, continued in relative isolation from the developed countries until fairly late in the nineteenth century (largely for technological reasons), but since the 1890's have been subjected to their impact and resulting colonial partition. Still others, mostly in South Asia, were already colonial at the beginning of the modern economic epoch, and were not fully freed until after World War II. Some, like those in East Asia (e.g., China, Thailand) were politically independent, but their sovereignty was severely limited. In view of these differences in timing, character, and source of impact of the developed countries in combination with the marked differences in structural and system characteristics of historical heritage among the various groups of underdeveloped countries, the variety of mixtures and the resulting characteristics of economic systems represented by the underdeveloped countries in the world today must be wide indeed. It is probably much wider than among the developed countries, where the dominance of the modern component dictates considerable similarity, because it is drawn from one and the same current source of economic advance in the modern technology.

I do not feel competent to discuss the methods by which this variegated underdeveloped world can be effectively classified for the analysis of the structure of economic organization and thus for what might be called the economic system elements.[6] It may well be that if these countries were carefully examined, some types of organization and system would emerge as common to several units reflecting their long-term past (e.g., the intensive agriculture empire; the tribal extensive agriculture complex, largely self-sufficient and with little exchange except for administrative or ritualistic purposes; the almost feudal structure of some of the more developed units). These different types of economic system could then be combined with the various types of modern sectors reflecting the impact of developed countries. Such a classification would probably involve the application of several economic systems with different weights to the several groups of underdeveloped countries. But again, I can only suggest; I cannot provide specific indications of the relation between stages of growth—in this case in different sequences among the underdeveloped countries, as well as changes in the technology and history of the impact of the developed societies—and the economic system prevailing in these underdeveloped societies.

The suggestion that the economic structure of underdeveloped countries may represent combinations of economic systems—some of which belong to a past different from that of the pres-

[6] For an interesting attempt at such a classification which groups underdeveloped countries by the major obstacle to their economic modernization and growth, see John K. Galbraith, "Underdevelopment: An Approach to Classification," in David Krivine, ed., *Fiscal and Monetary Problems in Developing Countries,* Proceedings of the 3rd Rehovoth Conference (New York, 1967), pp. 19–38 and discussion, pp. 38–45.

ently developed countries—with a modern component representing the impact of the present, may apply to Communist underdeveloped countries also. Unless the Communist system is taken in the literal meaning of its official theory, permitting no significant variants and claiming to exhaust the full economic meaning of the life of the country in which it is supposedly operating, its major components cannot be conceived in isolation from their embodiment, first in the historical experience of the pioneer, viz., the Soviet Union. As a result, the modifications of the system in other Communist countries can be quite marked; and in the underdeveloped countries, like China, may be associated with their distinctive historical heritages—as well as with their emergence as Communist *follower* countries. It may therefore help in comparative analysis to recognize that significant variants exist not only for the free-market economy but also for the Communist system; and that these variants in the underdeveloped Communist countries, like those in the underdeveloped non-Communist countries, may reflect elements of the historical past—although not necessarily the same elements or with the same weight.

5. System Deviation and Delayed Entry

The main issue in this section is whether the formation of a new variant of an economic system, or better, of a new type of economic system, may not be a link in the process of *spread* of modern economic growth in a world of competing political entities like nation-states. If we view the primary source of modern economic growth as a transnational stock of technological and social knowledge available for exploitation by any society that gears itself for this purpose, and if in the course of historical change in the structure of the various nation-states, the preparation for exploitation of the growth potential involves a change not only from a country's own past arrangements but also from those followed by previously developed countries, then a *new* system may be generated. In a sense, the new system is a response, sufficiently successful to merit recognition and attention, to opportunities of economic growth, a function of the latter, a new installment in the spread of modern economic growth. More specifically, if the new economic system emerges fairly late in the spread of modern economic growth, and the carrier is therefore a relative latecomer, it can be viewed as a deviation from the prevalent organizational pattern and a function of delayed entry, of the pressures that the backwardness implicit in such delayed entry exercises (in addition to the opportunities that it may provide).[7]

It would be tempting to set up a model in which prolonged delay in entry into modern economic growth produces greater pressure of increasing backwardness—so that those units that make a belated entry rely increasingly upon the power of the state in response to this greater pressure to catch up. The increasing exercise of this power may eventually lead to an economic system sufficiently different to be recognized as new, and to a pattern of industrialization that also differs markedly in its sequence from that followed by the pioneer and early follower countries. This model could be expanded by adding the proposition that the delayed entry, with the consequences just suggested, was in turn due to a greater "lack of preparedness," i.e., a greater difference between the social and economic institutions of the country under review and those of the pioneer and early follower developed countries at the early stages of their modernization. It would follow that radical changes would have to be made in these institutions; and indeed radical political and institutional changes often precede the successful entry into modern economic growth by the latecomers. Given such radical political changes, the new state would presumably feel a greater responsibility for catching up and participate more actively in the economic growth process. Thus the connection between delayed entry and the emergence of a new economic system is *via* the greater role of the state for two reasons: the greater pressure (as well as opportunity) of backwardness, and the greater need

[7] The similarity of such an approach which links deviant forms of the economic system to delayed entry in the process of modern economic growth to Alexander Gerschenkron's hypothesis is obvious (see his paper, "Economic Backwardness in Historical Perspective," published in 1952 and reprinted a decade later in his collection of essays under the same title [Cambridge, Mass.: Harvard University Press, 1962], pp. 5–30; and the supplementary discussion in the same volume, "The Approach to European Industrialization: A Postscript," pp. 353–64). However, we do not claim that our approach is a logical extension of Professor Gerschenkron's hypothesis.

to eradicate the old and inappropriate economic and social institutions.

The model explains the greater reliance on the powers of the state, and hence some of the development policies and patterns of the latecomers in the period of transition from underdevelopment to development. However, it fails to yield a new economic system as a necessary, or even as a likely, result—assuming that our definition of an economic system is not so narrow that a limited variant would have to be viewed as new (in which case a different system would be generated by practically every country that enters modern economic growth).

This inadequacy of the model is illustrated by the cases of Japan and Russia, both latecomers in the historical spread of the modern economic system. Japan was under much greater pressure to exploit the potential of modern economic growth than the earlier entrants in Europe and the United States, for its national independence was in danger, and the repetition of India's and China's experience threatened as a grave possibility. Furthermore, since its economic and social institutions were so far removed from those of the pioneer and early follower European countries and of their offshoots overseas, and radical, indeed revolutionary, changes were essential, Japan was a most conspicuous case—far more so than Russia. As is well known, the state did play a crucial role in Japan in the early periods of the Meiji Era, introducing a series of major changes in the political, legal, social, and economic institutions and itself engaging in several modern productive activities. Yet all this was done to facilitate the formation of a market economy, a system that despite some interesting differences is not so unlike those characterizing the other developed countries as to be recognized as a new economic system. In contrast, Russia, where backwardness was far less of a danger, where social institutions were far more akin to those of the developed West, and where an earlier attempt at modernization and entry had followed rather customary and nonrevolutionary patterns, ended with a violent overthrow of the existing social and institutional framework and a radically different and *new* economic system. In achieving modern economic growth, it became sufficiently successful to merit attention and raise problems of comparative analysis.

The link between the spread of modern economic growth and

the emergence of a new economic system, which we have not yet specified in the model, can be suggested, even if the suggestion bears all the earmarks of hindsight wisdom. Let us assume that in the course of its development and spread, modern economic growth generated an ideology that combines a great admiration for the technological attainments of the epoch with an equally great abhorrence of the social institutions, the system within which these attainments had been channelled previously —an ideology that considers the existing social system not only a dispensable part of the modern economic epoch but one that actually limits the full use of its technological potential; and that entertains this dogma with a fervor that justifies the use of an authoritarian minority party to pursue any policies, no matter how violent, in order to overthrow rather than gradually modify the existing system, i.e., one that is aimed at a new system (however ill-defined) rather than at some variant. The real question is whether such a specifically formulated ideology is a necessary consequence of the spread of modern economic growth—as distinct from a generally critical ideology that does not contain radically violent, authoritarian elements. Let me assume that such an ideological twist is a *possible* result of the institutional and human upheavals created by dynamic modern economic growth.

Given this specific ideological product of the evolution and spread of modern economic growth (i.e., of the epoch), the new economic system *may* emerge if the party-carrier of such ideology attains control; and having attained it, experiments with the new economic system sufficiently to demonstrate significant success—in the sense that it can raise the country's aggregate product rapidly and appreciably through the adoption of modern material technology at an adequately rapid and cumulative rate. The shift of power can be achieved in a country only if previous efforts to exploit the potential modern economic growth under the old system were not successful enough to build up group interests within that system which could effectively resist violent change in the political and social structure; and only if the country has had enough of an awareness of modern economic growth so that a significant minority group has been imbued with the specific ideology suggested. Success, after coming to power, depends in turn upon various special conditions if it is to be sufficiently marked, and the new system sufficiently different, to warrant recognition and become the concern in comparative analysis of the type emphasized in this volume. This violent change and attempt at a new system must occur in a *large* country—for only a large country can reap the benefits of economic growth in terms of world power and influence; and only a large country can effect the necessary revolutionary departures without being forced to compromise by the larger and less deviant developed nation-states. Furthermore, this violent change must occur in a large country that remains large despite the strains imposed upon it by the violent upheaval; and this means a country where past history has created a community of culture and feelings that have provided a sufficient substratum of unity. Whether we would be as much concerned with the Soviet economy as a new economic system if the results had been similar to those for the Austro-Hungarian Empire after World War I is a moot question; and it is a serious question, because such an outcome would imply that this type of entry, this attempt to exploit the potentials of modern economic growth, is too destructive of national viability to be practicable. Finally, the violent overthrow in a large country with an established history and unity that can stand the strain without decomposition into separate parts must also occur at a high enough level of development of modern technology, so that an authoritarian minority party can dominate the country by exercising repressive force long enough to mobilize the economic resources for a rapid transformation. Even more important, the effective application of this technology, which can be borrowed, must be achieved without reliance upon the skill of the labor force (which is very low to begin with) and upon the loyalty of the majority of the labor force (which, particularly if we include the agricultural classes, is questionable). Only with the tractors, the heavy producers' goods, and the capital-intensive infrastructure was the minority party in Russia able forcefully and rapidly to transform the technological base of the country. It could do so, furthermore, under a new system that initially and for a considerable period ran counter to the immediate economic and other interests of the majority of the population—however much these

interests may have been transformed later by attachment to the
new bases of the economic and social system once these were
created.

All these speculative notions may not stand up under scrutiny
in the light of greater knowledge of the relevant stretch of economic, political, and intellectual history. But they are advanced
as a preliminary attempt to illustrate the possible interplay of
stages in the spread of the modern economic epoch with some
specific singular elements, in giving rise to a new economic system.[8]

I would like to emphasize again that our recognition of a different economic system as new is a reflection not merely of its
difference from the prevalent system but also of its *weight* in the
world—and this means its success in a society large enough to
affect the balance of power in this competitive world. If this is
true, it is not only the economic system of socialism that interests us. Such a system, in the sense of state ownership of means
of production and control over economic activity, including
whatever planning may be fancied, can theoretically also permit
political freedom, many political parties, democratic decisions
on the choice of plans, and so forth. In realistic terms, our interest concerns the new economic system operated by a Communist authoritarian party, with complete repression of political activity, and fairly tight restraints on the choice not only of
economic plans but of all other issues of society. And it is because of this distinctive combination of political authoritarianism, an ideology that stresses economic growth as measured
by material output, with the tight control of the relations among
men in the social sphere and in cultural creativity, that the
Communist system interests us. This role of the Communist system affects the economic fate not only of the countries that
adopt it—and these are important because of their very size—

---

[8] The elements—size and national viability of the country; failure in
adopting modern economic growth and yet sufficient participation to have
an effective Communist party; a level of technology that permits the transformation despite the disloyalty and resistance of much of the population—
are singular in that each is the result of a vast complex of antecedent
causes not likely to recur or occur at more than one place in the world.
They are not chance, in that they are not the product of a vast variety of
uncorrelated unbiased elements, each of which is too small to warrant
identification and study.

but also of others, since the relations among them are more affected by the political ideology than by the purely economic aspects of the system. It is in order to try to explain the emergence of the new economic system, as exemplified by the U.S.S.R., not to formulate a socialist or Communist economic system abstractly defined, that the discussion above suggested the relevant interplay among the stages in the spread of modern economic growth, the delayed entry on the part of some nation-states, and the possible breakthrough to a new system based partly on the specific ideology generated by past economic growth, and partly on a combination of the singular elements that permit such a successful breakthrough.

6. Change in Later Growth

Implied in the discussion just presented is a view of the breakthrough to a new economic system as a contingency that might not have occurred if some of the required singular components had not been present at the appropriate stage of spread of the modern economic epoch; and a view in which the chances of such concurrence are slight, not too favorable, and clearly not inevitable. This conclusion is hardly surprising if, as has been argued with respect to the U.S.S.R., a new system, differentiating itself from the old by hostility, can be successful only in a large country that possesses the national unity to withstand a great deal of pounding. The distribution of nation-states in the world is skewed: a few (not more than a dozen) are very large (say with a population well over 50 million, to use the current scale), and many (over a hundred) are quite small (say with a population appreciably less than 20 million). Hence the number of units within which a successful breakthrough to a new economic system can occur is limited; and in view of the variety of further singular requirements, the chances that even one would be successful cannot, in the nature of the case, be high.

But whatever the probability of the contingency, once the breakthrough to a new system occurs and is successful enough to be recognized as an effective response to the potentials of modern economic growth, the new system begins its own process of internal modification and external spread. We shall not deal here with the spread of the new system beyond the country of origin—except in its possible bearing upon internal evolution within the pioneer country.

This new economic system, which originated in a belated response to the unexploited potentials of modern technology and modern economic growth, applied an essentially negative ideology to experiment with alternative ways of allocating resources under a different set of political and social institutions, and successfully made a rapid transition to a much higher level of aggregate economic performance and technology. Will it not then have served its purpose and be subject to substantial modification, particularly if the system fails to induce the still higher level of economic performance already attained in the other developed countries? In other words, is the new economic system, as exemplified in the Soviet Union so far, compatible with attainment of a higher level of economic performance, of another stage of economic growth? We should not overlook, of course, the possibility that the modifications required for further economic growth need not be made (although there presumably would be pressure in that direction).

This issue of compatibility between the Soviet Communist system and further economic growth and attainment is a question of *what* change, *how much* of that change, and how much in economic growth. Here we face the difficulty implied in our earlier discussion, viz., of identifying the nature and gauging the magnitude of any change that we would recognize as a variant in any economic system, to be related to an identified stage of economic growth. This difficulty led us to a rather sketchy and illustrative discussion of variants in the market-economy system of non-Communist developed countries (Section 3); and of the various types of combination of modern sector and traditional components in the systems represented by underdeveloped countries (Section 4). We had no such difficulty in associating different types of economic system with different stages of growth, when the latter represented sequences of major economic epochs and epochal innovations (Section 2); or when we discussed the emergence of a sharply contrasting new economic system, as exemplified by Soviet Communism (Section 5). But here, when we ask what changes in this new economic system would be required for a further advance in economic growth, we face the problem of identifying the organizational and system aspects necessary for some specific stage of growth. Whether or not we can resolve the difficulty, it should at least be recognized as a central problem in a comparative analysis of economic systems, if the latter are to be conceived as more than extreme abstractions (free-market economy, centralized command economy, and so forth) unaffected by realistic variants.

We can only illustrate the difficulty by reference to both parts of the compatibility issue, the system and the stage of growth. Every functioning economic system undergoes *some* changes as the components that it organizes change in the course of growth, and hence the very principle of organization is necessarily modified in its application. Changes have already occurred in Soviet Communism over the four decades since its crystallization in the first five-year plan. However one would weigh the element of historical accident in the brutality of Stalinist dictatorship, one could reasonably argue that the internal policies followed during the period of forceful wrecking of older institutions and of older economic and social groups had to change. Some of the organizational features had to be modified once the new economic bases made it possible for new group and class interests to emerge, and the latter could pursue a policy unconcerned with the pressure for removal of internal resistance or for external catching-up. In the sense that the functions of the new economic system in the later decades would differ somewhat from those in the earlier decades, there would be a change. But how should we evaluate this change; how much weight should we assign to the observable changes? The question calls for criteria in identifying and measuring changes in an economic system; and one wonders how far comparative analysis can proceed without such criteria for identifying the components of the system and measuring their magnitude. Was the shift from Stalinism to post-Stalinism—with the broadening of the decision base in planning from a small party faction to a wider group which may be more responsive to the interests and desires of a larger fraction of the population—a change in the new system? And how significant was this widening of the decision base in terms of allowing greater play of various interests and conceptions of the needs of economy and society? Would we consider some of the recent reforms, or even the Yugoslav type of organization, significant new variants, assuming the continued monopolization by the Communist party of political and cultural life? Obviously we need some testable typology of variants of the new economic system (as we do for the non-Communist economies) before we can trace the relation of these variants to stages of economic growth.

If it is difficult to define a change in the economic system, in this case the Communist, it is also difficult to define levels of economic performance and stages of growth (within the complex of modern economic growth). Assume that the Soviet Union allows for a moderate rise in per capita supply of consumer goods, but increases total and per capita output by concentrating on the production of military goods, producers' equipment, space exploration, output for foreign power diplomacy—while still controlling the country's political life, press, arts, education, man's choice of career, and at intervals tightening the Iron Curtain. Obviously, marked increases and higher levels of aggregate economic product can be attained in this way with practically no change in the Soviet Communist system, unless one argues that devotion of the greater share of input to increasing output along the lines suggested would arouse such a reaction in the population that further economic growth would necessarily be reoriented to the desires of the people.

The issue of compatibility can thus be rephrased. What change in the Soviet Communist system should be recognized as a major modification rather than a minor variant, and does the next stage or even simply further economic growth require this major modification? Such a requirement may be claimed by saying that the members of the Communist society will not cooperate in *further* economic growth unless the modification is forthcoming, e.g., unless they are given a more important role in decisions about consumption and production plans. The validity of this basis for the requirement, and hence incompatibility with further growth, can be determined, if at all, only by close students of the Soviet society and economy. Or it may be argued that greater freedom of economic, social, and cultural life is indispensable if the higher stage of economic growth is to generate further innovations and thus sustain itself. However, this is a condition of growth of the most advanced pioneer country and not a general requirement for all participants in an advanced stage of growth. The U.S.S.R. may attain a higher level of per capita growth, and even of consumption, while retaining its authoritarian structure, by continuing to adopt the innovations generated in the freer and more creative economies of the West. Finally, it may be claimed that further economic growth involves, *by definition*, much greater freedom of members of society to participate in decisions on economic plans, and in choices between economic and other aspects of social life. In that sense the kind of economic growth illustrated in the preceding paragraph is no growth at all. But this only means that *if* we *define* more advanced stages of economic growth as those in which pluralistic and decentralized decisions can be given adequate weight, then it follows that the Soviet Communist system is incompatible with further economic growth. But this is a value judgment and belongs to a different level of discourse.

Little in this discussion of the compatibility issue bears on the *likelihood* of significant changes in Soviet Communism. Exploring the latter would mean taking into account pressures for change generated within the Soviet Union—partly by its economic growth, partly by its continued coexistence with the non-Communist developed countries and the demonstration effect of the latter at least on some groups within Soviet society, partly by the evolution of the Communist system elsewhere (whether in demonstration of the advantages of modification, or of such disadvantages of accentuation as have occurred in Mainland China). But exploration of recent trends, viewed as sources of pressure for change, while possibly relevant as illustrations of linkages between changes in economic system and stages in spread of an economic epoch, would take us too far afield, and is, in any case, beyond my competence.

7. Postscript

The rather disjointed discussion in this paper dealt with selected topics in the broad field of the relation between phases of economic growth and economic system. The field was broad because of a decision to view an economic system not merely as a clear-cut, extreme formulation of some single principle of organization regardless of the parts being organized and hence of the variant ways in which one and the same principle would be applied; but as a concept permitting significant variants. With these variants viewed as important elements in comparative analysis, their association with stages of economic growth would reveal a variety of links. These could be covered here only illustratively and with emphasis on definitional and conceptual aspects.

The discussion was perforce illustrative, because I had neither an established typology of these significant variants of economic systems nor the empirical data by which they would be linked with equally well identified and measured phases of economic growth—although for modern economic growth, the supply of well-organized data and ad hoc hypotheses on phases of growth is richer than that bearing upon economic systems in their significant variants.

That our discussion was so largely in the nature of semantic clarification was perhaps inevitable—for in a field as broad as that outlined in the topic, clarification of meanings is the first indispensable step. It is only to the extent that some agreement is secured in this first step that further analysis and empirical testing become possible.

How much further analysis in the field can proceed, only the future will show. But the main import of this paper is to suggest that the broad social and ideological implications of the measures of economic performance and growth must be carefully noted in any empirical references to phases of growth (particularly within a given economic epoch), and that the typology of the significant variants of economic systems must be a major concern before the relation between phases of growth and economic system can be fruitfully studied.

Data for Quantitative
Economic Analysis: Problems
of Demand and Supply

---

1. The Demand for Economic Measures

Given the complexity of modern economic society, the interdependence among groups within a country's economy, and the close economic ties between a given country and much of the rest of the world, a strong interest in and continuous demand for economic information are to be expected. The demand is for quantitative measures relating to meaningful categories which represent important aspects of economic performance and components of economic structure.

Four conditions for a widespread and continuous demand for economic measures may be explicitly formulated. The first is recognition by members of society, individually or in their group capacity, that their own economic fortunes are interrelated with those of the rest of society; and that the economic fortunes of their country are interrelated with those of much of the rest of the world. This realization of being a part of a large, complex system forces a strong interest in the performance and

Extended version of a lecture at the Federation of Swedish Industries in December, 1971. Reprinted from a pamphlet published by the Federation (Stockholm, 1972).

structure of a much wider economic community—the kind of interest that in different conditions in earlier times was focused on the estate, or the village, or the city and its periphery. The second is the acceptance of meaningful categories within which the economic performance and structure of these wide-flung and complex aggregates can be subsumed. For much economic measurement the relevant categories and concepts are those provided partly in the system of national economic accounts—and these categories and concepts are in turn taken from economic theory and analysis—and partly in related systems of financial flows, sectoral analyses, and the like. Product, income, production sectors, labor, capital, the price level, money, credit, taxes, balance of international payments, and various other concepts and categories formally established in economic theory and accepted in widespread discourse, if only in rough outline, are indispensable, since economic measures are their quantitative expression. Such concepts and categories provide guidance in summarizing the variegated inputs and outputs in economic activity, or the different components of economic structure. The third condition is the recognition that these relevant aspects of economic performance and structure can be measured, and thus expressed in agreed-upon quantitative terms; and that the understanding of economic interdependencies is greatly enhanced by the possibility of weighing the different aspects and components, of measuring the costs of, and returns from, factors affecting the outcome in different directions, of establishing the analytical and possibly the policy "trade-offs."

These three conditions are reinforced by the addition of a fourth, viz., the belief that the institutional channels within which economic forces operate can be modified, if the observed results are unsatisfactory; and that much can be done to offset undesirable aspects of economic performance and structure. This may be seen by the opposite assumption, viz., the belief in *inexorable* economic laws, which would dictate complete adjustment of society to avoid violating them, and bar substantial modification and adaptation of institutions to changing consequences of economic performance (as was the position in some of the vulgar variants of Classical and Marxian economics). One is not much interested in what one cannot help but endure. The belief in the possibility of varied and changing adjustments in the institutional channels of economic activity, in response to changing consequences (both positive and negative) of economic growth and structure, is a powerful incentive toward expanding economic measurement. In countries with governments active in modifying the economic process as it evolves in the market (and this includes practically all economically developed countries), this fourth condition of interest in, and demand for, a wide range of economic measures is clearly present.

These four conditions produced a demand for economic measures that varied in scope in the past among countries at different levels of economic development and with different social and political structures. The spread of the demand for economic measures among the population—assuming that they recognize their membership in and dependence upon a wider economic system—is partly a function of their education and even more of their belief in the *possible uses* to which the more tested knowledge can be put. This, in turn, depends upon the political structure of a country, which determines whether policy-relevant knowledge should be accessible or monopolized in the hands of a small group. Even in an economically developed country, if major economic and social decisions were dominated by a monolithic party, relatively little interest in economic measures would be evinced by wider groups in the population. An authoritarian political system which limits the sources of the policy decision process would also almost automatically limit economic information and analysis as well. The situation is different in a political democracy with a plurality of interest groups and general freedom of access to and use of socially important information. Likewise, real changes or differences in the *degree of interdependence* would affect the scope of the desired economic measures: the self-subsistent farm in a traditional agricultural economy, with little contact even with the domestic urban centers, let alone with other countries, is hardly a base for a strong interest in nationwide or worldwide economic performance and structure. And there are, finally, real differences and changes in *measurability,* essentially in availability of mechanisms that would generate socially acceptable consensus on relative weights of various inputs and outputs, a point to be covered below in dealing with the supply of quantitative data. Such differences in measurability would be reflected in the demand for economic measures, the demand being weak when the very course and nature of economic activity does not foster a quantitative approach. In short, there are variations and changes in the effect of each of the four conditions. These variations and changes are due either to differences and changes in the real extent of interdependence and of measurability within the economy; or to differences and changes in the consensus on the relevant categories and aspects that should be measured; or to differences and changes in the degree to which policy modifications of economic performance and structure are within the control of the several groups within society.

To put it briefly, the demand for economic data, in the scope and variety of the measures called for, is a function of the relevant economic and social structure, of the organized knowledge that exists of economic society, and of the degree to which demand is encouraged by the political and ideological structure. To deal with these variations and changes in detail would be tantamount to reviewing past and current differences among economic societies with respect to all these characteristics—a task not feasible here, and perhaps not necessary. The major conclusion that we wish to retain, for consideration of the problems of supply of economic data discussed below, is that the demand for economic measures varies in space and particularly changes over time, as the relevant economic framework changes in the process of growth and as our knowledge of it also changes with the cumulation of tested analysis and recorded experience.

The dependence of demand on changing knowledge, and correspondingly changing perception of the policy potentials, is especially to be stressed. Much of the widespread use of economic measures is for current *orientation*—to establish what happened in terms of some meaningful categories and relevant to recognizable group and nationwide interests within the community. But such orientation is dependent upon accepted assumptions and theories—assumptions as to final goals of economic activity and as to tolerable ways of attaining them, and upon theories as to the relations among various aspects of economic performance and structure in their contribution to the final goals. These assumptions and theories are, in fact, established in a formal body of economic and social theory. Changes in the latter, resulting from uses of economic measures for consistent *analysis*, which go well beyond the uses for current orientation, and from changes in observed economic experience, will, with some time lag, be reflected in changes in the measures needed for current orientation. Likewise, uses for orientation are often generated by the search for *policy modifications or adjustments*, if the orientation reveals undesirable aspects of economic performance and structure. But the policy adjustments, in turn, depend on the existing and accepted body of economic analysis and theory that has to be applied, combined with the additional specification and extrapolation involved in weighing policy costs and returns. Changes in that body of analysis and theory would modify the direction of the current orientation, and hence the character of economic measures demanded.

One could perhaps distinguish three types of demand for and use of economic measures: for current orientation; for analytical uses, limited to scholarly pursuit within the discipline; and for policy exploration and application, involving specification and extrapolation not required for other types of use.[1] But these three types of use and demand are interrelated in the sense that wide demand for current orientation reflects, if with some lag, the theoretical concepts and assumptions involved in analytical uses, and even some of the results of policy exploration; while the latter are dependent upon the analytical uses for identifying the tested relations to be employed in further identification and exploration. The *central* position of the *analytical* uses of economic measures, in their long-term effects on uses for current orientation and policy application, is fairly clear. We return to this point below, when, in considering the problems of supply, we deal with the relations between the supply of primary data and the generation of economic measures.

---

[1] For more detailed discussion of this, and several other points touched upon here, see my "Quantitative Economic Research: Trends and Problems," in *Economic Research: Retrospect and Prospect*, Fiftieth Anniversary Colloquium VII (New York: National Bureau of Economic Research, 1972). But some of the problems in the supply of primary data discussed below are not dealt with there.

2. *Supply of Primary Data*

Since economic measures are quantitative expressions of analytically oriented concepts and categories, an effective way to derive such measures would be one similar to that used in the experimental sciences. The experiment, embodying an analytical model, is carried through, yielding the data that reveal either the validity or the inadequacy of the model. In the latter case, the model is modified and tested in a modified experiment. Even so, the data yielded by the experiments are raw, subject as they are to measurement errors, and require further treatment to be converted into properly interpretable measures. But at least there is an experimental design that uses the model as a guide to isolate and limit the substance or process to be treated and measured; and there is a battery of tools and controls that permit close specification of the variables allowed to affect the measured outcome.

No such experimental isolation and manipulation is possible in economics. But while this obvious limitation has been referred to repeatedly, some consequences may not have been clearly enough perceived, and warrant a brief comment. The consequences are viewed here from the standpoint of analytical uses of economic measures that are aimed at establishing tested and interrelated generalizations, at distinguishing the common and persistent from the variable and transient, and hence that permit understanding and policy based on established causative connections with known limits to their validity.

The first consequence of the impossibility of experimental treatment is a great loss in data economy and hence a vastly greater demand for *observational* data than would have been needed if *experimental* treatment were possible. The implication of being able to use an analytical hypothesis as a guide in identifying important factors and variables, and then using the latter in controlled (according to the hypothesis) manipulations and other means of introducing the assumed determinants, is that only a limited body of processes and data is involved. This dispenses with the need to collect a vast amount of observational data in the hope that when these are converted into meaningful measures, and then subjected to comparative analysis, they will represent quasi-experimental situations in which the common element is revealed, the variable distinguished, and both associated with the relevant determining factors. The point may be illustrated by asking how many millions of statistical observations of falling bodies under experimentally *uncontrolled* conditions would be needed before even a glimmer of the law of gravitation would emerge—if it ever would; and how much observational data we could dispense with if we could isolate an experimental national economy and subject it to various manipulative injections of inputs and policies to observe the effects on growth, stability, and equity. It is because of this huge demand for observational, and hence for primary raw data, to permit tested analysis, that the difficulties with the *supply* of primary data are so crucial in the field of economics and other social science disciplines.

The second consequence of the impossibility of experimental testing is the proliferation of competing hypotheses that survive for long periods of time. Such longevity in continuous conflict is found partly because, for lack of experimental complement, even the formulation of the hypotheses is not sufficiently precise and thus allows a variety of exceptions which are not damaging enough to kill; and partly because, even when the formulation is precise enough for empirical testing, the hypotheses require too demanding a variety of data. The longevity of theoretical hypotheses in economics is truly impressive, when one observes that Classical and Marxian theories of economic growth, generated well before the modern economic epoch was adequately revealed, still persist in somewhat modified variants. They survive despite the numerous and major disparities between the projected trends and the observed long-term movements, and despite the patent neglect of technological change, surely a most important permissive factor in modern economic growth. And yet, considering the pressure for some guidance for measurement and policy, an incomplete and hence partly wrong theory may be preferable to no theory at all; at least it yields a body of concepts and categories that can be used for *preliminary* guidance, no matter what revisions the ensuing results call for. Still, the impossibility of experimental, i.e., highly discriminating, testing leads to a great lengthening, a slowing down of the interplay between the generation of analytical hypotheses and their testing—a lack of economy similar to that in the requirements for primary data. For just as experiments economize on data, so are they economical in the rapidity with which they can reject a hypothesis as either incomplete or downright wrong. The resulting inefficiency in economics in the reformulation of and competition among differing hypotheses becomes all the more burdensome because of the rapid change in economic performance and structure, at least in modern times—shifting parameters and loci of the pressing policy problems.

Granted the impossibility of the experimental approach in economics and other social science disciplines, there are many natural science disciplines that also rely exclusively on observational data, the nature of their subject not permitting experimental manipulation (e.g., astronomy). We come, therefore, to what are perhaps the most crucial questions in our discussion. Who provides the observational primary data used by economic analysts in deriving economic measures? How are they provided? What control does the economic analyst exercise over the supply and character of the observational primary data in his field?

By and large, the primary data relating to economic activity and structure, unlike the data in the observational natural sciences, are not provided by trained professionals (e.g., collected by the astronomers in their observatories). They are supplied by the active participants in economic activity—the people who report to the census on their occupations and incomes; the business firms that report on sales, wages, and profits; and the governmental and other public agencies that report on their activity, personnel, payrolls, and the like. In all these cases it is the participant who reports on his activity, characteristics, or status. To be sure, some data are not recorded by the actual participant, but by some administrative agency empowered to observe the specific activity, e.g., the data on commodity imports and exports as observed by customs officers, although even here much of the information comes from the active participant, not from the customs officer. Or some data which *cannot* be adequately provided by the active participants are collected by professional technicians—e.g., in the crop-cutting surveys used in some countries to estimate the various major crops. And yet the overwhelming proportion of the flow of primary economic data comes from and is provided by the participants in economic activity and social life—individuals, firms, public agencies, reporting on their own characteristics and doings.

The major reason for this somewhat paradoxical situation (paradoxical by comparison with the observational practices in the natural sciences, in which there is typically a sharp distinction between the observer and the subject of observation) is the prohibitive cost of securing a comparable volume of data by other means. Placing professional observers within the household, the firm, or the public agency, to collect the minimum primary data on employment, income, consumption, and the like, would require an impossibly large input of human resources— even disregarding the problem of acceptability to the observed and compatibility between the latter and the observer. The provision of such independent observation even on a *sample* basis would still be prohibitively costly in sheer volume of inputs; and the sampling itself would have to depend on some census-based frame. While a natural science faces a somewhat similar problem in attempting to provide technically organized observations of the full range of its universe, the latter is relatively fixed and the observations have a cumulative impact on the formulation of an adequate theory. In the economic discipline the observed reality changes rapidly; and the flow of observational data must be continuous and representative in order to be useful. Recent developments in communication promise a greatly reduced effort in collecting primary data, and, once these are secured, a greatly reduced cost in treating them; while sampling procedures reduce the need for complete coverage. Nevertheless, the active participant remains the major source of data.

Two important consequences of the dependence of the flow of economic primary data on reporting by the active participants may be suggested (the full exploration of these consequences requires more knowledge than is presently at hand). The first relates to the quality of the resulting primary data; the second to their supply, given the quality.

Obviously, since the data are provided by an active participant, not by a technically trained and professional observer, quality will vary considerably. Particularly with quantitative data, presumably and hopefully relevant to a clearly and meaningfully defined category, there is, in addition to the possible conscious biases, the sheer difficulty of establishing a reliable magnitude—or of establishing a magnitude at all. The education of the participants; the extent to which the organization of economic activity involves adequate accounting as a matter of course; the simplicity or complexity of the activity or component whose magnitude is to be measured; and the capacity for maintaining the quality in observational data reported over a long period are all obviously relevant conditions. It should be clear that, in such reporting, the resulting primary data must differ greatly in quality, depending upon the extent of what might be called inherent quantification of economic activity and of social life in general. This is a function of modern economic growth, and is much less prevalent in the less-developed and traditionally organized countries. It is also dependent on the complexity of the concept or category for which a quantitative datum is being sought.

It scarcely needs to be stressed that in the less-developed countries the quality of economic data supplied by the active participants is likely to be poor, partly because of the inadequate quantification implicit in the very course of their economic activity, partly because of lack of experience in collecting such data and in acquiring the minimum levels of skill and consistency. Striking illustrations can be provided from the current experience of the less-developed countries, and also from the early periods of the presently developed countries. Several African countries encountered difficulties in securing a simple census count of population in recent years; and in the United States in the early nineteenth century, the censuses of manufacturing suffered critical breakdowns. It should be remembered that while the less-developed countries face difficulties in securing adequate quality statistics on seemingly simple aspects of economic production and structure, the developed countries face no less weighty difficulties in securing adequate quality of some economic data. The difficulties in the developed countries are related to highly complex activities and products that may loom large in the total flows and aggregate structure. The reporting on the complex quality characteristics of many advanced occupations in a country like the United States, or for that matter on the prices of complex commodities, is of a kind that makes interpretation difficult. If a peasant in a less-developed country finds it difficult to report accurately on his output, a big firm in a developed country may also have considerable difficulty, or may have to invest much effort in reporting properly on its net income—which involves allowances (required by the proper economic concept) for the effects of differential price changes in raw materials and in finished product, or in capital input and product output. The point is that quality of data is relative to what *should* be measured and reported, and the latter may differ in complexity with the level of economic development, making for more complex and hence more difficult measurement targets with rise in the level of economic growth.

The provision of economic data by the active participants may be a burden that they are reluctant to accept. The burden is twofold: the organization of information to provide the required data may be costly, and the disclosure of information to others may be viewed as a loss of privacy, regrettable particularly in a competitive society or in a world in which such information may be used against the participant. Added to this is the large cost of converting the information into useful measures— useful to society, to the economic analysts, and to the reporting units themselves. All this suggests that the primary economic data will be provided by the active participants *only if* they recognize that by doing so they may benefit themselves, as individuals or as members of a society that recognizes the data as an indispensable basis for social organization and policy illumination and is willing to assume the costs of collecting, organizing, and disseminating the data. The supply of the data—their collection from willing reporting units and organization of the results for wider effective use—is thus contingent upon a balance of expected collective good over the private and social burdens. This balance can be struck only by the sovereign government authority.

The dominance of government, in its various divisions, in the collection of primary economic and social data, and in their organization for wider use, is obvious from a glance at the statistical abstract of any country, be it an open market democracy or an authoritarian Communist country, an economically developed nation or a less-developed one. To be sure, in many developed market economies data are collected and organized for their members by industrial associations, trade unions, professional societies and the like—in recognition of the value of such data for their memberships and of the possible use of the data in presenting a case for the members to the country at large. Many large individual firms, in view of their public standing, do, in fact, collect and publish a fair amount of data on their activities. But, even though no comparative inventory can be presented here, it can be claimed that the dominant part of the primary data is collected, assembled, and organized for widespread use by the various branches of governments; and that it is the statistical branches of the governments that are largely responsible for the flow of basic primary data on which the economic analyst relies.

The point to be stressed here is that this central role of government is a direct consequence of the need for large amounts of observational (rather than small amounts of experimental) data, and of the dependence on the active participants in economic activity and structure for such data. Only the sovereign government can vouch for the consensus on the socially necessary character of the data; only it has the economic and other resources required for extensive data collection, tabulation, and publication—resource inputs far beyond the capacity of any single scholar, groups of scholars, or private research institutions. And only the government has unlimited life and can maintain the continuity of data flow. Moreover, the requirement that the data, when assembled and tabulated, be treated as a public good, not as a private asset of some limited group, makes the profit-oriented firms (in a country in which the latter operate) unsuitable carriers for such activity.

The dominant role of government as the collector and provider of the primary economic data may, in turn, affect the quality of the data—particularly in countries in which the canons by which information is secured may be corrupted by political expediency; and in which the government has limited capacity to wrestle with the difficulties of adequately organizing and carrying through the necessary programs. But the major consequence that we would like to stress is that bearing on the *supply* of primary data, assuming that they satisfy some minimum standard of quality. Here the role of the government is crucial, since in many situations only the government has the power to decide on the collection of data and to assume responsibility for their release for analytical and orientation uses. That this is the case is illustrated (negatively) by the decisions of some Communist governments to impose a blackout on all basic economic data, on the excuse that they may be a tool in the hands of enemies, external and possibly internal. To illustrate further, governments even in the non-Communist countries are often reluctant to publish bodies of data which may (or may not) raise awkward questions concerning deficiencies in social and economic performance. The use of primary economic data, when converted into economic measures, for comparative analysis of a wide variety of countries with differing governmental, political, and ideological structures, is particularly affected by the different situations with respect to the quality and availability of such data; and by the prohibition, in some countries, of the critical discussion of the domestic data and of the results they suggest, that would serve to limit the conscious and unconscious biases in the quality, and particularly, in the supply of data.

Setting aside such possible biases and concentrating our attention on the more freely organized economically developed countries, where conditions for government responsibility for widespread collection, organization, and publication of primary data are most favorable, we observe that even then there are major limitations on the supply—as viewed from the standpoint of effective economic analysis. These limitations are, in a sense, imposed by the requirement that the data be widely viewed as indispensable for orientation, understanding, and perhaps for needed policy amelioration with respect to a major aspect of economic (or social) activity or structure. The decisions to collect and disseminate data, therefore, reflect judgments as to what should be illuminated by quantitative primary data—given the feasibility of securing sufficiently reliable data in the first place. Such judgments, as exercised by the governments subjected to a variety of pressures, do not necessarily represent prompt and sensitive responses to emerging policy problems or evolving analytical questions. There is usually a substantial lag in the decision by the government to secure a new body of relevant data in response to a newly emerging problem, because the latter must attain sufficient magnitude before it is viewed by the government as warranting new data collection. Then, since a long period of data accumulation is required before adequate analysis can be carried through, the consequence is that the supply of primary data at any one time, even in countries placing high value on widespread and critically examined statistics, is deficient with respect to the currently emerging and hence especially pressing problems in economic policy and economic analysis.

Needless to say, the *supply* of data (regardless of quality) in the less-developed countries, relative to the major economic problems to be analyzed, is inadequate. Quantification is difficult, and resources for building up the required supply were in the past and are currently limited. Nor need one stress that in Communist and other authoritarian countries, the supply of primary economic data available for economic analysis is likely to be limited and biased; and that the restrictions on critical analysis *within* these countries only aggravate the problem. Not so obvious, and yet important, are the limitations on the supply of primary economic data, in both timing and coverage, in the more freely organized, democratically oriented, economically developed countries. Given the dominance of the government, basic data may be collected regularly and effectively because they form part of the recognized organizational framework of the society, but they may be subject to only superficial review by the economic analysts (e.g., the periodic population census in the United States, required by the political and electoral system, is a treasure house of accumulated data that economic analysts have only recently begun to study seriously). On the other hand, data on some important aspect of economic activity may be lacking, because the problems involved were recognized as important only after a substantial time lag (as was the case with unemployment statistics in the United States in the 1930's and income distribution data in the recent two decades). It is perhaps valid to say that the flow of primary data on the *distributive* aspects of economic growth even today in the advanced economic democracies leaves much to be desired. Such data will have to be extended markedly before adequate economic analysis—rather than rough and ready, and too often dogmatic, statements that reflect inevitable biases—is possible.

That lags occur in the flow of primary economic data, even in open and advanced economies, is not surprising. Such lags, and the resulting gaps in the supply of primary data needed for policy- and analysis-oriented economic measures, follow from the close tie between the government as the consensus-certifying arm of society, and the need for such consensus if data are to be secured from the active participants in economic and social activity. But they also follow from the inability to foresee many major changes with which economic and social life abounds, to foresee in time to call for the data-flow required for their illumination and analysis. This inability is a reflection of the limited capacity of economic analysis to encompass the changing course of economic life, to prevent "surprises," and accordingly to convert the primary data, the raw material, into fully relevant and meaningful measures. We come at this point to direct consideration of the relation between primary data and economic measures.

3. *Primary Data and Economic Measures*

The data reported by participants in economic activity, even if fully reliable and continuously provided, are only the raw material for economic measures. Since the latter are the quantitative counterparts of economic concepts and categories, they cannot, in the nature of the case, be directly provided by individuals, firms, or even government agencies. It is not merely a matter of aggregation, the need for which, in a comprehensive and articulated measure of a complex economy's performance and structure, cannot be satisfied in the reporting by individual active participants. It is impossible, even in the search for less aggregative measures, to request data that would automatically and neatly fit into a relatively sophisticated economic measure. One can ask an adult whether he was employed, for wages, during the last month, and in what capacity, but not whether he is a member of the labor force. One can ask a firm what price it charged for its product, but not whether it is a price in a monopolistic or competitive market. What the respondents provide, and the governments and related agencies collect, tabulate, and publish, and what fills the bulk of statistical abstracts and census volumes are not economic measures but primary data—which may, of course, carry economic connotations, because they are the customary raw material for economic measures.

The distinction between primary data and economic measures is important if we are to understand the effects of limitations in the supply of data on quantitative economic analysis. The tonnage of steel produced during a given year in a given country constitutes a primary datum, which may be the raw material for the derivation of an estimate of capital formation—an economic measure. But steel tonnage is not an economic measure, since it does not represent, in itself, a quantitative expression of any analytically derived economic concept. It may be looked upon as mainly an economic datum (although it may also be viewed as an engineering, or geographical, or ecological datum, in alternative uses) because people think—for good or bad, but mostly inadequate reasons—that steel output is a potentially significant index of economic performance. Similarly, output of wheat is a primary datum, but it is not the economic measure of production of consumer goods, of which it is a part. The price of milk is a primary datum; the cost of living is an economic measure. The gross profit reported by a firm is a primary datum; the estimate of the firm's profits, adjusted to correspond to the economic concept of net profit, is an economic measure. It follows that, given the quality and supply limitations on the flow of primary data, and even assuming unrealistically high quality and supply, a series of important steps is needed in the conversion of primary data into economic measures. These steps should be explicitly noted, for the extent to which they have been followed and the results used will in turn affect the further supply of primary data—with respect to both their quality and the completeness of their coverage. It is in the conversion of primary data to relevant economic measures—relevant to meaningful analysis—that economists, in pursuing such analysis, exercise their influence on and attain some control over the quality and quantity of primary data.

Before the raw primary data can be converted into economic measures, they must be scrutinized and their reliability for gauging the activity or aspect of structure that is being covered must be evaluated. The scope of the data must be compared with the coverage required by the economic measure, and adjustments must be derived to compensate for inadequacies in coverage. In the case of complicated measures, problems of internal classification of a variety of units and groups of products or activities among significant categories within the economic aggregate or index must be resolved. Whether some of these steps are taken by an economic analyst or by a government statistician, they must be taken in full cognizance of the requirements of the concepts and implied structural relations formulated in economic theory and analysis. The eventual judgment as to the bearing of any limitations in reliability, coverage, and relevance to analytical categories, must be that of the economic analyst who uses the measures in orienting interpretation or in analysis aimed at testing some established or newly formulated hypotheses. Under some conditions, formal statistical tests are possible, but these conditions are not widely encountered in the collection of primary economic data. Consequently, it remains the responsibility of the economic analyst to judge whether the data fed into the economic measure are reliable enough and of sufficient scope to justify the conclusions claimed from the analysis.

While this requirement of intensive scrutiny of the primary data used in deriving economic measures has not always been observed by economists, there has been marked progress as evidenced by the increasing reliability of increasingly complex economic measures derived by trained economists from the governmental statistics of the freely organized, economically developed countries. Substantial progress in this respect has also been made in a number of the less-developed countries. The widening use of economic measures in interpretive or generalizing analysis is even more important, for this involves testing not merely the reliability and scope of the primary data, but also the adequacy of the conceptual structure that underlies the measures, and thus the very theories and assumptions within the framework of economic analysis itself.

The use of economic measures to interpret current changes in or to establish general and variable features of some economic process, or to test directly a specific hypothesis, represents, implicitly or explicitly, a valuable test of the relevance and effectiveness of the underlying economic concepts and thus also of the basic assumptions and theoretical relations. If the tests reveal the inadequacy of the existing concepts and hypotheses, demand will be generated for new primary data on the variables newly introduced to adjust and modify the older hypotheses and concepts. To cite a recent example: the use of various long-term measures in the analysis of economic growth has raised questions as to the adequacy of material capital as the major factor in accounting for growth; and has led to a greater emphasis on investment in human capital. This has generated interest in primary data on education, and brought a growing pressure on government and society to supply such primary data more fully and continuously than has been done. To use an older example: the finding, from rather simple data on occupational and industrial structure, of the large increase in the share of the labor force attached to services led to pressure for more data, particularly on the distributive trades, and to the introduction of the relevant census in the United States in the 1920's.

These are examples of one set of empirically derived findings effecting a shift of emphasis on and of demand for additional primary data on previously neglected sectors or aspects. Examples can be cited of revisions of theoretical hypotheses, forced upon economic analysts by major events, observable even without elaborate statistics. These revisions, having emerged, called for new primary data, because they stressed the importance of new economic measures for which the pre-existing supply of primary data was not adequate. Thus the emergence of the Keynesian theory, by stressing final demand, forced the development of gross national product accounting to what is called the final-use level (distinguishing household purchases, government consumption, and capital formation) in addition to the more widespread earlier estimates, usually based on factor shares by production sectors. This shift to the final-use level called for new primary data by which continuous and acceptable estimates of the final-use categories could be derived.

While examples can easily be multiplied by exploration into the history of the discipline, the illustrations suffice to suggest the reality of the link between the derivation and *uses* of economic measures in various types of economic analysis, the implicit testing of pre-existing theories and assumptions (even when no direct testing of hypotheses is involved), and the fresh insights into the limitations of pre-existing theories, the shifts of weights with possible increase in weights of components conventionally neglected because they have been relatively small, and the nature of such current changes as have not been allowed for in the available analytical framework. It is through these analytical uses of economic measures that the economic discipline has affected the views of society and government with regard to the changing variety of socially-necessary, primary data. Through them it has attained a measure of influence and control, modifying the accepted views of both government and the wide circles of participants in economic activity that are the major source of primary data. It is by affecting *demand* that quantitatively oriented economic analysis affects the *supply* of primary data—and hence, the feasibility of securing the raw materials for an adequate flow of economic measures. We have thus come full circle in our discussion: having begun with a comment on conditions that determine demand for economic measures, and thus implicitly for the primary data needed for the latter, we have now suggested that the effective demand is shaped by the uses of economic measures in economic analysis. It is, in good part, determined in the continuous interplay between the formulation and reformulation of assumptions, hypotheses, and measurement tools, and their use in quantitative analysis—the latter representing the crucial test, whether the analysis be for current orientation, generalization, or some policy exploration.

Three concluding comments are perhaps appropriate. First, the neglect of empirically oriented, quantitative analysis, i.e., one based on economic measures derivable from existing primary data, results in an accumulation of significant problems, in a widening lag in the supply of primary data and of relevant economic measures. The belief that some basic principles of economic behavior will suffice neglects the fact that there is frequent change in the concrete conditions under which such behavior occurs, and within which general laws derived therefrom operate; and that it is these changing conditions that have to be continuously studied, and their impact analyzed. In retrospect, it seems clear that the long period spanning the second half of the nineteenth century and the early part of the twentieth century, during which economic theory relied only slightly on quantitative analysis, and there was little of the latter, left a legacy of accumulated problems and a stock of primary data that proved to be woefully deficient, when the recent acceleration in quantitative analysis began some three to four decades ago.

Second, there were and still are severe constraints on the volume of empirically oriented, quantitative analysis in economics.

The number of competent analysts who could be spared from the pressures of current policy problems is small; the institutional relations among academic economics, statistical and analytical work in government departments (and more recently in international agencies also), and whatever economic research is carried on within private firms, have been less than optimal in encouraging the necessary collaboration. I refer again to freely organized, economically developed, countries. Conditions for such research in authoritarian and particularly Communist countries, and in the less-developed countries, are, of course, unfavorable in additional respects. The small number of scholars that characterized previous decades has expanded since World War II; but there is a prevailing lack of systematic institutional provisions for quantitative analysis and for cooperation among academic, government, and business economics. This must be kept in mind in evaluating the slow pace in the past and the gaps in the present. The impressive acceleration in the volume of quantitative analysis, in the underlying collection of primary data, and in the relevant body of economic measures have all been from low bases.

Finally, so long as the analytical framework of the discipline is changing—and it must change if it is not to stagnate—there will be *some* gaps in the supply of primary data. Changes in the concepts and in the definitions of relevant economic measures, containing as they will new elements, will call for new data, which will not be there. No matter how much more is known, an intellectual discipline that is still alive has frontiers on the new partly unknown, for which ready data are not available and must be sought—in new experiments in the experimental sciences, in new technically controlled observations in the observational natural sciences, and in new primary data and new variants of economic measures in the field of economics. The task, of course, is to widen the scope of the tested known by sustained attempts to exploit the data and hypotheses already available—and push the frontiers of the new beyond the presently knowable.

The Gap: Concept,
Measurement, Trends

1. Concept

SUBSTANCE (GAP IN WHAT?) · By rich nations we presumably mean those that command a volume of economic goods that, relative to population, is significantly larger than some acceptable level. By analogy, those nations are poor whose command of economic goods, on a per capita basis, is so much below that acceptable level as to imply major shortcomings and deprivation. This command over goods may be approximated by the stock of material assets, preferably supplemented by some valuation of the human resources at the nation's disposal. But the effective magnitude of such productive assets is best revealed by the annual output which they, in fact, serve to produce. Despite several vexing problems of definition and interpretation, the long-term level of per capita national product is still a reasonable criterion of the wealth and poverty of nations—long-term meaning periods long enough to obviate distortion by transient disturbances and fluctuations.

But some nations, particularly smaller ones, can show a sus-

Reprinted from Gustav Ranis, ed., *The Gap Between Rich and Poor Nations* (London: The Macmillan Press Ltd., 1972), pp. 3–43. The paper was presented at a conference of the International Economic Association at Bled, Yugoslavia, in August–September, 1970.

tained high level of per capita product because they are richly endowed with a natural resource that is desired—and often discovered and operated—by others, and in return for which they receive a large rent. This kind of wealth differs significantly from that of nations whose economy and society are geared to the utilization of the technological potential of modern economic growth. While some economically developed and modernized countries may also have a natural-resource comparative advantage, we should, in considering the gap between rich and poor countries, exclude those that are rich merely because of the bounty of nature, of luck.

We propose to limit the rich nations here to those whose high per capita product is due to an economy and a society that are capable of significant and widespread utilization of the potentials of modern technology—the economically developed nations. Since no low per capita product nations are economically developed in this sense, the gap between rich and poor is reformulated into a gap between the economically developed nations and the *poor*, less-developed nations (less-developed by definition).[1] As just indicated, some less-developed nations may be windfall rich; other less-developed nations, whose levels of modernization, industrialization, and adoption of modern technology are below those of the developed nations, may have per capita products that place them well above the poor, without windfall riches. Yet the most significant gap for analysis and policy is that between the economically developed and the poor, less-developed countries (LDCs). Of course, it still remains to draw the per capita product line (or band) below which "poverty" lies; but this can be done best with the help of the statistical data in the next section.

This reformulation of the gap is important because it emphasizes the association between the disparity in per capita product and those in economic structures and institutions, in noneconomic structures, and in social ideology (i.e., views on man and nature prevalent in various societies). The gap is not merely be-

---

[1] This statement implies that the potential of modern economic growth can also be effectively realized and a high per capita product attained in countries without a great natural resource endowment. Japan is the most conspicuous example, but others are the Netherlands, Denmark, Switzerland, and even Italy.

tween rich and poor, but between the industrialized, urbanized, mechanized, modernized countries with distinctive economic institutions, demographic processes, political characteristics, and ideological patterns on the one hand; and the largely rural, agricultural, traditional countries, with only small nuclei of modern industry, modern firms, modern government, and modern views on the other. Difficult as it may be to establish the specific connection between economic development, as measured by some index of aggregate product, and economic and social structures, institutions, and ideological notions, the evidence on such historical association is too weighty to be denied or neglected. And the association provides a basis for interpreting and analyzing the aggregative gap.

BASE (GAP BETWEEN WHOM?) · The importance of the aggregative and structural gap depends upon the magnitude and number of societies at either end—what might be called the population base. If, despite what we know, we were to assume that of 3.3 billion of world population, divided among more than 150 states and dependencies (in the mid-1960's), only one country, with some 3 million population, was developed; and only one other, also with a population of 3 million, was poor and less-developed (and all others were within a range of, say, $500 to $600 per capita product and of rather similar structure), the gap—relating to less than 1 per cent of mankind—would hardly deserve much interest. If the modern economic growth process did not affect a substantial group of nations, and if poverty, caused by the failure to exploit modern economic growth, did not afflict a large proportion of humanity, the gap suggested by the illustration would be viewed as the result of some unusual combination of circumstances—perhaps as an analytical curiosity, but not a significant economic and social problem. It is the nature of modern scholarship to neglect mere intellectual curiosities and concentrate on questions with empirical weight that, at least potentially, seems large.

Given a large population base at each end of the gap, what is the extent of diversity and divisiveness within each base? If, again contrary to reality, we were to assume that there is one large developed country, with a population of, say, 1 billion, and one large poor, less-developed country, with a population, say, of 2 billion (leaving only 300 million for all other nations), the population base of the gap would be large but there would be no diversity or divisiveness at either end (assuming that each country is a fairly unified society). The actual gap, currently observed and illustrated by relevant statistics, is characterized by the many developed, as well as many poor, less-developed countries, and the numerous divergencies among them.

The diversity and divisiveness among nations at both ends are important particularly with reference to the interrelations or movements *across* the gap, a third aspect of the concept to be noted below. The diversity may relate to size, with major effects on propensity to engage in foreign trade; to level of development (*within* the range indicated by the grouping into developed, and poor, less-developed); and to the ideology that governs economic life. The organization of mankind into nations and the multiplicity of nations imply emphasis on the nation's interest as the overriding priority and permit a divisive cumulation of heritage of past history among nations. The gap is thus not merely between the aggregative and structural aspects of economic and social performances of two large groups within the world population, but between the two groups, subdivided into many relatively independent and differing units. There is thus a multiplicity of binary gaps; and the movements across the gap can assume a wide variety of combinations, affected partly by the complementary and partly by the competitive relations among the nations at either end and across the gap.

ASSOCIATION AND ISOLATION · Much of the interest in the gap lies in its effect on the flows across the gap—between the rich, developed, and poor, less-developed nations—and on the flows within the rich and the poor groups themselves—at least as affected by the gap.

One extreme assumption is that no such flows—either across the gap or within either end—exist; that the two groups are completely isolated from each other and indeed have no knowledge of each other's existence (and that the same is true of the several countries at either end). This is not an entirely unrealistic assumption with respect to much of past history. Until the European explorations of the late fifteenth century, the societies in Middle America lived without knowing Europeans or being known by them; and did not know of, and were not known to, the societies in Africa. Such cases of complete (or almost complete) isolation were numerous in past history; and their scarcity is a feature of only the recent century. The other extreme assumption—of fully developed and relatively easy economic and other flows across the gap (and within the groups at either end)—is a condition that has only been approached, and is far from fully attained even today.

Isolation or association, the extent and ease of international movements may apply to economic flows—of productive resources, such as man, capital, know-how, etc.; of commodities and services in foreign trade; of monetary and other claims; of consumption patterns via the demonstration effects; and the like. They may relate to flows of intangibles—of knowledge, education, cultural innovations—all fundamental in shaping social and economic life. Finally, the flows may represent exercise of political power—cooperative or aggressive—involving at times substantial flows of economic goods but not of economic activities per se. All these flows and the association or isolation that they spell, condition the co-existence of nations at both ends of the gap. They affect the social and economic stability among the poor countries; the rivalries of developed countries for preferential position with respect to the poor and less-developed; and the task of optimizing the economic flows, to enhance the growth prospects of the poor while preserving the pioneering potentials of the developed countries themselves.

2. Measurement

Measuring all aspects of the aggregate and structural gap, let alone of the flows across it, is an enormous task and can hardly be attempted here. Furthermore, many of the major quantitative characteristics of the current gap are well known; and it would serve little purpose to demonstrate what is already established. Under the circumstances, it seemed best to select for discussion a few statistical findings.

IDENTIFICATION AND BASE · We identify the developed and poor, less-developed countries primarily by their per capita product, using the recent estimates by Hagen and Hawrylyshyn of GDP in market prices, in U.S. dollars in 1965 (see Table 1, which contains the specific references). The H–H estimates are based largely on United Nations data, supplemented by a few special sources for the Communist countries.

Developed countries are defined as those with a per capita product in 1965 of $1,000 or more—with two significant exceptions. The first is the exclusion of a few countries with a high per capita product due largely to natural or location advantages (this meant excluding Puerto Rico, Kuwait, and Qatar). Second, although Japan's per capita product is given as only $870, we included it among the developed countries because, in view of its scarcity of industrial and natural resources, such a per capita product is a clear indication of a high level of modernization and development. As thus defined, the developed group comprises, among non-Communist countries, Europe excluding Ireland, Spain, Portugal, Greece, Malta; North America; Australia and New Zealand; Japan; and Israel; among the Communist countries—the U.S.S.R., East Germany, and Czechoslovakia. It differs from the United Nations definition of non-Communist developed countries by excluding some European countries and South Africa (excluded here because its high per capita income is for its small white population, not its total population). The developed countries, so defined, account for about 861 million people, with a per capita product of some $1,900, or 26 per cent of world population, but 79 per cent of world product.

The "poor" less-developed countries, narrowly defined, comprise all countries with a per capita product in 1965 of $120 or less. This definition segregates many populous countries and accounts for most of the population of sub-Saharan Africa and Asia. The population of this group in 1965 was 1,726 million, or 53 per cent of world population. Its per capita product was only $95—about one-twentieth of that for the developed group; and its share in world product was 7.9 per cent.

These two groups account for about 80 per cent of world population (and for an even higher percentage of world product)—leaving somewhat over 20 per cent with a per capita product ranging between $121 and $1,000. Thus, the relative magnitude, in terms of population (and product) of the developed countries on the one hand, and of the "poor" less-developed countries on the other, would be only slightly affected if we shifted the "pov-

PER CAPITA GROSS DOMESTIC PRODUCT
(AT MARKET PRICES) AND BY MAJOR REGIONS, 1965
(population in millions; per capita GDP in U.S. $)

				Regions				
	World (1)	Sub-Saharan Africa (2)	Asia (3)	Middle East (4)	Latin America (5)	Europe (6)	Oceania (7)	North America (8)
1. Total population	3,271	223	1,789	110	243	675	17.4	214
Developed Countries								
2. Population	861 (262)	0	98.0	2.6	0	532 (262)	14.0	214
3. Per capita GDP	1,892 (1,166)	0	870	1,407	0	1,455 (1,166)	2,033	3,441
4. % of population of region	26.3 (8.0)	0	5.5	2.4	0	78.9 (38.8)	80.3	100
Less-Developed Countries (grouped by per capita GDP)								
$80 or less								
5. Population	267 (19.0)	80.1	178 (19.0)	7.2	0	0	2.2	0
6. Per capita GDP	65.6 (70)	58.4	69.5 (70)	54.0	0	0	50.0	0
7. % of population of region	8.2 (0.6)	35.9	9.9 (1.1)	6.6	0	0	12.3	0
$81–$120								
8. Population	1,459 (713)	93.5	1,347 (713)	13.5	4.7	0	0	0
9. Per capita GDP	100 (100)	92.3	101 (100)	103	85.1	0	0	0
10. % of population of region	44.6 (21.8)	41.9	75.3 (39.9)	12.3	1.9	0	0	0
"Poor" LDCs, narrow definition (per capita GDP of $120 or less)								
11. Population	1,726 (732)	174	1,525 (732)	20.8	4.7	0	2.2	0
12. Per capita GDP	95 (99)	77	97 (99)	86	85	0	50	0
13. % of population of region	52.8 (22.4)	77.8	85.2 (41.0)	18.9	1.9	0	12.3	0

Table 1. Distribution of World Population by Per Capita Gross Domestic Product
(at market prices) and by Major Regions, 1965 (Continued)
(population in millions; per capita GDP in U.S. $)

					Regions			
	World (1)	Sub-Saharan Africa (2)	Asia (3)	Middle East (4)	Latin America (5)	Europe (6)	Oceania (7)	North America (8)
$121–$180								
14. Population	121	5.4	82.2	29.6	3.8	0	0	0
15. Per capita GDP	147	147	142	159	166	0	0	0
16. % of population of region	3.7	2.4	4.6	26.9	1.6	0	0	0
$181–$300								
17. Population	241 (1.9)	25.3	67.4	52.4	93.6	(1.9)	0.8	0
18. Per capita GDP	259 (185)	258	266	237	268	(185)	300	0
19. % of population of region	7.4 (0.1)	11.3	3.8	47.7	38.5	(0.3)	4.8	0
"Poor" LDCs, wide definition (per capita GDP of $300 or less)								
20. Population	2,089 (734)	204	1,675 (732)	103	102	(1.9)	3.0	0
21. Per capita GDP	117 (99)	101	106 (99)	184	255	(185)	50	0
22. % of population of region	63.9 (22.4)	91.5	93.7 (41.0)	93.5	42.0	(0.3)	17.1	0
$301–$450								
23. Population	88.5 (19.5)	0.5	13.2	2.4	42.9	29.1 (19.5)	0.5	0
24. Per capita GDP	349 (371)	448	324	323	334	380 (370)	435	0
25. % of population of region	2.7 (0.6)	0.2	0.7	2.2	17.6	4.3 (2.9)	2.6	0
$451 or more								
26. Population	233 (76.4)	18.4	2.6	2.1	98.1 (7.6)	112 (68.8)	0	0

All LDCs

29. Population	2,410 (830)	223	1,691 (732)	107	243 (7.6)	143 (90.2)	3.4	0
30. Per capita GDP	179 (164)	142	108 (99)	216	411 (530)	655 (662)	162	0
31. % of population of region	73.7 (25.3)	100	94.5 (41.0)	97.6	100 (3.1)	21.1 (13.4)	19.7	0

Entries in parentheses refer to Communist countries (included in relevant totals). We classified Yugoslavia and Cuba with the usual list of Communist countries in Asia and Eastern Europe.

The underlying estimates are from Everett E. Hagen and Oli Hawrylyshyn, "Analysis of World Income and Growth, 1955–1965," *Economic Development and Cultural Change*, Vol. 18, no. 1, Part II, October, 1969. These are based largely on United Nations estimates, supplemented by auxiliary sources (particularly for the Communist countries); and use conventional conversion rates to U.S. dollars in 1965. The estimates for the individual countries are given in Tables 3B, pp. 16–19; 4B, pp. 23–25; 5B, pp. 31–33; 6B, pp. 36–37; 7B, p. 39; and 8B, p. 41. The estimates for Communist countries have been adjusted to conform to the international GDP concept.

The regions distinguished here conform to the continental divisions, with the following exceptions. Sub-Saharan Africa includes all of Africa except Sudan, Egypt, Libya, Tunisia, Algeria, and Morocco. The latter, together with Aden, Gaza Strip, Muscat and Oman, Yemen, Bahrain, Jordan, Syria, Lebanon, Iraq, Saudi Arabia, Kuwait, Qatar, and Israel, constitute the Middle East. Europe includes Asiatic U.S.S.R., but excludes Turkey, which is covered under Asia. Latin Amer-

ica is the Western Hemisphere, except Canada and the United States (the latter two constituting North America), and therefore includes minor population groups (e.g., in Greenland) not usually included under Latin America.

The developed countries include most countries with per capita gross domestic product of $1,000 or more and Japan, for which per capita GDP was given as $870. However, we excluded those countries with per capita GDP above $1,000 in which this high level is due to some exceptional natural resource endowment or some advantageous strategic location. These countries—the Netherlands Antilles, Puerto Rico, Kuwait, and Qatar—were placed among the less-developed. The developed countries include most of Europe (except some in Eastern and Southern Europe and Ireland), Australia and New Zealand, North America, Japan, and Israel (whose per capita product is set at over $1,400, and would be well over $1,000 even allowing for unrequited imports). The definition differs from that used by the United Nations in excluding South Africa, where the high income of the much larger non-white population is offset by the low income of the white population (the per capita GDP is set at less than $600); and in excluding parts of Europe (Greece, Portugal, Spain, Ireland).

erty" line upward. A wider definition of the "poor" LDCs, with the per capita product line set at $300 rather than at $120, would mean a group accounting for 2,089 rather than 1,726 million, or 64 rather than 53 per cent of world population, but its per capita product would still be only $117 (compared with $95 for the narrower definition). This more widely defined "poor" group accounts for almost all the population of Asia and sub-Saharan Africa, and for a substantial part of the Latin American population.

Two characteristics of the population bases of the gap, familiar though they may be, bear repetition, for their implications are still to be fully explored. The first, given the $120 per capita as a reasonably low line for defining "poverty" (of which more in the next section), is the relatively large size of the base at the lower end of the gap. That the "poor" less-developed countries (narrowly defined) account for as much as 53 per cent of world population is to be ascribed largely to the populousness of the countries within the context of the Sinic and Indian civilizations (Mainland China, India, Pakistan, and Indonesia—the four alone accounting for 1,295 million in 1965). This, in turn, must be traced to the capacity of these two civilizations to sustain a large and growing population in the past—in ways in which this was not done in Africa, or in the Americas, or even in Europe; and this capacity could hardly have been due to greater natural endowments in Asia. But if the economic and social institutions were responsible, their role in the present economic position of these countries is in question. The second characteristic of the base is that almost all developed countries at the upper end are members of the European civilization complex, either in Europe or their offshoots overseas or in Asia (Israel). Indeed, only Japan can be said to be the one developed country effectively outside the European origin matrix. To be sure, some countries in Europe and offshoots overseas (e.g., Argentina) are not among the developed. Nevertheless, a question remains as to the extent to which some elements of "Europeanness" are a *necessary* if not *sufficient* condition for attaining the status of a developed country; and as to the special conditions in Japan that have provided an adequate substitute or analogue. In short, the identification of the bases at both ends of the gap, while indicating their large size in proportion to world population, also raises

questions concerning the historically conditioned social and institutional determinants of the difference in development between the two groups of countries.

MAGNITUDE OF THE AGGREGATE GAP · The estimates shown in
Table 1 have been converted from domestic currencies to U.S.
dollars by conventional exchange rates, modified in case of multiple exchange rates or violent distortions. Such exchange rates
differ substantially from approximations to real purchasing
power parities of the monetary units, and a wide literature has
emerged that deals with the problem and attempts modifications.[2] But the findings of the few usable studies, those by the
OEEC for Western European countries compared with the
United States, can easily be summarized.

First, even if exchange rates are assumed to reflect purchasing
power parities of goods entering foreign trade, the price structures of the latter do not fully represent the prices of the wider
range of goods entering countrywide output and comprising
gross domestic product; and more important, the degree of non-
representation differs among countries at different levels of development and hence of per capita product (as determined by
exchange rate conversion). The overstatement (or understatement) of the prices in the wider range of GDP is apparently
smaller (or greater) for the country with the lower per capita
product (country B) than for that with the higher per capita
product (country A). Hence, a shift from conversion by exchange rates to conversion by purchasing power parities for a
wider range of goods *reduces* the disparity among countries in
per capita product. This finding would probably also hold for
factor costs (rather than prices of final products), but I know of
no empirical study containing such a comparison (except incidentally in approximating prices of final goods, when the latter
are services of some one factor).

Second, the use of price levels for a broad range of goods for

---

[2] For a brief review and some attempts at solution, see Wilfred Becker-
man, "International Comparisons of Real Incomes," *OECD Development
Center Studies* (Paris, 1966). See also the discussion in Simon Kuznets,
Modern Economic Growth: Rate, Structure, and Spread (New Haven,
Conn.: Yale University Press, 1966), pp. 374–84 (referred to below as
MEG).

the two countries (or sets of countries) yields different relative disparities in their per capita products (as compared with those attained by conversion by exchange rates), depending upon which country's price structure is applied to one and the same set of quantities. If the price structure of the low per capita product country (B) is used, the reduction in the disparity measured by conversion by exchange rates is moderate (the low ratio is raised about 25 per cent for 1950 and less than 20 per cent for 1955, for the sample of Western European countries relative to the United States—see *MEG*, Table 7.3, pp. 376–77). If the price structure of the high per capita product country (A) is used, the disparity is narrowed appreciably—the more so the lower country B's per capita product. Thus for Italy, the lowest per capita product country studied in the OEEC investigation, the ratio of its per capita product to that of the United States as 100, on the exchange conversion basis, was 16 in 1950 and 19 in 1955; with the shift to conversion by the Italian price structure, the ratio increased moderately to 18 in 1950 and 20 in 1955; with the shift to conversion by U.S. prices, it rose to 30 in 1950 and to 35 in 1955.

These findings are due to two underlying associations. The first is the negative association between quantity and price structures within each country—more of the relatively cheaper goods (or resources) are used than of the relatively expensive— the obvious result of efficiency in use of resources and of responsiveness of final demand to relative prices. The second is the negative association in the process of growth (and hence presumably in disparities among countries that are, at the time of comparison, at different levels of growth) between movements of quantities and movements of prices—the higher priced goods growing more than the cheaper goods and their prices declining more (or rising less). Consequently when we value the quantities of country B by the prices of country A, we assign high prices to relatively abundant goods and resources, and low prices to relatively scarce goods and resources (e.g., high prices to labor and agricultural products and low prices to machinery, etc). And when we value quantities in country A by prices of country B, we assign high prices to machinery and capital and low prices to agricultural products and labor. Obviously the upward effects of such valuation by another country's price structure are far greater when this other country is a more-developed, higher per capita product nation, than when it is less-developed. Similar results are found for aggregate growth rates over time: the growth rate is much greater (the disparity is greater) when the weights are *initial* year prices (analogous to prices of country B) than when the weights are *terminal* year prices (analogous to prices of country A).

Third, judging by the sample of the European countries and the United States, the disparity among countries as revealed by exchange rate conversion and that found with direct purchasing power comparisons, is either moderately affected and relatively independent of the country's per capita product when prices of country B are used; or is increasingly reduced the lower country B's per capita product, when prices of country A are used. But even in the latter case, the disparities still remain large despite a possible reduction of a half or six-tenths. Given a gap of over 30 to 1 between the United States and the poor, less-developed countries, or one of 20 to 1 between all developed countries and the poor, less-developed countries, reduction to 15 or even 10 for the former or to 10 or even 7 for the latter, still leaves us with a large gap. And the adjustment has only a slight effect on the relative ranking of countries, taken in substantial groups.

These brief comments on the wide field of international purchasing power parities, which is still to be explored adequately in empirical study, can be supplemented by one, rather speculative observation. The difference between the aggregative gap when measured by the price structure of country A and the gap when that of country B is used—a problem from the standpoint of formal index number theory—may be analytically revealing. That the relative gap is much narrower when the price weights of country A are used indicates that the gap looks narrower when it is viewed by observers in country A, in the light of that country's judgments as to values of resources and goods; and the same gap looks much wider when it is viewed by observers in country B, using this particular country's judgments as to relative values of goods and resources. Either as a measure of differences in productive capacity or of differences in welfare satisfiable by economic goods, the gap looks wider when judged by the value weights of the "poorer," less-developed country rather than by those of the more-developed country.

This comment would be truly significant if the price weights adequately measured productivity assignable to the various factors or reflected the views of the country's population of welfare assignable to various final goods. Needless to say, the prices represent only rough approximations to relative productivity of factors or to welfare weights of final goods. Considering the distortions in factor markets and the effects of income inequalities in all countries, and both perhaps greater in the less-developed than in the developed countries, one may doubt that the price structures properly reflect the underlying productivity and welfare ratios. Yet, given the conformity of the behavior of the various price structures to expectations on economically rational grounds, it is hard to deny that the different magnitudes of the gap corresponding to shifts in price structure, i.e., position of the observer, have some significance. The loss in potential productivity and welfare looms larger in the less-developed countries, that view themselves as sustaining this loss than in the more-developed countries, which appraise the same loss in terms of their own scales of prices and values. A question remains as to the size and social position of the relevant observer classes in the two groups of countries, who may be expected to be aware of the values and quantities involved in the comparison.

STRUCTURAL ASPECTS OF THE GAP · Despite the difficult index number problems, we may reasonably conclude that the per capita product gap is wide, indicating a much lower capacity to produce and to consume in the poor, less-developed countries than in the developed. This conclusion is strongly reinforced by the structural characteristics associated with the level of per capita product—ranging from the purely economic, such as education of the labor force and mechanical energy available per capita; or distribution of labor force and product among major production sectors; or consumption of final goods, ranging from "necessities" to "luxuries"; to noneconomic processes and characteristics, such as the demographic rates of births, deaths, and migration, or to conditions of life reflected in extent of urbanization, literacy of population, etc. Wide differences in per capita product are accompanied by wide differences in the characteristics of economic and social structure. If in the developed coun-

Table 2. Structural Aspects Associated with Per Capita Income or Product, Late 1950's and Early 1960's

A. Large Sample of Non-Communist Countries, Late 1950's

	Developed		Classes by per capita national income, 1956–58	Less-Developed		
NI, 1956–58 GDP, 1965	$575 to 1,000 ($811 to 1,410)	$1,000 & over ($1,410 & over)	Total	Under $100 (under $133)	$100 to 200 ($133 to 266)	Total
	(1)	(2)	(3)	(4)	(5)	(6)
1. Average per capita income (1956–58 $)	760	1,366	1,063	72	161	102
2. Equivalent, GDP in 1965 $	1,072	1,926	1,500	96	214	135
3. Per capita energy consumption, kilos of coal equivalent, 1956–58	2,710	3,900	3,305	114	265	164
4. Percentage of population literate, 15 years of age & over (about 1950)	94	98	96	29	51	36
5. School enrolment (excl. pre-primary and higher education) as % of four-fifths of 5–19 age group (one year, 1956–58)	84	91	87	37	48	41
6. Percentage of male labor force in agriculture (about 1956)	21	17	19	74	64	71
7. Percentage of national income originating in agriculture (latest year)	10.9	11.4	11.15	40.8	33.4	38.3
8. Relative product per worker, agriculture (line 7: line 6)	0.52	0.67	0.59	0.55	0.52	0.54
9. Relative product per worker in non-agriculture (100 minus line 7):(100 minus line 6)	1.13	1.07	1.10	2.28	1.85	2.13
10. Intersectoral ratio, line 9: line 8	2.17	1.60	1.86	4.15	3.56	3.94
11. Level of urbanization (% of population in metrop. communities of over 100,000), 1955	39	43	41	9	14	11
12. Expectation of life (yrs.) at birth, 1955–58	67.7	70.6	69.1	41.7	50.0	44.5
13. Infant mortality (per 1,000), 1955–58	41.9	24.9	33.4	180	131	164
14. Per capita calorie consumption, latest year	2,944	3,153	3,048	2,070	2,240	2,127
15. Starchy staples as % of calories consumed, latest year	53	45	49	77	70	75

Table 2. STRUCTURAL ASPECTS ASSOCIATED WITH PER CAPITA INCOME OR PRODUCT, LATE 1950's AND EARLY 1960's (Continued)

B. Vital Rates, Structure of Labor Force, and Extent of Urbanization, World by Regions, Early 1960's

	Vital crude rates per 1,000 1960–64			Percentage shares in labor force			Percentage shares in population		
	Birth rates	Death rates	RNI	A	I–	S+	Rural & small towns	20,000 to 500,000	Over 500,000
	(1)	(2)	(3)	(4)	(5)	(6)	(7)	(8)	(9)
Developed Regions									
16. Europe (Western & Northern, plus Italy)	18.2	10.8	7.4	15.4	44.1	40.5	48.2	27.7	24.1
17. North America	23	9	14	8	39	53	42.0	21.5	36.5
18. Australia & New Zealand	23	9	14	12	40	48	35.4	23.7	40.9
19. Japan	17	7	10	33	28	39	54.0	19.7	26.3
20. All non-Communist (lines 16–19)	19.8	9.5	10.3	16.2	39.4	44.4	46.7	24.1	29.2
21. U.S.S.R.	23	7	16	45	28	27	63.6	23.9	12.5
22. All developed (lines 20 & 21)	20.7	8.8	11.9	25.3	35.8	38.9	51.3	24.1	24.6
"Poor" LDCs, Narrow Definition									
23. Sub-Saharan Africa excl. South Africa	48.5	25.1	23.4	81.6	7.3	11.1	92.7	6.7	0.6
24. Mainland China	35	21	14	75	10	15	86.2	6.5	7.3
25. Middle South & Southeast Asia	41.5	20.2	21.3	72.1	12.4	15.5	87.0	8.1	4.9
26. Total, non-Communist incl. Melanesia	42.9	21.1	21.8	74.1	11.3	14.6	88.1	7.9	4.0
27. Total, incl. Melanesia	39.8	21.1	18.7	74.5	10.7	14.8	87.3	7.4	5.3
Next Group of LDCs (add for "Poor," Wide Definition)									
28. North Africa	43	19	24	71	10	19	74.4	14.8	10.8
29. South West Asia	42	18	24	69	14	17	77.2	17.0	5.8
30. Middle East (28–29)	42.5	18.5	24.0	70.0	11.9	18.1	75.7	15.9	8.4
31. Other East Asia	39	15	24	62	12	26	70.5	17.3	12.2
32. Tropical Latin America	43	15	28	61.7	13.9	24.4	72.7	15.8	11.5
33. Total above (lines 30–32)	42.1	16.5	25.6						
"Poor" LDCs, Wide Definition									
34. Non-Communist	42.7	20.1	22.6	71.8	11.8	16.4	84.7	9.6	5.7
35. All	40.2	20.4	19.8	73.0	11.1	15.9	85.2	8.6	6.2
All Other LDCs									
36. South Africa	42	19	23	37	29	34	67.6	17.6	14.8

| 39. South Europe (excl. Italy) | 22.5 | 8.3 | 14.2 | 50 | 26 | 24 | 66.4 | 20.8 | 12.8 |
| 40. Total incl. Melanesia (36–39) | 28.2 | 11.0 | 17.2 | 45.6 | 27.4 | 27.0 | 66.1 | 19.7 | 14.2 |

Lines 1, 3–7, 11–15, columns 1–2 and 4–5: Underlying data are from *Report on the World Social Situation* (New York: United Nations, 1961), Chapter III, Table 1, p. 41 (and following discussion and tables).

Line 2: National income in 1956–58 prices was converted to gross domestic product at market prices, in 1965 prices (both in U.S. dollars) in three steps. First, we calculated the ratio for the late 1950's of gross domestic product at market prices to national income (the difference being indirect taxes minus subsidies, capital consumption charges, and net factor income from abroad). This ratio was calculated separately for the low and high income countries (both limited to those in which the net income from abroad was relatively negligible) on the basis of *Yearbook of National Accounts Statistics 1968*, Vol. II, *International Tables* (New York: United Nations, 1969), Table 1. The average ratio of GDP at market prices to NI was about 1.165 for the low per capita product countries and 1.24 for the high per capita product countries. Next, we calculated the change in the general price level (implicit in gross national product) from 1956–58 to 1965 for the United States, based on the *Economic Report of the President* (Washington, D.C., February, 1968), Table B–3, p. 212. It was 14.1 per cent. Finally, the adjustment factor for the high per capita countries, derived as (1.24×1.141), was 1.41; for the low per capita product countries it was (1.165×1.141), or 1.33.

Panel A, columns 3 and 6: For the developed countries, we weighted the entries in columns 1 and 2 equally, judging by the rough population magnitudes in the two income class groups (non-Communist countries). For the "poor," less-developed countries (wide definition) the weights for columns 4 and 5 were 2 and 1 respectively, as suggested by the population for the non-Communist countries in Table 1.

Panel B: The regional groupings in the three sources from which

the demographic and labor force data were taken are identical. We tried to fit these groups roughly into the categories distinguished in our Table 1, shifting Italy out of Southern Europe (with the remainder classified under less-developed countries).

The rough consilience is indicated by comparison of the population totals underlying Panel B with those shown in Table 1 (for 1965). For the developed countries, the total underlying Panel B is 831 million, compared with 861 in Table 1; for the "poor" LDCs, narrow definition, it is 1,823 million in Panel B compared with 1,726 in Table 1; for the "poor" LDCs, wide definition, it is 2,149 million in Panel B and 2,089 million in Table 1; and for "other" LDCs, it is 305 million in Panel B and 322 in Table 1.

Columns 1–3: The vital rates in columns 1 and 2 and underlying population totals are from *Demographic Yearbook 1965* (New York: United Nations, 1967), Table 1, p. 103 (and relevant tables for Italy in the same volume). Rates for larger groups were calculated by weighting the rates for the sub-components by the arithmetic mean of the population for 1960 and 1965.

Columns 4–6: Underlying data are from Samuel Baum, "The World's Labour Force and Its Industrial Distribution," *International Labour Review*, Vol. 95, nos. 1–2, January–February, 1967, 96–112. I— includes mining, manufacturing, construction, electric power, gas and water. Transport and communications are included with services in S+. Agriculture includes related industries, such as fishing, forestry, and hunting. Weighting is by total labor force.

Columns 7–9: Underlying data are from Population Studies No. 44, *Growth of the World's Urban and Rural Population, 1920–2000* (New York: United Nations, 1969), Tables 47, 48, 49, and 51, pp. 115–17 and 119; and for Italy, Tables 41 and 43, pp. 98–100 and 102–3. Weighting is by total population in 1960.

tries the literacy ratio is close to 100 per cent and in the poor LDCs (narrow definition) it is below 30 per cent; if in the developed countries labor force attached to agriculture is less than 25 per cent of the total and in the poor LDCs it is 75 per cent; if the crude death rates in the poor LDCs are twice as high as in the developed countries, then greater reality is imparted to the conclusion that the aggregative gap in economic capacity and performance is wide, and is not a statistical illusion.

A large number of structural characteristics, economic and social, associated with the gap in per capita product, can be measured. However, the documentation for a recent year or period in Table 2—from which the statistics in the preceding paragraph were taken—presents a choice limited to a few characteristics of wide import for which data are easily available. (A more comprehensive survey and discussion are provided in *MEG*, Chapter 8, pp. 400–60.) Although it is unnecessary to discuss even the few characteristics given in Table 2, let alone others—the major ones are fairly familiar—it may be useful to comment on some problems of interpretation of the gap, which the differences in economic and social structure suggest.

First, the gap, whether in per capita product or in associated structural characteristics, is relative—the levels for the poor LDCs are low (or high, depending upon the characteristics) compared with those for the developed countries. This does not mean that they are low (or high) compared with some other standard. To illustrate: Table 2 shows that per capita calorie consumption is a third lower in the poor LDCs than in the developed countries (line 14); and more recent data confirm this disparity.[3] This does not mean that calorie consumption in the LDCs is low relative to requirements set by some nutritional standards. Indeed, in many "poor" LDCs, according to the table cited in footnote 3, the ratio of calorie consumption to requirements is close to 100 per cent (e.g., Pakistan—98 per cent, Ceylon—99 per cent, Ethiopia—95 per cent, Uganda—97 per cent); and in many LDCs the net protein intake is at or above the required level. Disregarding the problem of unequal distribution of food consumption *within* countries, the averages do

---

[3] See *1967 Report on the World Social Situation* (New York: United Nations, 1969), Table 2, pp. 36–37.

not suggest any significant *gap* in the calorie consumption of LDCs with respect to requirements. Not so paradoxically, one may interpret the excess of calorie consumption over requirements in the developed countries as a deficiency with respect to desirable standards. Table 2 also shows much lower levels of formal education in the LDCs (line 5); and the proportion of people in these countries who have completed higher education is also probably much lower. But it does not follow that there is a shortage with respect to the requirement standards of the actual or proximately higher level of productive capacity. The comment is intended to draw attention to the absolute levels at the low end of the gap and to the value of relating these levels to such potentially meaningful criteria as mentioned above, rather than to the levels at the high end of the gap. The latter comparison implies unrealistically that the developed countries represent an optimum with respect not only to per capita product, but also to the various economic and social characteristics that they display.

Second, the associations between per capita product and *some structural* characteristics are close and consistent. Thus as we move from the "poor" LDCs (narrow definition) to the next group of LDCs, then to the "non-poor" LDCs, and to the developed countries, the crude death rates drop from 21 to 16 to 11 and to 9 per thousand; [4] the share of labor force in agriculture declines from 75 to 62 to 46 to 25 per cent, while that in the I−sector rises from 11 to 14 to 27 to 36 per cent; and the share of population in rural areas and small towns declines from 87 to 73 to 66 to 51 per cent (see Table 2, lines 22, 27, 33, and 40). Even within the "poor" LDCs (narrow definition), the lower per capita product for sub-Saharan Africa is associated with higher death rates, higher proportions of labor force in agriculture, and greater "rurality" of population than in the Asian countries with their somewhat higher per capita product (see Table 2, lines 23 and 25, and for per capita product Table 1, line 12, columns 2 and 3). But even here there is one significant exception: the U.S.S.R., with an appreciably higher per capita product than the

---

[4] The sequence and differences for death rates adjusted for age and sex differentials would be even wider, because the higher birth rates in the LDCs result in an age structure dominated by the younger age classes, with lower age-specific mortality rates.

top group of LDCs in Latin America, shows as high a proportion of labor force in agriculture and the same extent of rurality (see Table 2, lines 21 and 37, column 4 and 7, and for per capita product, Table 1, line 3, column 6, in parentheses, and line 27, column 5). For other characteristics, the association is not consistent. Thus while birth rates are, in general, higher in the LDCs than in the developed countries, Latin America, with a larger per capita product than the Asian countries, shows distinctly higher birth rates; and among the developed countries, the overseas offshoots in North America and Oceania, with much higher per capita product, show significantly higher birth rates than Europe and Japan (see Table 2, line 32 compared with line 25, and lines 17–18 compared with lines 16 and 19, column 1).

Even when the association between per capita product and a structural characteristic or process is close and consistent, per capita product, in itself, should not be interpreted as a direct cause. For example, high death rates for low per capita product countries do not necessarily mean that the low consumption levels due to low per capita product are the major, direct cause of high death rates. The latter may reflect the wide inequality in income distribution in the LDCs, or the general state of economic and social institutions, or the prevailing views which may place a low value on health and life. In short, a complex of factors may result, at one and the same time, in low per capita GDP and in high death rates, with no crucial causal connection between the two. Still, a close and consistent association between per capita product and specific characteristics means that the former is a good index of the latter—and can be used to generalize cross-section results from a limited sample, and infer levels of these characteristics when they are not directly available.

Third, the association between per capita product and a structural characteristic is often viewed as a basis for extrapolating forward the expected results of a change in per capita product (usually its rise in the process of growth), or estimating backward the change in the characteristic in the past as per capita product grew. But a single cross section is not a reliable basis for projections *over time* because technological changes and related changes in conditions of life and tastes may shift the cross-section function to a higher or lower level, and such shifts are not reflected in the association within one cross section. For example, the close inverse correlation between per capita product and death rates in the 1960's does not imply ("predict") the decline between the late 1930's and the mid-1950's in crude death rates in many countries in Asia, Africa, and even Latin America despite the absence of significant rises in per capita product; and it is highly probable that death rates will also decline in those LDCs in which these rates are comparatively high today, even if per capita product fails to rise. A technological revolution that reduces death rates without large economic inputs or without a radical modification of the social structure means a downward shift of the cross section, a lowering of death rates without any economic and social changes that would result in a higher per capita product and a more modern social structure. Such gains, with respect to some undesirable corollaries of low per capita product at the lower end of the gap, are not unexpected; but they are necessarily limited and may not reduce the structural gap significantly. The latter may require a significant reduction of the aggregative gap, largely by a higher growth rate of the lower than of the higher per capita product groups.

DIVERSITY AND DIVISIVENESS · Table 3 shows twenty-one countries in the developed group and thirty-nine in the "poor" LDC group (narrow definition), even though we exclude units with less than one million population. Almost all the countries are sovereign states, but include a few territories like Mozambique and Angola; and there are some 120 such units in the world. This multiplicity of sovereign entities, of societies that consider themselves distinct from the rest of the world and their own decision makers (actually or potentially), affects the interpretation and measurement of the aggregate and structural gaps.

First, when we distinguish individual countries or subgroups within the developed group, or within the "poor" LDCs, we observe a range of relative magnitudes of the aggregate gap, i.e., a disparity in per capita product. As Table 1 shows, per capita GDP for the North American region of the developed countries, at $3,441, is over twice as large as that for developed Europe, and about four times as large as that for Japan; whereas within

Table 3. DISTRIBUTION OF COUNTRIES, WITH POPULATION OF
1 MILLION AND OVER, BY SIZE OF POPULATION, DEVELOPED AND
LESS-DEVELOPED, NON-COMMUNIST AND COMMUNIST COUNTRIES, 1965

	Size of Population Groups (in millions)							
	1.0 to 2.99 (1)	3.0 to 5.99 (2)	6.0 to 9.99 (3)	10.0 to 19.99 (4)	20.0 to 49.99 (5)	50.0 to 99.99 (6)	100 & over (7)	Total (8)
Developed Countries								
1. Number	2	4	3	5 (2)	1	4	2 (1)	21 (3)
2. Population	5.2	19.0	24.5	74.4 (31.2)	48.9	263.2	425 (231)	860.0 (262.0)
"Poor" LDCs, Narrow Definition								
3. Number	7 (1)	12	4	8 (2)	4	0	4 (1)	39 (4)
4. Population	12.3 (1.1)	50.1	30.3	112.0 (31.0)	119.7	0	1,395 (700)	1,719.0 (732.0)
"Poor" LDCs, Wide Definition								
5. Number	15 (2)	20	8	12 (2)	9	1	4 (1)	69 (5)
6. Population	28.1 (3.0)	84.1	59.2	160.8 (31.0)	268	81.3	1,395 (700)	2,077.0 (734.0)
Other LDCs								
7. Number	10	3	7 (2)	6 (3)	4 (1)	0	0	30 (6)
8. Population	20.2	11.9	60.3 (15.8)	96.0 (48.7)	126.1 (31.4)	0	0	314.0 (95.9)
All LDCs								
9. Number	25 (2)	23	15 (2)	18 (5)	13 (1)	1	4 (1)	99 (11)
10. Population	48.3 (3.0)	96.0	119.5 (15.8)	256.8 (79.7)	394 (31.4)	81.3	1,395 (700)	2,391.0 (830.0)
World (excluding countries with population less than 1.0)								
All Countries								
11. Number	27	27	18	23	14	5	6	120
12. Population	53.5	115	144	331	443	345	1,820	3,251
Non-Communist Countries								
13. Number	25	27	16	16	13	5	4	106
14. Population	50.5	115	128	220	412	345	889	2,159
Communist Countries								
15. Number	2	0	2	7	1	0	2	14
16. Population	3.0	0	15.8	111	31.4	0	931	1,092

Entries in parentheses in lines 1–10 relate to the number and population of the Communist countries (included in the relevant totals). Cuba was classified among the Communist countries.

For underlying population totals see the Hagen-Hawrylyshyn paper cited in the notes to Table 1.

even the "poor" (narrowly defined) LDC group, the per capita GDP for a sizable population group in sub-Saharan Africa and Asia (of some 260 million) is only about $65. The range in per capita product between North America and this latter group is over 50 to 1, whereas the range between Japan and the populous less-developed countries of Asia is less than 9 to 1. The range in the gap can obviously vary once we recognize the diversity in per capita product within the developed and less-developed groups themselves; and presumably large differences in such relative gaps in per capita product imply similar differences in the gaps in the associated characteristics of economic and social structure. These variations in the "distance" represented by the aggregate and structural gaps are important and should be kept in mind as a necessary supplement to the overall group averages employed in the discussion.

Second, of more interest because it introduces characteristics not mentioned so far, is the diversity among the countries in size. Table 3 provides a condensed illustration of this diversity, with size measured in terms of population (and, to repeat, excluding units with less than one million each, an omission of about 20 million of the world population in 1965 of 3,271 million); but similar diversity would be shown with size measured in terms of area or total economic product.

Within the developed group, two of the twenty-one countries (the United States and the U.S.S.R.) account for about a half, while at the other extreme, six countries, with less than 6 million each, account for less than 3 per cent of the group's total population. The size inequalities are even wider among the less-developed countries. Thus of the thirty-nine countries in the "poor" LDC group (narrow definition), four (Mainland China, India, Pakistan, and Indonesia) account for 1.4 out of 1.72 billion population, whereas nineteen countries, with less than 6 million each, account together for 62 million, or less than 4 per cent of the total. One should note the many small countries within the less-developed group—a result perhaps of the inability to overcome initial divisiveness and to form, through unification, somewhat larger national units.

The importance of size for economic growth attainments and prospects lies in the inevitably greater dependence of small than of large units upon foreign trade (shown by the close inverse correlation between size and proportion of foreign trade to domestic product for countries in which free foreign trade is permitted); and in the problems of organization and integration that large countries face, particularly if they are less-developed and their unifying infrastructures consequently are far less advanced than those of an economically developed country. With special reference to the gap one should note that if the small countries must rely on foreign trade and other forms of international division proportionately much more than the large countries, which can count on large internal markets; if the small countries trade mostly with a large country, rather than among themselves—as is usually the case; and if the small less-developed countries, like all other less-developed countries, trade with one or two large *developed* countries, the inequality represented by the gap—a gap in per capita product magnified by a gap in size—becomes particularly conspicuous. Such inequality in dependence between a small LDC, with exports amounting say to a quarter of domestic product and going to a large developed country in which such imports (or exports to pay for them) represent a fraction of one per cent of total foreign trade, and even less of domestic product, is clearly potential of great strain —for the smaller trading partner. And it may be observed from Table 3 that, if we use 6 million population as a dividing line, as many as forty-six non-Communist small countries are presumably trading primarily with six sizable developed non-Communist countries (with population over 20 million). The strain between the small and large exists also among the Communist countries even though their foreign trade propensity is generally lower than that of non-Communist countries of similar size and level of development.

Finally, in addition to per capita product and size, other characteristics show great diversity at both ends of the gap. Of these, Tables 1 and 3 illustrate only one—the distinction between Communist and non-Communist countries, which reflects a major type of divisiveness in the current world, a major difference in key aspects of economic and social organization. There are Communist countries within both the developed group and the "poor" less-developed group (narrowly defined); and some of these are large and some are small. Given the pervasive presence of at least two "worlds" at both ends of the gap, there is a conspicuous division among countries, and within any gap observed, with respect not only to several major characteristics of economic and social organization, but also to views as to the optimal pattern of movement toward higher levels of economic and social performance.

COMMODITY TRADE FLOWS ACROSS THE GAP · Foreign trade in commodities appears, at least in casual observation, still to be the flow among countries least subject to the type of interventionary restraint that affects even the flow of services, let alone of productive resources, or of such intangibles as elements of the stock of human knowledge and culture. Foreign trade is also an economic flow closely related to economic performance and growth, and is one for which worldwide data are at hand. For these reasons flows across the gap are illustrated only for foreign trade in commodities (Table 4).[5]

Two factors affecting the proportion of commodity trade to total output have already been noted. Communist countries, with their governmental control over foreign trade, are characterized by lower trade proportions than non-Communist countries. In Table 4 the ratio for the former of the total of exports and imports to GDP is 10.7 per cent, contrasted with one for the non-Communist countries of 20.5 per cent (in both cases the ratio of the sums of exports and imports to the sums of GDP); and the difference would probably be even more marked if the foreign trade in services could be included, given the lesser importance of finance and transport as well as of tourist services in the international flows to and from the Communist countries. Part of the difference can be attributed to a lower proportion of small countries and a lower per capita product within the Communist bloc—both of which would make for a lower foreign trade ratio. But the magnitude of the difference, the sharp de-

---

[5] For a more detailed discussion see Simon Kuznets, "Quantitative Aspects of the Economic Growth of Nations: IX. Level and Structure of Foreign Trade—Comparisons for Recent Years," *Economic Development and Cultural Change*, Vol. XIII, no. 1, Part II, October, 1964. In recent years exports of services were about a quarter of the exports of commodities, and imports of services about a sixth of the imports of commodities. Total trade in services tends to be a somewhat higher proportion of total trade in commodities in the more-developed than in the less-developed countries (see e.g., Table 1, pp. 4–5).

Table 4. COMMODITY FOREIGN TRADE, 1965, PROPORTION TO GROSS DOMESTIC PRODUCT AND STRUCTURE OF EXPORTS BY ECONOMIC CLASSES OF PROVENANCE AND DESTINATION

A. Proportion to GDP, Market Prices

	Total GDP in group	GDP covered by I&E	Proportion to GDP, %			Proportion to world trade, %
			I	E	I&E	
	(1)	(2)	(3)	(4)	(5)	(6)
	Billion $					
Non-Communist Countries						
Developed						
1. Europe (Western, Northern, Italy)	469.5	469.5	17.4	16.0	33.4	41.4
2. North America	737.1	737.1	4.3	4.8	9.1	17.8
3. Japan	85.2	85.2	9.6	9.9	19.5	4.4
4. Total (incl. Australia, New Zealand, Israel)	1,323.9	1,323.9	9.6	9.3	18.9	66.2
"Poor" LDCs, Narrow Definition						
5. Sub-Saharan Africa	13.3	12.8	22.2	19.7	41.9	1.4
6. Middle South & Southeast Asia	75.4	72.7	7.6	4.7	12.3	2.4
7. Total (incl. Melanesia)	91.0	87.6	10.4	7.3	17.7	4.1
"Poor" LDCs, Wide Definition						
8. Sub-Saharan Africa	20.6	20.1	24.0	23.1	47.1	2.5
9. Asia	105.0	102.3	9.6	7.5	17.1	4.6
10. Middle East	18.9	18.7	21.8	25.5	47.3	2.3
11. Latin America	26.1	26.1	7.0	8.9	15.9	1.1
12. Total (incl. Melanesia)	171.0	167.3	12.4	11.6	24.0	10.6
All LDCs						
13. Sub-Saharan Africa	31.7	31.1	23.5	20.0	43.5	3.6
14. Asia	110.7	107.9	13.0	10.3	23.3	6.6
15. Middle East	23.1	20.6	23.6	27.4	51.0	2.8
16. Latin America	96.0	92.6	11.3	12.9	24.2	5.9
17. Europe	33.7	33.7	18.4	7.5	25.9	2.3
18. All LDCs (non-Communist), incl. Oceania	295.7	286.3	15.0	13.1	28.1	21.3
Communist Countries						
19. Developed (U.S.S.R., Czechoslo-						

B. Structure of Exports by Economic Class of Region of Provenance and Destination

Regions of Provenance	Economic Class I (1)	Economic Class II (2)	Economic Class III (3)	Total (4)	U.S.S.R. (5)	Eastern Europe (6)	Asia III (7)
							Regions of Destination
Values of Exports (Billion $)							
22. Ec. Cl. I	95.74	26.99	4.99	127.72	1.63	2.45	0.91
23. Ec. Cl. II	26.11	7.65	2.39	36.15	1.08	0.80	0.51
24. Ec. Cl. III	4.68	2.94	13.77	21.39	5.10	7.97	0.70
25. Total	126.53	37.58	21.15	185.26	7.81	11.22	2.12
Shares in Total Exports Sent Out (%)							
26. Ec. Cl. I	75.0	21.1	3.9	100.0	1.28	1.92	0.71
27. Ec. Cl. II	72.2	21.2	6.6	100.0	2.99	2.21	1.41
28. Ec. Cl. III	21.9	13.7	64.4	100.0	23.84	37.26	3.27
Shares in Total Exports Received (%)							
29. From Class I	75.7	71.8	23.6		20.9	21.8	42.9
30. From Class II	20.6	20.4	11.3		13.8	7.1	24.1
31. From Class III	3.7	7.8	65.1		65.3	71.1	33.0
32. Total	100.0	100.0	100.0		100.0	100.0	100.0

Panel A: The underlying data for imports (c.i.f.) and exports (f.o.b.), in U.S. dollars, for individual countries are from *Yearbook of International Trade Statistics, 1967* (New York: United Nations, 1969), Summary Table A, pp. 12–19, and from Table 1 of the country tables for Iran, Afghanistan, Iraq, and Saudi Arabia. The data for individual countries were combined into the groups set up in Table 1.

The gross domestic product estimates are from the source cited for Table 1.

Panel B: The underlying data are from the *Yearbook of International Trade Statistics, 1967,* Summary Table B, pp. 20–33. Economic Class I includes the United States, Canada, Western Europe, Australia, New Zealand, South Africa, Japan. However, Western Europe, as defined in the source, includes, in addition to the non-Communist developed countries, the less-developed countries (such as Portugal, Spain, and Greece), as well as Turkey, classified by us under Asia, and Yugoslavia, classified by us as Communist. Nevertheless, the proportional difference between the trade of what we define as non-Communist developed countries and Economic Class I is minor, one or two percentage points at most. Economic Class III covers the Communist countries—U.S.S.R. and other Eastern Europe, and the four in Asia. Economic Class II, the rest of the world, is roughly coterminous with what we define as non-Communist, less-developed countries, but it includes Cuba, classified by us as Communist.

cline in trade proportions in the countries into which the Communist organization was introduced, and the obvious effects of control over foreign trade, all suggest that the major source of lower propensity to trade probably lies in the Communist organization of economic activity.

The second, and most dominant factor, is size. The paper cited in footnote 5 shows for a large sample of non-Communist countries proportions of commodity trade to GNP for countries classified by size of either population or GNP. For some twelve groups of countries, the foreign trade proportion ranges from a low of 12 to a high of 109 per cent; for groups classified by size of population it ranges from 17 to 81 per cent, or about two-thirds of the full range; for groups by size of GNP it ranges from 19 to 73 per cent, over half of the full range (see Table 2, Panel B, p. 10). Further analysis shows that the narrower range of effect for countries grouped by size of GNP is due to the reduction of the inverse correlation with total GNP by the positive correlation of foreign trade proportions with GNP *per capita*. It is therefore the size factor that explains the somewhat lower trade proportion for the total of developed countries than that for the "poor" LDCs (wide definition, but not the narrow) or than that for all the LDCs—19, 24, and 28 per cent respectively (Table 4, column 5, lines 4, 12, and 18). For the one developed group that contains a fair number of small countries, Western Europe, the foreign trade proportion, 33.4 per cent, is among the highest, surpassed only by sub-Saharan Africa and the Middle East with their many very small countries (column 5, lines 1, 10, and 13).

But the most relevant finding, bearing directly upon flows *across* the gap, is in Panel B of Table 4, which shows exports by provenance and destination for economic classes of countries, of which Class I is quite close to the non-Communist developed countries as we define them; and Class II is close to the non-Communist LDCs (taken as a whole). If we exclude the Communist countries, whose share in total world foreign trade (and in the trade of the large subdivisions of the non-Communist countries) is small, we find that of the total exports of LDCs to non-Communist countries (93.5 per cent of their total exports) about eight-tenths were sent to developed countries and less than two-tenths to other LDCs. Likewise, of the total imports (exports received) by LDCs from non-Communist countries (92 per cent of their total imports), about eight-tenths were received from the developed countries, and only about two-tenths from the other LDCs. To put it crudely, the LDCs depend on the developed countries for eight-tenths of their foreign trade, which means overall about a fifth of their output. By contrast, the developed countries send about eight-tenths of their exports to non-Communist countries (about 96 per cent of their total exports), to other developed countries; and receive about eight-tenths of their imports from non-Communist countries (96 per cent of the total) from other developed countries. The developed countries are thus dependent on the non-Communist LDCs only for about two-tenths of their trade (other than that with the Communist bloc), or roughly speaking, less than four per cent of their total domestic output. As already mentioned, this contrast is even wider for individual large developed and small less-developed countries.

Finally, Panel B indicates that among the Communist countries (Economic Class III), the developed and less-developed countries within Europe are fairly closely tied in: most of the exports received by Eastern Europe and the U.S.S.R. originate within the Communist bloc (71 per cent of all exports received by Eastern Europe and 65 per cent of all exports received by the U.S.S.R., line 31, columns 5 and 6). But the Asian Communist countries (dominated by Mainland China) receive only a third of their imports (exports received) from the Communist bloc, and close to a half from the non-Communist developed countries (column 7, lines 29–31). Presumably, the allocation of exports originating in the U.S.S.R. and Eastern Europe also differs from that for Communist Asia.

3. Long-Term Trends

We deal here with the gap between the developed and the "poor" LDCs (largely narrow definition), and view the movement over the past century to century and a quarter, the period of modern economic growth for most presently developed countries. The following major trends can be suggested: (1) widening of the absolute, and even relative gap, in per capita product; (2) widening of the gap in some aspects of economic and social structure, but not in others; (3) increasing interdependence among nations combined with increasing diversity and divisiveness—the former associated with continuing major improvements in transport and communication and advancing technology; the latter with the growing number of sovereign units, and of large developed nations, and increasing diversity in political and ideological orientation.

WIDENING GAP IN PER CAPITA PRODUCT · The evidence, while limited in reliable details, is compelling. Most of the presently developed countries entered into modern economic growth about a century ago, or more. The typical growth rates in per capita product for these countries meant multiplication over a century by a factor of 5, implying an annual growth rate of about 1.6 per cent (see *MEG*, Table 2.5, pp. 64–65). In none of the "poor" LDCs (narrow definition) did per capita product rise at such a rate over a century; and, indeed, if we work back from the mid-1950's when the per capita product of this group was between $80 and $90 (in 1965 $), a *doubling* over a century would have brought the per capita down to between $40 and $45. But even doubling is too large a factor, at least for the "narrowly poor" countries of today. Of these we have an approximation only for India, for which the suggested rise from the 1860's to mid-1955 is about two-thirds, or a multiplication factor of 1.8 per century.[6] For Egypt (within the range of the "poor," wider definition), the records suggest practically no growth in per capita product (but considerable growth in population) between 1895–99 and the mid- or late 1950's; and only for Ghana, another country within the widely defined "poor" LDCs, do some estimates suggest a substantial growth in product (amounting to almost a tripling between 1890 and the 1950's).[7]

[6] See M. Mukherjee, *National Income of India: Trends and Structure* (Calcutta, 1969), Table 2.5, p. 61. An even lower estimate is suggested in Krishan G. Saini, "The Growth of the Indian Economy: 1860–1960," *The Review of Income and Wealth*, September, 1969, 247–63.

[7] The estimates for Egypt are extrapolations back from 1945–49 on the basis of indexes of agricultural output, their relation to labor force engaged in agriculture, and the ratio of product per worker in the A and non-A sectors. Those for Ghana are taken largely from R. Szereszewski, *Structural Changes in the Economy of Ghana, 1891–1911* (London, 1965). For details see Simon Kuznets, *Economic Growth of Nations: Total Output and Production Structure* (Cambridge, Mass.: Harvard University Press, 1971), Chapter I, Table 3, pp. 30–33.

A reasonable conjecture is that, in comparison with the quin-tupling of the per capita product of developed countries over the last century, the per capita product of the "poor" LDCs rose two-thirds at most; and that this relation would hold roughly, even if we were to measure the century back from 1965 (rather than from the mid-1950's). This suggests that the gap that ex-isted at the beginning of the century tripled in 100 years. Since the present relative gap is either 20 to 1 or 16 to 1, depending upon the definition of "poor" at the lower end (see Table 1), a century ago the average per capita product of developed coun-tries (taken together) was already from 5 to 7 times as high as the per capita product of the current "poor" LDCs. However, this widening of the gap was not due to a decline or stagnation of the per capita product of the LDCs as a whole; even if it had quadrupled over the century, the absolute and relative gap would have widened. In fact, if the records can be trusted, the per capita product of many LDCs rose substantially and for no such country can a significant long-term decline be found.

As Tables 5 and 6 (limited to non-Communist countries) indi-cate, even in the post-World War II period, when there was a marked acceleration in the growth of per capita product of the LDCs—with some growth rates more than 2 per cent per year, i.e., higher than the 1.6 per cent for the developed countries over the past century—the gap continued to spread. The reason for this is that the growth rate of per capita product for the de-veloped countries, more than 3 per cent per year in this period, rose even more. It should be noted that the rate of growth of *total* product was higher for the LDCs than for the developed countries—at least for the longer periods of 15 and 10 years (Table 5, lines 1 and 2, columns 5 and 6); it is the higher growth rate of population in the LDCs that yields a lower rate of growth of per capita product—although no necessary causal as-sociation is involved.

The gap in per capita product between the developed coun-tries and the LDCs appears to have widened also in the Com-munist bloc, at least as suggested by the comparison between the U.S.S.R. and China over the period since the early 1950's. According to rough estimates by western scholars, net domestic product per capita for Mainland China rose only 20 per cent be-tween 1952 and 1965 or 1.4 per cent per year (although it rose 32 per cent from 1952 to 1958). By contrast, in the U.S.S.R. per

Table 5. Growth of Gross Domestic Product, Total and Per Capita, Non-Communist Countries, 1950–1967

	1950–52 (1)	1955–57 (2)	1960–62 (3)	1965–67 (4)	Growth Per Year (%)		
					Col. 1–3 (5)	Col. 2–4 (6)	Col. 1–4 (7)
Gross Domestic Product (1963 $ factor costs, in billions)							
1. Developed countries	654	798	959	1,232	3.90	4.44	4.31
2. Less-developed countries	116.3	147.2	185.5	231.9	4.78	4.65	4.71
3. East & Southeast Asia (excl. Japan)	53.5	65.5	80.4	99.4	4.16	4.26	4.22
4. Latin America	42.5	54.5	69.4	87.9	5.03	4.90	4.96
Population (in millions)							
5. Developed countries	589	626	669	711	1.28	1.28	1.26
6. Less-developed countries	1,082	1,200	1,356	1,542	2.28	2.54	2.39
7. East & Southeast Asia (excl. Japan)	685	759	853	961	2.22	2.39	2.28
8. Latin America	162	185	211	244	2.68	2.82	2.77
GDP per Capita (1963 $ FC)							
9. Developed countries	1,111	1,274	1,433	1,733	2.59	3.12	3.01
10. Less-developed countries	107.5	122.6	136.8	150.4	2.44	2.07	2.27
11. East & Southeast Asia	78.1	86.3	94.2	103.4	1.90	1.83	1.89
12. Latin America	262	295	329	361	2.29	2.03	2.13
Relative Gap							
13. Line 9: Line 10	10.3	10.4	10.5	11.5			
14. Line 9: Line 11	14.2	14.8	15.2	16.8			
15. Line 9: Line 12	4.2	4.3	4.4	4.8			

Comparison of Growth Rates of GDP Per Capita, Moving GDP (G) Weights and Fixed Population (P) Weights

	Developed Countries			Less-Developed Countries	
	G	P	P, excl. Japan	G	P
	(1)	(2)	(3)	(4)	(5)
16. 1955–57 to 1965–67	3.13	3.69	2.88	2.03	1.86
17. 1950–52 to 1965–67	3.03	3.57	2.86	2.13	1.94

Total and per capita gross domestic product are from *Yearbook of National Accounts Statistics, 1968*, Vol. II, *International Tables* (New York: United Nations, 1969), Table 7B, pp. 119–25 (for annual indexes from 1950 to 1967); and Table 2B, pp. 54–59, for estimates of 1963 total gross domestic product, at factor costs, in U.S. dollars for the non-Communist countries. Population indexes were derived by dividing the indexes for total GDP by those for per capita GDP. The absolute totals for population in 1963 are from *Demographic Yearbook 1967* (New York: United Nations, 1968), Table 1 and Table 4 for individual countries excluded or shifted for comparability with product.

The entries in columns 1–4 were derived by applying arithmetic means of the indexes for the years indicated in the headings to the absolute totals of GDP and population in 1963. The per capita GDP was derived by division.

Developed countries in the source include all of non-Communist Europe (plus Cyprus and Turkey), North America, Oceania, Japan, Israel, and South Africa. The less-developed countries include East and Southeast Asia (excluding Japan); the Middle East (Southwest Asia excluding Cyprus, Turkey, and Israel); Africa (except South Africa), and Latin America (including the Caribbean).

Lines 16–17: When changing per capita GDP is derived by dividing total GDP by total population (as is done in lines 9–12), and a region comprises subregions with different levels of GDP per capita, the per capita average can change because of a shift in weights of population among subgroups with different per capita GDP levels. The per capita levels are thus derived by the use of different and moving GDP and population weights. One can remove the effect of shifts in relative population weights, as well as the effect of a percentage change in the higher per capita GDP levels, by weighting the growth rates in per capita for each subregion separately by fixed population weights. This was done for the population weight calculation, using the 1963 population totals.

Entries in columns **1 and 4, lines 16–17** are comparable with those in lines 9 and 10, columns 5–7, except that here developed countries had to be limited to the sum of EEC and EFTA countries in Europe, North America, Oceania, and Japan, and the less-developed countries to the sum of E and SE Asia (excluding Japan) and Latin America. For countries included under EEC and EFTA in Europe see the notes to the *Yearbook of National Accounts Statistics*, Table 7B, referred to above.

capita product rose 5.2 per cent per year from 1950 to 1958 and 3.5 per cent from 1958 to 1964.[8]

The continuous widening of the gap between the developed and the "poor" less-developed countries may seem puzzling, given some obvious economic implications of a wide gap. The latter implies a large potential of material technology, and of social and institutional inventions, as yet unexploited by the LDCs; and correspondingly the possibility of a much higher growth rate for the LDCs, once whatever barriers prevented it in the past are removed. But growth potentials at different levels of material technology (and associated social and institutional structures) may differ; and those at higher levels of technology are not necessarily more limited than at the lower levels—assuming that additions at the former may be of limited relevance to additions at the latter. To use the recent decades as an illustration: the emergence of atomic energy, electronic industries, space exploration, and some new chemicals, may mean little to the proximate growth potentials of the "poor" LDCs. The growth rates that these new industries generate in the developed countries need not be lower than the potential growth rates of the "poor" LDCs, even with relatively successful exploitation of the modern technology relevant to their condition and needs. Similar reasoning applies to possible differences in growth potentials between the "advanced" levels of material technology and those relevant to the LDCs, as they might have been in the nineteenth and earlier twentieth centuries.[9]

Three further comments on the post-World War II widening of the gap are relevant. First, the greater growth of population in the "poor" LDCs than in the developed countries is largely the result of a recent sharp decline in the death rates, accompanied by continued high birth rates. This more rapid popula-

---

[8] The estimates for China are from Nai-Ruenn Chen and Walter Galenson, *The Chinese Economy under Communism* (Chicago: Aldine Publishing Co., 1969), Table VII–2, p. 169. Those for the U.S.S.R. are from the 89th Congress, 2nd Session, Joint Economic Committee Print, *New Directions in the Soviet Economy*, Part II–A (Washington, 1966), Table 2, p. 105 (in a paper by Stanley H. Cohn).

[9] For a discussion of this point in application to the case of Japan see Simon Kuznets, "Notes on Japan's Economic Growth," in Lawrence Klein and Kazushi Ohkawa, eds., *Economic Growth: The Japanese Experience since the Meiji Era*, for the Economic Growth Center of Yale University (Homewood: Richard R. Irwin, 1968), pp. 388–95.

tion growth than in developed regions is a recent phenomenon, which has emerged only since the early 1940's. Before then and back to the late eighteenth century, population in developed countries had grown more rapidly than in the less-developed (each group taken as a whole).

Second, the trends in per capita product in Table 5 for developed and less-developed countries, taken as groups, are affected by shifts of population weights, as well as by the difference in absolute per capita product, both *within* the groups. Thus, the percentage growth rate for per capita product of the United States has a large weight within the developed group because the U.S. per capita is so high; and a shift in population in favor of the United States will raise per capita product for the developed group as a whole, even if per capita product for each subregion taken separately remains constant. Likewise, Latin America, with the highest per capita product among the LDCs, will have a similar effect on the per capita product for the group as a whole. There is much to be said for weighting per capita growth rates for each subregion by a constant share of population—so that a 20 per cent rise in per capita product will be weighted the same for members of different nations or subregions. (Indeed, one might argue that these percentage rises, or declines, should be weighted more heavily, the lower the per capita product.) Lines 16–17 of Table 5 show that if we use fixed population weights, the growth rate of per capita product for the developed group as a whole is greater than shown in the calculation based directly on the comprehensive indexes (3.57 instead of 3.03 per cent for the longest period of coverage, line 17, columns 1 and 2), whereas the same adjustment reduces the growth rate for the LDCs (1.94 instead of 2.13 per cent). The per capita product growth rate of the LDCs in this population-weighted calculation is still lower than that for the developed countries, even if we exclude Japan from the latter (it is then 1.94 compared with 2.86 per cent).[10]

Finally, the details in Table 6 on the sectoral shares reveal that the larger weight of the A and smaller weights of the I and S sectors in the LDCs, combined with the generally higher

---

[10] For more detailed discussion of this point see the next paper in this volume, "Problems in Comparing Recent Growth Rates for Developed and Less-Developed Countries."

Table 6. Growth of Gross Domestic Product, by Three Major Production Sectors, Non-Communist Countries, 1950–67

	1950–52 (1)	1955–57 (2)	1960–62 (3)	1965–67 (4)	Growth per Year (%)		
					Col. 1–3 (5)	Col. 2–4 (6)	Col. 1–4 (7)
Agriculture and Related Industries (A Sector)							
GDP Originating (bill. $, 1963 FC)							
1. Developed countries	54.7	59.8	67.3	74.8	2.10	2.26	2.11
2. LDCs	45.5	54.2	63.8	71.8	3.44	2.85	3.09
3. East & Southeast Asia (excl. Japan)	26.9	31.6	37.0	40.5	3.24	2.51	2.76
4. Latin America	10.4	12.5	14.9	17.8	3.66	3.60	3.65
GDP Originating in A, per capita of total population ($, 1963 FC)							
5. Developed countries	92.8	95.5	100.6	105.2	0.80	0.97	0.83
6. LDCs	42.1	45.2	47.1	46.6	1.13	0.30	0.68
7. East & Southeast Asia (excl. Japan)	39.3	41.7	43.3	42.2	1.00	0.12	0.47
8. Latin America	64.1	67.6	70.7	73.1	0.96	0.76	0.86
Relative Gap							
9. Line 5: Line 6	2.20	2.11	2.14	2.26			
10. Line 5: Line 7	2.36	2.29	2.32	2.49			
11. Line 5: Line 8	1.45	1.41	1.42	1.44			
Industry Sector (I Sector)							
GDP Originating (bill. $, 1963 FC)							
12. Developed countries	298	373	447	592	4.14	4.73	4.68
13. LDCs	29.9	41.6	57.2	77.4	6.70	6.41	6.55
14. East & Southeast Asia (excl. Japan)	10.1	14.0	19.1	26.9	6.58	6.75	6.73
15. Latin America	14.5	19.7	26.6	34.7	6.26	5.82	5.99

GDP Originating in I, per capita of total population ($, 1963 FC)

16. Developed countries	507	596	668	832	2.82	3.40	3.38
17. LDCs	27.7	34.7	42.2	50.2	4.32	3.77	4.06
18. East & Southeast Asia (excl. Japan)	14.8	18.4	22.4	28.0	4.34	4.33	4.36
19. Latin America	89.7	106.5	126.3	142.4	3.48	2.94	3.13

Relative Gap

20. Line 16: Line 17	18.3	17.2	15.8	16.6
21. Line 16: Line 18	34.3	32.3	29.8	29.7
22. Line 16: Line 19	5.6	5.6	5.3	5.8

Service Sector (S Sector)

GDP Originating (bill. of $, 1963 FC)

23. Developed countries	302	365	445	566	3.95	4.48	4.28
24. LDCs	40.8	51.4	64.5	82.6	4.69	4.86	4.81
25. East & Southeast Asia (excl. Japan)	16.5	19.9	24.3	32.0	3.95	4.86	4.51
26. Latin America	17.5	22.3	27.8	35.4	4.74	4.73	4.72

GDP Originating in S, per capita of total populaton ($, 1963 FC)

27. Developed countries	512	583	665	796	2.64	3.16	2.98
28. LDCs	37.7	42.8	47.6	53.6	2.35	2.26	2.36
29. East & Southeast Asia (excl. Japan)	24.1	26.2	28.5	33.3	1.69	2.42	2.18
30. Latin America	108	120	132	145	2.01	1.87	1.90

Relative Gap

31. Line 27: Line 28	13.6	13.6	14.0	14.9
32. Line 27: Line 29	21.3	22.3	23.3	23.9
33. Line 27: Line 30	4.7	4.8	5.0	5.5

The underlying data are from the sources cited in the notes to Table 5.

The I sector includes mining, manufacturing, electric power, gas, and water, construction, and transport and communications. The S sector includes trade, professional and government services, and all other services. The A sector includes besides agriculture such related industries as fishing, hunting, and forestry.

For the methods of calculation see the notes to Table 5.

growth rates of the I sector (as well as of the S), would produce a lower growth rate of *total* per capita product in the LDCs— even if the rate of growth of per capita output of each sector taken separately were the *same* in the two groups of countries. If technological or other constraints restrict the growth rates of the A sector to lower levels than those of the I sector (the S sector may be left out because fully adequate bases for measurement of its "real" output are still to be established), the LDCs, in order to match or exceed the growth rates of per capita product of the developed countries, would have to attain much higher rates of growth in either the A or the I sector, and most likely in both. With substantial growth rate of product per capita in the developed countries, achievement of such high rates in both the A and the I sectors of the LDCs, particularly in the former, is a difficult task.[11]

TRENDS IN STRUCTURAL GAP · The long-term widening of the gap in per capita product was obviously accompanied by a widening of the gap in some aspects of economic structure. Thus if the rise in per capita product in the course of modern economic growth was associated with a marked decline in the share of the A sector in product and in labor force, the slower rise of per capita product in the LDCs than in the developed countries was likely to be accompanied by a lesser decline in the share of the A sector in labor force and in product, widening the gap in the production structure (between the A and non-A sectors).

[11] The effects of this difference in weights of the A and I sectors can be shown in a simple calculation based on Table 6. The relative gap between the developed countries and the Asian subregion in per capita product of the A sector barely changed between 1950–52 and 1965–67 (from 2.36 to 2.49, line 10); that for per capita product of the I sector dropped appreciably (from 34.3 to 29.7, line 21). But if we combine the A and I sectors, the relative gap in the combined per capita product rises from 11.1 to 13.4, by about a fifth. Likewise, the gap in per capita product of the A sector between the developed countries and Latin America remained unchanged (1.45 and 1.44, line 11); and that in per capita product of the I sector barely changed (5.6 and 5.8, line 22). But when the two are combined, the gap rises from 3.9 to 4.3, about a tenth.

Moreover, these effects of the small weights of the I and the large weights of the A sector would be accentuated if we were to allow for the higher prices of I sector products relative to A sector products in the LDCs (i.e., apply the world market price structure, or that characterizing more-developed countries).

This trend can be readily documented in terms of shares in labor force. The share of the A sector in the total labor force in the non-Communist developed countries (Europe, North America, Australia and New Zealand, Japan, and Union of South Africa) declined from 56 per cent in 1880 to 48 in 1900 and to 23 in 1960; whereas the share in the non-Communist LDCs (all other countries) was 78 per cent in 1900, 77 in 1930, and 71 in 1960.[12] In 1880 the spread between 56 per cent in the A sector in the developed countries and probably about 80 per cent in the LDCs was 24 percentage points; in 1960, the two percentages were 23 and 71, a spread of 48 percentage points. And presumably the disparity in the share of the A sector in total product also widened (for the movement of this share in developed countries see *MEG*, Table 3.1, pp. 88–93). The decline in the share of the A sector in labor force must have been accompanied by a drop in the share of rural and small-town population, a rise in urbanization, and increasing divergence in this respect also between developed countries and LDCs. Evidence on this point is available, limited, however, to the period 1920–60. In 1920, 70.7 per cent of the population of the developed regions (all of Europe, North America, the U.S.S.R., Japan, and Australia and New Zealand) were in rural areas and small towns (less than 20,000); and 13.7 per cent were in large cities (over 500,-000). In the same year 93.9 per cent of the population in the LDCs (rest of the world) were in rural-small town areas and 1.4 per cent in large cities. The spread in percentage points was 23.2 for shares of rural-small town areas and 12.3 for shares of large cities. By 1960, the share of rural-small town population dropped to 54.2 per cent for developed regions, but was still 84.0 per cent for the LDCs, and the spread widened to 29.8 percentage points; while the share of large cities population rose to 22.3 per cent in developed countries but to only 6.9 per cent in the LDCs, and the spread widened to 15.4 percentage points.[13]

There should have been, at least among the non-Communist

[12] See P. Bairoch and J.M. Limbor, "Changes in the Industrial Distribution of the World Labour Force by Region, 1880–1960," *International Labour Review*, Vol. 98, no. 4, October, 1968, Table IV, pp. 320–21 and Table V, p. 324.

[13] See *Growth of the World's Urban and Rural Population, 1920–2000* (New York: United Nations, 1969), Tables 47, 48, and 51, pp. 115–16, and 119. Temperate South America was shifted to the less-developed regions.

countries, a widening disparity in other aspects of the production structure, e.g., in the distribution of factors and output among various types of organization, and of productive establishments (by status of workers, scale of enterprise, type of ownership, etc.) The growth of per capita product in the developed countries must have been accompanied by changes in the character of organization of the economic unit and the scale of the production unit, which accentuated the existing differences in this respect from the less-developed regions of the world.

Although the statistical measures indicate widening divergence in such structural aspects as shares of non-A sectors, of urban population, of large-scale economic units, etc., important elements of convergence do exist. The rises, limited as they are, in the shares of the I sector within the LDCs may be associated with the emergence of modern technology, of the modern infrastructure, and of some modern industry; and this emergence, although it brings only a modicum of modern technology and economy within the boundaries of a less-developed country, represents a significant movement *toward* developed status—even if the share in the developed countries of such modern elements has increased more, absolutely or proportionately to aggregate product. And the A sector, the rural population, and the small-scale economic units may be affected by these nuclei of modern economy and technology in ways that are not reflected in the types of shares cited above.

Yet in some aspects of economic and social structure this penetration of elements of modern economic growth brings about a *measurable* convergence between the LDCs and developed countries, even though the disparity in per capita product widens. Thus the increasing involvement of less-developed regions in the network of international trade must have raised their foreign trade proportions and brought them closer in this respect to the developed countries which had had, in earlier times, higher foreign trade proportions—a point to which we will return in the next section—and in some, in many ways more important, noneconomic aspects of social structure convergence also took place. Thus, as already observed in the discussion of Tables 5 and 6 in connection with the post-World War II growth of developed and less-developed regions, the death rates in many of the latter regions declined markedly, and more than in the developed countries. Comparison of death rates, and perhaps even morbidity rates, between the 1920's and the 1960's—a period over which the gap in per capita product must have widened—would show marked convergence (except for some LDCs in Africa). Literacy, with its rapid rise in the less-developed countries, and its approach to practically the 100 per cent ceiling in developed countries, would also show convergence; and so would proportions of population receiving primary education.

Finally, there is much evidence of convergence in political and ideological aspects, uncertain as an economist's judgment of such aspects must be. We can particularly interpret the shift from colonial status to political independence and national sovereignty, which began after World War I and spread rapidly and widely after World War II, as an instance of convergence between the LDCs and the developed countries with respect to the formal character of political structure. Before World War II, and even more before World War I, most of the low-income, less-developed countries were colonial in status; and although some developed units (such as Canada, Australia, and New Zealand) were also colonies, the character of their relationship to the mother country was quite different. The shift to national sovereignty that occurred is clearly a major case of convergence in political form that accompanied divergence in economic performance and some aspects of economic structure.

Analogous to the shift in political form was the movement toward what might be called modern ideology. The often referred to "revolution of rising expectations" that is assumed to characterize the less-developed regions of the world means that their populations (or groups within them) have begun to emphasize material (economic) achievement, and are accepting the belief in the capacity of modern technology and society to reach high levels of material output per capita, and expect that these material attainments can and should be secured. All these are typical views on the modern economy and society that have evolved in the developed countries (largely from experience with the impressive achievements of modern technology), and are quite different from the views held by pre-modern societies and by traditional societies even in recent times. This represents a significant convergence, which, in combination with the widening gap in economic per capita performance, may have some explosive possibilities. But I know of no measures of such expectations among the populations of the less-developed countries or of the dissatisfaction produced by the widening gap, when combined with a significant rise in the absolute per capita product and consumption.

TRENDS IN INTERDEPENDENCE AND DIVISIVENESS · The rapid advance in technology, characteristic of modern economic growth, both facilitated and induced larger flows among nations, and also across the gap between the developed and the less-developed countries. And these larger flows made for greater mutual dependence of nations than in earlier times when groups of nations could live isolated from each other. The continuing technological revolution in transport and communication, from the application of steam to land and water transport, to the internal combustion engine on land and in the air, to the recent emergence of jet and rocket propulsion in space; the spread of electric and short wave power in communication—let alone a host of subsidiary inventions in preservation and storage and reproduction—had an obvious and profound effect on the ease with which goods, people, and ideas could be moved across long distances and among widely separated nations. Growing materials-technology, and the readiness of population in developed countries to accept new goods, created a continuing economic (in addition to political) stimulus for the developed countries to reach out to the less-developed in the search for the resources that the new technology made accessible and valuable (e.g., petroleum and uranium ores, previously of little value) and for which potential markets within the developed countries could be large. This dependence of developed countries on the resources of the less-developed, although mitigated by the capacity of modern technology to produce substitutes, obviously has grown in comparison with the state of relative isolation a century to a century and a quarter ago. Concomitantly, although the less-developed countries were often unwilling parties to the establishment of trade and political ties that sometimes limited their freedom of decision, the growing exploitation of their natural resources and their closer acquaintance with modern goods, technology, and society in turn increased the dependence of these LDCs on the rest of the world, largely the developed countries.

Such growing interdependence was reflected not only in economic and material flows but also in the spread of consumer tastes and social inventions and philosophy. For foreign trade in commodities this process can be readily measured, with the help of long-term estimates of the total volume of foreign commodity trade since the early nineteenth century; and subdivided between the developed and less-developed for more recent periods. Between 1820 and 1850, volume of world foreign trade *per capita* grew over 42 per cent per decade; between 1850 and 1880, 38 per cent; between 1870 and 1900 about 30 per cent; between 1881 and 1913, 34 per cent.[14] Since the growth of per capita product in the developed countries was less than 20 per cent per decade, and for the world as a whole, including the less-developed countries, must have been much lower, the proportion of foreign trade to total output rose markedly between the early nineteenth century and 1913, demonstrating greater involvement and interdependence among nations. The proportion of world commodity trade to output (i.e., of combined exports and imports to world product) must have risen from a few percentage points in 1800 to about a third in 1913 (see *Paper X*, p. 7).

Even in the period from 1913 to 1963, which was affected by two world wars and a major world depression, the volume of world trade per capita grew 14.4 per cent per decade (*Paper X*, Table 1), and this rate would probably be raised one or two percentage points if we were to add the four years to 1967. Even at this much reduced level, the growth rate of world trade per capita was probably not far short, if at all, of the growth rate of world output per capita—which means that although the trade proportion for the world did not rise, by the late 1960's for the world as a whole (if not for some distinct regions) it was not significantly below the peak before World War I.

The *shares* of the less-developed part of the world (all except Western Europe and North America from 1800 to the 1870's, excluding also Oceania, South Africa, and Japan for later years,

[14] See Simon Kuznets, "Quantitative Aspects of the Economic Growth of Nations: X. Level and Structure of Foreign Trade: Long-Term Trends," *Economic Development and Cultural Change*, Vol. 15, no. 2, Part II, January, 1967, Table 1, p. 4; referred to in the text as *Paper X*.

and excluding the Communist countries after 1913) in this rapidly growing volume of world foreign trade remained constant
in the nineteenth century—at either 20 or 30 per cent, depending upon the estimate—and tended to rise slowly from the beginning of the twentieth century to just before World War II
(*Paper X*, Table 2, pp. 11–12). This meant that the volume of
foreign trade of the less-developed part of the world grew at
equally high or higher rates than that of the developed countries
through most of the long period back to the early nineteenth
century if not in the recent decade. Indeed, direct calculations
for 1876–80 to 1913, and even for 1913 to 1963, show decadal
rates of growth in the *per capita* volume of foreign trade of 28.6
and 11.0 per cent respectively for the LDCs, and 25.6 and 10.4
per cent respectively for the developed countries (*Paper X*,
Table 3, p. 16, based on a somewhat different set from that cited
above). The foreign trade *proportions* therefore rose much more
in the LDCs than in the developed countries—which was only
natural for those less-developed countries that entered the network of foreign trade for the first time during this long period.
Since it was widespread, it is a good index of increasing engagement. Moreover, if in the earlier periods foreign trade proportions were lower in the less-developed regions than in the developed countries, these trade proportions in the LDCs moved
closer to those in the developed regions—convergence in another aspect of economic structure despite widening per capita
product differentials (as already noted in the preceding section).
However, in the post-World War II decade the foreign trade
proportion for the LDCs rose less than that for the developed
countries; and for Latin America it even declined over a longer
period.[15]

[15] *Paper X*, Table 3, p. 16, shows that between 1913 and 1963 per capita
volume of foreign trade for all non-Communist LDCs grew 11.0 per cent
per decade, but that for Latin America *declined* whereas that for Asia and
Africa (excluding Japan and the Union of South Africa) grew 14.8 per cent
per decade. For the post-World War II decade from 1955–57 to 1965–67,
we derived the growth rates for the country groupings in Table 5 from
quantum indexes of exports and imports given in *Yearbook of International
Trade Statistics 1967* (New York: United Nations, 1969), Table C, pp.
32–33, and extrapolated back to 1955 by the indexes in the *Yearbook of International Trade Statistics 1959* (New York, 1960), Table C, pp. 28–29.
Classes I and II in the 1967 *Yearbook* and developed and less-developed
categories in the 1959 *Yearbook* were taken to represent developed and

Two final brief comments on this trend toward increasing interdependence may be added. First, technological and related breakthroughs in transport, communication, and the stock of general knowledge have enormously facilitated and affected not only the peaceful types of flows, but also the exercise of political pressure, or military power—particularly of the developed countries vis-à-vis each other or in relation to the less-developed regions. The consequences, combined with increasing divisiveness, are obvious and need not be discussed here; but clearly the enormous economic magnitudes involved in major wars and explicable largely in terms of the complex technology of producing, transporting, and delivering weapons, played a major role in the disruption and retardation of the growth of the international trade network. Second and much less obvious are the possible worldwide effects of increasing power of modern technology, even when exercised within the boundaries of the developed countries proper. The pollution of air streams by jets and atomic weapon tests and the heat pollution of the atmosphere by power plants, while largely originating in the developed regions, spread across the globe and affect even distant less-developed regions. These unforeseen, and certainly unintended, effects of the application of modern technology, com-

---

less-developed regions (non-Communist). The regional groupings in the two *Yearbooks* are similar.

Growth Rates per Year, GDP and Foreign Trade for 1955–57 to

1965–67, Non-Communist Countries

	GDP (from Table 5)	Exports	Imports
	(1)	(2)	(3)
1. Developed countries	4.44	6.80	7.79
2. LDCs	4.65	5.12	4.18
3. Asia (E and SE)	4.26	4.01	5.03
4. Latin America	4.90	3.53	2.21

The marked decline in the foreign trade proportion for Latin America, particularly in the import proportion, is clear. Yet for Asia, the proportion of exports declines slightly but the import proportion rises; and the trade proportions for the developed countries rise noticeably. However, such movements over the post-World War II decade should be interpreted in the perspective of much longer trends, back to the 1920's, to 1913, or even further. In this longer perspective, the foreign trade proportion rose more in the LDCs than in the developed countries before 1913; and for Asia-Africa, but not Latin America, even for the long stretch from 1913 to date.

bined with the rapid consumption, chiefly by developed regions, of the apparently non-reproducible and non-replaceable natural resources of the world, suggest a dependence of the rest of the world on the technology of the developed regions—not only on its bounty, but also on its adverse effects on ecology of the world, which means a dependence also on its capacity to provide substitutes and to offset such adverse effects.

These trends toward increasing interdependence assume particular weight when viewed together with the trends toward increasing divisiveness—which have emerged, if not concurrently, since World War I. This divisiveness, particularly with respect to political structure and ideological positions, is a difficult subject for an economist. Yet it is too important to be passed by without comment. Let me then conclude with a few brief remarks, which are offered as notes on trends that seem of direct bearing upon the economic gap between rich and poor nations, although no claim is made that these trends have been closely scrutinized.

First, although the rapid dissolution of colonial empires and attainment of national sovereignty by the former colonies promise many potential benefits, they also mean a multiplication of foci of decision, a large addition to the number of nations (many small), and thus, at least in the short run, a great increase in points of friction and division. Our earlier comment on the many small countries in the world, and particularly in the less-developed regions, illustrated in Table 3, should be repeated here. The colonial liberation movement has added, since World War II alone, at least twenty-six new nations in sub-Saharan Africa (not counting Southern Rhodesia); at least five in North Africa and the Middle East, eleven in Asia—counting only countries with over a million population and outside the Communist bloc (see the source used for Table 1). Thus, over 40 of some 120 units counted in Table 3 have attained political sovereignty at most only two decades ago. The number, particularly in the Middle East, would be even larger if we extended the period to the World War I decade.

To be sure, we cannot say that the conflicts among or within these new nations (e.g., between India and Pakistan, or North and South Vietnam, or the internal revolts in the Sudan, the Congo, and Nigeria) are a more divisive element than the ten-

sions, incidents, and squabbles in the past among colonial powers in their struggles for protection or extension of their spheres
of interest. But regardless of how one compares the two situations, the significance of the gap between poor and rich nations
must be considered in the light of the recent large increase in
the number of these poor nations of most diverse historical origin; the continuing struggles to establish a viable political
framework within many of them, as well as the unresolved conflicts that emerged when many of these new nations attained independence; and the prospect that many will continue to be relatively small and a few extremely large, with all the problems of
independent economic growth that such size characteristics
suggest.

Second, the number of *large, developed* countries implies increased divisiveness so long as the organization of national
states persists and newly developed large national states claim
their "rightful" share in the world. Pax Britannica lasted as long
as Great Britain was the only truly developed large country, but
it eroded rapidly in the last quarter of the nineteenth century,
by which time Germany, France, and the United States joined
the ranks of large, developed nations. If one may speak of a
trend when so few units are involved, there has been an increase in divisiveness associated with the rise in the number of
large economically developed societies organized politically into
sovereign nations with competing claims as to their position in
an already divided world. That a large country can, in a short
time and without substantial industrialization, move toward
greater economic (and hence political) power, and thus have
unsettling and divisive effects is illustrated by the recent history
of the relations between Mainland China and the rest of the
world.

Third, the emergence after World War I of the U.S.S.R., and
its rapid attainment of substantial industrialization, if not of
complete economic and social development, meant, as already
indicated, the beginning of a major fissure in the world. For a
century and a quarter before 1917, although modern economic
growth, as it was spreading, was accompanied by tensions and
wars among economically advanced nations or between them
and some less-developed units, no ideological cleavage emerged
in the major organizational form of society in which economic

development was taking place. Even the Marxian doctrine adhered to by some social groups within developed countries envisioned socialism as a final phase of development after the breakdown of capitalism, but did not consider the possibility of by-passing the long evolution of capitalist, free-market, democratic society. Against this background, the U.S.S.R., a large nation that, having industrialized, operated under an ideology hostile to that of all other developed countries and thus served as an exponent of an alternative road from pre-modern to modern economic organization, was something new; and inevitably increased the divisiveness in the world. The significance of its effect on less-developed countries through competing claims and policies needs no expounding. We do not intend here to pass judgment on the validity of ideological claims, or to indicate whether such divisiveness, particularly among the developed countries, is beneficial for the economic growth of less-developed regions. The reference is simply to obvious facts of political and ideological life on the international canvas of the world, which must be considered in analyzing various aspects of the economic gap.

Problems in Comparing
Recent Growth Rates
for Developed and
Less-Developed Countries

1. Introduction

The discussion may be introduced by a brief summary of the readily available aggregative measures for the post-World War II period, for the more-developed, or simply developed (i.e., industrialized and with a relatively high per capita product), and less-developed countries. The measures are annual indexes for 1950–68 of GDP, at constant (1963) factor costs, for these two groups of countries. Table 1 is based on the data as given, including available series on population. The notes to the table, which covers the entire non-Communist world, indicate the scope of each group.

Because the first quinquennium after 1950 may still have been significantly affected by residual consequences of World War II, and particularly by recovery following the shift in political status toward independence among the less-developed countries, greater weight should be assigned to the rates for the period

Reprinted from *Economic Development and Cultural Change*, Vol. 20, no. 2, January, 1972, 185–209.

from 1954–58 to 1964–68 (line 6) as reflections of aggregate growth. In that period total product in both the developed and less-developed countries grew at about the same rate—4.6–4.7 per cent per year, or almost 60 per cent per decade. But population in the developed countries grew less than 1.2 per cent per year, or less than 13 per cent per decade; whereas that in the less-developed countries grew about 2.4 per cent per year, or more than 27 per cent per decade. As a result, per capita product in the less-developed countries rose about 2.2 per cent per year, whereas that in the developed countries grew almost 3.4 per cent per year, and the relative disparity in per capita product between the two groups of countries widened somewhat, from a multiple of 10.7 to one of 12.0. The comparison of growth rates for the full period, from 1950–54 to 1964–68, yields similar results.[1]

Before we raise questions about the acceptability of these findings, three comments might prevent misunderstanding. First, the growth rates for both developed and less-developed countries greatly exceed those of modern economic growth in the historical past, indicating a marked acceleration of growth in both groups. Second, regardless of whether the gap in per capita product between the developed and less-developed countries is of major significance, it must be stressed that the recent widening occurred not because the less-developed countries failed to grow rapidly but because the developed countries grew at a greatly accelerated rate. Third, although the discussion that follows raises serious questions about the comparability of magnitudes like those shown in Table 1, it is intended to facilitate the derivation of more comparable measures—not to deny all significance to the crude measures now available.

[1] See *Yearbook of National Accounts Statistics*, Vol. II, *International Tables* (New York: United Nations, 1970), Table 4B (hereafter cited as *International Tables*). Table 4B shows growth rates for GDP, total and per capita, for several periods, for the developed and less-developed country groups (also for several subgroups and many countries). The rates were calculated from exponential curves fitted to the annual underlying data by least squares. We hesitated to use them in our analysis because the basic assumptions of least squares do not fit the characteristics of historical time series (in which errors are not random) and, if applied to annual data for short periods, yield results too sensitive to any large, transient disturbances in the data. We limited the use of these rates to Table 4, for comparison with rates derived from other sets of estimates.

Table 1. GROSS DOMESTIC PRODUCT, POPULATION, AND PRODUCT PER CAPITA, NON-COMMUNIST DEVELOPED (DC) AND LESS-DEVELOPED (LDC) COUNTRIES, 1950–68

	Gross domestic product factor cost		Population		Product per capita	
	DC (1)	LDC (2)	DC (3)	LDC (4)	DC (5)	LDC (6)
	Absolute Value					
	(Billions 1963 $)		(Millions)		(1963 $)	
1. 1950–54	675	124.7	579	1,132	1,167	110.1
2. 1954–58	785	150.7	603	1,237	1,301	121.8
3. 1959–63	953	189.5	639	1,391	1,491	136.3
4. 1964–68	1,229	237.8	678	1,569	1,812	151.6
	Growth Rates per Year (%)					
5. 1950–54 to 1959–63	3.90	4.77	1.11	2.31	2.77	2.40
6. 1954–58 to 1964–68	4.59	4.67	1.17	2.40	3.38	2.21
7. 1950–54 to 1964–68	4.37	4.72	1.13	2.36	3.20	2.31

Developed countries include all of non-Communist Europe (excluding Cyprus and Turkey), Canada, the United States, Japan, Australia, New Zealand, Fiji, Israel, and South Africa. Less-developed ("developing") countries include non-Communist East and Southeast Asia (excluding Japan), the Middle East (Southwest Asia including Cyprus and Turkey and excluding Israel), Africa (excluding South Africa), Latin America (excluding Cuba and including the rest of the Caribbean), and the rest of Oceania. The countries included in the various regions are listed in *International Tables,* Table 1B (see n. 1 above).

Cols. 1–2: Estimates of 1963 GDP at factor cost, in U.S. dollars, are from ibid., Table 1B. These were extrapolated to the periods indicated in the stubs by use of geometric means of the annual indexes given in ibid., Table 6B.

Cols. 3–4: Estimates of population in 1963 are from *Demographic Yearbook, 1968* (New York: United Nations, 1970), Table 1; for countries excluded or shifted for comparability with product, Table 4. Population indexes were derived by dividing the indexes for GDP by those for GDP per capita given in *International Tables,* Table 6B.

Cols. 5–6: Derived from cols. 1–4 by division.

The questions can be most conveniently discussed under three heads: (*a*) the definition of developed and less-developed countries (DCs and LDCs for short) and the reliability of the estimates, particularly those of gross product for the LDCs; (*b*) the weighting of the per capita growth rates for subareal units in deriving per capita growth rates for aggregative totals for the DCs and LDCs; (*c*) the weighting of sectoral growth rates within the areas or countries in deriving the growth rate for total product (the sectors being those in the production system, e.g., agriculture, manufacturing, etc.), and possible allowance for the increasing weight of intermediate products resulting from urbanization.

2. Scope and Reliability

In the United Nations classification used in Table 1, developed countries include all of non-Communist Europe. That Greece or Portugal should be included, while Argentina in Latin America is considered less-developed, raises a question about the criteria used. The OECD Research Centre includes Greece and Spain in its compilation of statistics for the less-developed countries; while the Pearson Commission on International Development includes Portugal in addition to these. The International Labour Office, like the United Nations, includes all of Europe in the developed group but also includes "Temperate South America," that is, Argentina, Chile, Uruguay, the Falkland Islands, and, surprisingly, Paraguay.[2]

The rationale for treating all of the non-Communist world as comprising just two groups—developed and less-developed—is not clear. Economic development is a gradual process and not without setbacks, and at any one time a number of countries are neither clearly in the developed group nor clearly so low on the per capita product scale as to belong to the populous group of less-developed regions. If one must divide the non-Communist world into the two categories, there will obviously be borderline cases; although even then, if a set of fairly objective criteria were applied to individual countries, incongruities like those mentioned above would be eliminated.

But this problem cannot be handled adequately here; and we resolve it, for the present purposes, somewhat arbitrarily. Since the United Nations provides indexes of GDP, total and per capita, not only for the developed and less-developed groups but also for several regions within each, we can, by means of the lat-

---

[2] For the OECD compilations and the Pearson Commission Report, see references cited in the notes to Tables 3 and 4. The International Labour Organization (ILO) classification can be found in Samuel Baum, "The World's Labour Force and Its Industrial Distribution, 1950 and 1960," *International Labour Review*, Vol. 95, January–February, 1967, 3–19.

ter, not only remove components that do not seem to us to fit but also check on the reliability and weighting problems.

In Table 2 we take advantage of the total output indexes for the several regions among the developed countries, supplementing them by an index for Japan. To be sure, even these regional indexes contain an admixture of countries that can hardly be considered developed: EFTA includes Portugal, and Oceania includes Fiji. But the adjustment to eliminate these would have minor effects and hardly warrants the calculations involved. Using the regional indexes as they stand, we derive a new total for developed countries which excludes almost all of non-Communist Europe that does not properly belong to the developed group, judging by its per capita product and degree of industrialization. It also excludes Israel, a minor omission in terms of relative magnitudes; and South Africa, hardly a properly defined developed country, considering its low per capita income for *total* population (not just the white minority).

Two conclusions are suggested by Table 2. First, while the average per capita product is between 7 and 8 per cent larger than that for the more comprehensive total in Table 1 (cf. Table 2, line 20, cols. 2–4, with Table 1, col. 5, lines 2–4), the growth rates are about the same. Thus, for the span from 1954–58 to 1964–68, the growth rates per year for GDP are 4.6 and 4.5 per cent, those for population about 1.2 per cent, and those for per capita product, 3.4 and 3.3 per cent. Second and more important, the developed regions within the total in Table 2 are markedly different, with respect to both the level of per capita product and the growth rates of population, per capita product, and total product. These differences indicate that the system by which the regions are weighted is a significant factor in determining the growth rates for the totals of all developed countries. If the per capita product levels or the growth rates were roughly the same for all regions, the weighting system would be unimportant.

When we turn to regions within the less-developed group, for which separate annual indexes are given, we also find that the two major regions, East and Southeast Asia (ESEA) and Latin America (LA), differ markedly with respect to per capita product, which is more than three times larger in the latter than in the former; and the growth rate of per capita product is dis-

Table 2. Gross Domestic Product, Population, and Product Per Capita, Selected Developed Regions, 1950–68

	Absolute values				Growth rates per year (%)		
	1950–54 (1)	1954–58 (2)	1959–63 (3)	1964–68 (4)	1950–54 to 1959–63 (5)	1954–58 to 1964–68 (6)	1950–54 to 1964–68 (7)
	GDP (factor cost, bill. 1963 $)						
1. EEC	123.2	155.4	201.6	257.9	5.62	5.20	5.42
2. EFTA	91.1	102.8	121.1	145.8	3.21	3.55	3.41
3. Japan	nc	32.7	51.7	84.8	nc	10.01	nc
4. NA	407.5	458.6	532.0	677.5	3.01	3.98	3.90
5. O	14.4	16.4	19.9	25.7	3.70	4.58	4.24
6. All regions above (DCR)	nc	766.0	926.4	1,191.8	nc	4.52	nc
7. All regions excl. Japan (DCR – J)	636.3	733.3	874.7	1,107.0	3.60	4.20	4.03
	Population (mill.)						
8. EEC	160.1	166.1	174.0	182.9	0.93	0.97	0.96
9. EFTA	90.2	91.9	94.9	98.8	0.56	0.72	0.65
10. J	nc	89.9	93.9	98.8	nc	0.95	nc
11. NA	172.3	184.7	201.7	216.6	1.77	1.60	1.65
12. O	10.9	12.0	13.4	14.7	2.27	2.10	2.17
13. DCR	nc	544.6	577.9	611.8	nc	1.17	nc
14. DCR – J	433.4	454.7	484.0	513.0	1.23	1.21	1.21

Product per capita (1963 $)

15. EEC	770	935	1,158	1,410	4.64	4.19	4.42
16. EFTA	1,011	1,119	1,277	1,476	2.63	2.81	2.74
17. J	nc	365	551	858	nc	9.97	nc
18. NA	2,366	2,483	2,637	3,128	1.22	2.34	2.02
19. O	1,318	1,372	1,494	1,746	1.40	2.43	2.03
20. DCR	nc	1,407	1,603	1,948	nc	3.31	nc
21. DCR − J	1,468	1,613	1,807	2,158	2.34	2.96	2.79

nc = not calculated. The estimates are derived from the sources and by the procedures indicated in the note to Table 1. For Japan, the underlying indexes of total and per capita GDP (in market prices), from Table 7 of International Tables (see n. 1 above), were applied to total and per capita GDP at factor costs in 1963, from ibid., Table 1B. Population was derived from these indexes and totals (and is virtually identical with that shown in the Demographic Yearbook, various issues).

European Economic Community—Includes Belgium, France, Germany, Italy, Luxembourg, and the Netherlands.

European Free Trade Association—Includes Austria, Denmark, Finland, Iceland, Norway, Portugal, Sweden, Switzerland, and the United Kingdom.

North America—Limited to Canada and the United States.

Oceania—Includes Fiji, in addition to Australia and New Zealand, but the addition is minor in terms of either product or population.

tinctly higher in Latin America (see Table 3, lines 7–8). But a question arises concerning the reliability of the estimates for the *residual* area implied in the UN indexes of gross product for all less-developed countries and for the two regions for which annual indexes are given (ESEA and LA). This residual area (AME)—which is roughly the total of Africa and the Middle East (as defined by the United Nations with the proper exclusions)—shows a much higher growth rate of per capita product than either ESEA or LA (line 9). In view of the dominant weight of Africa in this residual, with respect to both population and per capita product, and its poor growth record associated with political turmoil, the results are not plausible. Alternative growth rates of per capita product, based on the OECD indexes, for roughly the same area for a slightly different period (for which we recalculated the growth rates in the UN estimates) are about a fifth lower (see lines 10–14, particularly lines 12 and 14). The comparison uses identical estimates of population, and the difference is due exclusively to the higher growth rate of the UN estimates of total product. Because the reliability of the estimates for the residual area is in question, an alternative total for the less-developed countries, limited to ESEA and LA, is used for lines 15–17.

This problem of the reliability of the product estimates for the less-developed regions, as suggested by lack of consistency among estimates for the same regions and periods prepared by different international agencies, is further illustrated in Table 4. We compare the growth rates published in the recent UN *Yearbook of National Accounts Statistics* with those shown in the Pearson Commission report, based apparently on data in the files of the International Bank for Reconstruction and Development, and with rates calculated for similar periods from the OECD indexes. The discrepancies are particularly striking for Africa: for the period as a whole, the growth rates of per capita product based on UN estimates are about a third higher than those of the Pearson Commission and two-thirds higher than those of the OECD. Even for Latin America, the UN growth rates tend to be higher than those based on the OECD and Pearson Commission estimates. It is disturbing to find such differentials in growth rates for major regions of the world published by the several international agencies; and one would wish

LESS-DEVELOPED REGIONS, 1950–68

A. Regions as Given in UN Source (or Derived)

	Absolute values				Growth rates per year (%)		
	1950–54 (1)	1954–58 (2)	1959–63 (3)	1964–68 (4)	1950–54 to 1959–63 (5)	1954–58 to 1964–68 (6)	1950–54 to 1964–68 (7)
	GDP (factor cost, bill. 1963 $)						
1. ESEA	55.8	65.3	79.5	98.8	4.00	4.23	4.16
2. LA	41.7	52.0	67.0	85.1	5.40	5.04	5.22
3. AME°	27.1	33.4	43.0	54.0	5.26	4.91	5.04
	Population (mill.)						
4. ESEA	696	755	848	964	2.22	2.47	2.35
5. LA	166	185	213	245	2.80	2.82	2.82
6. AME	270	297	330	360	2.25	1.93	2.08
	Product per capita (1963 $)						
7. ESEA	80.1	86.4	93.7	102	1.75	1.71	1.77
8. LA	252	281	315	348	2.53	2.16	2.34
9. AME	101	113	131	150	2.94	2.92	2.90

B. Comparison of UN and OECD Estimates for AME, 1950–67

	Absolute values				Growth rates per year (%)		
	1950–52 (1)	1955–57 (2)	1960–62 (3)	1965–67 (4)	1950–52 to 1960–62 (5)	1955–57 to 1965–67 (6)	1950–52 to 1965–67 (7)
	Based on UN indexes of GDP						
10. GDP (bill. 1963 $)	25.8	33.1	42.9	53.4	5.20	4.91	4.97
11. Population (mill.)	265	293	327	356	2.14	1.96	1.99
12. Product per capita (1963 $)	97.5	113	131	150	3.00	2.90	2.92
	Based on OECD indexes of GDP						
13. GDP (bill. 1963 $)	27.4	34.3	43.1	53.2	4.62	4.49	4.51
14. Product per capita (1963 $)	104	117	132	149	2.43	2.48	2.47

Table 3. Gross Domestic Product, Population, and Product Per Capita, Less-Developed Regions, 1950–68 (Continued)

C. Alternative Total for LDCR

	Absolute values				Growth rates per year (%)		
	1950–54 (1)	1954–58 (2)	1959–63 (3)	1964–68 (4)	1950–54 to 1959–63 (5)	1954–58 to 1964–68 (6)	1950–54 to 1964–68 (7)
15. GDP (bill. 1963 $)	97.5	117.3	146.5	183.8	4.62	4.60	4.63
16. Population (mill.)	862	940	1,061	1,209	2.33	2.54	2.44
17. Product per capita (1963 $)	113	125	138	152	2.24	2.00	2.14

Lines 1–2, 4–5, 7–8: Derived from the sources and by the procedures indicated in the note to Table 1.

Lines 3, 6, 9: Obtained by subtracting GDP for ESEA and LA from the total for the LDCs, shown in Table 1, performing the same subtraction for population, and calculating product per capita from the residuals. Given the geographical scope of the LDCs and of the two regions, the residual should represent Africa (excluding South Africa), the Middle East (excluding Israel), and less-developed Oceania (excluding Fiji).

Lines 10–14: To check the growth rates in lines 3, 6, and 9, we compared the results based on the UN indexes of GDP with those based on the indexes given in *National Accounts of Less Developed Countries, 1950–1966* (Paris: OECD Development Centre, July, 1968); *National Accounts of Less Developed Countries, 1959–1968* (Paris: OECD Development Centre, July, 1970), Table 1b. The periods differ from those for lines 1–9 because the OECD data are not available for the full span. Line 14 is derived from line 13 and the population totals in line 11 (which are taken as identical), so that the comparison is of the GDP indexes alone. The absolute total GDP for 1963, taken from the UN source, is also identical in the comparison.

Lines 15–17: Limited to the sum of ESEA and LA (shown in lines 1–2 and 4–5) with a new product per capita derived from the product and population totals.

* Residual area, roughly the total of Africa and the Middle East.

	Gross domestic product			Product per capita		
	1950's (1)	1960's (2)	1950–67 or 1950–68 (3)	1950's (4)	1960's (5)	1950–67 or 1950–68 (6)
East and Southeast Asia						
1. UN	4.0	4.4	4.2	1.9	1.9	1.9
2. PC	4.0	4.7	4.3	1.9	2.1	2.0
Latin America						
3. UN	5.5	4.9	5.3	2.6	1.9	2.4
4. OECD	4.9	4.7	4.8	2.0	1.7	1.9
5. PC	5.0	4.5	4.8	2.1	1.6	1.8
Africa (excl. South Africa)						
6. UN	4.9	4.2	4.6	2.7	1.7	2.3
7. OECD	4.0	3.3	3.8	1.8	0.8	1.4
8. PC	4.0	4.0	4.0	1.7	1.6	1.7
Middle East (incl. Israel)						
9. UN	6.9	6.5	6.5	4.1	4.0	3.8
10. PC	6.0	7.2	6.5	2.9	4.2	3.4

The periods covered are: UN estimates, 1950–60, 1960–68, and 1950–
68; OECD estimates, 1950–52 to 1960–62, 1960–62 to 1966–68, and 1950–
52 to 1966–68; Pearson Commission estimates, 1950–60, 1960–67, and
1950–67. The United Nations growth rates are from *International Tables,*
Table 4B (see n. 1 above). "The method of calculation used is an exponential curve fitted to the data by least squares" (p. 148). The OECD growth
rates were calculated from the regional annual indexes by means of a
straight log line between the terminal three-year averages. The indexes
for 1950–52 are from *National Accounts of Less Developed Countries,
1950–1966,* Tables C, E; for 1960–62 and 1966–68, from *National Accounts
of Less Developed Countries, 1959–1968,* Table 1b (for total product),
Table 3b (for per capita product), Table 2b (for population, when needed).
The Pearson Commission growth rates are from L. B. Pearson, *Partners in
Development: Report of the Commission on International Development*
(New York: Frederick A. Praeger, 1969), Table 1, pp. 358–59. The rates
for South Asia and East Asia, shown separately, were combined by using
GDP and population shown in the later OECD source as weights. These
weights, which relate to 1960, were applied to the growth rates for the
three periods, and the combined growth rate for per capita product was
derived from the combined rates for total product and for population. The
Pearson Commission report does not indicate how the growth rates were
computed and cites the World Bank as the source.

that the estimating work behind these results could be unified in
some way to produce a single set of acceptable measures. For
the present, we proceed with the UN estimates for ESEA and
LA, omitting the residual estimates as subject to too much error,
and thus exclude Africa and the Middle East from our discussion of the less-developed group.

3. *The Weighting of Regions or Countries*

The indexes of the combined totals for GDP, published by the United Nations and other international agencies, are derived by compiling indexes for subregions or individual countries, multiplying them by a set of fixed weights (in the UN calculations, GDP in factor costs, 1963 $), summing the results, and dividing by the sum of weights. In this procedure the growth rates of *per capita product* of the regions (and of the countries) are weighted by the shares of the regions (or the countries) in *total product,* modified by the differential movement of the population of the regions or countries covered, relative to the movement of the total population. Is this the proper system of weights, or should growth rates of per capita product in separate regions or countries be weighted by fixed population—not allowing for differences in per capita product or for disparities in relative growth of population? One may legitimately argue that the growth rate of a country's per capita product should be given the weight of the underlying population, not a greater weight because of a higher per capita product or because of a greater growth of population over the period. Indeed, in welfare terms, when two countries show the same percentage rise in per capita product, the rate for the country with lower per capita product might well be given a larger weight than that for the one with higher per capita product. Nor should the differential rate of population growth of a country (relative to the growth rate of total population for the region or group) affect the per capita product growth rate for the total region or group.

A brief algebraic exposition may clarify the argument. Designate:

Y_1, Y_2, Y = products of subregions 1 and 2, and total, respectively (for simplicity we limit the illustration to two regions so that $Y_1 + Y_2 = Y$);

P_1, P_2, P = populations of subregions 1 and 2, and total, with $P_1 + P_2 = P$;

I_1, I_2, I = per capita products for subregions 1 and 2, and total, with $I_1 = Y_1 / P_1$, $I_2 = Y_2 / P_2$, $I = Y / P$;

r_1, r_2, r = growth rates of products in subregions 1 and 2, and total;

g_1, g_2, g = growth rates of populations in subregions 1 and 2, and total;

$k_1 k_2, k$ = growth rates of per capita products in subregions 1 and 2, and total, with $1+k_1 = (1+r_1)/(1+g_1)$, $1+k_2 = (1+r_2)/(1+g_2)$, $1+k = (1+r)/(1+g)$.

Then when we follow the conventional calculation for combined totals:

$$(1+k)\cdot Y/P = [Y_1(1+r_1) + Y_2(1+r_2)] : [P_1(1+g_1) + P_2(1+g_2)]. \tag{1}$$

By simplifying, we derive:

$$1+k = \left(\frac{1+r_1}{1+g}\cdot\frac{Y_1}{Y}\right) + \left(\frac{1+r_2}{1+g}\cdot\frac{Y_2}{Y}\right). \tag{2}$$

If we set $a_1 = (1+g_1)/(1+g)$, and $a_2 = (1+g_2)/(1+g)$, equation (2) can be rewritten as:

$$1+k = \left(\frac{1+r_1}{1+g_1}\cdot\frac{Y_1}{Y}\cdot a_1\right) + \left(\frac{1+r_2}{1+g_2}\cdot\frac{Y_2}{Y}\cdot a_2\right), \tag{3}$$

and this in turn can be simplified:

$$1+k = [(1+k_1)\cdot(P_1/P)\cdot(I_1/I)\cdot a_1] + [(1+k_2)\cdot(P_2/P)\cdot(I_2/I)\cdot a_2]. \tag{4}$$

In the conventional calculation, the growth rate of per capita product for the total region (group) is a weighted mean of the growth rates of per capita product for the subregions (two in this illustration, but they can be extended to n)—the weights being (a) the subregion's share in population, multiplied by (b) the ratio of the per capita income of the subregion to that for the total region or group, and further multiplied by (c) the ratio of the growth rate of the subregion's population to the growth rate of total population for the region or group.

The aggregate growth rates of per capita product derived by the conventional calculation will be *higher* than those weighted by total population alone if the higher per capita product subregions have a higher growth rate than the lower per capita product subregions; or if the population of the higher per capita product subregions is growing more rapidly than the population of the lower per capita product subregions; or if any combination of the two yields a positive excess.

In the alternative calculation, using superscripts to distinguish the alternative average:

$$1+k' = (1+k_1)(P_1/P) + (1+k_2)(P_2/P). \tag{5}$$

Using this weighted mean, which from many standpoints is preferable to the weighted mean in equation (4), and retaining the same population growth rates over the period, we derive:

$$
\begin{aligned}
1+r' &= (1+k')(1+g) \\
&= (1+k_1)(1+g_1)(P_1/P) + (1+k_2)(1+g_2)(P_2/P) \\
&= (1+r_1)(P_1/P) + (1+r_2)(P_2/P).
\end{aligned}
\tag{6}
$$

The weighted growth rate of total product in equation (6) combines growth rates for two (or n) subregions *without* allowing for the effect of different levels of per capita product in the subregions. Furthermore, the calculation does not permit the greater growth rate of the higher per capita product subregion, as measured by its *total* product, to inflate the growth rate of the product of the whole region or group.

Thus, when the GDP totals for all regions or countries are combined in the conventional procedure, the rise in the product of one (say LA) is treated as if it redounds to the direct benefit of the others (say ESEA). The alternative procedure denies the relevance of this *pooling of product* and suggests, instead, the pooling of population numbers as the proper base for weighting the growth of per capita product of populations of different size. This alternative procedure, of course, permits the derivation of variants in which a given percentage rise in per capita product is assigned *more* than the population weight when the initial per capita product is low.[3]

[3] One simple way to allow for greater welfare equivalents of a proportional increase in per capita product at lower than at higher per capita product is to make them directly inverse to these levels. This variant, using double superscripts to designate the resulting weighted average, would then be:

$$1+k'' = \frac{(1+k_1)(P_1/P)(1/I_1) + (1+k_2)(P_2/P)(1/I_2)}{(P_1/P)(1/I_1) + (P_2/P)(1/I_2)} \tag{7}$$

As already indicated in the comment on Table 2, the differences between the rates derived by the conventional and alternative procedures will be sizable if per capita products of the several regions or countries differ in level and rate of growth. The relevant comparisons, for the regions within the developed and less-developed groups, are summarized in Table 5.

For the developed group, the alternative weighting *raises* the growth rates of both total and per capita product. This is not surprising, since in the conventional calculation the low growth rates for North America and Oceania, with their high per capita product and large weight in the *product* total, are assigned much heavier weights than when they are weighted by population alone; whereas the other developed regions, particularly Japan, which show high growth rates in per capita product and have relatively low per capita product, are assigned heavier weights in the alternative calculation than in the conventional procedure. Thus, even when Japan is excluded, the alternative calculation raises the growth rate of per capita product for the recent period from 2.96 to 3.10 per cent (lines 2 and 5, col. 3). When Japan is included, the effect is much more striking, the rate rising from 3.31 to 4.07 per cent.

For the less-developed group, the effect is the opposite: the alternative calculation *reduces* the growth rate in per capita product. Here the LA region with the higher per capita product shows distinctly higher growth rates of per capita product than the ESEA region, and the former is assigned a much lower weight when fixed population totals rather than shares in total product are used. An additional factor here is the greater population growth in LA than in ESEA, which raises the growth rate of the per capita product of the less-developed group in the conventional but not in the alternative calculation. The growth rate of per capita product drops substantially over the more recent period, from 2.00 to 1.80 per cent, and the drop is even greater,

---

This weighted average growth rate of per capita product, like that in equation (5), could be calculated for the regions and countries covered in Tables 5 and 6. But since the resulting adjustments probably would be only slightly greater than those now shown, it did not seem useful to load the paper with tentative calculations. There is also a question whether the specific assumption, while the simplest, is the most appropriate. In any case, it is the analytical question of the possible bases for deriving the average growth rate of per capita product, even within a single country—not the specific magnitudes and estimational assumptions—that is important.

	1954–58 to 1964–68			1950–54 to 1964–68		
	GDP (1)	Popula-tion (2)	Product per capita (3)	GDP (4)	Popula-tion (5)	Product per capita (6)
Weighted by product, changing population						
1. DCR	4.52	1.17	3.31	nc	nc	nc
2. DCR − J	4.20	1.21	2.96	4.03	1.21	2.79
3. LDCR	4.60	2.54	2.00	4.63	2.44	2.14
Weighted by constant population						
4. DCR	5.29	1.17	4.07	nc	nc	nc
5. DCR − J	4.35	1.21	3.10	4.28	1.21	3.03
6. LDCR	4.39	2.54	1.80	4.37	2.44	1.88

nc = not calculated.
Lines 1–2: From Table 2, lines 6–7, 13–14, and 20–21, cols. 6–7.
Line 3: From Table 3, lines 15–17, cols. 6–7.
Lines 4–6: See the text for the rationale of the calculations. The entries in cols. 3 and 6 are averages of the growth rates of per capita product of the subregions (five or four for the DCs, two for the LDCs), weighted by their population at the midpoint of the period (1959–63 for 1954–58 to 1964–68, and the geometric mean of 1954–58 and 1959–63 for 1950–54 to 1964–68), given in Tables 2–3. Entries in cols. 1 and 4 were derived by multiplying the relatives of the rates in cols. 3 and 6 by the relatives of those in cols. 2 and 5.

from 2.14 to 1.88 per cent, for the longer period (see lines 3 and 6, cols. 3 and 6).

The discussion of the weights of regions applies equally to the weights of individual countries within a region. The rise in the per capita product of Brazil cannot be treated as of direct benefit to the per capita product of Mexico, and vice versa—even if the countries are within the same region. We therefore extended the alternative calculation to compare the effects with the revisions of the rates shown in lines 4–6 of Table 5.

In Table 6 regional growth rates calculated by weighting growth rates for individual countries by constant population are compared with those yielded by the conventional procedure. The calculation had to be made for a somewhat shorter period, to assure complete time coverage for a sufficient number of countries, but the results can easily be applied to the period covered in our earlier tables. Also, to reduce tabular matter, the comparison is limited to the more recent period, 1954–58 to 1964–68.

The alternative weighting tends to *raise* the overall growth rate of per capita product in the developed regions and to *lower* the overall growth rate of per capita product of ESEA, the

Table 6. GROWTH RATES, COUNTRIES WITHIN THE DEVELOPED AND
LESS-DEVELOPED GROUPS, VARIANT WEIGHTING, 1955–57 TO
1965–67 AND 1954–58 TO 1964–68 (PERCENTAGE PER YEAR)

	Weighted by total product, changing population (conventional procedure)			Weighted by country population (constant for period)		
	GDP (1)	Population (2)	Product per capita (3)	GDP (4)	Population (5)	Product per capita (6)
DC, 1955–57 to 1965–67						
1. EEC (5 countries, 1960–62 pop. = 173.2 mill.)	4.97	1.01	3.92	4.99	1.01	3.94
2. EFTA (9 countries, 1960–62 pop. = 94.7 mill.)	3.46	0.74	2.70	3.59	0.74	2.83
3. NA (2 countries, 1960–62 pop. = 202.0 mill.)	3.86	1.60	2.23	3.88	1.60	2.24
4. O (2 countries, 1960–62 pop. = 12.9 mill.)	4.50	2.09	2.35	4.49	2.09	2.35
5. DCR (above)	4.20	1.23	2.93	4.24	1.23	2.97
DC, 1954–58 to 1964–68						
6. DCR − J	4.35	1.21	3.10	4.39	1.21	3.14
LDC, 1955–57 to 1965–67						
7. ESEA (10 countries, 1960–62 pop. = 761.5 mill.)	3.94	2.41	1.49	3.71	2.41	1.27
8. LA (17 countries, 1960–62 pop. = 199.5 mill.)	4.75	2.91	1.79	4.91	2.91	1.94
9. LDCR (above)	4.11	2.52	1.55	3.96	2.52	1.41
LDC, 1954–58 to 1964–68						
10. LDCR	4.39	2.54	1.80	4.24	2.54	1.66

Lines 1–4, 7–8: The countries covered are Belgium, France, West Germany, Italy, and the Netherlands in line 1; Austria, Denmark, Finland, Iceland, Norway, Portugal, Sweden, Switzerland, and the United Kingdom in line 2; Canada and the United States in line 3; Australia and New Zealand in line 4; Burma, Ceylon, China (Taiwan), India, Indonesia, South Korea, Malaysia, Pakistan, the Philippines, and Thailand in line 7; and Argentina, Bolivia, Brazil, Chile, Colombia, Dominican Republic, Ecuador, El Salvador, Guatemala, Jamaica, Honduras, Mexico, Nicaragua, Paraguay, Peru, Uruguay, and Venezuela in line 8. Col. 1: Estimates of 1963 GDP at factor cost, in U.S. dollars, for individual countries are from *International Tables,* Table 1B (see n. 1 above). These were extrapolated to the periods indicated by GDP (or a similar aggregative total) in the local currency, at constant prices, taken from *Individual Country Data* (see n. 6 below) or unpublished data obtained from the Statistical Office of the United Nations. Cols. 2, 5: Estimates of population of the individual countries for the periods indicated are from the *Demographic Yearbook, 1968,* Table 4, and *Demographic Yearbook, 1965,* Table 4. Col. 3: Per capita product was derived by division. Col. 4: Derived by multiplication of the relatives of entries in cols. 5–6. Col. 6: Averages of the growth rates for individual countries, each weighted by its population in 1960–62 (derived from the sources cited above for cols. 2 and 5).

Line 5: Col. 3 is based on lines 1–4, col. 3, weighted by the region's

major less-developed region. The implication is that the growth rates of per capita product, or of population, are negatively correlated with the initial level of per capita product—within the several developed regions, whereas the correlation is positive within the ESEA, if not within the LA, region.

This finding can be easily illustrated. Within EEC, it is Italy (with the lowest per capita product) that shows one of the highest growth rates in per capita product; within EFTA, Portugal (with the lowest per capita product) also shows a high growth rate in per capita product, whereas the United Kingdom and Switzerland (with higher per capita product) show lower growth rates in the latter; and, within the North American region, the same is true of Canada compared with the United States. By contrast, within ESEA, the low per capita product countries (Indonesia and India) show rather low rates of growth of per capita product, whereas the countries with higher per capita product (Taiwan, Korea, and Thailand) show high growth rates in the latter. We thus end up with a growth rate in per capita product for the less-developed regions of about 1.7 per cent per year for 1954–58 to 1964–68, compared with a rate in Table 1 of 2.2 per cent and in Table 3 of 2.0 per cent; whereas for the developed regions, excluding Japan, the rate rises from 3.0 per cent in Table 2 to over 3.1 per cent in Table 6.

The reasoning can be extended to different groups *within* one country, with different per capita product (or income) and possibly different rates of growth in their per capita product (or in their relative number, or in both). Here, however, the conventional procedure may be more justified—in that the rise in income of one domestic group can redound to the benefit of the others, *if* the additional income is invested in capital that would

population in 1960–62; cols. 2 and 5 are based on total population of the countries covered in 1955–57 and 1965–67; and col. 1 is derived by multiplication of the relatives of the rates in cols. 2–3. Col. 6 is the mean of the growth rates for individual countries covered in lines 1–4, each weighted by its population in 1960–62. Col. 4 is derived by multiplication of the relatives of the rates in cols. 5–6.

Line 6: Cols. 1–3 are from Table 5, line 5, cols. 1–3. Cols. 4 and 6 were derived by adding the absolute differences between cols. 1 and 4, and 3 and 6 of line 5 to cols. 1 and 3, respectively, of this line.

Line 9: See note to line 5 above. The regional data are from lines 7–8.

Line 10: Cols. 1–3 are from Table 5, line 6, cols. 1–3. Cols. 4 and 6 were derived by adding the absolute differences between cols. 1 and 4 and 3 and 6 of line 9 to cols. 1 and 3, respectively, of this line.

raise the productivity of every member of that country. But from the standpoint of human welfare (rather than social productivity) it can still be argued that, if the total product of a country rises solely because the product or income of a small high-income group rises (while the per capita income of the large low-income group remains constant), the growth rate should be computed by the alternative procedure—in which the growth rates of per capita income would be weighted by fixed population, not by shares in total income. With any widening in the inequality in distribution of product among given ordinal groups within the economy, or greater growth in relative numbers of the low-income groups, the alternative procedure would yield lower growth rates of the countrywide per capita product than those obtained in the conventional calculation.

The matter is relevant here because of the suspicion that inequality in the distribution of income within many less-developed countries has widened in the recent decade to decade and a half. It would take us too far afield to try to test this conjecture by statistical evidence. We can only suggest the possibility and indicate that it may mean a further sizable reduction in the properly weighted rate of growth of per capita product for the less-developed countries.

A simple, if extreme, illustration will suffice. Assume, realistically, that the initial share of the top 10 per cent of the population within a less-developed country is 40 per cent of the product.[4] Assume further that in the conventional calculation the product per capita of the country grew 2 per cent per year, or 22 per cent over the decade, and that this growth was concentrated in the hands of the top 10 per cent of the population. The growth rate in per capita product, in the alternative procedure, would then be $(0.9 \times 1.0) + [0.1(121.9 - 60):40]$, or 1.05475, that is, 5.475 per cent for the decade, or 0.53 per cent per year. In this illustration the conventional growth rate of 2.0 per cent per year is reduced about three-fourths.

To be sure, this shift is extreme and could not continue for long without causing the economy to break down. However, a

[4] According to ECLA estimates of a "conjectural" distribution for Latin America (relating presumably to the late 1950's or early 1960's), the top 5 per cent of the population received 33 per cent of the personal income (see *The Economic Development of Latin America in the Post-War Period* [New York: United Nations, 1964], p. 65, Table 67). A 40 per cent share for the top 10 per cent is then moderate.

more moderate widening of inequality over a long period is quite feasible; and the illustration suffices in suggesting that, if the distinction among economic groups within the country is important, the indiscriminate pooling of their income is questionable. Even a moderate widening in the inequality of the distribution of income among these groups can affect significantly the properly weighted rate of growth in per capita income.

These comments on the size distribution of income in the less-developed countries apply also to the intra-country regional income differentials, which are usually wider, proportionally, than in the developed countries. This is particularly true of the large less-developed countries, whose populations dominate the totals for Asia and for the LDCs. Yet these intra-country regional differentials tend to widen in the early phase of growth and to grow smaller eventually.[5]

4. Weighting the Sectoral Growth Rates, and Other Adjustments

The growth rate of a country's or region's total product can be viewed as a weighted average of the growth rates of output in the different sectors of the area's productive system. With the latter distinguished, we can observe marked differences in sectoral rates of growth and consider the proper system of weights for these rates, assuming that they are acceptable. For reasons suggested below, the questions raised are particularly relevant to the evaluation of aggregate growth for the less-developed regions—which are of most interest to us here. A related question bears on the effects of industrialization and urbanization on the proportion of intermediate products possibly included in the conventional definition of gross domestic product.

In Table 7 we summarize the sectoral shares and growth rates for the two large less-developed regions and, for comparison, one developed region. The five components shown and grouped into the three major sectors could be subdivided further (see note, Table 7 for definitions of the sectors and their subdivisions). Within OI we could distinguish mining, electricity, gas, and water, construction, and transport and communication.

---

[5] Jeffrey G. Williamson, "Regional Inequality and the Process of National Development: A Description of the Patterns," *Economic Development and Cultural Change*, Vol. 13, no. 4, Part 2, July, 1965, 44–45 particularly.

	A (1)	M (2)	OI (3)	I (4)	T (5)	OS (6)	S (7)	Total (8)
	Shares in GDP (%)							
	ESEA							
1. 1954–58	48.7	13.5	7.8	21.3	11.8	18.2	30.0	100.0
2. 1964–68	40.9	15.3	11.7	27.0	12.6	19.5	32.1	100.0
LA								
3. 1954–58	20.8	20.5	14.6	35.1	16.8	27.4	44.2	100.0
4. 1964–68	18.0	23.9	15.0	38.9	17.2	25.9	43.1	100.0
LDCR								
5. 1954–58	35.6	16.8	11.0	27.8	14.1	22.5	36.6	100.0
6. 1964–68	29.7	19.5	13.3	32.8	14.9	22.6	37.5	100.0
EEC (for comparison)								
7. 1954–58	10.3	31.2	18.3	49.5	11.4	28.9	40.2	100.0
8. 1964–68	8.0	35.3	17.9	53.2	11.8	27.0	38.8	100.0
	Growth Rates per Year (%)							
	GDP							
9. ESEA	2.42	5.48	8.61	6.72	4.94	4.96	4.95	4.23
10. LA	3.56	6.68	5.34	6.14	5.29	4.44	4.77	5.04
11. LDCR	2.72	6.17	6.65	6.36	5.12	4.65	4.83	4.60
12. EEC	2.55	6.49	5.00	5.96	5.62	4.51	4.83	5.20
	GDP per capita							
13. ESEA	−0.05	2.93	5.99	4.14	2.41	2.42	2.42	1.71
14. LA	0.72	3.76	2.45	3.23	2.41	1.58	1.90	2.16
15. LDCR	0.18	3.54	4.01	3.72	2.51	2.05	2.23	2.00
16. LDCR (weighted by pop.)	0.10	3.10	5.28	3.96	2.41	2.25	2.32	1.80

Column designations: *A*, agriculture, forestry, hunting, and fishing; *M*, manufacturing (both large- and small-scale); *OI*, other components of the *I* sector (viz., mining and quarrying, construction, electricity, gas, water, and sanitary services, and transportation, storage, and communication); *I*, the sum of *M* and *OI*; *T*, wholesale and retail trade; *OS*, other components of the *S* sector (viz., banking, insurance, and real estate, ownership of dwellings, public administration and defense, and all other services [education, medical and health, recreation and entertainment, domestic services, hotels and restaurants, laundries, barber shops, and other personal services, and religious institutions, welfare, legal services, trade associations, etc.]); *S*, the sum of *T* and *OS*. (For the relation between the UN classification used here and the International Standard Industrial Classification, see *Studies in Methods*, no. 2, *A System of National Accounts and Supporting Tables* [New York: United Nations, 1953], appendix 1, p. 40.)

Lines 1–8: Calculated from Table 6B of *International Tables* (see n. 1 above). Geometric means of indexes for the subdivisions for 1954–58 and 1964–68 were multiplied by the 1963 weights in total GDP, and percentage shares calculated.

Lines 9–12: Computed from the growth rate for GDP and the relative changes in shares from 1954–58 to 1964–68. A proportional change in the percentage share (reduced to an annual basis) multiplied by the growth rate per year of total product yields the growth rate of the given component. Entries in col. 8 of lines 9–11 are from Table 3, lines 1, 2, and 15, col. 6; in col. 8 of line 12, from Table 2, line 1, col. 6.

Lines 13–15: Computed from lines 9–11 and the growth rates for population in Table 3, lines 4, 5, and 16, col. 6.

Within *OS*, by using tables for individual countries, we could distinguish finance, income from dwellings, government and defense, and private services groups. But the present classification serves our purpose, which is to raise questions about comparability aspects, without entertaining unrealistic hope that these questions can be answered—even with the investment of considerable effort—with the present limitations on the data.

The findings in Table 7 are fairly familiar. The first is the contrast between the less-developed and developed countries in the relative weights of the *A* and *I* sectors, with the shares of the former much larger and those of the latter much smaller in the LDCs than in the DCs. The second is the shift in structure away from the *A* sector and toward the *I* sector when per capita product grows; even in the short period covered, the shares of the *A* sector decline and those of the *I* sector rise in all regions (see lines 1–8, cols. 1 and 4), and this shift would be observed also in the other developed regions. This means, of course, that over the period the growth rates of the *I* sector, and partly also of the S sector, are much greater than those of the *A* sector in both the LDCs and the DCs. Third, if the *A* sector tends to grow more slowly than the other sectors, a greater initial (or average) weight of the *A* sector retards the growth rate of the economy. And it is interesting to note that the growth rate of total product for the developed region EEC, 5.20 per cent per year, is much higher than that for the LDCR, 4.60 per cent per year (lines 11–12, col. 8). Yet the growth rates in the EEC region for the *A*, *I*, and S sectors (2.55, 5.96, and 4.83 per cent, respectively) are either lower than or equal to the corresponding rates in the LDCR (2.72, 6.36, and 4.83 per cent). The EEC rate of growth of total product is higher than that in the LDCR because in the former the *I* and S sectors have greater weight than the *A* sector. One cannot venture to claim, without documentation, that the growth rates of sectoral output have some realistic upper limits that are distinctly lower for the *A* than for the *I* sector and perhaps for the S sector. But if there is some such element in the comparison of the growth potentials of the *A* and the *I* sectors, the constraints on the aggregate growth rate of the

Line 16: Computed by weighting the sectoral growth rates for ESEA and LA (lines 13–14) by population in the middle of the period, i.e., in 1959–63 (given in Table 3, lines 4–5, col. 3).

LDCs, with their much larger weight of the A sector, are much greater than on the growth rate of the DCs.

1. Are the weights used in combining the sectoral outputs and growth rates comparable for the LDCs and the DCs? The ratios of prices of industrial products to those of agricultural products are generally much higher in the less-developed than in the developed countries, according to a few tested price comparisons available. Consequently, the I (and perhaps the S) sector has a greater weight in the current price estimates for the LDCs than it would have in those for the DCs; and some adjustment to assure better comparability is called for.

In comparing the 1950 price structures of the United States and other *developed* but lower per capita product countries, we find that, with the I/A ratio in the United States set at 1.0, the geometric mean of the I/A ratios for eight European countries in 1950 is 1.37.[6] We can compare the price structures for 1962 in six Latin American capital cities with those in Los Angeles and Houston; and the I/A ratio (geometric mean) for the former is 1.56 (1.0 for the two U.S. cities). Similar calculations yield a mean S/A price ratio of 0.76 for the European countries, but

---

[6] Simon Kuznets, *Economic Growth of Nations: Total Output and Production Structure* (Cambridge, Mass.: Harvard University Press, 1971), Table 20, p. 137. The price ratios underlying the 1950 structure (for the United States and Europe) are geometric means of prices weighted by domestic and U.S. quantities; those underlying the 1962 structure (for the two U.S. cities and the Latin American capital cities) are weighted by a common set of Latin American quantities. In a recent study (*Economic Progress and Policy in Developing Countries* [New York: W. W. Norton & Co., 1970]), Angus Maddison attempted to convert gross product estimates by sector in less-developed countries to comparability with those of the developed countries (particularly the United States) by weighting measures of commodity output, for the A sector and for industry (mining, manufacturing, and electric power, water, and gas), by U.S. prices. The results, however, contradict both the direct price comparisons and our expectations concerning the differential comparative advantage of LDCs vs. DCs with respect to agricultural and industrial products, and one hesitates to accept them. We calculated several implicit I/A price ratios by comparing the ratios of the Maddison "converted" estimates of GDP originating in 1965 in the I and the A sectors with the ratios derived from estimates in domestic currency. (The Maddison estimates are from his Table A-10, p. 294; those in the currency of the country are from *Yearbook of National Accounts Statistics, 1969*, Vol. 1, *Individual Country Data* [New York: United Nations, 1970], hereafter cited as *Individual Country Data*.) The implicit ratios for Argentina, Brazil, Chile, and Colombia are significantly below one; and that for Peru is the only ratio above one. Yet for all these countries the I/A ratios based on price comparisons range from 1.3 (for Lima, Peru) to 1.9 (for Buenos Aires, Argentina).

1.43 for the Latin American capital cities. A major limitation of these comparisons is that they are of prices of finished products, not of gross product originating within specific sectors. For example, the price of food (largely an *A* sector product and so classified) includes costs of distribution and transportation (either *S* or *I* sector products), and the price of clothing (largely an *I* sector product) includes the costs of cotton and wool (products of the *A* sector). We have no data by which the sectoral structure of factor costs in the LDCs could be compared with that in the DCs—although there is some evidence that the ratios of *I* and of *S* factor costs to *A* factor costs are much higher in the less-developed than in the developed countries.

In the circumstances, we can only attach some rough but realistic weights to our observations; and for illustrative purposes we set the ratio of *I* to *A* prices in the LDCs at about 1.5, compared with 1.0 in the DCs—probably a moderate allowance, particularly for the LDCs attempting to foster industrialization and limit industrial imports by tariffs, quotas, and other restrictions. This means that the weight of the *I* sector relative to the *A* sector in the LDCs is 1.5 times that in the DCs. For comparison with the growth rate of total product in the DCs, that for the LDCs should be recalculated with the *I* sector growth rate assigned two-thirds of the weight now used. One may argue that the present high valuation of the *I* sector products reflects the judgment of the LDC societies and that there is no ground for modifying it. But to the extent that this higher price is the result of designed intervention, and that industrial imports are available and a lower *I*/*A* price ratio is feasible, this adjustment for comparability has merit.

We also make an adjustment for the *S*/*A* price ratio, although the basis is much weaker because of the heterogeneity of the subcomponents in the *S* sector and the difficulties in comparing prices of qualitatively similar factors or goods in this category. Perhaps these difficulties explain the differences between the *S*/*A* ratios of less than one for the United States–Europe comparison and those above one for the Latin American capital cities. We adopted a ratio of 1.25 to 1.0—although this is only a guess.

These two adjustments are applied to derive lines 4–5 of Table 8. First, the growth rates of total product for ESEA and LA were recalculated by using the sectoral growth rates in

Table 7 and the reduced shares for the I and S sectors in 1959–63 (yielding line 4); and the per capita growth rates were derived by division of the relatives of the recalculated total product rates by those for population (in line 2).

The adjustment reduces the growth rate of total product for ESEA by about 7 per cent; that for LA by about 2 per cent (lines 4, 1, cols. 1, 2). The reduction of the rate is greater, relatively, for ESEA because of the wider contrast for ESEA than for LA between the low growth rate of the A sector and the high growth rates of the I and S sectors. One should also note that the relative reduction for both regions is appreciably greater in the growth rate for *per capita* product than in the rate for *total* product (cf. lines 1 and 4 with lines 3 and 5). This is an obvious result of the high rate of population growth in both regions and suggests clearly that minor proportional changes in the growth rate of total product for the LDC regions will mean much greater proportional changes in the growth rates of per capita product. This would not be the case for the DC regions, since the growth rates of their populations are low relative to the growth rates of their total product.

If we adjust for a differential sectoral price structure, as was done here, we should also allow for the possible movement of this structure over the period (without its being reflected in the constant price estimates) toward that prevailing in the DCs and on the international markets. In other words the adjustment, say for the I sector, might involve a reduction of its weight to $1.0/1.7$ in earlier years, and to $1.0/1.3$ in the later years. But no evidence of such movement is at hand; and, with the rapid extensive growth of the I sector in the LDCs, it is hardly likely that *relative* efficiency (relative to the DCs) would improve significantly over a period as short as a decade and a half.

2. The S sector contains heterogeneous components such as trade, financial returns, income from dwellings, government service and defense, domestic and personal services, business services, professional services, and services of religious and charitable institutions (see note, Table 7). It is difficult not only to compare prices or factor costs but even to decide how much of the output shown (with estimates often based on inputs) is in the nature of final product and not the cost of urbanization and modernization. Such questions are particularly relevant in the LDCs, in some of which the high growth rate of the S sector

Table 8. Growth Rates in Total Product and Product per Capita, Alternative Treatment of *I* and *S* Sectors and Allowance for Effects of Urbanization, Less-Developed Regions, 1954–58 to 1964–68 (Percentage per Year)

	ESEA (1)	LA (2)	LDCR (3)
Growth rates from Tables 3, 7:			
1. Total product	4.23	5.04	4.60
2. Population	2.47	2.82	nc
3. Per capita product	1.71	2.16	1.80
Adjustment 1 (growth rates, with weight of *I* sector reduced a third, and weight of *S* sector reduced a fifth):			
4. Total product	3.93	4.91	nc
5. Per capita product	1.43	2.03	1.55
Adjustment 2 (growth rates, with weight of *I* sector reduced a third, *S* sector omitted for ESEA, and allowance for increased urbanization in LA):			
6. Total product	3.54	4.48	nc
7. Per capita product	1.04	1.61	1.15
Proportional change in growth rates due to adjustment 2:			
8. Total product	−0.163	−0.111	nc
9. Per capita product	−0.392	−0.255	−0.361

nc = not calculated.

Lines 1–3: Growth rates for ESEA and LA from Table 7, lines 13, 14, and 16 (col. 3 weighted by population, here and in all other lines, the weights being 0.8 for ESEA and 0.2 for LA). Population growth rates are from Table 3, lines 4–5.

Lines 4–5: For the rationale of adjustments see the text. The calculation involves combining the sectoral growth rates with the new weights (the shares for the A sector unchanged and those for the *I* and *S* sectors reduced); deriving new growth rates for total product (in line 4) for ESEA and LA; and then obtaining new growth rates for product per capita by dividing the relatives of the rates for total product by the relatives of the rates for population (given in line 2).

Lines 6–7: The additional adjustment here is the complete exclusion for ESEA of the S sector, which shows a growth rate much higher than those for total product and for the combination of the *I* and *A* sectors. This omission in fact assumes that the S sector product grew at the same rate as the sum of the A and *I* sectors.

For LA there is evidence of marked urbanization over the period. *Growth of the World's Urban and Rural Population, 1920–2000* (New York: United Nations, 1969) shows a decline in the proportion of rural and small-town population in the total from 75 per cent in 1950 to 67 per cent in 1960 (see Tables 47 and 48, summing the totals for the four regions of Latin America). Assuming that real product per head (i.e., product disregarding cost differentials for the same goods) was twice as high in the agglomerated localities (i.e., those over 20,000 in population) as in the rural and small-town areas—and that the cost or price differential between the two types of areas was about 1.5 to 1.0 (for the agglomerated and rural areas, respectively)—a shift from 75 to 67 per cent rural implies a price inflation due to urbanization of about 4.17 per cent per decade. The allowance for such inflation, not reflected in any adjustment so far, reduces the annual growth rate of total product from 4.91 per cent (line 4, col. 2) to 4.48 per cent (line 6, col. 2). The adjustment for LA just described implies a ratio of product per capita in the *I* + *S* and *A* sectors of roughly three to one (two to one in comparable prices and three to one allowing for the urban-

tends to raise the growth rate of total and per capita product. As Table 7 shows, the growth rates of both the trade and other services components in ESEA are almost 5 per cent per year (line 9, cols. 5–6), distinctly higher than that of the aggregate, 4.2 per cent. Without accepting physiocratic, Classical, and Marxian notions of the primacy of commodities and the dubious value of services not embodied in commodities, one may still legitimately ask whether these high growth rates of many components of the S sector represent growth of real final product.[7] Nor are hidden costs or intermediate products limited to the S sector; the additional burden of transportation and fabrication resulting from urbanization (as far as food and other A sector products are involved) means an increased intermediate product component in the I sector in the accepted economic accounting.

The proper response to such doubts would be, of course, a detailed examination of the components of the S and other sectors, country by country, in an attempt to evaluate the significance of the recorded increases for welfare or growth. But this is not feasible here, and we limited ourselves to two crude adjustments, for the ESEA and LA regions, respectively.

---

rural price or cost differential). This ratio of three to one is similar to that found for LA when we compare the sectoral distribution of GDP (excluding pure property income components, such as finance and income from dwellings) with that of labor force (adjusted to exclude women in agriculture). This ratio was found to be 3.0 in 1950–51 and 2.9 in 1960–61. (The underlying product data are from the sources used in this paper. The data on labor force are from P. Bairoch and J. M. Limbor, "Changes in the Industrial Distribution of the World Labour Force by Regions, 1880–1960," *International Labour Review*, Vol. 98, October, 1968, Table F, p. 332.)

Lines 8–9: Calculated directly from lines 6 and 1, and 7 and 3.

---

[7] In the LA region the share of the S sector is quite high, well over 40 per cent of total product in both 1954–58 and 1964–68, compared with 40 per cent or less in the developed EEC region (Table 7, lines 3–4 and 7–8, col. 7). Also, the share of trade in total product rose over the period, and its growth rate, 5.3 per cent per year, is higher than the 5.0 per cent growth rate for total product (Table 7, line 10). The UN estimates for Africa (excluding South Africa) and the Middle East show growth rates for 1950–68 of the other-services component of the S sector distinctly higher than the rates for total product (5.7 and 4.6 per cent, respectively, for Africa; and 8.9 and 6.5 per cent, respectively, for the Middle East; see *International Tables*, n. 1 above). The large share of the S sector in the total product of the LDCs and the tendency for its share—or those of its major components (trade and other services)—to rise in the recent period suggest the need for a reexamination of the basis of the estimates and of the meaning of the results for evaluation of the growth process.

For ESEA we omitted the S sector completely, in addition to reducing the weight of the I sector by one-third. This omission, in fact, implies that the rate of growth of the output of the S sector is the same as that of the combined A and I sectors, with the weight of the latter reduced. As line 6, column 1 of Table 8 shows, this means scaling down the growth rate of the output of the S sector to 3.54 per cent per year (from the 4.95 per cent rate in Table 7, line 9, col. 7).

For the LA region a different adjustment was used, suggested by the wide disparity shown in the region between sectoral product per worker in the A and other sectors (see note to lines 6–7, Table 8). A rather marked shift of population toward urban communities of 20,000 population and over during the decade 1950–60, and probably also during the 1954–58 to 1964–68 span, means that the proportion of total final consumption at the higher relative prices of urban communities introduced an element of inflation (or an increased proportion of intermediate products) even into the constant price estimates—and the reweighting of sectoral outputs in lines 4–5 of Table 8, which is constant over the period, does not take care of the problem. The allowances of a two-to-one differential in per capita final consumption in rural and urban communities, at the same prices, and of a price differential of 1.5 to 1.0 are suggested by data for the United States for 1935–36 and 1960 (used in *Economic Growth of Nations,* cited in n. 6). At both dates, the ratio of per *family* consumption in urban communities to that on farms is close to two to one, and the ratio for per *capita* consumption would be much greater; while the implicit differential price ratio is about 1.5 to 1.0. Our approximation to the proportion of such inflation, 4.17 per cent of GDP over the decade, may be too high in that it is based on the equating of final household consumption with GDP, but it may be too low because it is based on an incomplete measure of urbanization and because it neglects other possible sources of an increased proportion of intermediate products. As an order of magnitude, it suggests a reduction in the GDP growth rate of less than a tenth, but one in the growth rate of per capita product of over two-tenths (see Table 8, col. 2, lines 4 and 6 for total product and lines 5 and 7 for per capita product).

The adjustments in lines 4–5 of Table 8 are designed to improve comparability between growth rates for the LDCs and the

DCs. However, those in lines 6–7 may also be relevant to the measures for the developed countries; but this relevance would have to be explored before the adjustments are made. This means asking whether the contribution of the S sector to the growth of real product is questionable also in the DCs; and whether the proportion of intermediate products in GDP, as measured, has risen significantly over the period. An adequate investigation of this question is not feasible here. But undoubtedly the use of the illustrative assumptions underlying lines 4–7 of Table 8 would yield results for the developed regions that would tend to increase the relative disparity in *per capita* growth rates between the LDCs and the DCs. For identical adjustments applied to the growth rates of *total* product of the DCs would mean a smaller proportional adjustment of the growth rates of their *per capita* product, because their population growth rate is much lower than their total product growth rate (the latter is almost the same as that of the LDCs). Thus, using the EEC region as an example, we calculated the effect of the adjustment in line 6 for the LA region. An allowance for inflation in measured GDP of 4.17 per cent over the decade would reduce the growth rate of GDP for the EEC region from 5.20 per cent per year to 4.77 per cent and reduce the growth rate of per capita product from 4.18 to 3.76 per cent. The latter growth rates may be compared with 2.03 and 1.61 per cent for LA (lines 5 and 7, col. 2). Thus, the identical adjustment reduced the growth rate in per capita product of the LA region by over two-tenths and that of the EEC region by only about one-tenth. The results for other developed regions would be similar.

5. *Summary*

Table 9 recapitulates the successive approximate adjustments in the rate of growth of per capita product for the 1954–58 to 1964–68 span. It thus provides a useful summary of the findings. Four broad aspects of these findings deserve emphasis:

1. The differences among the several international agencies in their allocation of the non-Communist countries to the developed and less-developed ("developing") groups introduce difficulties into the comparison. More disturbing are the large discrepancies in the growth rates yielded by the estimates of the several agencies for some of the major less-developed regions, in

particular Africa and the Middle East. One cannot avoid the conclusion that, except for a few countries elsewhere, acceptable estimates cover only Latin America and South and Southeast Asia among the less-developed areas—and the quality of the estimates differs somewhat even for those. A major effort to secure greater consistency and better coverage is required if the quantitative comparative study of the growth of less-developed countries is to be built on a relatively firm foundation.

2. The conventional procedure, in which growth rates of per capita product for larger groups are derived from the sum of products in the numerator and the sum of populations in the denominator, implies a greater weight of the per capita growth rate of subareas with a higher initial per capita product or a higher growth rate of population—both relative to those in the other subareas. Such weighting in deriving an average rate of growth for per capita product may be questioned from the standpoint of changes in welfare and other implications for the subareas or subgroups within the broader areas and wider population totals. The alternative procedure—deriving per capita growth rates *separately* for each subarea or country, and then weighting them by constant population—seems distinctly preferable for various analytical purposes. The shift from the conventional to the alternative procedure reduces the average growth rate of per capita product of the LDCs substantially but raises somewhat the growth rate of per capita product of the DCs (cf. line 2 with lines 3–4, Table 9).

3. The preceding argument applies not only within such broad totals as all LDCs or subregions within the latter but even within individual countries. The greater weight assigned to the proportional increase in per capita income of the upper income groups, or of the richer regions, within a country, which is the result of the conventional aggregation of all incomes (or product) and all population, may not reflect properly the proportional rises in per capita income among the distinct groups or regions (which may better be reflected by population, or some other weights, not by total output). For many analytical purposes it may be advisable to abandon the conventional procedure's assumption that the rise of any group's income redounds to the benefit of all—even within a country. The reweighting and adjustment, however, call for data not readily

	East and Southeast Asia (1)	Latin America (2)	Less-developed countries (3)	Developed countries	
				Incl. Japan (4)	Excl. Japan (5)
1. Total as reported in UN sources (conventional weighting)	1.71	2.16	2.21	3.38	nc
2. Omitting some regions and countries (for better definition and greater reliability)	1.71	2.16	2.00	3.31	2.96
3. Weighting regions by constant population	1.71	2.16	1.80	4.07	3.10
4. Adjusting for individual country weights (constant population)	1.46	2.34	1.64	4.11	3.14
5. Adjusting for possible changes in internal income inequality within countries	ne	ne	ne	ne	ne
6. Adjusting for changed weights of *I* and *S* sectors relative to *A* sector (LDCs only)	1.22	2.20	1.42	4.11	3.14
7. Adjusting for changed weight of *I* sector and other effects in Table 8	0.89	1.74	1.06	ne	ne

nc = not calculated; ne = not estimated.

Line 1: Cols. 3–4 from Table 1, line 6, cols. 5–6. Cols. 1–2 from line 2 below.

Line 2: Omissions intended to adjust for improper classification and inconsistency of estimates for some areas. The less-developed group is limited to ESEA and LA, and the developed group to EEC, EFTA, NA, Oceania, and Japan. (From Table 2, lines 20–21, col. 6; and Table 3, lines 7, 8, and 17, col. 6.)

Line 3: Cols. 3–5 from Table 5, lines 4–6, col. 3; cols. 1–2 from line 2 above.

Line 4: Cols. 1–2 from cols. 1–2 of line 3 above, adjusted by the proportional differences between cols. 6 and 3, lines 7–8, Table 6; cols. 3 and 5 from Table 6, lines 6 and 10; col. 4 derived from col. 5 and line 3, cols. 4–5.

Line 6: Line 4, adjusted by the proportional changes in Table 8, lines 3 and 5.

Line 7: Line 4, adjusted by the proportional changes in Table 8, lines 3 and 7.

available; and we could not make the adjustments for these differences *within* countries.

4. Compared with the sectoral price structure of developed countries, that of the less-developed countries assigns greater weight to the *I* (and possibly the *S*) sector, relative to that for the *A* sector. A crude reweighting for the LDCs reduces the growth rate of total product substantially and that of per capita product even more (see lines 4 and 6, Table 9). Another adjust-

ment, relating largely to the possible rise in the proportion of intermediate products included in the gross product in the accepted economic accounting, was made for the less-developed regions. It substantially lowered the growth rate of total product and that of per capita product even more (see lines 6–7, Table 9). Such an adjustment for the developed countries, not attempted here, is not likely to produce a similarly substantial reduction in the growth rate of *per capita* product (even if the adjustment were the same for the growth rate of total product), because the growth rate of population is so much lower than in the LDCs.

The cumulative result of all these adjustments is to reduce the rate of growth of per capita product in the LDCs to about half of the rate shown in the UN estimates, and thus to one-third of the rate for the developed countries, even excluding Japan.

One should note, in conclusion, that other sources of possible downward adjustment have not been explored. As indicated, no study was made of the changes over time in the size distribution or regional distribution of income within the less-developed countries. Also, inclusion of Africa—with per capita product levels and growth rates apparently not much higher than in East and Southeast Asia and with its large population relative either to that of the Middle East or even of Latin America—would only augment the reduction of the growth rate of per capita product for the LDCs when weighted by constant population. On the other hand, we have not examined fully the downward adjustments that might be made in the growth rates for the developed countries.

But rather than dwell on substantive findings, we feel it is more important to stress the need for continuous critical examination and adjustment of the growing number of aggregative measures that are becoming available. While such critical evaluation and adjustment are needed for both developed and less-developed countries, the preceding discussion suggests that the downward adjustment in the present measures of growth rates in per capita product may be greater for the LDCs. Examination of the factors underlying these adjustments is urgently needed, in view of the acute growth problems of the less-developed regions and despite the marked acceleration even in their adjusted growth rates.